Lovers and Madmen

A True Story of Passion, Politics and Air Piracy

Julienne Eden Busic

To John —
my first boyfriend
(but fortunately for my
social life, not my last)
Here's to all the
good memories!
Love
Julie

Writers Club Press

San Jose New York Lincoln Shanghai

Gearhart
Dec 31, 2000

Lovers and Madmen

Published by Writers Club Press
an imprint of iUniverse.com, Inc.

For information address:
iUniverse.com, Inc.
620 North 48th Street
Suite 201
Lincoln, NE 68504-3467
www.iuniverse.com

Book cover designed by Kristina Babić

ISBN: 0-595-00758-9

Printed in the United States of America

To my parents,
without whom none of this would have been possible.

"Lovers and madmen have such seething brains,
such shaping fantasies, that apprehend
more than mere reason ever comprehends.
The lunatic, the lover and the poet
are of imagination all compact."

W. Shakespeare, A Midsummer Night's Dream

Part One

"Whatever is done from love always occurs beyond good and evil."
Nietzsche

Vienna, Austria, 1969–Girls always know when they're being stalked and we were. We stopped in front of a window, he stopped in front of a window. We started walking and so did he. When we slowed our pace, the shadow just behind us also slowed imperceptibly. Though he was subtle and did an exceptional job of appearing uninterested, indeed, unaware of our existence, there was a tangible and undeniable interconnection between our movements. The only enigma here was the object of his affections: Joanne or I. When we came to a stoplight, he smoothly eased up beside me and asked: Are you from England? No, I'm not, I told him. I'm American. We spoke in German, mine was better. His had the sound of a machine whose parts were not synchronized. Joanne rolled her eyes as she looked him up and down, whispered to me to get rid of him, but I was contrary, I let him walk with us. The sky became dark and we all turned different colors.

He had a look of poverty about him, the bright, red sweater with a black and white slash across the front, olive threadbare pants, too short in the leg, dark socks and black shoes with felony pointed toes. Black hair, oily or wet, falling over his forehead. He smelled of alcohol, but was not drunk, just serenely confident. Dark eyes, angular face, a Picasso face, not handsome but intense, an air of suppressed danger or excitement, which Joanne totally failed to apprehend. She whispered on, but I had left her, had formed a provisional government with the man at my side.

But what of myself? What kind of a picture did I present? What he saw was a rounded girl in her late teens or early twenties, wearing a red plastic raincoat with a long and incongruous leather shoelace tied in a bow around the waist. If it hadn't been hidden, I could say the attraction was the long blonde hair. I can't because my hair was stuffed into a knit cap. But we were somehow strangely drawn together, like a car out of control is drawn towards a tree or a brick wall.

His name is Zvonko but his friends and family call him Taik. He tried to get too familiar with me as we stood in a doorway out of the rain. He hooked his index fingers under my leather shoelace, a proprietary gesture I viewed with disfavor, and I told him so immediately. I don't remember where Joanne was, but she must have been there, because she was sitting next to me on the streetcar we took home together late that night after leaving him behind at the station. And she was with me earlier in his student dorm room, where I took off my cap, letting my hair tumble out, my glory. He had no reaction whatsoever. Joanne sat down and laughed, resigned to the situation, while Taik stuck his head under a faucet and sputtered, shook his head, spit, dried his face. A small student room, two beds, a sink , a chair, a table, books everywhere. He made us coffee. All the while, two other dark-haired girls who had been waiting in his room for him when he arrived sat on one of the beds, knees firmly pressed together, hands folded. They talked to each other in some strange language, sibilant but exotic. He was in complete control, orchestrating this odd encounter with great ease and assurance, a sun surrounded by his small planets.

My grandfather was a German, born in the Ukraine; it was from him that I inherited my love of foreign languages, which I began practicing at an early age and was attempting to continue to perfect in Austria. My father, therefore, whose son he is, can scarcely be critical of another foreigner in the family. But it seems I am getting ahead of myself, have us already married, whereas I am simply waiting for Taik to call, which he had promised me to do before three the next day. He is already four hours late, but somehow his arrogance endears him to me. Only this morning, I had decided he was unworthy. My father would find fault with his teeth, and one of his eyes is smaller than the other. But he is so inexcusably late that his faults become virtues, I desire him for having the insight to place himself above me. I need a myth to which I can dedicate my life.

When he finally calls and we see each other again, I feel an overwhelming relief. We look at each other with surprise, with delight. Both of us have undergone transformations since we last met, we are like sleek dogs, brushed and shiny, we have to make instant re-evaluations, take ourselves more seriously; I know it and so does he and we also know it about each other. To our initial curiosity is added a tangible physical current, which repels and attracts at the same time. A solemnity takes possession of me, a rising to the occasion, the little American girl sinks down, as though thrown into the sea with weights, and in her place emerges—what? I don't yet know; I only know that he demands something from me, without words, and that I am able to pry it like a hard nut from deep within the shell of myself and offer it to him without thought.

But I am living in Vienna and the Viennese seem threatened by foreigners of certain types. They advertise apartments for rent and state, in bold black and white: "No Eastern Europeans, Negroes or Turks." And they have a term for the Croatians. Croatians? Since yesterday, I am no longer ignorant of this term, because Taik happens to be one of these: a Croatian. When he told me, I was unsure what my reaction should be. Was this cause for sympathy, pity, envy? Should I refer him to a doctor, did he worship gold spiders? I was perplexed. But Croatia, it turns out, is a geographical location and the inhabitants are Croatians. When I tell an Austrian girlfriend I met a Croatian, she says: "Oh, a Tschusche!" The origin of the term in unknown, it defies etymological analysis, but to the Viennese, "Tschusche" is more or less synonymous with small, dark, greasy, shifty and lazy, as well as illiterate, fertile, and dishonest. A "Tschusche" also has at least a few gold teeth.

Milena, the cleaning woman at the hospital where I work as a nurse, fits the above description perfectly. But she is a Serbian, from the same country as Taik, Yugoslavia, only a different republic. I point this out to the other nurses. They want to consider Taik different for my sake, but their hearts are not in it. Meanwhile, while we talk, Milena is protesting loudly that she did empty the bedpans, but that they are full again, she can't empty them every ten minutes, she has other work to do; we shake our heads knowing that the bedpans, at least Herr Oberthaler's, have not been emptied all afternoon. He is incapable of anything vaguely resembling a bowel movement without his morning enema. He had had it, had deposited a few embarrassed pellets, and they were still lying accusingly in the plastic pan on his bedstand. Lazy, lying Milena!

But if it sounds as though Taik and I have had little on which to build a firm and lasting relationship, this is true in the practical sense of the word; however, we seem to know each other by divination. I watch him with fanatical dedication when he speaks his language, not understanding the meaning of his words, but understanding, by watching, the meaning of him. His absorption with his subject, the way he smokes his cigarette, sucking in the smoke as though it fuels his speech, impatiently, loath to be interrupted. His eyes, which are often opaque, looking into part of nothingness. Our eyes meet; at least, they seem to meet, but his consciousness, of which the eyes are a physical focus, often eludes me. Sitting by his side, I am, nonetheless, a part of his engagement with the world.

I do not know what he is saying, he only rarely directs comments at me in German, but already I am making myself unobtrusive, drawing my elbows in, willing my stomach not to growl, my chair not to squeak. I dread disrupting the orderly pattern of my new universe.

But one night when we were together, I rebelled. He gave me an ultimatum. I laughed in his face, he said it had been nice knowing me, I seconded it. He walked away, toward the opera, and I walked the other way, in the direction of home. When I turned around, he was looking over his shoulder at me; we both were ashamed, but had gone too far, had declared ourselves, and now our wills were set against each other.

At certain moments, one is struck with the certainty that something critical is happening, that life is taking off on its own, like a planet spinning off its orbit, and that one has been catapulted into space. A sound, a smell, the slight movement of a hand in a window, anything can trigger this knowledge, this overwhelming sense of powerlessness in the face of something bigger than oneself. So it is as I walk away from Taik. And yet I keep walking, saying to myself: "What a tragedy!" over and over, not crying, just shaking my head at the absurdity of a world into which we are all placed, replaced and displaced so randomly. I fall into bed, a deep despair settles on me, entombing my head in my pillow. I sleep, I am ashamed to say, the sleep of the dead.

The next morning I wake thinking of the telephone. It is in my landlady's sitting room, which is separated from ours by a double door. Just before it rings, there is a strange clicking noise and immediately thereafter, the shrill buzz. Frau Kus is seldom in her sitting room. She is the proverbial Viennese Hausfrau, always working on something that can be worn, smelled, or eaten. Most of these activities take place in the kitchen or the laundry room, so that I am the first to hear the telephone. I prefer to answer it before she gets the chance, as she tends to pass judgment on my caller based on his or her command of the German language.

One of my boyfriends, an Austrian through and through, was pronounced "lower class" because of his pronunciation. It seems he left off the endings of many of his words, transforming, for example, "ich habe" into "ee hob". Even I eventually took exception to this practice and eased him gracefully out of my life. But the thought of Frau Kus answering a call from Taik filled me with horror. I would have to tell her he was Croatian, from Yugoslavia, she would crunch her lips, weave her fingers together underneath her vast bosom and say, or maybe not say, just think, "A Tschusche!" I couldn't bear it. She wouldn't even rent her apartment to one. But I needn't have worried; he doesn't call.

The subject of the ultimatum hasn't really been on my mind, probably because it was not the reason for our separation. The separation occurred for the simple reason that our wills, for the first time, were in opposition and neither of us could afford to surrender power. Only when one has power can it be absolutely or partially surrendered, only then can one be magnanimous, gracious about it. We were both of us still powerless against one another, unsure of the efficacy of our respective weapons.

I go often to sit in the park and think about it all, looking at the trees, one particular tree. The name of the tree I do not know; it is very leafy, and its branches are thin and spidery, with tiny offshoots radiating out in all directions, so many, in fact, that the entire tree is bent over, as if in grief; the branches hang low to the ground and sway to and fro in the wind like corpses hanging from the end of a rope, bloodless, disembodied. There is a look about this movement which is inhuman; it is immediately identifiable as such, it has no center, no focus, no heart or mind from which the meaning is derived. And so the branches sway back and forth, touching me deeply because they have died without ever having really lived.

Taik and I have shared many tender moments; however, the tenderness has not come from any kind of physical intimacy, but, rather, from a feeling that we recognize ourselves in one another; when we praise the other, admire or extol the virtues of the other, we somehow feel that we are, in fact, speaking about ourselves, and we cannot fail to experience great tenderness because of this. I suspect that Taik finally calls for this very reason: he misses himself. But he sees me, I think, as an unfinished replicate, as a bud on the same branch, perhaps, which has not yet burst into bloom, as he has, or perhaps as a shadow, attached to him at all times, rendering a physical copy of his every curve and angle, which, depending on the sun, contracts or stretches into an attenuated line in danger of disappearing. But whatever form the shadow takes, it always includes him in his totality, as well as me in mine.

Heavy darkness, the musky smell of mown and molding grass, which cuts through this dark blanket as though both are smells or both sights—the awkward weight of Taik lies upon me, makes me passive. The concrete is cold on my cheek, and smooth like marble; one of my arms hangs limp to the ground, there is no room for it, while the other is wedged between my thigh and the slight rise of ground beneath which we lie. The hedge around us is dense and thick. The seeds must have been planted very closely together, causing the adult bushes to push against one another, become entangled, their appendages locked in abandoned embraces. Some of them appear to have bizarrely human qualities. One has a pair of eyes, wild eyes, the whites shimmering against the dark foliage, eyes that do not blink. It has a nose and mouth as well; they are fixed as if in stone. This face, unlike the rest of the branched body, does not move in the faint wind that has come up. I ease my face very close to this other face; it suddenly becomes undeniably a human face, I don't know exactly what gives it away. I am hesitant to interrupt Taik, but I have no other choice. I shove him away, jump to my feet and point to the hedge. I start to run. He runs after me, we hold hands, my hair is flying behind me like a sail in the wind. "Keep running!", he says. "Don't look back!" He could have a gun!" We run until we are out of the park and then we stop, breathless, thrilled. I have surrendered to his ultimatum, but since I remember little of it, I do not feel diminished. We kiss, a long, conspiratorial act. It is immortalized by the question he asks me, in all seriousness, immediately afterward. "Are you a spy?" This is what I was born to hear.

Others might say I was born twenty years ago in Eugene, Oregon, to be the dutiful daughter of Richard and Jeanne Schultz. We lived there in a seedy student complex called Amazon Flats while my father finished his graduate degree at the university. During the day, I played with the little neighbor girl, Donna, and my mother pushed me back and forth in the rickety swing set in the courtyard, which was covered sparsely with brown grass, either dead or dying. When I fell, gravel would stick to my knees. My mother, Jeanne Claire, was a budding and beautiful dramatic actress, the toast of the University drama department, whose picture still hangs in the lobby of the theatre building, reminding one of the glories she could have possessed one day, had she not surrendered everything for the love of equally blonde and beautiful Dick Schultz, classics scholar and son of a German immigrant and a firm Scandinavian mother.

Brothers came along with amazing regularity. First Ricky, whom I initially detested with a child's omnipotent rage for usurping my position, and beat whenever I had the opportunity. We seldom drove in our car because we couldn't be left alone in the back seat. We couldn't be left alone anywhere at all. My mother the actress often burst into tears, not able to understand my passionate loathing, saying over and over that we should love each other, we were, after all, brother and sister. The beatings continued until Ricky got too big and, ultimately, incredibly lovable.

Next came Stewart the introspective, who rarely talked and developed into an authority on any number of things, but mostly plants, who could bend his legs back until they reached behind his ears, and did, often, as he watched the little black and white television we were first on our block to possess. Stewart escaped my beatings. I had gotten too old for such undirected anger. Besides, he, too, with his quiet smiles and unassuming manner, could no more be beaten than a newborn puppy, a bunny rabbit, or any other terminally endearing creature.

Last was William, known cryptically as Todd, before whom lay a long and successful career deconstructing mental illnesses both in the classroom and in the psychiatric ward. Todd was the recipient of any nurturing instincts I might have harbored in my primordial genes. I threw him in the air, I hugged and kissed him until he screamed or wet his pants, I hung him upside down until his face turned red.

So there we were, the beautiful actress mother who gave it all up for love, but somehow was unable to surrender completely to the domestic, who never taught me to knit or sew or cook or embroider or make jams and jellies because she didn't care about all that and neither did I. She did agree on several occasions to act in certain of my grade school plays, as an offstage voice that screams. That scream alone would have guaranteed her career in films and theater. And then the professor father with his dry wit and urbane manner, holed up in his den doing translations of Euripides and Aristophanes, surrounded by his library of Balzac, Proust, Voltaire—how as I child I had loved the poor father Goriot in Balzac! And the three brothers, all of us living together and growing, but on parallel planes, whose individual existences were apprehended by the others but didn't exactly touch. I felt my life was more, larger, bursting forth from a space too small to contain it.

In fact, one life was not enough for me, I had several other and more desirable lives, one of which was spent with a family of great wealth and influence, owners of a large horse ranch in which thoroughbreds and jumpers were raised, trained and shown. I was informally adopted by the couple, an older, kindly man and his much younger, peroxided wife, and wherever they went, introduced as their natural daughter. My hair was always arranged in one long braid, identical to my "adoptive" mother. We sometimes took pictures with our braids hanging over their shoulders, more like sisters than mother and daughter. At night, I slept on the couch and woke early, reading horse books until my "parents" got up, which was usually very late. After the weekend was over, I was returned to another couple, even though they could obviously see that the three of them plus the three brothers did not belong together, that I was destined for a different, a more significant life than the one I was forced to lead in their square house on their boxy street, side by side with young, divorced mothers who had overnight guests in cars with crumpled fenders or older, overweight couples whose dogs, cats or birds had become their children, who spoke baby talk to them and treated real children like ruined adults.

There was another life, too, but it was somewhat vague. It always included a foreign country and some sort of intrigue for which my capabilities were particularly suited, be it foreign languages, an iron will, a propensity for taking risks without shedding tears, or attracting men who could later be squeezed for information. Taik's question, then, did not come as a surprise, even though I was not, in fact, a spy. He recognized that I would have been equal to such a profession and that was good enough for me.

He walked me home after the terror in the park. A few cars crawled by from time to time, some weaving as their drivers would have, had the drivers been walking like the two of us. The air was damp. He held my hand, or perhaps had his arm around my shoulder. It is all the same; the feeling was one of intimacy, more intimate than anything that had been done earlier on the stone bench. He spoke of a decaying village, of mutilations, a friend's father hanging from the porch of his house, Catholic priests murdered by Serb soldiers and buried in a cave near his house, of eating cornmeal mush for months on end, and an egg once a month, if at all. Chocolates were dropped from the air by Americans, that he remembered vividly. He spoke of excruciating toothaches which, after a number of years, simply became part of his life; in fact, he could not imagine being without pain, so much had he assimilated it into everything he did, the way he talked, the way he moved his whole body. The absence of pain would somehow have taken the sharp edge off life, an edge he needed to drive him on, to enable him to survive other outrages which would come later with depressing regularity. He talked and talked and I nodded my head from time to time, dizzy with information, and though I could hardly have understood, I drank in what I heard in his voice, I felt the blood moving in his hand, matched my vein to his, made myself at home, in a manner of speaking, as I began to persuade myself that I had not yet had one commensurate to my desires and capabilities.

I have a secret bond with Milena, merely because she is from Yugoslavia. When the other nurses aren't around, I treat her as an equal, we enjoy a clandestine camaraderie, we slap each other on the back, we exchange conspiratorial looks. Milena is uncertain to what she can ascribe this sudden change of status, but this does not prevent her from exploiting it to its fullest potential. She hasn't buttered the bread for the "Jause" or afternoon snack. Head Nurse Erni asks her snidely why not. Milena, edging towards me, proclaims: "I just finished with the bedpans!", and looks to me confidently for confirmation. For once, she is telling the truth. "Well, at least go wash your hands before you do the bread!", a thought Head Nurse Erni is certain would never have occurred to the hapless Milena.

I practice the few words of Croatian I know with poor Milena throughout the day. She speaks Serbian, but the two languages are similar enough to be understood. Twenty times a day I ask her what she's doing, how she is, what she said. She assumes that my ability to ask a question endows me with the same ability to understand the answer and launches invariably into a long-winded monologue, punctuated by a short glottal stop at the end of each sentence.

The nurses often call me over to translate; how easy it is to deceive people into believing one knows what one is doing! I perpetuate the charade, inventing Milena's answers, asking her what she's doing, how she is, instead of, as I am requested, where the plastic gloves that were on top of the medicine cabinet have disappeared to. But because of

Taik, I carry an albatross around my neck. My obsession with anything having the slightest connection to his world has made me a slave to Milena and to the nurses, who have come to depend upon me as chief labor mediator. Just yesterday, I was even asked to translate for the Czech patient, Herr Kubilek, as Czech and Croatian were related, or so they understood.

I make other friends from Taik's world as well. Benjamin the enigmatic, whom we awaken in the middle of the night to keep us company, and Milan, for example, who is a wanted man in Yugoslavia and a tax consultant in Vienna.

We are in his garret, eight floors up, one hundred ninety two steps, no elevator, no indoor toilet, no shower, no hot water. He has an impressive stereo/radio set which overwhelms the few other pieces of furniture, the queen-sized bed, the square card table with one short leg, propped up by an old nylon sock tied around the bottom, the three scratched chairs, the hot plate, the cracked dishes on a shelf by the sink. A small, streaked window looks out onto a postage stamp courtyard below, containing four garbage cans, two without lids, and a broken tricycle. The stereo is out of place, just as Milan is out of place in this apartment, in Vienna, just as Taik is out of place with me, and I am out of place with both of them and the apartment. But we sprawl so comfortably throughout the room. I have laid myself down on the bed, clothes on, hands under my head. Milan sits with his feet on the edge of the table. Taik is in his underwear, white briefs, and nothing else, opposite Milan, smoking, talking feverishly. His right leg is bent in such a way that he is partially exposed, yet he talks on, oblivious. My eyes wander over him from top to bottom, like two feathers swinging slowly to the ground. I somehow understand that he has sat this way many times before in front of many other girls, that this is something he does, something that is natural to him, a biological necessity.

"Come here!", I tell him as I hold out my arms. He turns around, startled to hear a voice behind him, surprised that someone has entered the room without his knowing. Recognition dawns on him. It is I! He smiles indulgently, gets up from the chair and jumps on the bed. I bounce high in the air, what fine springs this mattress has! We settle down, having found the same rhythm; the bed is at rest, we are at rest, Milan snores next to us, we all are on our own.

Sometimes I catch Taik with other women, walking hand in hand with a tall, dark, pale girl dressed in an Austrian dirndl, but I suspect she is not Austrian, she is too gloomy, too intense. He is talking to her animatedly and she listens enthralled, as I always do, but I am whizzing by on the back of a motorbike and cannot watch what happens afterwards. I tell my pal Helmut to drive around the block, to pass them once again. Helmut, my partner in conspiracy, who lusts after me but figures if he can't have me, he will assist in breaking my heart over the one that can. He turns the corners at such an angle that I cry out. My hair is caught in my mouth, the wind whips it out again, but I am oblivious to the wet strands, I want only to see Taik one time and for him to see me. When our eyes meet, he will know that wherever he goes and whatever he does, he can never escape, trick, or take advantage of me, the woman of the western world, because where I come from, the Balkan deceits he is accustomed to practicing are incomprehensible, thus totally ineffectual. But he is gone, and his pale-faced girl with him. We return to Helmut's apartment to plot further action.

The next night, I am waiting for Gerhard in the underground passage by the Opera, sitting at a metal table, drinking a "Grosser Brauner", a large coffee made with milk. Joanne has come along, but she has no date, she is waiting with me, dressed in a tiny dress and tiny shoes, her eyes darting back and forth like those of a small animal. Joanne is tiny all over, her tininess is not self-conscious, she is simply condensed into the tiniest essence of herself that is psychologically and physically possible, for her an effortless operation. "Guten Abend", I hear behind me. We turn and see Taik, his friend and Joanne's sometime date, Branko, and another girl, a bundle of movement, who can't stand still at all as we talk, who grabs Taik's elbow, pushes her hair behind her ears, laughs in inappropriate places, who makes everybody but Taik nervous, irritable. "This is Heidi Kunkler" he tells me. So what, I long to say, get this bitch out of my sight. He invites us to the "Twelve Apostles Cellar", the site of our first date, a heresy. I decline, tell him I have a prior commitment. They wander off, as arbitrarily as they had come, and my whole world is ruined.

Gerhard, Rudi, Joanne and I sit in the "Griechenbeisl", a small pub near Saint Stephen's church, not long after my world has been ruined. We are drinking glasses of white wine, teaching Joanne rude phrases in German, laughing at her pronunciation, liking her for laughing at herself as well. Taik, the same tall, pale dirndled girl, this time in a dark dress and sweater, and Branko, come in the door. I stop laughing and look at him with cool suspicion, as though he had been hired by a jealous husband to follow my movements and this was his gang. They sit diagonally from us, and I notice with satisfaction that the pale girl is looking at me miserably. Taik waits for our dates to go to the restroom and comes over to the table.

"Guten Abend", he tells me with a slight bow of his head, ever the cavalier. "Guten Abend", I answer with a slight bow of mine. "Those two guys are pitiful, aren't they?" He says this as though he and I are the only two people in the world with the insight and intelligence to realize just how pitiful they are, we are the only ones with the necessary knowledge and instincts. "They are, aren't they?" I actually say this, against all intentions, all desire. He returns to his table, after having made a date with me for the following afternoon. The two of us are apart from the rest of the world once again.

But Taik leaves town unexpectedly and then returns weeks later, without an explanation, without so much as a regret that he has had to spend so much time apart from me, his fate, his destiny. And now he will have to spend even more, he will learn as we sit in "Uncle Max's", a self-service restaurant one floor beneath street level, where Anka, a woman from Taik's village in Croatia, works as a waitress. We often go there just so that Taik can feel at home.

Branko, Joanne, Taik and I are at a corner table, drinking coffee, talking desultorily about this and that. Taik is crumpling and uncrumpling an empty cigarette pack. Joanne and Branko are attempting, as usual, to communicate with each other in the few words of German each knows, but today this does not amuse me, today everything that is not absolutely vital should not happen at all. The man at the table next to us should not be concerned with the fact that his girlfriend has not shown up, he ought to stop looking at his watch, craning his neck in the direction of the door, huffing and puffing, resenting us for being two couples. It should not be raining outside, as we have had more than enough rain this week and everybody is getting sick of it, babies are cranky, shopkeepers dispense with their otherwise obligatory "Grüss Gott" when one enters, socks get wet as water soaks through canvas tennis shoes one insists on wearing in spite of the weather. Taik takes a pen out of his pocket and writes on a matchcover, something I don't understand, in Croatian. He gets up and says something to Anka, who gives him a sad smile which makes me suspect melodrama. The fact is, I am leaving tomorrow, my ticket to America is about to expire. A simple fact. I am packing my suitcases, taking a taxi to the airport, waiting on one of the benches for my flight to be called, boarding the plane and arriving, some hours later, in New York. What more can be said about this? And if any more were said, it would change nothing.

Branko picks up the matchcover and holds it out to me. He points to the words and says: "Taik very sad." This means to me that he has never been this sad before, and probably will never be this sad again the rest of his life, but I still do not know what he has written on the matchbook. Taik returns and sits down. I tell him it's time to leave. I am crying. The matchbook remains on the table, in my place; we all see it but nobody dares to pick it up. My inclination is to cover it with a napkin, as though it were a horrible highway accident, a dead pet, a pool of blood, a tiny abortion.

We are walking to the streetcar stop where we will catch the "E" train, which takes us straight down the Wiedner Hauptstrasse, where we will alight, five stops later, to walk up the hill to our apartment, past the little bakery which also sells cartons of orange drink, fresh milk and marzipan, past the automat full of cheap wines in ocean green bottles, past the restaurant, always empty, but never going bankrupt, before which two fly-encrusted black dogs, mother and son or father and daughter, from the looks of it, sprawl indolently day in and day out. Past all these things, past, the past. I am standing at the streetcar stop now, Taik is next to me, not looking at me or at anything else in particular. He is looking at nothing and I am feeling nothing, willing it, really, defending myself against an untenable position with my guns drawn. The last few minutes escape me completely. If I am ever asked to describe them, I shall have to invent an appropriately maudlin version, one in which we fell sobbing into one another's arms, lacking the words to communicate the depth of our devotion and commitment, but trying, anyway, as all people do. It shall have us pondering the uncertainties of love and life, the arguments for and against destiny, chance, and luck. My face is covered with tears, they run down the front of my coat in rivers, in torrents. I try to talk but choke, gasp, fail to cough out what is killing me. This is what I will say happened in those few last minutes. And who knows? Perhaps this is the truest version of all.

"Every person is a prison—also a refuge". Nietzsche

Gearhart, Oregon, 1969–I close my eyes and try to imagine what is happening in Vienna without me. Life is going on, I have no doubt of that, but the quality of life has changed. People are forced to move differently down the streets I frequented, they do not walk around me but through me, my space is no longer reserved for me but has been appropriated by others in odd clothing, some smiling, some well aware of what they are doing to me. There are no legs hanging out the window of the apartment on Blechturm-gasse 26, the bordello has gone out of business. And I doubt that anyone has borrowed the yellowed copies of Georges Simenon mysteries in translation from the seedy book store down the street, the one which serves as a modified flophouse for all the local down-on-their-luck intellectuals in crumpled overcoats smoking small cigars. Nobody is riding in the milk truck at three in the morning save the regular driver, and the horse, Fritzi, is trying to bite someone else's shoulder, not mine. Nobody is sitting high up on a hill on the outskirts of town looking across the Danube at the plains of Hungary in the distance, legs crossed, little bits of prickly grass scratching at the upper thighs, and, if there should be somebody there, it is not I, which invalidates whatever is happening with that other strange person who has tried to take my place.

My letters to Taik do not come back, yet I receive no answer. They are sent to Milan's address, to be forwarded to Taik in Sweden, where he is to spend the summer. Although I am home now, it somehow does not include me completely as it did in the past. There is an excess, an over-lapping, a spilling out which defies definition.

I tell Ed not to grab my crotch as I walk by him in his wheelchair. He laughs and wheels himself behind the door, where he assumes he is invisible. An asylum patient in his younger years, he is now a patient in the nursing home in which I work, as are Toivo, the old, hunchbacked Norwegian who urges me politely to touch his genitals when I give him showers, Emma, the genteel Englishwoman who, embarrassed at her lack of bowel control, hides her messes between her dentures and the roof of her mouth, and Vera, pregnant now for five years, stomach swollen as in the last stages of gestation, cradling a stuffed baby in her arms, rocking it to sleep all day long. I call my parents daily. Do I have a letter from him? I ask. No letters, never a letter. I do not despair, how-ever; the six thousand miles that separate us are like a curtain hanging between us, blocking our view, but when we are ready to see each other, we will push this curtain aside. It is as simple as that.

Ed is threatening to throw his urinal bottle at me, but he hesitates because I have his "Playboy" magazine in my hand, the one with the pictorial on Hawaiian women, one of whom he has named Genevieve Genevieve. The filmy liquid splashes against the side of the bottle as he approaches, one hand holding it high, the other maneuvering the wheelchair. He tells me he thought I was working down in the whore-house and Genevieve Genevieve was there, too, except that he needs the magazine because otherwise they'll come through the wall and kill him. He stops the wheelchair, an anguished look on his face. Then he laughs, remembers who he is, comes after me again. Put down the bottle and I'll give you the magazine, I tell him. But don't go around showing the pictures to the women or I'll take it away for good, OK? I look up and my roommate is standing in the doorway, a letter in her hand. It is a flimsy, airmail letter, the kind you fold over and lick shut, the kind that only has room for a few words. I walk on feathery legs out into the hall. Ed is chuckling as he leafs through his magazine and considers, for just a second, whether he should show Genevieve Genevieve to my roommate. He decides in the negative.

I am leaning against the wall, opening the flaps carefully. Of course it is from Taik, from Vienna. I peel the many corners back, smooth the sheet carefully before I begin to read. He's coming to America! I look at my roommate. I jump around in circles, squealing, she squeals in sympathy, we both jump and squeal until the head nurse emerges from her office. Taik is coming to America! Well, that's fine, I think that's a fine idea; I compose myself, become a thinking adult. The head nurse tells me politely to shut up and get back to work, so I go to Ed and spin him around in his wheelchair until he grabs my crotch fiercely and begs me to stop. And I stop, believe me, I stop.

An old boyfriend, Jim, has come to visit from down south, arriving in his old beat-up van, wearing his faded jeans, his khaki work shirt, looking tan and healthy, but still with a disreputable air about him. Long, brown hair, moustache, bright white teeth. He is incredibly handsome and, for a moment, I feel nostalgic. Then I remember some of the rotten things he did to me before he realized he was in love with me and I hold them all against him, regardless of the time that has passed. He has driven all the way up to see me and expects to be entertained. I ask him if he would like to take Ed out for an ice cream cone and a drive to the Cove to watch the surfers. He says sure. We pick up Ed, maneuver him out of his wheelchair into the van, and head for the Dairy Queen. Ed wants a vanilla cone. He is laughing all the way, dripping ice cream down his chin and onto his shirt. He has the window seat, but is looking straight ahead, eyes frozen. Jim is being a laid-back hippie, taking it all in stride, making small talk with Ed about the Mother of God and Genevieve Genevieve. Ed has not tried to grab my crotch, which amazes me. He does, after all, have a sense of propriety.

I try to tell Jim about Taik, but what's the use, I need a different language, one which we do not share, so I give up, tell him Vienna stories to make him laugh, about the man in the bar who claimed he could write on a piece of paper a sentence in any language in the world for the price of one beer. I asked him to write "Peter Piper picked a peck of pickled peppers" in Tagalog, which he did, immediately. How did you know it was really correct? Jim asks. You don't know Tagalog. I am irritated. Ed sits quietly, contemplating the nature of things. I am quiet. No more stories for Jim, who has never been out of Oregon or seen anything of this wild world and its mysteries. I will tell stories to Ed later, who is much more receptive to what I say.

Portland, Oregon, 1969. My grandmother has become sick and must go into the hospital, leaving grandfather at home. I am enlisted to stay one month with him. I will receive fifty dollars. Taik has written that he needs cigarettes, and not the Austrian variety, either. He wants Marlboros. He also needs more money for his ticket to America. Fifty dollars will buy him plenty of cigarettes and pay for a goodly portion of his ticket, so I go without for a month, I stay at home with Grandpa, devising chores to keep him busy. I give him a broom and send him outside to sweep leaves four or five times a day. I send him down into the basement to straighten things up. I have him dry the dishes, fold the laundry. He still manages to get lost and the police bring him home. Does this nice gentleman live here? they ask. Grandpa enjoys a fine reputation in the community. He is polite and congenial, even though he does not know his name or where he lives. He chats pleasantly with Dad when he comes by to check on us. After Dad leaves, he whispers to me: "Who was that man?"

Eugene, Oregon, 1969. When Taik has received his cigarettes and money, he writes and thanks me profusely. He plans on arriving in America in a matter of months, probably in November, but he will be living in Ohio with friends who have refugee status. And I am back in school at the University of Oregon, where I have taped a picture of Tito, the Yugoslav president, on the wall of our apartment, and on his chest have written "Tito is a fascist." The time is ripe for such statements, we are all in revolt without quite knowing why, all clinging together in a state of extreme alienation, but I am perhaps touched less deeply than others by injustice because I have not yet discovered the art of suffering vicariously

I try to find ways to summon Taik's presence. I look down at the raw scar on my wrist, the only visible scar he has given me. He is carrying me along the Danube, he can barely walk from the weight. We are rollicking drunk, moving along like a strange insect who has been stunned by a rolled newspaper. His lit cigarette is resting comfortably on my wrist. I look down at it, curious, a bit perplexed, ask him to move the cigarette, not a bit irritated, flattered, in fact ,that he is so lost in me that all else has escaped his concentration. He wants to know if I could ever love him. I do not yet fathom the answer to this question but tell him yes nonetheless. And in the morning he is amazed that he still likes me. It usually isn't the case, I am told. But I am cranky and tired and I don't care.

I go down almost every night to Max's tavern, down the alley from our apartment. I never study, but my grades do not suffer, my classes seem to go on without me, filling in for me, covering for me when I am not there. I develop crushes on John, a Communist from Marblehead, Massachusetts, who writes proletarian plays and lets me read them. We smoke pot together and look at books on Hieronymus Bosch. Then there is another John, from San Francisco, but he turns out to be gay. George is in between these two, the angst-filled philosopher, the one besieged by Weltschmerz, by his own admission, who is kind and gentle and boring and who cries when I won't let him kiss me one rainy night as we lean against the wall of an old building. Tom, a blond who looks like my twin brother, comes into my life for just an instant and is gone again, in his psychedelic van. His parting advice to me is that, if I should ever hear him knocking at my door again, don't open it.

But the image of Taik is continually present in my mind, invalidating all other levels of experience to which I am exposed. Tom and John and John and George, as well as Brandy, who lectures me about having a dog on a leash, and James, who is enchanted with me for telling him I want to know him as no other ever has, who is hooked already by this little game—they are like beads on a string, little plastic beads meant to adorn, but not too expensively, not too extravagantly, whose loss one does not feel longer than a minute or so when the string finally breaks and they all go scattering across the floor.

The letters I receive from Taik contain no timeless statements, but it is what lies beneath, what I know with certainty unsupported by fact lies beneath, which gives them their great significance. I keep them in a special place, under my bed. If I were to show with my thumb and fore-finger how high the stack of letters is, there would hardly be a space between the two. It isn't important, it isn't critical. He knows his place and I know mine and no mile-high stack of letters someone else might have received from some other lover has any bearing on the two of us. Everything is out of his control, though he doesn't realize this yet. There is a power and a knowledge within me which will not be denied.

I go to a big demonstration against the war in Vietnam. Many of my friends are there, and they all wave and smile. I stand impatiently a few feet before a podium from which an impassioned speech is being given. Mary is with me, the one who refused to talk to her fiance when he returned from Vietnam, who called him a murderer, a piece of garbage, a non-human. She is yelling slogans along with most of the others standing around us, caught up in the hysteria which carries one along like a wave. Even I yell slogans, though I am mortally embarrassed, not because I object to the triteness of the words I yell, but because I have no feelings about what is happening in Vietnam. What do I care about:? I try to make a list in my mind. It is a short one. It consists, it seems, of one word: Taik.

"A human being who strives for something great considers everyone he meets on his way either as a means or as a delay and obstacle—or as a temporary resting place." Nietzsche

Cleveland, Ohio, 1970–Melody and I sit in a parking lot waiting for Taik to come out of the factory. It is three in the morning, a humid, unbearably hot evening in Cleveland, on the banks of the Cuyahoga River, the one that caught fire not long ago. We are stuck to the car seat, deep half moons of sweat are spreading under our arms, our hair clings willfully to our cheeks and the back of our necks. I hate Cleveland already. Whatever position I assume is too hot, too wet; too many parts are touching too many other parts of my body. Melody is losing patience, with me, with the conversation Branko and I carry on in German, with the sound of machinery cutting through the humidity in a maddening staccato, with the idea of going to Europe in general. She wants to go home to Gearhart, to her house up on a hill, overlooking the ocean, where deer come every morning and stand poised outside the kitchen window to be fed, where the only sounds of machinery she hears are those of the electric can opener in the kitchen.

I get out of the car and walk back and forth, leaving Melody and Branko to get on with each other any way they can. I predict already that they will be in love before the week is over; how else can they survive this heat and humidity? I am already in love, with the dark shape that suddenly comes running across the gravel and grabs me, hugs me fiercely in his arms. His T-shirt clings to him, there is a film of moisture covering his face and arms which mingles with mine as we touch; we are slick, slippery. He tells me with wonder that I am skinny, as though he had resigned himself long ago that I would be forever plump, that he would have to rent a wheelbarrow as we grew older to transport me from place to place. He laughs at my shoes, saying only the old women in his village would wear such shoes, and only if they had nothing else. How's my dress? I want to know. He looks at it very seriously and pronounces it merely OK. But he also is in love and nothing about dresses or shoes has the slightest importance to either of us, we are talking just to convince ourselves we did not imagine each other long ago.

He tells me he got off work because his boss thinks his sister is coming from Europe and that he must pick her up at the airport. What is this place where you work? I ask. He dismisses the question as irrelevant. He is as suited to a factory as a leg is to a sleeve and any curiosity he might at one time have had for the mysterious interplay between labor and capital has long since disappeared.

We drive down Superior Avenue, through a gritty ghetto where people hang out doorways, even at this hour, yelling back and forth, where most houses are lit, windows open, radios playing, children crying, moaning really, as though besieged by some dull pain. Taik tells me to roll up the window, lock the door. We move through the streets as though under siege, and when we emerge, onto a cobbled street lined with tall, leafy trees, the car slows down and finally stops. This is where I live now, he tells me ironically. In this beaten-down house only feet from the ghetto, porch stairs collapsing, roof slanted in embarrassment, grass dead or dying—in this tomb he now lives, emerging like a vampire at night and sleeping in the daylight hours, hoping nobody discovers him and drives a stake through his heart.

It is only two in the afternoon and already I have eaten about half a pound of prosciutto, or prsut, a home-cured Croatian specialty, endless slices of bread: rye, pumpernickel, a doughy French at one house, served in triangles, rectangles, with and without crust, and big, heavy slabs. In addition, I have had two pieces of apple strudel, one piece of cheese strudel, one piece of spinach pie, three poppyseed pastries, and a big marzipan peach. With this I drank four cups of Turkish coffee, all with at least three spoonfuls of sugar per cup, two plum brandies, a glass of white wine and a peach brandy. I sit on the edge of a sofa covered with plastic, in danger of slipping off onto the floor, like a beached whale coming in on a wave. No thank you, I am fine, I tell the Croatian hostess, but she ignores me and puts two large slices of chocolate cake on my plate. The coffee will be ready in a minute she tells me conspiratorially. What, I wonder, are we conspiring about?

Taik sits with the husband and talks politics. Every so often I understand an international word, such as revolution. At each house I am put through my paces. What are you, Taik asks me smugly. Ja sam vijestica. I am a witch. Everybody bursts out laughing without fail and my glass is filled, my plate loaded down. When we finally return to the sad house he now lives in, I go to the bathroom and throw up. The colors coming out of me make me dizzy and proud at the same time.

We sit at the kitchen table, Taik is in his underwear, his newly-arrived sister, Zdravka, is standing at the stove, hair pulled into a long ponytail, bare feet, stirring a huge pot. The temperature is well over ninety, and so is the humidity. She tells me we will eat in about half an hour, but I say no, flatly no. She looks up in surprise, No, I say more feebly. I go into the bedroom and lie down, wish to die.

When I come out again, Taik sits in my lap, he finds this flouting of tradition endlessly amusing, and I laugh along with him, happy to have him so close. Much of the surface of his body is in contact with mine, and this never fails to please me. I look around to make sure everybody sees that he is sitting in my lap with his arm around me. My legs are going to sleep, but I would rather they be paralyzed for life than tell him to move.

I'm going to Zagreb in a few months, as soon as we get settled in Vienna, I tell him. Zagreb is the capital of Croatia. I had never had the idea of going there until five seconds earlier, but as soon as he hears this, I know I have heard something of importance. You are? he asks. He is thinking and I must wait for what comes next. I wait and wait and nothing comes, he has become like stone, like an animal frozen in fear or anticipation, all senses heightened. Would you do something for me there? he finally asks. Sure, I say without expression, knowing by instinct that any show of enthusiasm or eagerness will cause the offer to be withdrawn. Anything I can do for him is fine with me.

There is no further mention of the favor I am to do for Taik. We lie in bed, looking at old pictures he has brought with him from Europe. He has a snapshot of an old girlfriend, Andrea, who sprawls seductively across a couch, her nakedness only partially covered by a scarf, looking vixenish, whorish. He eyes are like cat's eyes, slanted and green, narrowed as she looks into the camera. Taik tells me she is rich and crazy, she'll do anything for him, she doesn't work, she just goes out looking for interesting and dangerous people, she has no meaning, no passion in her life and anybody who can give her one or the other or both she will make any sacrifice for. What has she done for you? I want to know. Nothing, he says, but she would if I asked her. He has asked me, though, not her, and I'm going to do it, if only I can find out what it is.

Melody and I are invited to a Croatian wedding, to be held in the Croatian Hall just off St. Clair Avenue. Nevenko and Mara are getting married, even though they have lived together for a number of years, first in Berlin, then here in Cleveland, where they arrived as refugees. Mara is sick now, sick and pale, sick from Cleveland, homesick, for the bright blue water which surrounds her island of Pag, for the air so clear and crisp, the fresh food, the pounds of glistening fish pulled in on her father's boat every day. Nevenko cannot make her laugh anymore. She gets up in the morning and already the day is over, time holds no promise for her now, it contains no mystery, no possibilities, it is simply a unit of measure designed to make one's days pass as quickly as possible. By the time she counts the minutes and hours, the sun has gone down and she can turn out the lights, go to bed, scoot way over so Nevenko cannot accidentally touch her as she sleeps. But they are getting married in spite of everything.

A long table has been set up at one end of the hall, covered with a snowy tablecloth. In the center sits the happy couple, and on either side, the family members and close friends. Mara smiles frozenly, her hands lie on the table like dead animals. Something is wrong here, I tell Taik.

People stare at Melody and me, in a friendly way, at our clothing, our way of talking, of handling ourselves in this crowd. I am wearing the shoes only old women in Taik's village would wear. They are heavy and brown, with thick laces and squared-off toes. My dress is gold corduroy. The Croatian women are in their finery, long pastel gowns, silver heels, gold purses, a lot of jewelry, on the fingers, the wrists, around the neck, two or three gold chains on some, long, dangly earrings, some so heavy that the earlobes much stretch to accommodate the weight. Faces brightly made up, powdered, blushed, all shades of lipstick, deep magenta, mauve, frosts of all colors. When they smile, the gold teeth most of them have flash in the light, like beacons signalling a lost ship.

Their husbands stand apart in a corner near the bar. They rarely dance, they leave the merriment to the women, they have important issues to discuss in their drunken profundity, issues such as revolution and assassination. Their shirts, as the evening goes on, begin to come untucked, first one corner, then the whole shirt. The jackets have been removed hours before, after the first few glasses of wine. So many red faces, broken capillaries. An argument breaks out, there is blood on the floor, mixed with a spilled glass of red wine, people are escorted out, hustled out, really. Mara sits motionless at her special place in the center of the table, a queen in exile.

A woman has asked me to dance, she has taken my hand and pulled me onto the dance floor. I feel my face redden, I am suffused with warmth. I stand in the middle of the room, my hand encircled by that of the woman who invited me. Where is Taik and why won't he rescue me from this shameful situation, this outrage! We don't dance with other women in America, I tell her as politely as I can. Her face falls, like shifting concrete, her smile, her air of frivolity desert her completely, she is suddenly a broken woman, a stupid immigrant, she has committed the ultimate faux pas, made a donkey of herself. I read this in her expression in a matter of seconds, the time it takes her to drop my hand and turn away to run off the floor. I am relieved that I do not have to dance with a woman after all and when Taik asks me where she went so suddenly, I say I don't know. When I see her later in the evening, she averts her eyes. I notice she has spilled something red down the front of her dress, but she is too drunk to care.

Violich is a huge man, both in height and physique, but nonetheless, there is a smallness about him, shrinking into himself, as though his inner essence is incapable of supporting such a large frame. He has no teeth, not a single tooth in his mouth. He has refused to have dentures fitted, for some perverse reason he wants to be reminded day after day of the circumstances under which those teeth were lost. When he smiles, he smiles with his lips pressed together and if something is especially funny, he laughs out loud, mouth wide open, but covered with a hand so that the dark cavern is not exposed.

Taik will not tell me exactly how her lost his teeth, only that they were lost in prison in Yugoslavia. I imagine his teeth still there, looking for their master, roaming around aimlessly, down dark corridors, either together as a top and bottom, gnashing against each other, or as individuals, spread out so as to cover more territory. He can't eat too many things, I comment. More than he got before, says Taik. Violich's wife hovers around him like a troubled hen, bringing dishes and taking them away, cutting fruit into small pieces and mashing them as unobtrusively as possible. He accepts this as his due, teeth or not, and scolds her when she allows his glass of wine to become empty.

From time to time, he shakes his head violently, perhaps he hears something which bothers him, or is trying to bring himself to his senses. All his gestures are quick, disjointed, without a sense of origin or destination, as though he is simply crisscrossing the globe, retracing his steps, intersecting an old route, one which he may or may not recognize.

His wife has brought a plate piled high with pieces of poppy pastry. Eat, eat, she tells us. He regards the pile with a weary, tolerant smile, as if to say that even though this excess is possible from a logistical point of view, it is unacceptable from an aesthetic one. I would like to take a piece, my stomach has stretched out and I am continually hungry, but I am afraid of Taik's reaction. So I fold my hands in my lap and try to make some sense out of what he and Taik are saying. After about two hours, I give up and take three pieces of pastry. I also allow his wife to fill my wine glass. All the while, I am urged to continue to eat and drink, so I do until everything is gone and so are we.

What was your impression of Violich? Taik asks me on the way to his sad house. Only half alive, I say, or half dead. Behind his eyes is a city with all the buildings burned down. I feel strongly that he should get some teeth. I want to hold this against him but cannot find a way to justify my need. If only for the sake of his wife, who has to look at him every day.

We go to Croatian bars every night, the ones on St. Clair Avenue. Each one has a jukebox and at least two pool tables. Melody and I sit at the counter, allowing all of Taik's friends to buy us drinks, to gather around us, try to speak English with us, flirt, but not too blatantly, they are not foolish, play our requests on the jukebox. I choose "El Condor Pasa" over and over again, I have decided this is to be our song, the song which will remind me of Taik when we are separated, which will provide me with an appropriate framework for the suffering I will have to undergo. I'd rather be a hammer than a nail, yes I would. The plaintive voices cut through me, into my heart, like a humming wire. Taik is shooting pool, he is bending over, intense, doesn't know I am alive. I am overcome with love for him, I want to flatten myself against him until we are welded together, until we are one.

Branko is driving us to Akron in his tiny car. He and Melody are in the front seat, Taik and I squeezed into the back. His legs are draped over mine, he leans against the window, smoking cigarettes and telling me stories about his village, Gorica. And Ikina walked all hunched over, he tells me, he couldn't help it, he had a problem with his spine, and the first time his future daughter-in-law saw him, she naturally wanted to make a good impression so she goes over, she doesn't know about his spine, and bends down and asks him what he's looking for on the ground and can she help him find it. After that, Ikina did all he could to embarrass her. He'd sit in the doorway mending his own socks so the whole village would see that she was lazy and didn't take care of her husband's poor widowed father. He'd come out and spread a newspaper on the grass and eat off it because, he said, she never got the dishes clean. Things like that. The daughter-in-law cried, begged forgiveness, promised him anything, but he wouldn't budge. Finally she gave up and stopped talking to everybody, even her husband. Taik laughs as he tells this, it is so fresh in his mind, even though he has not been allowed to go home for many years. Another man used to throw his wife out the window when he got drunk, we used to hear her screaming all the time in the middle of the night. It's a good thing the houses are only two stories high, he says, she just rolled down the hill, there was grass right underneath the window. The women in our village are much tougher than you American women, he tells me. My mother had me under a tree and went back to work planting tobacco a half hour later.

The car has come to a stop in front of a small, white house, neatly kept and enclosed, as if it were a vicious animal presenting a false face to the public, by a high, barbed-wire fence. We get out of the car, go through the gate and up to the door. We knock. Behind the thin curtains of one of the windows, we see movement, hurried movement, but very purposeful. The door opens and we are greeted by a small. bespectacled man. He is wiping his hands on a dishtowel, he has just finished doing the dishes. He and Taik go into a room and leave the three of us behind in the kitchen, sitting at the table, each with a glass of slivovitz before us. There is an enormous tension in the air, an indefinable quality of evolution, of things developing, changing. Perhaps it is revolution after all. The door opens and Taik asks me to come in. Branko and Melody sit like statues, ask no questions, show no curiosity about any of this. They are drinking their slivovitz, which has transported them to a different level of consciousness, where absences are cause for amusement and not concern.

This is Milan Antic, Taik tells me. Antic smiles hugely, his glasses have steamed up in excitement, so that I am unable to see his eyes. He grips my hand so tightly I wince, tells me how important this mission is, could be, will be, in a fractured English I barely understand, all consonants, the words thrown together like a bunch of bad beans in a pot. I understand, I say solemnly, summoning forth a decorum, a dignity and purposefulness I do not in reality possess. My hands are folded in front of me, my back is straight, my eyes look directly into his. What if this is an historic moment? I ask myself. Don't forget anything that has happened here, remember the softness of the leather chair on which I rest my hand for one quick moment, the feel of the slight wind against my cheek from the open window, the cars honking in the distance, so forlorn, don't forget how Taik looks, standing against the bookcase, like a king or a president on vacation. His shoes need to be polished, one lace is tied together, it has broken, but this does not affect his bearing at all. The three of us could be making history, changing the world in some yet undetermined manner, causing terrible or wonderful things to happen, who knows? Antic hands me the leaflet. Here it is, he says. Already I am imagining what will be written about this piece of paper and who will write it.

There are three thick packets in all, wrapped in heavy brown paper and taped shut, each containing one thousand leaflets. Each packet weighs approximately ten pounds, and I begin to worry that I will have to pay extra at the airport, that I will be forced to get rid of some of my clothes or books. I have placed the precious packets at the bottom of my suitcase, where they lie like sleeping bombs, waiting to be activated by the right press of the switch, the right finger.

On our way back, Taik is talking non-stop, as he always does when he rides in a car. He cannot drive himself, and he feels it is his responsibility to entertain the driver and the passengers for as long as the drive lasts. I remember the last time the two of us parted, the sense of loss that settled on me like a cold and heavy blanket.

If you have no other alternative, just give them my name, he tells me. But it won't come to that, there won't be any problems. I nod my head, even after he has stopped talking. Nothing will happen to me, I'll be outside the country, he says. But what will happen to me? I think for just a moment before criticizing myself. Nothing will happen to me, either. Nothing will happen.

Have a good trip, good-bye, good-bye, we all exchange greetings, Branko kisses Melody, Taik and I embrace for a long time, like good friends or brother and sister, like soldiers, one of whom finally gets to go to the front, the one who didn't really want to be a soldier. I have brought a book by John Fowles,"The Magus". I settle in my seat, find the faces of Taik and Branko in the terminal, they are like bugs under glass, wave at them, though I know they can't see me, continue to wave until the plane slowly taxis away down the runway. Some kind of event is being set into motion and I find myself both spectator and participant, I act and am acted upon; because of this, it is impossible to attach guilt.

It is exactly like flying in this plane, I realize. I fly and am flown. With what could I possibly be indicted?

Vienna, Austria, 1970. Vienna, you fancy old friend, you reprobate, you prig, what have you done in my absence to distinguish yourself, how have you rehabilitated yourself? Your streets are still like bursting veins, barely containing the life pressed into them; they swell and pulse like an overburdened heart. There is something excessive about you, something which wants to spill over but never can; you simmer, you don't boil. Is this what you have learned from the past century, that your voluptuousness causes you not to be caressed, but raped? So you have tightened your stays, forced your succulent flesh into a space far too small. You have not changed at all. Even the birds in the trees sing as though they are choking.

Frau Kus is bubbling over with excitement that I have returned, bringing with me a new friend, Melody, whom she likes immediately for her beautiful skin. So eine schöne Haut, says Frau Kus as she runs her index finger over Melody's cheek. We have unpacked our suitcases, washed our hands and faces, and now Melody must be taught how to run the hot water, how to light the gas stove. I pull her to the window and point out the apartment across the street. The couple who lives there told Frau Kus I was a whore because I sat in the window drying my hair with my feet hanging out. I embellish the story so that Melody will like Vienna more quickly. If I can be accused of being a whore, anything is possible in Vienna, a notion that gives her endless pleasure. Frau Kus bustles around our rooms, setting things in order, moving a bowl here, a lamp there, even patting empty spaces, as though she perceives a disorder in nothingness. I am home again, where everything began and will continue.

Meanwhile, I continue, as though Taik would approve, to pursue connections to what I perceive as his world. One of these takes place in the Prater, Vienna's huge and renowned amusement park, a lovely garden on the surface, filled with a profusion of colors, shapes, and fragrances, a dizzying phantasmagoria of frantic activity and movement, which inspires and enervates and seems to expose its every aspect simultaneously, like a cubist painting which is both coming and going at the same speed. But this as a deception, because there is a dimension which remains hidden until the rides close down, until the cafes empty of red-cheeked beer drinkers in green loden jackets and feathered hats, and young parents with cranky babies whose noses are dripping, whose bedtimes have long since passed, until the giant ferris wheel ceases its revolutions, comes to a complete stop like a dying dinosaur. It is then that everybody heads for the last streetcar, trickles out onto the streets in tired little rivers, surrendering this lovely garden to the creatures thriving below the surface, the maggots whose importance is always underestimated. After all, they were here before the babies and young mothers, before the apes, before the consciousness of human or animal existence. They thrive in the bowels of every organism, small and large, they cause a necessary disintegration and decay, they cleanse the system of impurities by becoming impure themselves.

But it is still early, the garden is still in bloom. Melody and I watch the pony ride. There are five men leading the ponies by their reins, five ponies, each carrying a small child on its back. The smell of horsehair, manure, hay assails me. I am ecstatically content bathing in these fragrances, but Melody is impatient, she wants to go on the bumper cars, the giant ferris wheel, she wants to buy fry bread, a white wurst, an ice cream in a paper cone. Around and around go the ponies, circling forever, never reaching a destination. But what of the men leading these ponies, men who are conscious of the destination never reached, who are not sated by the flake of hay at the end of the evening? I search their faces. Most are like the ponies, like appendages of the ponies, a fifth leg, a second head. There are two, however, who are different. They are laughing as they walk the circle, yelling across to each other, they catch our eyes as they pass by, wink, smirk. Both are dark and swarthy, black hair, black eyes, black clothes, black, scuffed shoes with pointed toes. My heart is feeling cramped, as though my chest cannot contain so large an organ. I realize, I hope fervently, that the two are possibly Croatian, perhaps guest workers, refugees, exiles. Suddenly there is a bond between us, I create one at that very moment, withdraw from the rest of humanity crowding around me, narrow my eyes, my self.

The two have gotten the message we have sent. The taller one points to his watch and holds up one finger. I nod in comprehension. We will come back at one o'clock to meet them, they will be off work. I take Melody for a white wurst and a piece of Sachertorte, just in case she is inclined to raise objections to the rendezvous, but she is content, willing to indulge me as I have indulged her.

Their names are Sasha and Alexa and they are from Yugoslavia, but they are not Croatians, they are Serbian, the ones Taik told me were in control of the government which had oppressed, imprisoned, even killed Croatians who were in opposition. It is hard to imagine these two being capable of such infamy, these pony guides with the ragged clothing and faces. Just as it is clear that the majority of Serbs are decent and good people as well, and Taik has said as much to me on several occasions. How are you? I ask them in Croatian. They are surprised that I speak a language they understand and answer volubly, just as Milena used to do. Alexa takes my hand and Sasha takes Melody's. They have made their choices, so we set off to a beer hall. The walkways are empty now, the stands have closed down, locked up, the rides are silent; yet in this silence something moves, something menacing, like a fish going belly up in a still pool of water.

Time passes, I am unsure how, perhaps it is aided by the glasses of wine we drink and forget, perhaps we are enchanted by the exotic quality of the decadent garden at rest, or benumbed. We find ourselves alone, Alexa and I, on a park bench in the middle of the Prater, not far from the beer hall. Melody and Sasha have disappeared, but I do not call for them. There is a feeling to their disappearance; they are nowhere near, their absence transmits information of an intangible sort, tells me my calls would be in vain, that I am absolutely alone with Alexa.

He says something to me which I wish so much to understand, because it is connected somehow with the long, sharp knife he pulls suddenly out of his pocket and holds out in front of me. It reminds me of a fang, a malevolent fang. Something I have once heard floats in and out of my memory at the sight of it, about Serbs and knives. I try to recapture it, as one tries to recapture a fading dream when one first awakes, but I cannot, it is gone. The knife is not, however; Alexa continues to hold it out, to fondle it with the cushiony part of his thumb.

As if by mutual assent, we rise and begin to walk. He has put the knife back in his pocket. My mind is suddenly very clear, the curtain of fog has lifted, exposing a tidy scene on a cramped stage across which I walk unsteadily. Suddenly, from the audience, I cry out. Watch out for that man, I cry. But neither of them hears me, they continue to walk along the empty path, empty even of sound.

We are back at the pony ride, but the ponies are gone. All that remains are the trampled ring and the spokes from which the ponies were attached. It is as though everything has died, the ponies, the children, the parents hanging over the fence watching; it is like a tomb, a mausoleum. I have to go, I tell Alexa in English. It's too bad if he doesn't understand, I am back in my world now, I am out of patience. He mutters something, not to me but to himself, and guides me around the back of the building. I yank my arm away and he yanks it back. There is a sudden sharpness pressing into my back, through the material of my coat. I turn around to see the knife again. I say to Alexa, OK, let's go, let's go up these stairs looming in front of us, I think in terror. He is pacified, I pat his arm, the one not holding the knife. We slowly climb the stairs and, at the top, we stop for a moment. He puts the knife back into his pocket, then opens the door. In the blackness, I hear movement, sighs, people rolling over, but spread out, as though we are in a large dormitory. A disembodied voice speaks to Alexa, and he tells this voice everything is under control, he has merely come to rape me and then he will leave, leave them to go back to sleep again. This what he must have said.

He pushes me over to a bed, he pushes me down onto it. I try in confusion to decide what to take off first, to deny him the opportunity to make the choice. But suddenly, the door opens and a woman bursts into the room. The lights go on. She begins to yell in German, she is the pony woman, the one who runs the ride, the owner, the boss, the saviour. She wants to know what in the hell is going on here, anyway. I jump up, run over to her, we are confederates, my grandfather was a German, I have my degree in German, I am from a good family and my father is a university professor. Poor, poor me, what am I doing in a place like this with these heathens, these animals? This old woman gives me a look of pure contempt and tells me to get out and never come back. I run, I fly down the stairs, across the pavement, out into the street, my heart pounding. I am in the middle of the street, waving down cars, a taxi, an American on vacation. A taxi stops, I get in, give my address, a very good one, in a good section of Vienna, any fool knows that, especially a taxi driver. Someone tried to rape me, I tell the driver. I am bursting with indignation and outrage. He turns around and gives me a long look. What do you expect running around the Prater at three in the morning! he says. Well, I say, well, and then I am quiet.

I decide I am much safer with Milan, the wanted man, who has taken me out to a Croatian restaurant near the Danube where a trio of musicians strolls from table to table playing folk music. I have ordered a Balkan plate, small rolls of spicy meat, paprika rice, skewered beef and pickled cabbage and carrots. Milan has invited a group of Austrian co-workers along, with whom he chats knowledgeably in his thick accent. I am not dressed appropriately, I wear a pair of pants and a long smock, and around the waist I have tied my favorite long leather shoelace. The others are in their finery. Milan is in a smart suit, freshly-shined Italian shoes, crisp white shirt. I am drinking Zilavka, a tart, topaz-colored white wine from Croatia.

The musicians stop at our table, but Milan ignores them, continues talking, smoking his cigarette. They sing and play, they court him, but he refuses to be seduced. I like the looks of the tall guitar player, he is dark with a long moustache, a ruddy face. His fingers are slender and delicate, and the way they move up and down the strings is undeniably erotic. I excuse myself and go to the restroom, where I feel dizzy all of a sudden and sit down on the floor.

I moan, my head between my legs. When I look up, the guitar player stands over me. Are you all right, he asks in German? No, I'm sick. Ooooohhhhhh.... I continue. If only I could make some interesting conversation.

Will you meet me tomorrow? he asks. I am surprised, but I say yes and then he leaves. When I return to the table, I do not tell Milan, but he looks at me strangely, as though he had been in the restroom with me and the guitar player the entire time, as though he knows how these things go, or should go or have gone. I don't understand why I feel ashamed, but I also feel excited. This is a Croatian restaurant and I have an engagement with a Croatian musician the next day. The guitar player sits down for a break and as he smokes his cigarette, he narrow his eyes at me, he releases the smoke from his mouth slowly, as though he were sending me signals.

We are leaving. Milan takes my arm, leads me towards the door. I am swept up in the crowd, up and out of the restaurant. From the street, I look back through the window. The guitar player is standing at the bar, watching us as we go down the cobbled walkway. Milan drops me off at my streetcar stop, he is strangely silent. I pretend that I notice nothing, I pretend to be innocent, although I feel I will be punished for what I have done. But what is it that I have done? A nameless guilt overcomes me. What exactly is it that I have done?

I write a letter to Taik when I arrive home, even though I have no place to send it, tell him I was at a Croatian restaurant, where musicians played folk music, Milan took me, the wanted man, actually a second cousin to Taik. I ramble on and on, giving him little details of the evening, tell him about the color of the Zilavka, its tartness which made my tongue shrivel up. When I finish I am not purged. I throw the letter away. Then I take it out of the wastebasket and tear it up, flush it down the toilet. My dreams, once I finally drop off to sleep, frighten me. They concern a drawing which is in more dimensions that science has discovered.

Ivan, the guitar player, has not always been one, he has spent most of his life in Dalmatia on a fishing boat, he tells me when we see each other again. It is unclear to me why he is now playing a guitar in a Croatian restaurant in Vienna, and he says he can't speak German well enough to explain. We sit in a long booth somewhere in the fourth district, not far from the Prater. It reminds me of a truck stop, it has no European flavor to it whatsoever; in fact, I am surprised that there are no plastic ketchup and mustard containers on the tables. Off-white formica tops, tiled floors, waitresses leaning against the counter, a little oasis of backroads America deep in the bowels of Europe.

We have finished our dinner, Ivan, I, and a Croatian friend of his who has joined us, a stocky man with curly brown hair, who smokes continually and talks too loud. I am talking loud as well, telling him Tito is a traitor and has been bad for Croatians and that they are terribly oppressed. Ivan listens intently, adding nothing.

What do you think of the Croatian movement for independence? I ask Ivan. This is something I had heard something of from Taik. He says that he doesn't know much about it. Well, you're Croatian, aren't you? I persist. Why wouldn't you be a supporter? His friend interrupts me, says the supporters of Croatian independence killed lots of people in the last war. I yell at him that Croatians were Partisans, too, and many were killed by the Serbs and later even by the Partisans, weren't they? It was a war, after all. All the guilt wasn't just on one side. And what about today, I say, what's happening today?

Who is this idiot? I ask Ivan. I don't want to talk to him anymore. I turn my back to both of them, stare off into space. I'm still aware, though, that I have a full glass of wine in front of me, and I drink it down.

Somehow I get home. Melody is already asleep. I fall into bed until the alarm wakes me. As I climb out of bed, I try to remember what happened the night before and feel vague misgivings. Everything is fuzzy, undefined. But I am angry at Ivan and everybody like him. I don't want to see him again, or perhaps I want to see him so that I can tell him he makes me sick. I postpone a final decision on this matter, my stomach is churning, my head aches, the inside of my mouth is like a scouring pad. Ivan can't even pretend he isn't Croatian because his name gives him away. Ivan is Croatian for John, Jovan is the Serbian variant. Well, my name is Julienne and I am not French. This is quite funny to me, for some reason. I go to the refrigerator and down a pint of cold milk, go out the door, down the stairs and to work.

Some people could make quite a case about a young girl working in a candle shop, especially in Vienna, birthplace of Freud. This thought diverts me until I reach the front door. I open it, walk in and prepare myself for another multi-lingual day, a day of being different.

We have discovered "Leopold's", a pub/restaurant not far from the University. It has an outside terrace where people can sit in sunny weather and drink beer. The clientele here is international, and mostly young. Our attraction is that we are Americans, and, therefore, wealthy, cosmopolitan, and always ready for a good time. First we meet Dave, a salesman from England, who is married to Marta, a Czech refugee with blonde hair severely pulled back into a bun. Marta speaks English and they both can get by in German. Then there is Ralf, a cello player for a Viennese symphony orchestra, Norwegian, big, burly, with a long moustache curled at the ends. Helmut is an Austrian, born and raised in Vienna, who scorns his own and aspires always to friendships with those he feels are equal to his grandiose schemes in life, paramount is which, by his own admission, marrying a rich American girl. He works in a photography shop on the main street, the Kärtner-strasse, where he caters to tourists who can't seem to figure out how to load their exotic cameras bought a week before leaving on their first European vacation. Clive is Swedish, a ruddy-faced Swedish medical student, best friend of Ralf, who gets drunk and abuses the head-waiter every night without fail just before closing. Sober, he is an articulate delight, but drunk, an abusive monster, who is so unfair to Tony that the Austrian customers regularly stand up in protest against him, telling him too shut up and to go back to whatever country he comes from. I hide my face, pretend I am sitting at the table by sheer chance, look beseechingly at poor Tony, who, to his credit, does not hold grudges, even against Clive, whom he serves politely every evening until the ultimate confrontation. Nobody has been able to explain this animosity towards Tony, not even Clive in his sober moments. It just overcomes him, he says, he can't help himself, he sees that smirking face and he gets so mad he wants to punch him.

Even though Clive and I spend time together, he's not a boyfriend, he is just filling in, he is safe, entertaining, even a bit complex. Almost every night, Clive and I share a taxi home from "Leopold's". They are cheap and we are usually too impatient to wait for a streetcar and have drunk too much beer to want to walk. So we climb in, heavy and weaving, and are transported, like large bloated fish, to our apartments. I learn that Clive also dislikes taxi drivers when he has been drinking, suspects them of trying to take advantage of him because he is a foreigner. He tells one of them, in precise German, that he is an idiot and a stupid asshole for not being able to do anything in life but drive a beat-up car around the city day after day.

When I get out, I lean into the car and tell the taxi driver that Clive is dying of cancer, that he has only a few more months to live and this is why he talks the way he does. The taxi driver says he hopes he dies tomorrow and speeds off. But Clive never yells at me, he becomes affectionate and sentimental when he has been drinking, asks me questions such as, would I marry him if he asked me, things like that, which he never remembers the next day. And I never try to refresh his memory, we both know it is only a scene to be replayed whenever necessary.

One night a Croatian joins our table at "Leopold's", or at least he says he is one. His mother works at a Viennese newspaper as a correspondent. He doesn't fit in with our group, he is too reserved, he sits too straight in his chair, he sips his beer instead of gulping it, his hair is cut too precisely, like a mathematical equation. But he says the enchanted word, "Croatian", and I warm to him immediately, regale him with bits of information I have picked up, that there will soon be a revolution in Croatia, that Tito should be sentenced to death for all the tortures and murders he has commissioned, that his correspondent mother, if she has any principles at all, should be reporting on the situation of her own nation in Yugoslavia at every opportunity. But before I know it, I am in a taxi with Clive.

Who was that guy you were talking to? he asks me. I don't know, I tell him, he just came and sat at our table. I thought he knew Dave and Marta. But I don't really believe that. I don't care where he came from, I am always happy to have someone listen to my views on Croatia. Taik would have been very proud of me, I think with satisfaction as we bounce along. For once, Clive does not curse the taxi driver. Clive is sometimes completely unpredictable. If he thinks the car is bouncing too much, he goes into a rage, and sometimes even refuses to pay the driver. Thank you, he tells this one when we reach his apartment, that was a very pleasant trip. I wish you were the rule rather than the exception. He bows and gives me a wink. It's a shame Clive does not suffer more. I feel there is nothing to learn from him.

There is a sign in a candy shop near the center of town: Help wanted, English-speaking. I apply and get the job. The candle shop has become oppressing. Margaret, from England, also works with me. She is engaged to a Spaniard and speaks Spanish as well as German and English. In our shop, we sell every imaginable chocolate known to mankind. One, a triple-layered concoction filled with raspberry jelly is called the "Hoheit", or majesty, a term which frequently occasions a snide monologue on my part about the Austrian predilection for titles. While Americans content themselves with Doctor (a Professor slipping in on occasion), the Austrians, loath to relinquish their fin de siecle grandeur, continue to assign titles to both people and objects. As the Austrian aristocracy has, if not disappeared, at least decreased substantially, titles are now bestowed upon their symbolic successors in the technological age. Thus, an engineer becomes Herr Diplom Ingeneur Tuchmann, or Mr. Diplomaed Engineer Tuchmann. High school teachers generally known to students and teachers alike by such names as "Bony Brady" or "Fast Legs Foster" assume the title of Herr or Frau Studienrat (in), or Mr./Mrs. Secondary School Teacher Schlutzer. Not to be excluded from this twentieth century nobility, the corner butcher becomes Herr Metzger Blockenstein, or Mr. Butcher Blockenstein, and the dairy salesgirl is transformed into Fraulein Meierin Humpelfratz, or Miss Milkmaid Humpelfratz. All this by way of elaboration on the chocolate triple-layered "Hoheit" and its humble origins.

Since I have renewed my acquaintance with Milan, the wanted man, we have decided to meet every Wednesday evening in a coffeehouse, where I teach him English for an hour and, afterwards, he teaches me Croatian. Before we begin, we observe a ritual. First we choose a secluded table without a window view, as we are easily prone to distraction. We then take up the menu, review the pastry list, which is always the same, and order a grilled cheese bread and some tea. I take out my tablet and pen. He has a red, leather notebook filled with voluminous notes in both English and Croatian. Laboriously I work on his pronunciation, which is horrendous. Our facial contortions occasion much laughter from neighboring tables as well as from the waiter, who has come to know us. Milan is hopeless with foreign languages, even though his German is fluent. He can't force his mouth to assume the shapes necessary to produce the sounds correctly. I, however, can, and my Croatian pronunciation, he tells me dourly, is near perfect. What are you eating? I ask him in Croatian. A piss of brett, he tells me in English. He insists on paying the bill every time we meet, as though to recompense me for the suffering his pronunciation has caused.

During this period, there are only a few letters from Taik, it is as though he feels the plan will fail if he acknowledges it or even my existence in any way, as though denying a deadly disease allows one automatically to live. I have told Melody everything about the leaflets, but she is not concerned, she wants to go to Zagreb anyway. Nothing will happen, will it? she asks me. I don't think so, but at least you know that it's a possibility, I tell her. And you can decide if you want to go. I do, she says. So that much is decided. We don't talk about it anymore, we treat it also like a disease and we want to live for a long, long time.

I would also like to discuss my assignment with Milan, but Taik has made me promise to tell nobody except Melody, and only if absolutely necessary. I would also like to know why he is a wanted man, what crimes he has been suspected of committing or, better, what crimes he has in actuality committed. Kindly Milan, with the triangular fingers, which are plump at the bottom and come to a benign point where the impeccable nails end. I want to know what these fingers have done, what possible evil they could possibly have perpetrated. But what do I mean by evil? I wonder to myself. It depends on who dies, who kills, what is changed and how. It also depends on who is looking at the body. Is it the mother or the mother of the one the body, once alive, caused to die? But I have eaten too much cheese-bread and drunk too much tea. My head is fuzzy. I don't know what to think. I want everything to be explained to me.

4

"Whoever fights monsters should see to it that in the process he does not become a monster. And when you look long into an abyss, the abyss also looks into you." Nietzsche

The Vienna-Zagreb Express, heading toward the Austrian-Slovenian border, 1970. In my shoulder bag, I have the packets of leaflets, wrapped in heavy blue paper. They are written in Croatian and signed "Croatian Revolutionary Youth". As soon as we are settled in our train compartment, I put the bag on the seat and cover it with my coat. The train is filled with guest workers going over the border into Yugoslavia for the weekend, drably dressed, in grays, blacks and dark blues. They bump against each other, impatient to be on their way; they remind me of bruised plums. The train jerks slowly out of the bright station, the cries and shouts fade away, as though they are weak watercolors instead of sounds, and we are plunged into a thick darkness. We snake forward, insubstantial yellow segments of a huge caterpillar.

The corridor is smoky, a babble of voices, languages spills into our compartment, bottles are passed back and forth. Strange faces press against our window, winking, waving, but mostly leering. But we are suddenly at Maribor, the border town in Slovenia. There is sudden, tense calm in the corridor. The plums move, as if of a single mind, to their sections, and their bottles disappear into tight pocket prisons. We are invaded by two of them, who speak in low voices and look at us with marbled eyes.

Get your passport ready, I tell Melody, who then asks me if I am going to leave the bag where it is. I check the reaction of the two men. They are sprawled in their seats, feigning nonchalance. I pity Melody for her naivete, for her obliviousness to the fact that these two are possibly, if not probably, seasoned agents sent to expose our plan and send us to prison for the rest of our lives. The bag lies like a corpse under my coat; I ease myself closer to it, rest my elbow on it.

But the men do not jump up, do not pull the coat from under my arm. Instead, the border police bursts into the compartment and asks for our passports. I yawn and hold them out, let my eyes linger for a moment on his gun and uniform. My elbow is frozen to the mound on the seat next to me. Our passports are opened, the pictures compared to the faces the policeman sees grimacing before him. Then he leaves. But wait a moment, he has taken our passports with him.

We are immediately subjected to intense scrutiny by our fellow travelers, who decide that we are of extreme danger to the well-being of their country and should be summarily arrested. They rise in unison and leave us alone to suffer. We squirm and protest to one another, in case we are being taped, though we feel silly about it, we don't believe such things really happen. I am sweating, I begin to feel nauseous at the thought of failing my mission before even arriving in Zagreb. I tell myself confusedly that I do not deserve to live any longer. The train jerks forward, pulling out of the station, leaving the bleak outpost to the tobacco farmers and widows selling cheese.

The train stops once again, and this unexpected deviation from what we believe to be routine procedure alarms us even more. We look out the window for a clue. A group of uniformed border policemen stands in the grass, milling around. An order is given, from where we do not know, and they swarm into the train. We spring back, rigid against our seats, waiting for our door to be torn open once again. I feel a loathing for the obscene mound upon which my elbow rests, but I have sworn to protect it, I cannot do otherwise. My bowels are threatening to decompose into small, sodden puddles, to lose their form, their substance, to simply collapse under the pressure. I listen for sounds in the corridor, anything that will prepare me for what is to come. The silence is deafening, it is composed of all the sounds in the world cancelling each other out.

Melody is frozen, her skin white, clammy to the touch. I pat her hand, tell her everything will be fine. She scoots closer to the door, as if to disassociate herself from me and the mound, refuses to answer me, thinks better of it, says she doesn't know what I'm talking about, just in case the compartment is taped, I assume. Melody is a good student.

Our policeman has returned, he looks in at us before opening the door, as though we are not human at all, but merely objects he has been sent to examine, he is a quality control inspector in a factory and we are the defective products he must either repair or destroy. He directs us to pull our suitcases down from the overhead shelf and to open them. I put mine on the seat and open it so that it covers the mound behind, I pull things out, socks, a nightgown, a plastic belt, drop them on the ground, laugh, pick them up, put them back in. Melody does not help him, she stands quietly and lets him look through her suitcase by himself, which he does, reluctantly, it seems, as though afraid to be contaminated by capitalist consumer goods.

Before I have a chance to close my suitcase, he is gone. I am unable to speak, afraid to believe he will not return with a gun and handcuffs. Melody and I look at each other, then out the door into the passageway. We see the policeman's back receding, the gun moving against his hip. He is finished, headed outside to mill around until the next border check. He has already forgotten the chubby Americans with revolution and enemy propaganda in their hearts as well as their suitcases.

Seconds later, the door opens, before we have had a chance to even close our suitcases, to congratulate ourselves. Our passports are held out to us and we grab them, put them away, out of sight. The guard's eyes tell us he is wise to us and we'd better watch our step because his government doesn't cater to American tourists who play dumb and break laws in foreign countries. Thank you, I tell him, and give him a look of bovine incomprehension only the guilty can have.

Suddenly I am alive again, my body tingles, the mound at my side has grown to incredible proportions, assumed an importance far eclipsing my own, eclipsing all of humanity's; it breathes under my elbow, which I now would not move for anything in the world. How could I have loathed this mound just moments earlier, how could I have been guilty of such a betrayal, I ask myself. Lovely mound, soft and warm mound, mound unequalled by all others. I am enraptured by you; in fact, I love you. We are across the border!

Zagreb, Croatia, 1970–At the train station, we are given the address of a family in Zagreb who rents rooms to tourists. The rooms are cheap and clean and, in addition, we have the opportunity of becoming acquainted with a Croatian family. Their name is Tonkovich, and the wife is called Jagica, or little strawberry. She tells us how to find the neboder, the skyscraper, which, because it is the only one in the city, has no name. It is simply the neboder and it sits in the middle of Republic Square, only ten minutes from the Tonkovich household.

We find the building without difficulty and decide that it must be cased thoroughly. We enter on the ground floor and take the elevator, which is self-service, to the top floor. No operator to identify us later. A good sign. The restaurant and dance floor are closed, but we are able to go out on the terrace and walk all the way around it. High wire mesh has been built on to the concrete wall, with a six-inch space between the two. The mesh is to prevent suicides, I remember having been told.

Twelve stories below us lies the square, filled with people moving in orderly lines, like a cross section of an ant farm. Banners flap from most building tops, banners celebrating the Yugoslav independence celebration scheduled for the following day, the largest celebration of the entire year. The square will be packed with people, Taik had told me, and the wind will blow the leaflets all over the city. The celebration will be ruined. They'll never catch you.

We take the elevator back down and walk across the square. On each street corner, there are at least one or two gypsies, squatting, crying, beseeching all who pass by. One old woman holds a child with no legs. Smiles, a radiant smile, she has excellent teeth, half white and half gold. Vendors sell buttons by the streetcar stop, buttons bearing familiar names of Croatian soccer teams, such as "Dinamo" or "Hajduk".

There is a huge open market place just above the square. We climb thick stone steps to reach it. Here everything is sold, from intricate embroidered blouses and carved wooden flutes to blood-red peppers in paper cones and squid squirming in large buckets of clouded water. The peasant women vie for our attention, fight over us, moaning and protesting as we move to a competitor's table and cheering as we return to theirs. When we decide upon our purchase, a pair of woven slippers, the victor grins a wide, toothless smile at us and immediately turns to smirk at the others.

I am at home, I have no sense at all of being in a strange place, though I am surrounded by faces whose landscape baffles me, by noises which have no origin that I can detect, by words, sounds which appear to have no cohesion. The arrangement of the streets makes no sense to me, one runs into the other in the middle, or veers off without architectural reason into a dead end. Store windows are filled with displays, but the stores are not open, look as though they haven't been open for years. There are stylish dresses in the shops which nobody wears on the streets as we walk through. But I have the sense that everybody understands the facade that must be maintained. Passersby seem to exchange knowing looks, even with the two of us. I understand everything and nothing at the same time. That seems to be the secret of this country and people, understanding everything about nothingness. And the secret is mine as well, though I do not deserve it. All my suffering has been inherited, I am just the bandage over the wound.

It is a clear and starry night, and when we look out the window from our table on top of the neboder, we see the mountains, black against the deepening sapphire of the sky, which surround Zagreb to the north. We are not inconspicuous, as we wish, we are almost completely alone in the large restaurant, we are too early. The waiters hover around us in various doorways, coyote-like, looking our way from time to time with devious amusement, coming over finally to ask us if we want another Turkish coffee or perhaps a glass of wine. Below us there is a large dance floor, the kind one remembers from high school days, the tiles scuffed, the colors faded, some of the edges curling up like little waves.

We sit disgusted at our table, where are the people, where are the dancers, the drinkers, the families out for a celebration on Yugoslav Independence Day? My bag lies on the ground beneath the table. I open it for a last check. It contains a book, Stendhal's On Love, my wallet and passport, a camera, and brown wool gloves, so that the bag will not be suspiciously empty after the leaflets are gone. I tap my fingers on the tablecloth, get up and look down upon the square, which is filling quickly with people.

Music suddenly issues forth from a number of strategically placed speakers. It is a live band, but they are hidden from view, perhaps to ensure that they are not mobbed, in typical decadent Western manner, by hordes of crazed girls on drugs. It is only with great resolve and imagination that I am able to convert what sounds like "Charming Truffles" being sung over and over into the more familiar "Jumping Jack Flash".

The room begins to fill and, within fifteen minutes, we have achieved near anonymity. The coyotes have turned their attention to other customers and we move from our table to another closer to the terrace.

When will you do it? Melody asks, and I tell her soon, as soon as people start going out on the terrace.

Another ten minutes and we are on the terrace ourselves, dodging entwined couples and large families with screeching children chasing one another around and around. I post Melody on the west end of the terrace and myself at the east end, so that we can see when one stretch of the terrace is free of people and potential witnesses.

It's clear now, Melody tells me. Time expands and contracts, and different forms seem to pass in and out in front of me as if on wheels. I look behind me, nobody there. The bag, as if by pre-arrangement, what a fine conspirator, removes itself to the ground to await further instructions. The leaflets fight their way out of the blue wrapping paper, leaving it in shreds and tatters, and come out to rest ponderously in my right hand. I stretch my arm out over the wall and release them all at once. I look down for a split second. The people below are a brightly colored smear, like dyed bacteria on a slide. An avalanche of leaflets descends slowly upon them.

My legs, buckling beneath me, threaten to send me sprawling onto the ground. I steady myself on the railing for a moment. Where is the bag, where is it, it is behind me, still on the ground, open like a dark cave or a wound, go get it, hurry up. Someone goes and gets it, it may have been I, I am not at all sure, but suddenly we are back at our table watching the dancers, my mouth is so dry, my whole body is this dry, there is not a drop of moisture in it whatsoever, the fright has sucked all the vital juices out of me. I am even unable to wet my pants like some people I have read about, who are so scared they lose all control. Melody is beside me, as always, but somehow I am not concerned about her, she is on automatic, nothing is happening with her, she is like that bag in my lap or the table upon which my elbows rest so heavily, so tensely.

Seconds later, the whine of sirens is heard everywhere. This pleases me and I smile to Melody, who is transfixed in her chair and seems not to recognize me. I notice many of the customers looking down upon the square, worried, anxious. A few try to take the elevator down, but it is locked already and nobody can leave. We are too smart to rush to the elevator, we have nothing to fear now, it is over, completed, accomplished; it cannot be taken back or changed, nor can anything that follows from it. I would like to take responsibility for the excitement, the drama, stand up and declare that it is I who has caused all the uproar, made the sirens scream, made the people run around on the streets below, it is I who is preventing everyone from leaving the dance hall; I have changed everybody's life at this moment. I am the controller of destinies.

There is an increase in activity suddenly, the kind one senses rather than sees. And then I do see it, a group of burly men with bulging pockets coming through the kitchen door onto the restaurant floor, see them fan out among the crowd, grabbing and shoving people indiscriminately, as one would grab hold of a cobweb or something just as insubstantial. Their eyes pause from time to time on the two of us, sitting so near the elevator, but they move on, they do not stop.

They go instead to others, whose papers are perhaps not in order or, worse yet, with no papers at all, those whose fathers fought against the Communists, those who are known to sing nationalist songs after one too many glasses of slivovitz. One by one, they are taken by the arm and pushed to the elevator, some are protesting, asking questions which are ignored, some are silent, some are in terror, shaking, faces red, or devoid totally of color, like dough, dough that has failed to rise. I ask myself what I have done, though I am uncomfortable thinking about it. I want to know where they are taking these innocent people, all innocent, because I am the guilty one, the one they are seeking, sitting right in front of them, sitting heavily, frozen to my chair, actually, a chair with six legs instead of the usual four.

But our turn finally comes, we are surrounded by four of these gray men, one gestures for us to get up, says something, to us and then to his comrades. I look at him blankly and Melody reaches for her eczema medicine to carry her through this crisis. We are out of our chairs, though, involuntarily we move from a sitting to a standing position, our arms are gripped on either side by these monsters who cannot speak English. I try to yank my arms away but the grip is incredibly strong, like a straitjacket.

We are taken down to the street in a service elevator in the kitchen. A thick hatred spreads throughout this small elevator, as though the four would rather kill us immediately instead of delivering us live to wherever we are being taken. In rapid succession, I tell the four that I want an attorney, I want to call the U.S. Consulate, that they have no right to take us anywhere and, finally, arrogantly, as so many Americans, that they ought to learn how to speak English.

From the elevator, we are hustled into a car and driven out onto the street. A large crowd waits on either side of the driveway, waits to see us, to look into our faces, to see the ones who have done this to them, for them. One young man is convinced of our guilt already, he presses his face against the window, yells something at us, his face is contorted, he is filled with loathing, anybody can see it, it has taken over his face, like a spreading sore.

5

"In all desire to know there is a drop of cruelty." Nietzsche

The waiting room in the police station is like a Greyhound bus depot, long wooden benches line the walls and people sit, lean, sprawl and lie sleeping on them, just as they do in any other bus depot. But the bus does not come; instead of embarking on a long journey, they are taking a short, perhaps a last trip. What have I done? I sit, miserable, watching the process I have set into motion. A young, blonde girl, dressed in tight, black pants and a gold sweater, hears us talking English and asks us if we know what is going on. I say we have no idea, we are being held unlawfully, arbitrarily, just as she is. She smiles a sad smile and takes a seat, crosses her legs and prepares for a long wait, bites her lip until the lipstick is gone.

One by one, each of us is called into an office. We are the last to be called, we have waited the longest, about three hours. I am taken to a room on the left and Melody to a room on the right. In my room, a dim room, lit by a feeble lamp and containing only a scratched desk and two chairs, sits a stocky man with a crewcut and flushed, red face.

Sit down, he tells me, in a thick accent. I see a telephone on the wall and demand to call the U.S. Consulate. Of course, he says in a soothing manner, but first I want to ask you a few questions. He is a smooth one, he looks like a peasant and that is part of his routine.

Where have you taken my friend? I ask. They are questioning her in another room, he says. And why are we here at all? I think you know why, this peasant tells me with a smile. He offers me a glass of cognac, he has had a hard day, he confides to me, a very hard day. I want to pour my own, I was not born yesterday, and he allows me, he humors me, but cannot resist saying I have watched too many spy movies. I rub the glass on the cuff of my coat, rub it until it shines. Then I pour myself a large shot, pour him one as well, which makes him smile. He toasts me, as though we are on a first date and he is trying to make a good, a favorable impression.

We drink in silence. Outside, the streets are quiet. A car slinks by from time to time, like a dog with its tail between its legs, and a radio plays softly above us. He watches me, says nothing, turns the glass around and around in his hand. The cognac has loosened me, melted my limbs, my tongue. What do you suspect us of, can you tell me that? He says that he can and will tell me, that somebody has dropped anti-state leaflets into the square, leaflets of a highly dangerous content, and that whoever did it faces a sentence of at least fifteen years in prison. Somebody will have to do these fifteen years. Who is this person?

The door opens and a head pops in. "Priznala je." I look at my interrogator, who is smiling indulgently. It seems your friend has admitted everything, he says. Melody has obviously been tortured and her fingernails torn off. Why else would she have admitted anything? But I have heard nothing, no screams, no moans, I have smelled nothing either, no singed flesh or burning hair. What has made her talk? Where is her eczema medicine? But it is my duty to extricate her from this situation. I threw the leaflets, I tell my captor, she is innocent of everything. I am so tired, I only want to sleep, to sleep or die. I want to cry as well, but my mother is so very far away.

Melody and I have been reunited, in a large, comfortable room, well-carpeted, well-lighted, not too bright, not too dim, a room three floors above the station, perhaps the room in which the radio had been playing a melancholy song hours before, before my guilt had been established. We sit in deep, plush armchairs, facing my interrogator, who has barricaded himself behind a heavy desk across the room. We are no longer drinking pals, sitting close to each other, so close that we can see the individual network of veins running across each other's faces. A young girl now sits between us, an interpreter, who has sheets of paper spread out on her lap, whose legs are crossed, causing the sheets to fall continually onto the floor. I want to tell her to uncross her legs, it would make everything much easier, but who am I to give anybody advice in my situation?

Please look at the leaflet and tell me what words you understand, the interpreter tells me, after listening to my interrogator. Suddenly he does not speak English anymore, he has forgotten everything, he is all business, does not want unmediated contact with me, everything must go through this pleasant, dark-haired girl who smiles apologetically whenever he asks her to relay a question to me, as though she, too, is here against her will, and perhaps she is.

I take a look, a long look, at the leaflet, I go through it word for word, try to erase all expression from my face, as though my recognition of this word or that will be immediately apparent to my interrogator simply by watching my face, the set of my lips, the number of times I blink, the way I tilt my head. I am surely not so stupid as to claim that I don't recognize the word revolution, which is much the same in English as in Croatian. Well, this means revolution, I tell him, pointing to the word "revolucija". I go down a few more sentences, point to another word "crna", and say that it means black. When I have finished going through the entire leaflet, these are the only two words that I have identified. My interrogator is not pleased with me and shows it. He makes a sound of disgust behind his desk, and says something nasty about me to the interpreter, I can tell, even though I can't understand him. The pleasant girl is uncomfortable, she answers him, but reluctantly, in case I can, in fact, speak Croatian, and might surprise her one day by quoting her words. She looks down at her lap, shuffles her papers, puts them in some kind of order, a different one. One of the papers falls to the floor and I pick it up, beat her to it. Thank you, she says, and then she is still.

Are you sure that is all you understand? my interrogator asks me directly. The friction between us is so strong that it cancels out the presence of all else in the room, our faces are both red, we are breathing heavily, we are like two machines shorting out on one another. Yes, I'm sure, I tell him. I am inexplicably sad that we cannot now be friends under any circumstances. Already I have fond memories of our first, pleasant hours together, drinking companionably together at the scratched desk, listening to muted music overhead as cars creep by on the street outside the window, two people with a goal, the same goal, in a way: rising to the occasion.

We are hungry, Melody and I, and tell him so. It has been many hours since we have eaten anything and the endless cups of coffee we have been drinking throughout the night, the cigarettes we light one after the other, have made us tense, irritable, disinclined to talk. We want something to eat or we won't talk to you anymore, I tell my interrogator, who sits motionless across from us, staring at the wall. He looks at me with surprise, then with a strange recognition. Go through the leaflet one more time, he says sweetly, and then I'll think about it. I refuse.

I look around the holding room they immediately move me to, expecting somebody I know, anybody at all, to appear, but I am alone. It occurs to me suddenly that it is November, that Christmas is coming and that I might well be spending it in prison. I sit for hours on this hard bench, locked in without even a glass of water or a cigarette. Melody is being held somewhere else, my interrogator has separated us, thrown me into this foul-smelling room in which the garbage lies piled in the corner, not even in a bag or a bucket, but free, piled so high that part of it has toppled over and threatens to multiply until the entire room is overrun.

There are noises outside the door, sounds of movement, people talking, a cart being dragged across the floor. The door opens, a young man comes inside and hands me a dented pan filled with amber liquid, a huge spoon, and a chunk of bread which has been torn off from a loaf. He makes polite conversation as he hands me these items, and when I fail to respond, he smiles, then laughs, a bit too heartily, and is gone. I fall upon this food, I am ravenous, I cannot get it into my mouth quickly enough. The only problem is getting the liquid and the bread into my mouth at the same time. I cannot seem to wait, to take things in sequence.

As I am finishing my meal, I hear a strange sound in the hallway, one which I have trouble at first identifying. And then I am overwhelmed because it is an unaccented English, the most soothing sound one can imagine, I am almost put to sleep by it on the spot, it sounds like smooth pebbles bumping gently against one another in a brook.

The door opens once again and a vision of a man walks in and takes a seat next to me. He is impeccably dressed, his nails are fastidiously cared for, his teeth are perfect, like little ivory boxes, his shoes are shined. I am overwhelmed with warmth, gratefulness, appreciation, I want to hold him, tell him how handsome he is, how well-dressed, how I admire him, how flawlessly he speaks English, I want to tell him any number of things, so happy am I that I am not alone any longer. I need help. Will he save me?

But he does not ask me what I did, or if I did it, he is not interested in getting to the bottom of the matter, in learning the identities of those who have so cruelly exploited me if I am, in fact, guilty. I am Wilson Orren, from the American Consulate, he tells me. We will be getting you a lawyer and have already notified your family about your situation. Is there anything you need to make you more comfortable while you're waiting for your case to be heard? You mean you can't get me out of here? I ask him. He is sorry, but we must let Yugoslav law take its course, we are not in America. It could be six months before I even go to court.

He is gone before I know it, gone with his bedside manner and his shiny shoes, his nails with the smooth half-moons resting above the closely-trimmed cuticle. The remains of the soup have dried at the bottom of the dented pan and on the huge spoon, and the bread crumbs lie embarrassed around me, on the table, in my lap, at my feet, the survivors of a beaten army. I sit quietly, a quietness has come over me which I cannot explain, I sit and try to discover what error has brought me to this place, what possible flaw of character, and what I must do to get out. But I do not know nearly enough to save myself, somebody, something else must save me, a stroke of fate, or perhaps the intervention of my interrogator, who surely still thinks about me and holds a soft spot in his heart for me after all we have been through. I feel a confusing bond with this interrogator. Perhaps it is he who is my savior after all.

Melody has returned, escorted by a guard who has been directed to take us to another location. We trot behind him but do not dare to ask him questions. When we begin to lag, he turns and yells at us to hurry up. Brzo, brzo, he says, and then he gives us an impish smile, as though to say that he is well aware of the comedic possibilities of the situation: two young Americans in jail in a totalitarian country, a series of misadventures, misunderstandings, before the mess is finally cleared up and they are sent packing, full of adventures for their families and friends back home. Hahaha, he is taking it all in stride and when we fail to smile at him, seems hurt and confused. So many hurt feelings around here, my interrogator with the red face, the apologetic interpreter, who is unable to provide him with the desired answers to his questions, and now our escort. What do they want of us, the truth? I suspect it is not so much the truth they want but, rather, the appearance of truth. It can be of much greater use in the long run.

Melody and I are separated once more. I sit with the guard in a small office room. He tries valiantly to make conversation, to amuse and entertain me as we endure this awkward silence, but I am unable to answer him, I do not dare to speak any Croatian words, lest I be indicted later for lying to my interrogator, for failing to identify these same words in the leaflets. We sit facing one another, but I am looking at the wall behind the guard, upon which hangs a large and colorful picture of President Tito, the one who some claim is an impostor. Supposedly the real Tito had gone to Moscow with only four fingers on one hand and returned, fifteen years later, with five.

My guard shuffles uncomfortably, crosses and recrosses his legs. Finally the tension becomes too unbearable. He pulls out his wallet and extracts three pictures from it. He holds them out to me one by one, his face is beaming. Here is something we both understand. I coo over the round-faced dumpling framed with blond curls, like little question marks, that stares out at me from the pictures. My daughter, he tells me. He leans back in his chair, hugely proud of what he has produced, relaxed, sure of himself. We are just two people now, one a father, the other a daughter, we both have a perfect understanding of the network of human love and aspiration which binds us together, even in this room. My guard. I feel a comfort in the possessive. They all belong to me.

Our suitcases are unpacked and inventoried in two large rooms across the courtyard from the prison itself. I am in one room with my guard and Melody is in another. The guard is talking to her, how silly, she understands nothing. Suddenly she screams, begins cursing at him, using the worst words I have ever heard her use, and I have heard many. I jump up and run into the other room, shaking off the hand of my guard, who is trying not to laugh. This son of a bitch won't give me my eczema medicine, this asshole, this fucking piece of shit, she runs behind him as he holds his hand up in the air, medicine aloft, he is laughing, so is my guard, though at least he is trying to hide it, even I am trying to hide it. Melody's face is white, not red, as one would expect, and she is trying vainly to jump up and snatch the medicine out of the guard's hand. She screams and screams, until she is out of breath, until her voice is hoarse, and then she falls in a heap into a chair. The look she gives her guard should be a crime in this country, and perhaps it is, perhaps we will be charged with this as well.

I am deloused for the first time in my life, taken bodily to a small closet room filled with stacks of gray linens, stripped naked, and covered with a white, vile powder which goes up my nose as well as in my ears and mouth as I tell my torturer to wait just a minute, what does she think she is doing? She, a small prune of a woman whose flesh hangs from her upper arms like layers of crepe, puts her hand over her mouth, closes her eyes in pantomime. The door to the closet is open and I stand exposed to anyone walking by, like a large loaf of floured bread ready to be popped into the oven.

Imagine them thinking I might have lice! I am indignant, filled with righteous indignation, I want to laugh but cannot, as it is a fully preposterous and objectionable proposition which has no place in my conception of self. I stand up straight, hands on hips, and wait patiently, patronizingly for my clothes to be returned to me. They are in a heap in the corner, covered also with a thin film of the white insecticide. The little prune hands my clothing to me piece by piece, first the blue knit top, which I pull over my head with lightning speed, and then my faded bell-bottom jeans. Before I am allowed to put on my heavy brown hiking shoes, the laces are removed, slowly, painstakingly, so that the full import of this procedure is not lost on me.

Imagine them thinking I might kill myself! Once again I am filled with indignation. Why should I want to kill myself, I who have so much to live for? What can be going on in these people's minds? Even if I were so inclined, the laces are far too short to hang myself, and they would hardly be sturdy enough to support my weight hanging from a rafter, they would break immediately and I would fall to the ground, would end up with just a headache, a bruised knee. And if I kill myself, what does it matter if I am infested with lice?.

I am taken to one of the cells as soon as I am dressed. Introductions are made, or perhaps explanations, and I am locked in with two others, a gaudy bleach-blonde in a rumpled housecoat and plastic slippers and an oily-skinned older woman who has not washed her hair in at least six months, whose fingers are stained deep mustard yellow. The two greet me effusively, pull out a chair for me, fetch yoghurt from the window sill and set it in front of me. They tell me to eat, eat, that much I understand, but I cannot, I can only nod and smile and try to keep my eyes open. Against my will, my head falls forward, I have not slept for at least twenty or thirty hours. My cellmates hustle me to a bed and the last words I hear before I drop off are "batsala letke". It seems everyone, even those locked away in these dark rooms, isolated, incommunicado, has heard about the leaflets I dropped. The news has spread to every dark corner of the city. Batsala letke, batsala letke. My cellmates' faces bend over me as I drift off to sleep, and though I am vaguely aware of the things they could do to me as I sleep, I allow myself to drift away, sleep at this moment is more important than possible death or disfigurement, more important than anything that is happening around me. Their voices drone on, their strange lullaby from far, far away and I am gone.

The next morning when I wake up, I refuse to relieve myself in the foul hole in the corner of the cell. I would rather burst. Not only because I am afraid of spattering myself, but because the curtain surrounding it is not even high enough to hide one's head. My bleach-blonde cellmate converses with us as she uses it. We can hear her and see her face at the same time, she is exposed on three different levels, sight and sound. And smell, too.

But I leave the cell fairly soon, I am taken to an office and introduced to a Mister Madirazza, the investigating judge. Melody is sitting across from him, covered with red sores, which she is scratching with a vengeance. Her eyes are red as well, as though the sores have spread even there. They won't give me my eczema medicine, she tells me with clenched teeth. I look at Mister Madirazza, who is smiling at both of us, allowing us to make our greetings, our small talk, before interrupting us. Why won't you give her the eczema medicine? I ask him. I am having somebody look for it, it has gotten very lost, he says. If they don't put us together in the same cell, I'll kill myself, Melody tells me in a monotone. Why don't you put us together in the same cell? I ask him. We need to be together. He tells us he has made arrangements also for that. He is so amenable to everything, so easy-going. Can I use your bathroom for a minute? He finds this highly entertaining, but does not laugh outright. Of course, I'll have my secretary show you where it is, he tells me, and calls her right away. I need some paper, too, I say a bit sheepishly, as though I am going a bit too far. But he is unfazed, he opens his desk drawer, pulls out a few Kleenexes and hands them over to me. After I relieve myself, and I take a goodly amount of time, I return to Mister Madirazza, who has made himself a new friend. We smile warmly at each other. It is such a fine world.

Mister Madirazza is as good as his word. Melody and I are moved to a smaller cell with two bunk beds, a hole in the corner, a huge pile of garbage in another corner, a lopsided table, and a rickety chair. There is a window high up, where nobody can reach it, it is streaked with dirt, the blue of the sky can barely be discerned, it is closer to a gray, the color of soggy newspaper. We are told that we will be interrogated each day by Mister Madirazza, but that today we have off, in order to become accustomed to our new surroundings. I assure Melody that since she is innocent of any wrongdoing, I will do all I can to get her released and returned to Vienna. We sit on the top bunk, our legs hanging over.

From time to time, the peephole in our door is opened and we see an eye peering in on us. Then a straw appears through the hole. We jump onto the floor and go over to the door. It is my waiter, the one who served me bean soup, he has a carton of orange juice and wants to share it with us. We each take a long drink from the straw. Then it is withdrawn, the peephole is closed once again, and we are cut off from the outside.

The garbage in the corner has no reason for being. I understand the toilet hole, the rickety chair and the lopsided table. They are to provide a semblance of normalcy, to trick the prisoner into thinking well of his captors. But the rotting garbage belies this notion, it ruins the smooth logic of the rest of the objects placed in this room with such fore-thought. I understand the window, even though it is too high to reach, even though the small pane is streaked with filth and the shapes which pass by it from time to time are unidentifiable. The garbage baffles me. I must give the matter some thought.

Melody is in the top bunk and I am in the bottom, we have arrived at this decision without any discussion, but I suspect it is because she prefers, both literally and figuratively, to be above everything that is happening to us. We are unable to sleep, but do not feel like talking, either, we want to be alone with our thoughts, which are perhaps too bleak to share. Do you hear that? she asks me. I do, in fact, hear something, but I deny it immediately. We lie tensely, waiting for the noise, which we know will come again, against our will. Do you hear that? she asks again, louder. It is a tiny rustling, as though a little piece of paper is being wadded up in some small hand and then unwadded once again. I picture a mass of little hands surrounding us in the darkness, wadding and unwadding little pieces of paper. The noise, though, becomes constant and we cannot possibly ignore it any longer.

Turn on the light, I tell Melody, who can reach it from the top bunk. The light goes on, it is blindingly bright, and it takes our eyes a few moments to adjust. When they do, we let out a ferocious scream in uni-son, which brings the guards immediately to our door. The floor is car-peted with huge beetles, scurrying madly in every direction, bumping into one another, trying blindly to escape the bright light, even attempting to climb the walls, which they are unable to do. Their hard shells make a clicking sound, like a bunch of crickets, as they fall to the ground. We are crying and screaming, looking in our blankets, our clothing, for any which might have made it up that far, shaking our hair, arms, legs.

The guards are laughing and running around the room, smashing the beetles with their heavy boots. They have not had so much fun in years. The ones they are unable to smash have disappeared into the garbage or the hole in the corner, clustered together in fear, just as we are, waiting out the storm. I scramble up into the top bunk, where I huddle with Melody, legs hanging over the bed. A beetle falls out of the blanket onto the ground, where it runs for safety, and makes it. We both scream again.

Don't turn out the lights, we tell the guards, or you'll be sorry. We act it out for them so there can be no misunderstanding. The guards leave the lights on, they are still laughing and talking to each other, no doubt making fun of us, the Americans who are used to better prisons. It is three thirty in the morning, and we do not sleep the rest of the night. There is no more rustling, no noises at all except the sound of our breathing, which takes some time to slow.

In the morning, Melody is ruthless. We've got to get out of here, she says. I know, I know, I tell her. I am the guilty one, the one with no comprehension of her crime. Issues of guilt and innocence assail me, perplex me and ultimately overwhelm me. I have done something, but what exactly have I done? I am the one who expects things to defy logic and rationality, to operate on a different level, one determined by myself.

I would like someone to explain to me when it is appropriate to distribute pieces of paper to the general public. It seems such a simple issue, why am I unable to get to the bottom of it? I am even unsure whether it is an ethical, moral, philosophical or political issue. Perhaps it is all four. If Taik were here, he would tell me, he would explain what is at stake here. I do not bother asking Melody what she thinks about all this. Besides, I was not born yesterday, the room is probably bugged. Instead, we take some paper from our property, tear it into fifty two pieces, and scratch numbers and suits on them with a fingernail so that we can play cards until the sun comes up, we play gin rummy and Melody beats me every time. But after a few hours of this, we begin to cry again and I go throw the papers into the hole.

I understand you had a difficult night, Mister Madirazza says. I laugh and shrug my shoulders. Already it is an amusing story to tell and not the tragedy it was the night before. I am moving you to a different room today, he tells us, and I apologize for your experience. Melody is cranky and in no mood to be appeased by Mister Madirazza, her eyebrows are so crinkled that they almost meet in the middle of her forehead. Melody is innocent of everything, I tell him, so please consider letting her go back to Vienna. She only came for the trip, she had nothing to do with the leaflets. He gives me an appraising look, leans back in his chair and joins his fingers together to make a little chapel.

Your attorney is here, waiting in another room. My secretary will take you there now. Melody stays behind with Mister Madirazza, and I cannot help but feel sorry for him because I see that Melody's mood is darkening by the minute, that she will soon erupt and ruin Mister Madirazza's day. Perhaps he has retrieved her medicine. I hope so, for his sake.

6

"'I have done that,' says my memory. 'I cannot have done that,' says my pride, and remains inexorable. Eventually—memory yields."
Nietzsche

My attorney is named Zorislav Dukat, and he has been retained by the American Consulate. Dr. Dukat is a kindly old man, in his seventies, at least, with a sharp nose, thin lips and a round head surrounded by a halo of white hair. He is short and fleshy and wears glasses so thick it is impossible to see the color of his eyes. But his English is excellent, it is the King's English, and he takes great pride in it. In fact, as I speak I get the feeling he experiences a certain disappointment in my particular dialect, as though he is lowering his usual standards in defending me. But he rises above it, he greets me heartily, sits me down, takes a paper and pencil and gets right down to business.

I tell him my sad story, of the boyfriend who has given me the leaflets, of my belief that they were advertisements for a book, of my ignorance of Yugoslav law which makes this an illegal act, I go through all the points of interest, the Croatian charm to which I succumbed, my reluctance to name the possessor of this charm, my apathy towards politics in general and Yugoslav politics specifically. Dr. Dukat writes and writes, looking up at me from time to time with eyebrows raised. Really! I tell him whenever I sense his disbelief, that's exactly how it happened!

When I am finished with Dr. Dukat, I am returned to my Mister Madirazza, who looks as though he has been waiting impatiently for me, so wide is his smile when the door opens and I walk in. Would you like to use my bathroom? he asks solicitously. Oh, no thank you, I'm fine. I arrange myself on the couch, get comfortable. It occurs to me that I may as well be in my own living room at home in Oregon instead of being interrogated in Yugoslavia for anti-state activities which could get me fifteen years in prison, and that, even though it is now December, it wouldn't actually be so bad to spend Christmas in the company of my Mister Madirazza. That is how content, how much at home I feel. The room is at a pleasant temperature, I have a glass of cool water in front of me, and there are no beetles crawling around on the floor under my feet. I am in a state of bliss in which nothing bad can possibly happen to me. Besides, I am too nice a person for that, anybody can see that I am here as a result of some monumental mistake, one over which I had no control. But who is the guilty person? Is anyone guilty? These questions overwhelm me; after all, I'm just a girl.

Mister Madirazza has some papers in front of him, which he shuffles through slowly until he finds the one he is looking for. Would you please look at this list of people and tell me if you recognize any of the names? he asks politely. All right, I say, and reach for this list. But I am afraid to look at the names, afraid that my expression may betray me. My palms are clammy now and my heart is beating more quickly. Sometimes when one stares at a word for long enough, the letters make no sense at all, they assume shapes and forms that are totally unrecognizable, they become gibberish. This is what I want. I start at the list, but before this phenomenon can take place, I have seen the first name on the list, recognized it and reacted to it, at least internally. Suddenly, I have to throw up, but what would my Mister Madirazza think? My stomach has taken on a personality, a will of its own, out of my control, it is heaving and surging like a ship in rough water.

The name at the top of the list is Milan's, the wanted man, the tax consultant, the avid English student. Branko is in fourth place, and another friend, Zvonko, whom we call "Cigo", is in second. And Benjamin Tolic is there as well. Taik's name is not even on this list, and I am somehow insulted by his exclusion, tempted to tell my mister Madirazza he has made a huge mistake, that the important one, the one they want, they have been too stupid to even include on this list!

I don't recognize any of these names, I tell him, trying to speak in a firm tone of voice. I am sorry, though, at the same time, that I cannot do something nice for my Mister Madirazza, who has been so nice to me and even keeps a stock of Kleenex for me in his desk drawer. His face falls, he looks as though he is going to cry. It occurs to me that he will perhaps lose his position, if he fails to break me down. And I, forever willing to suspend my will in order to view things objectively, feel sympathy for this man, can understand his situation. Nonetheless, I refuse to act.

After my interrogation, I am returned to a different cell, without Melody. It is a large cell and contains twelve double bunks along the walls at a right angle, two wooden picnic tables with benches in the center, a sink and a hole in the corner, surrounded by a low curtain. Next to the hole is a big bucket to flush the contents of the hole as needed.

As I enter the room, eleven women look up at me expectantly. Some are sitting at the tables, one is standing next to her bed, one is at the sink, two are pacing the floor. But when I come in, all activity stops. The guard speaks to them and they immediately barrage him with questions, which he answers in a patronizing tone of voice. "Kiss me, Kate!" yells one of the women at the table, and bursts into laughter. I am shown to my bunk, the top one closest to the cell door. Underneath me is an older, frazzled woman wearing a housecoat and plastic slippers, who is sewing on a square piece of cloth. I wonder what is going to be when she is finished. She looks at me with irritation, as though to say: You had better not toss and turn in your sleep or you've had it! The guard says a few more words to my cellmates before he turns and goes out the door. The turn of his key is unbelievably loud, it is like those strange noises which makes one jump just when one is on the verge of sleep, that sends electric jolts down one's spine. I have been allowed to keep a small bag of my belongings, a dress, a nightgown, some under-wear. It is a paltry collection of possessions and I am embarrassed that it is under scrutiny by my cellmates. One of the women laughs and I shoot her a dark, reckless look. The old hag! It's the one who yelled "Kiss me, Kate!". She'll be sorry.

I sit down on one of the wooden benches. At first, nobody wants to look at me, so I avert my eyes as well, I look around the cell, file away this detail and that for later, the fact that there are two windows, high above two of the top bunks, so high that one cannot look outside with-out climbing upon the bunks. All I am able to see through the glass is a patch of gray-blue and the angles of a red brick building, neither exhibiting any signs of life. There is a sink, hanging like a bad tooth from the crumbling wall, and there are heaters at each end of the room, hissing and fizzing from time to time but emitting little warmth. They are both covered with drying bits of cloth, yellowed socks, frayed nylons. A smell of laundromats pervades the cell, a musty, metallic smell, of cheap soap mixed with body odors, of something washed but not clean.

Two gypsies are in the cell with me, they have gotten up from the bench and parade past, speaking to each other but loud enough for the rest of the women to hear, in a cynical tone of voice, tossing their heads in my direction as they walk back and forth, back and forth. They are dressed in golds, bright reds, hung with every kind of jewelry, like Christmas trees, their hair is long and shiny, as though dressed with a thick oil. One is old and the other young, but they do not look much alike. And neither is subservient to the other, they are both in charge, the cadence to their voices tells me this. The other women try to ignore them, but it is difficult, I can see, they are too visible, too loud, too colorful, and they communicate a tension by their movements. None of the women gets up as the gypsies pace, they do not want to get into a collision. But they continue to talk, they do not allow themselves to be completely terrorized.

The younger one is quite beautiful and feline in her movements. She is heavily made up, lips red as a pounding heart, eyes darkly outlined, long nails painted red as well, but the polish is chipped. When she smiles, and it is a mocking smile, she shows a number of gold teeth. The both of them are wearing gold slippers and their toes, smooth and brown like little sand pebbles, are as fastidiously cared for as the rest of their bodies.

I want to make friends with these two but already I can see that they do not approve of me, especially the older one. She frowns and looks my way as she speaks. Once in a while I understand a word or two, such as "country" and "dissident"; the older one wants to catch me, wants me to react to something she has said, expose myself in front of everybody, hang myself, so to speak. There is no danger of this, however, I have managed to learn a few things, so she finally becomes bored with failure, comes to believe in my ignorance, and sits down heavily.

The old woman is here for stealing gold and the younger one for slitting the throat of the one they stole the gold from. This remarkable statement is offered in German by a small, red-haired woman next to me on the bench. Marica and Zorica, they are mother-in-law and daughter-in-law. I'm glad somebody speaks German, I tell her. I can't speak Croatian. That's what we heard, she says strangely. She tells me her name is Milica, and that she is innocent, that the authorities came to her house and stole things from her, then said she had stolen the things they had stolen from her from somebody else. It is a very confusing story, made the more so by her halting German. But I believe in her innocence already because she is my first friend.

Slavica is just an old whore, she tells me about one of the women standing by my bed. She robbed one of her customers. Slavica comes over to us and sits down. She looks young inside her eyes, but her face and body are old, parched, like a piece of bark peeled from a dying tree. She has an old "National Geographic" magazine in her hand. I wonder how on earth this magazine has come to be in this bleak cell. I suppose it is just as strange as my being here, flanked by Slavica and Milica, carrying on a conversation in two foreign languages in a foreign prison.

There is an article about hog-raising in the magazine, so I turn to it. On the first page are two huge sows, long ears hanging in the mud, smiles on their faces, looking just like humans. Milica has a pencil and, as natural as can be, I take it from her and write "Slavica" on one of the sows and "Julie" on the other. Slavica is delighted, she laughs uproariously, goes from woman to woman to show them the picture and, if the response is in her opinion inadequate, cuffs the offender lightly on the ear or about the head.

One of the women, Nada, a small, dark, shifty-eyed weasel, who has glared at me since I first arrived, who has not spoken a word to anybody, pushes Slavica away when she tries to show her the article, with her elbow, not even her hand, as though Slavica were a branch or a side of beef hanging in her way. The magazine falls to the ground and Nada follows right after it because Slavica has wound up and delivered a colossal blow right across the side of her head. She goes down and out like a beanbag, and even though she is clearly unconscious, Slavica delivers a number of kicks to her stomach, screaming in unison with the movements of her foot.

Nobody comes to open the cell door, nobody hears nor wants to hear the noise. The gypsies watch the beating disinterestedly, as though they are there solely to critique the techniques and have no emotional connection whatsoever. Zorica is smoking a cigarette as she watches.

She smiles languidly from time to time, lost in secret amusement. Two of the others talk softly with one another, not even looking up, denying what is happening around them. Milica is smoking and watching intently, saying a few words between puffs, but not in German. And I, the one who set this all in motion, pretend that everything is normal, that I am used to violence and that it does not faze or disgust me. I force my eyes away from the motion of Slavica's foot, but I cannot drown out the sounds she is making, she is grunting like a plowhorse pulling a heavy load.

And then, it seems like forever, she stops, she is exhausted, breathless, her face is red and swollen and her hair is mussed, it hangs over her eyes like a veil of broken capillaries. Her dignity has returned, she straightens her skirt, arranges her hair behind her ears and picks up the magazine, all very ladylike, lowering herself to the ground with knees together, back straight, as though her body were on a runner. Then she spits on Nada, who is still out cold, and sits back down on the bench.

Perhaps Nada is dead. She has not moved at all, I do not even detect the rise and fall of her chest. Everybody is ignoring her, as though she will disappear if her presence is denied long enough. The old gypsy even gets up and steps over her on her way to the toilet, as though she were an old dog dead on the highway.

My Mister Madirazza asks me the next morning how my first night in my new cell was, and I tell him it was fine, the women are very nice, the bed is just fair and it's a new experience eating everything with a big dented spoon out of a pan. Before I have a chance to ask, he opens his drawer and hands me some Kleenex. His solicitude makes me feel bad, I want to help him in some way, but what can I do? Your friend has been released, he tells me. I am surprised at this, wonder if he is playing a trick on me, but am afraid to ask him. Really, he says, she is leaving the country tomorrow. Meanwhile, she is staying with the American consul. So now I am all alone! I like the feeling of bearing this burden by myself. After all, I and nobody else has earned all the guilt.

7

"Madness is rare in individuals—but in groups, parties, nations, and ages it is the rule." Nietzsche

The peephole in the cell door has fallen open and since we all know this noise, we all want to be the first to look through it. But I am closest to the door, so I am the one who sees the door of the cell opposite ours open, I am the one who gasps at the sight of a group of men and little boys, some littler than others, crowded at the entrance. A few are no more than eight or ten years old, ragged little boys, but none is crying, they are trying to be men, like the ones in the cell with them, all together, men and little boys, doing their time, punished equally, but maybe some, as Orwell said, are more equal than others. Oh, look at the little boys, I tell Milica, who has not rushed to the door, little boys in jail! I am pushed out of the way because I have stopped looking to talk, I am cheating someone else out of their rightful look. But the guards hear us, they see that the peephole is open and it falls rudely back into place. Everyone grumbles and moves away from the door.

What kind of a place is this, I ask Milica, where little boys are in prison? I begin to feel a dread that all is not as it appears to be, but, in fact, much worse. In a place where children are put into prisons, what can I expect? Could even my Mister Madirazza be a monster, his every move a smoothly calculated one designed to lull me? Doctor Dukat is certainly part of the conspiracy, a conspiracy planned in detail to trick me into believing they are all decent people, that this is a decent and just country, and that I, as a law-abiding person by nature, should be anxious to cooperate with them in every way.

But I want to like everybody, I like the way my Mister Madirazza smiles at me every morning before the interrogations begin, as though he is really delighted to see me, I like Doctor Dukat's accent and his pompous air, which is, for the most part, for my amusement. I even like the Warden, Drug Nadzornik, who comes into the cell every morning with a hearty greeting and a few jokes for all of us. He is congenial, easygoing and takes an interest in us. But what kind of interest, I ask now, in light of my new knowledge, what does he want from us, what does he take us for? Oh, I am so confused, I want to believe so much and can believe so little, I am willing to forgive everyone for what they have done, nobody is perfect, least of all myself, but something is terribly wrong here and out of control. What justification can there possibly be for imprisoning children, or giving me fifteen years for passing out pieces of paper? What is this new definition of evil?

Nada isn't dead. She has a bruise which covers the whole side of her head, and it is quite colorful, not just the usual browns, yellows, and blues, but a lot of purple, and pink as well. She sits and glares at everybody, but furtively, without moving her head at all, only her eyes move, as though her body is encased in cement, as though she is buried alive. Nada is a snitch, Milica tells me. She deserves everything she gets, don't feel sorry. So nobody is sympathetic when she gets a letter from her husband, asking for a divorce. Hahaha, the stupid slut! Everyone is in high spirits now. There is nothing quite so intolerable as boredom. Great joy or great desperation at least affords the possibility of something happening, of a change in the monotony.

The daily routine in my cell is always the same, with slight variations depending on everybody's mood: at five in the morning, the lights go on, and since I am in the top bunk, they shine directly into my eyes, shocking me out of my sleep, disorienting me, throwing me too rapidly into the reality of my imprisonment. After rolling over a few times, stretching, making all the little sounds one makes before finally emerging from the bed, each one of us lines up in front of the picnic tables. Shortly thereafter, the cell door opens and a small, fair-haired woman enters, she is either a guard or assistant warden, I am not sure, and I don't know her name. She is a tyrant, a petty one, who yells at us to stand up straighter, threatens anyone caught in bed during the day, tells us the floor isn't clean enough, calls us names.

Milica is my interpreter of events. I only hear what she wants to tell me, so that all her prejudices become mine as well. The woman warden is a bitch and a tyrant, she ought to be hanged in the hot sun to die. Well, I share this view because the woman warden is always mean to me, she makes no concessions to the fact that I am American and don't understand her language. I ignore her when she speaks to me, I can't be expected to respond to something I don't understand, but this infuriates her, she comes up to me and yells directly into my face. I smile and say over and over, in English, that I don't understand her, sorry, she's wasting her time, I go on and on, elaborating on this theme, until she finally gives up, turns to somebody else. I savor this little victory, which is played out almost every morning, as she simply refuses to surrender. It is a question of relinquishing power and neither of us is willing to do this. But she cannot force me to understand, so I have the advantage. She can yell all she wants and I just smile. I win.

After our daily encounter with the woman warden, we pull the picnic tables and benches to the side, sweep the cell thoroughly, get a bucket full of water and a mop, and mop the cell floor. Everyone has her own job, and is expected to do it without being reminded or prompted. I have no job, but have taken it upon myself to wash the sink area. Actually, everyone has a job but the gypsies, they are exempt, nobody can tell them to do anything. While we clean, they lie back on their beds and smoke cigarettes like duchesses or queens. I never see them without their makeup and their costumes, it is a matter of pride, of maintaining their aura of separateness from the rest of us. Even when it is time to go to sleep, they wait until everyone is in bed before changing into their nightclothes. I suspect they never remove their makeup, but simply touch it up each morning. One day, it will simply flake off in sheets and fall to the ground, as though a snake were shedding its skin.

When the cleaning is finished, the coffee and our daily half a loaf ration of bread are delivered to the door. It is not real coffee, but chickory, and every morning without fail there is a lot of grumbling about this. Sometimes Milica takes her portion and dumps it directly into the toilet hole in the corner, she makes a big production out of it, does it very ostentatiously, with a flourish, when she has everyone's attention. I drink mine, though, because chickory is a new taste for me and I rather like it, and I like the bread as well, a dark bread with a thick, crunchy crust, still warm when we get it, it is baked right in the prison by trustees.

The rest of the morning is ours to do with as we like, except there is nothing to do. We are not allowed near our beds during the day, we can pace back and forth across the cell or sit on the picnic benches. Some women have papers to read, taken from a huge pile in the corner of the cell, papers meant to be torn into squares and used for toilet paper. Others write letters or talk about how they have been framed. They are all innocent, Milica tells me with a dry laugh. Our prison is just a holding facility, so that as soon as the women go to trial and get sentenced, they are sent away to the harsh labor camp.

Lunch is served, after a stultifyingly monotonous morning, at approximately twelve o'clock. By this time, we have worked up huge appetites sitting for five hours. This is good, because we are dealt out huge portions of a nameless soup which changes only as regards color; the taste, the texture, the ingredients are always the same. Or perhaps they are different but simply taste the same. I begin to throw mine in the toilet hole as well, Milica and I make a sort of ritual of it, it becomes one of the high points of our day. But after a few times of doing this, one of the women pulls me aside and asks if she can have my portion. Her name is Mira, she is a Serb, a bit mannish, short, dark hair. A thief, if Milica is to be believed, who stole two cows from a neighbor to avenge herself for the theft by her neighbor of a brand new tire she had found by the side of the road. So I agree to give her my soup. She is pretty skinny, actually, and must be hungry all the time, she eats constantly, and never gains a pound.

In the afternoon, after we have had our lunch, we either pace the floor or sit on the picnic benches. Once in a while, we are allowed to make some spending money if we choose, and big boxes of flattened tea boxes are brought into the cell. Our job is to open them up, glue the flaps together and throw them into another box. We are paid according to the number of boxes of flattened pieces we finish by the end of the day. When I am especially deadened by boredom, I help one of the others fold her boxes. I get the hang of it quickly and manage to fold more boxes than anyone else when we are finished for the day. I turn over my money to Nada, whom I am helping because I feel sorry for her from time to time, but she immediately complains about how I have done something, which causes Slavica to slap her off the bench.

You help her, try to be nice and she complains, Milica tells me, the little rat. Nada has no sense at all, never knows when to speak and when to be quiet, doesn't comprehend the importance of being quiet when one lacks strength and influence, doesn't understand the balance of power in our cell. She is always covered with bruises and scratches and is, I suspect, beginning to like the beatings and to provoke the assaults. She is lonely and this is the only attention she can get on a regular basis.

For our evening meal, we are given more of the same soup we have had for lunch. Even if we do not want it, we are required to line up with our pots and dented spoons for our portions, which are ladled out by male trustees from a huge kettle balanced precariously on top of a cart. After dinner, we can either pace back and forth some more or sit on the picnic benches. At nine o'clock, the lights go out and we must be in our beds. Sometimes I get up in the middle of the night and catch the young gypsy, Zorica, smoking cigarettes in the dark, waving the red tip back and forth, tracing patterns in the blackness like a tiny fireworks display. At these times, I feel there exists an strange affinity between the two of us, alone and awake in the dead of night. We do not need to speak; in fact, we cannot. We are simply unified in consciousness, both being, hearing, alert, awake, alive.

She sometimes offers me a cigarette. I go sit on the edge of her bed as we smoke. We ignore each other, pretend I am there next to her by sheer coincidence. But there is a bond. I wonder how far this bond will go, what it will transcend, if anything, what it is dependent upon. When I climb back up into my bed, Katarina awakens below me, growls at me, bounces on the bed in protest and lets out a long, despairing sigh. And then she is dead to the world.

Though we are supposed to get a daily exercise period, this is seldom the case. It is due, I suspect, to a complete lack of interest on the part of the prisoners as well as the guards. But I feel a need to get outside in the air, to look at the sky, hear sounds that are part of another world denied to me now, move my legs, stretch them until they ache. I ask Milica to request some exercise time from the guard, which she does when the chickory coffee and bread are delivered. At once, Kata, the old bag who is always yelling "Kiss me, Kate" apropos of nothing, begins to laugh. She is exhorting everybody to get on the walking shoes, to warm up, get the blood flowing! Meanwhile, she sits in her regular spot, knitting and holding court to the few women who are subservient to her.

Are you coming with me? I ask Milica. She sighs and puts on an old ragged sweater which has only two buttons, lights up a cigarette and stands by the door. Slavica joins us. We are a trio, apart from the others, and there is a subtle, and sometimes not so subtle, competition between us and Kata and her group. But we are younger and stronger and in the long run, we will prevail. Besides, Milica and Slavica know how to fight.

When the guard finally comes, I am happy to see that it is my friend who had what seems like years ago shared pictures of his daughter with me shortly after my arrest. He greets me with a big smile, grabs my elbow and pulls me along the hallway, to the wry amusement of the others. We go down some stairs and are suddenly out in the courtyard, which consists of a patch of dry land about one hundred feet long and forty feet wide. Posted at every corner is a guard with a long rifle pointed at us. I look around to see where we could possibly run to, how we could possibly escape these tall brick walls, but there is nothing, no exit to be seen save the door through which we came moments before. Slavica, the thieving whore, Milica, the accused burglar, and myself, distributor of pieces of paper. We are a dangerous trio indeed, and I laugh out loud, it is all so ludicrous.

Well, start walking, Milica tells me, you're the one who wants the exercise. The three of us begin to walk, back and forth, just like in our cell, except that the distance is longer. One of the guards, who, I notice with pleasure, is extremely handsome, winks at me each time I pass him, winks as he trains the rifle on my head. I look down in embarrassment, but enjoy this attention, want the exercise period to last for hours, until I drop. Now I will be sure to request exercise every day, twice a day if possible. Who knows what may develop from this small flirtation? At least I will have a reason to live in the event that I do get fifteen years. The guard and I can grow old together.

When we return to our cell, I am rejuvenated, I sit on the picnic bench and daydream about the handsome guard, about the possibility of touching him accidentally as I walk by, or being alone with him somehow, of staging an accident, a hundred possibilities present themselves to me. But suddenly I remember why I am in prison at all, it is because of my love for Taik. What is this mutiny within me which is scheming now to be alone with a guard who trains a rifle at my head as I pace back and forth in front of him and would surely shoot me the minute I make a false move? Someone who has perhaps shot or tortured friends of Taik's who may have been under his jurisdiction in the past? I have a sick feeling in my stomach. What can I possibly be thinking of? I sit at the bench pondering my treasonous inclinations.

Dear Mom and Dad, I write, after I have gorged myself with sandwiches, fruit and candy provided by the American Consulate, this cell is like a sociology class. I try to make the letters funny, to sound optimistic, I give them descriptions of each prisoner but omit the crime for which they are charged, I tell them about the food, the layout of the cell, the walks in the courtyard, I praise my attorney, my Mister Madirazza, for their fairness, their conscientiousness. All will be fine, don't worry, it's all a big mistake, a misunderstanding, I will laugh about it later when I'm home, it will be a story to tell my grandchildren.

I begin to cry as I write, but put my head on the picnic table immediately so that nobody will see, least of all Nada, the only other woman in the cell who cries. I keep my head there, resting on my hands, until the tears dry up, but it seems like hours, they just keep running down my face onto the table, making shallow puddles under my hands. When I finally raise my head, I can tell that my face is swollen, my eyes red, but I do not look around, I resume my writing as though everything were the same as before, as though the tears had flowed out of a foreign, an alien, heart, and not my own. Milica comes over to me and pats my arm. I could kill her and the look I give her tells her so. Small kindnesses at moments such as these harm instead of heal, strip the iron out of one's will. If I don't watch it, I will fall apart. Everybody just leave me alone.

Milica has made me promise that when I leave, I take with me all the particulars of the trumped up charges of which she has been accused, so that I can write a letter from Vienna to President Tito asking him to investigate her case and grant her a complete pardon. I get a piece of paper and a pencil and write in tiny letters the information she gives me. Then I tear the paper into small squares, about twenty of them. She hands me a pack of cigarettes, and we empty each one of its tobacco, then roll each square and place it inside the cigarette paper. After all the squares are in place, we return the tobacco to the cigarette, which takes all afternoon.

When we finish, we are very proud of ourselves, sure that we have thwarted the officials and that Milica will soon be free as a result of my brave intervention. But first I must be freed myself, and of this I am not certain. And if I am, there will be much to explain and assimilate: I feel at home with the gypsies and the whores, and, at the same time, I find myself incomprehensibly attracted to the armed guard who holds us prisoners, who would kill us in a moment if necessary. There are little boys in prison here. I threw pieces of paper. Taik is Croatian but it is virtually illegal to say so. They pulled out all of Violich's teeth. What did the little boys do? What, in fact, have I done? Why are we in prison? Everything is becoming clearer to me. It is not a good sign for my antagonists.

Dear Mom and Dad, I write, my trial is next week, and I am hopeful that I will be back in Vienna by Christmas. I think everybody has realized a mistake has been made. Meanwhile, I think of you often, I love you all very much and am sorry for all the worry I have caused you. Please write as often as you can. My attorney is very good and the Consulate is taking excellent care of me. All my love, your daughter, Julie. This time I do not sign it "your only daughter", as I sometimes do. I do not want to remind them.

I have stopped worrying about the undeveloped film they have confiscated from us, which, I had recalled with horror, contains a picture of Milan, Melody, and me at the Prater. If the film has been developed, I will find out in time, and it is pointless, anyway, to worry about something I cannot now change. The picture is so clear in my mind, so vivid, the colors of the flowers in the background, the type of smile Milan has on his face, one I know so well, the one he uses like an unloaded weapon to remind one of his potential for danger. Milan the wanted man. What is he capable of? Certainly more than I, with my Western opinions and indulgences, with my traveling iron and German camera I have never learned to operate.

One thing I am capable of, though, is remaining calm under pressure. I will tell the story to the judges, not the whole story, perhaps, that is impossible, but the core will be there, the core. I will trim everything, cut off all the edges, round them off, trim, trim, until I am left with only a few curled shavings from a monstrous tree. A man gave me the leaflets and I threw them. I don't speak Croatian. It is not illegal to throw leaflets in my country. I am sorry if I offended anybody and it won't happen again. That is all they are getting. Yes, his name is Taik, I don't know, I don't know. This will be my answer to most questions. And the best part is that I really don't know. The larger issues engulf me like a tidal wave gaining momentum by the second. My defense is that I'm so young and stupid. I'm sure everybody will agree.

Nada is heading for the toilet hole in the corner of the cell to relieve herself. For at least three days that I know of she has not defecated, she tries to hold it as long as possible. But now she can't hold it any longer, she is beaten, forced to capitulate. Everyone watches her voraciously, as hungry animals would watch a wounded bird or rabbit limping across a field. Nada knows she is in for it, her eyes are angry but she refuses to look at anyone directly. She goes over to the toilet hole, walks gingerly in, and pulls the curtain around her. As she squats, we can see her head above the height of the curtain, only her head, the rest is hidden, as though she were imprisoned in a box with a hole for her head to stick out of. Nobody talks, nobody wants to miss anything. It takes a few minutes, Nada is still hoping at the last minute to be able to hold it just a bit longer, her face is set, obstinate, she looks into the distance as if in a trance.

And then it happens, as it always does. I don't know if it is due to the food she eats, her dirty habits, the lack of any type of exercise—at any rate, the sounds that issue from the depths of her bowels are terrifying, as though her innards are being turned inside out and shaken violently. The revolution has begun, the revolution has begun! Kata, the old witch, screams out triumphantly. Everybody get under a table or bed! The rest join in, laughing, holding their noses, putting their index fingers in their ears, making sounds of disgust, anything to add to the torment Nada is being forced to endure. Meanwhile, Nada squats in the corner, looking stonily ahead of her until the upheaval of her bowels, the betrayal, has ended. Then she gets the bucket, fills it with water from the sink, and washes down whatever abomination it was that has been ejected from her.

Fill another bucket! orders Marica the gypsy, we want to sleep tonight without fear of being attacked by that monster! Make sure you wash it clear into the other building, the one reserved for the politicals! She laughs so hard at this that she begins to cough spasmodically and Zorica is forced to pound on her back for at least five minutes. The excitement over, we all return to what we had been doing: folding tea boxes for the government.

8

"There is an innocence in lying which is the sign of good faith in a cause." Nietzsche

My trial is next week. Dr. Dukat is convinced he can get me off, that nobody in their right mind could convict me of this crime, especially since I have now admitted the name of the "enemy of the state" who gave me the leaflets. Madirazza is happy, he has another success to place in his dossier. It seems more appropriate now to call him simply Madirazza, he is mine no longer. Our fragile bond has been snapped, and all because he asked something of me I feel he might not really have wanted to ask and I gave it.

But I must forget about this now, must prepare for trial. In my mind, I see the woman who just left to begin serving the eight years hard labor, how she looked as she went out the door, her brown box under her left hand, sort of hanging off her hip, eyes sad but not resigned. There was a rebellion brewing, I could see it by the way she took her leave—with a cold contempt, not for us, but for those who thought that she could be forced by anybody to do eight years in a hard labor camp. And I, too, share her contempt. I must be strong, strong like this. But fifteen years is more than I can fathom, almost as many years as I have lived my life.

I have been allowed to keep only one dress, a forest green knit bought from a street vendor in Venice for approximately five dollars. When I pull it out of the cardboard box under the bed, it is hopelessly wrinkled, and I forsake any hopes of being able to wear it at my trial. But Slavica takes matters into her capable hands, relieves me of my dress, sprinkles it with water, lays it out completely flat under my mattress and tells me that after I have slept on it for one night, it will be perfect. She is so pleased to be able to perform this service for me, pleased that she is so appreciated. Has nobody ever shown gratitude to Slavica the whore, even the customers whose desires she must somehow have slaked? She is like an organ grinder monkey doing tricks, running up and down a stick, making faces, so desperate for recognition. At the end of the day, she lies down quietly, as though her life force is seeping out of her like an old radio bleeding electrons, voice fading and full of static.

The unjustly-accused Milica is in a horrible mood and Nada has done something, I am unsure what, to provoke her. Without warning, which is so often the case in this cell, violence erupts. Milica lunges out of her seat on the bench, runs over to Nada's bed, where she is curled up in her usual fetal position, and drags her out onto the floor. Then she gets up onto the top bunk and pulls the entire window from its hinges, breaks off one of the panels and climbs back down. Meanwhile, Nada is in a ball, head buried between her arms, whining and waiting for her beating. She never lets out a healthy cry, it is always a whine or a keening sound, like a baby who does not know exactly what is wrong, but feels the need to express its existential indignation. Milica takes the panel in her right hand, raised it above her like a whip and begins to beat Nada over the head with it. Nada curls into an even tighter ball, she is disappearing before our eyes, metamor-phosing into a smooth globe of flesh covered in thin cloth. As Milica beats her, she calls her names, a snitch, an idiot, a moron, a retard. From time to time, Nada responds, she still has spirit, which I am forced to admire, in spite of everything. You're the moron, you're the retard! she says triumphantly, as though she has just discovered the truth, the real truth, of the matter. This only serves to speed up the tempo with which Milica beats her over the head. There is no blood, strangely enough, but bruises are already forming on Nada's hands and forehead. Milica gets tired before Nada passes out, so she stops, throws the piece of window frame onto Nada's bed, gives Nada a kick on the behind, and returns to the bench. We all are quiet afterwards, as though we ourselves had participated in the beating.

Disembodied sounds haunt me day and night, sounds without connections, or sounds which have lives of their own, which operate without attachments to object or person. They are like ghosts materializing from nothing, then disappearing again in a puff of vapor. I often hear a screech in the hallway late at night. It is possible that a person is making this horrific sound, but it is just as possible that it is simply a bucket being dragged down the cement floor. Yet somehow the screeching sound is unlike a bucket or a person, it is a sound which exists on its own, born from misery, giving voice to those who have been deprived, who listen motionless between their stained sheets, waiting, hating.

9

"What a time experiences as evil is usually an untimely echo of what was formerly experienced as good—the atavism of a more ancient ideal." Nietzsche

It is the day of my trial and everybody is excited in her own way. Kata and Slavica look ready to cry, especially Slavica, who stands near the door, as if waiting for an opportunity to bolt as soon as it is opened. Her long, skinny legs are in a scissors position, she looks so vulnerable, like a schoolgirl standing alone on a playground. I give her a quick hug, I even hug Kata, the witch, who, for the first time since I have known her, is speechless, dispenses with her usual "Kiss Me, Kate!" But Milica the innocent looks worst of all, sitting on the bench, smoking, looking at the floor, knees crossed, elbows at right angles, a fleshless pretzel taken prematurely off the coals. She won't look at me. Well, I won't look at her either, that's what she wants. There is no need to emphasize by a gesture her despair at the thought of not seeing me again. Her optimism that I will soon be gone is contagious and I take a quick look around my home, the cesspool in the corner, the spattered sheets, the uneven cement floor upon which my feet so often paced—just in case it is my last. I look at the walls, remembering the sound of tiny taps breaking the silence of our cell to communicate signs of hope, love, even rebellion, to those waiting expectantly on the other side. There are many ways of talking here, most often without the use of words. The greasy water in the soup bowl, the tiny pieces of pale green floating on top—there is an entire soliloquy contained in the picture this meal presents, day after day. So much to say, so many ways of saying it. But it is the day of my trial, the door closes behind me. The last face I see is the face of Slavica. It has fallen, the forces of gravity have exerted their pull upon her, laid claim. She forces a tiny smile, but only one half of her mouth moves. Everything is done in half-measures, it is a world of almost.

My green knit dress is impeccably pressed, just as Slavica told me it would be. But I have no nylon stockings, my legs are white and bare, and, against all odds, fat. The American Consulate has achieved the impossible: I have gained at least ten pounds in a totalitarian prison, where everybody else half starves to death. The shoes I wear are like big brown cows, whose tongues flap back and forth as I walk. I present a ludicrous picture, dread the first moment in the courtroom, which, I have been warned, will be filled with reporters, consular officials, Yugoslav government representatives.

My guard takes me by the elbow, we climb some stairs, and as we climb, our picture is taken by a group of photographers. I am startled, try to hide my face, not because I have qualms about my picture appearing in the paper; on the contrary, that is somehow an exciting prospect to me, but because I make such a comical impression, the green knit dress, the big, white legs, the oversized shoes with tongues hanging out. My face is like a full moon which never sets. My hair hangs in greasy ropes, as I have had no shampoo, only hard soap meant for scrubbing toilets or metal pipes. Nor have I had a shower in a month, for that matter. But I am used to the filth, I have gotten accustomed to scratching my arm and seeing, afterwards, the grime packed underneath my fingernails. Everyone in the cell is dirty, was dirty. I am just like the rest of them, but different as well. A comforting thought. Outcasts, but not among each other. I wish, really, to be taken back to my cell, to fold some tea boxes, joke with Slavica, watch the gypsies play their games. I feel so confused.

The first thing I feel like doing as I enter the courtroom is to laugh. For whom have they prepared this absurd spectacle? The room is large, ornate, pompous. There are five rows for observers and all seats are occupied, there is not an empty chair in the house. As I enter through prepared heavy door, all eyes turn towards me, bore into me like lasers, from my greasy hair down to the brown, docile cows carrying me across the room. I sense a feeling of disappointment sweeping over the observers, I can hear the thoughts swirling around in their heads: this can't be the one, it's impossible, this young, fat girl with the funny shoes and the hair hanging in slick vines over her shoulders? Nobody laughs outright, but there are hints of disbelieving smiles, of indulgent, omniscient, barely perceptible shakes of the head. But they are unaware that I share their disbelief, their sense of the absurd. My aesthetics are insulted as well at the sight of this comic scene, at the object of this farce, which so happens to be myself. Many take notes on small pads tightly in their laps, while others continue to stare at me shamelessly.

Facing the spectators are five judges, all bespectacled, who sit behind a large, elevated desk, four men and one woman. To describe them accurately is to simply say that they seem connected by an invisible thread. The looks they give me are uniform, their gestures automatic and identical. They act as a body of which they are the appendages, each, in this case, knowing exactly what the other is doing.

A single, a solitary chair has been placed in the middle of the courtroom, spaced halfway between the judges and the observers. This is where I am to sit, vulnerable and exposed, and as Dr. Dukat motions me to the chair, I find it hard to contain an uncontrollable urge to bolt from the room, to disappear, to remove myself as the object of ridicule and entertainment. But I do not bolt, I walk slowly to the chair and sit down, facing the five judges. I fold my legs as well, one foot behind the other, the way nice young ladies are taught to sit. But nice young ladies should not be in a Yugoslav courtroom on trial for disseminating enemy propaganda and advocating the overthrow of the government. My hands are damp and so are the places where my legs touch. I can feel the movement of the spectators behind me, they are like animals stretching in the sun, but I dare not turn around, I dare not do anything but look from the judges to Dr. Dukat and then back again to the judges, and then down at the floor, eyes downcast, the picture of abjection, misery, penitence. But I still am not sure what I could possibly have done, I do not comprehend the magnitude, if there is any, the evil of my act. It is like sentencing a lunatic to the electric chair.

The prosecutor has a crewcut, which I have always considered an American aberration, and a pair of dark-framed glasses, which he removes whenever he mentions my name, as though to say that he doesn't need glasses to see, see through me. After everything he says, Dr. Dukat jumps up from his chair and comes over to provide me with a translation. Because he is especially excited, he sprays me even more than usual as he talks, he gives me a veritable shower, but I am polite, I do not wipe the moisture from my face, my arm, I allow it to dry by itself, I suffer in silence. I think I have finally learned to suffer.

The questions I am asked are the same ones my Mister Madirazza has asked me during our many interrogation sessions. He has prepared me well, if unintentionally, for this onslaught. I wonder if he is in the courtroom, but somehow I know he is not, does not want to be a witness to this comedy or is it tragedy? I have at least accomplished this: I have made him share the guilt.

Not only does the prosecutor ask questions but the judges ask them as well, one after the other, one more probing than the last, about my knowledge of Croatian, of Croatian history, Yugoslav history, of the Second World War. How could I think the leaflets were harmless and non-political advertisements for a book when I myself admitted it was about atrocities committed by the Partisans after the war? A good, valid question. One I would ask myself. And I am suddenly irritated with Madirazza, whose good humor had prompted this admission from me, one which I am now to regret. But I had wanted to be helpful to him, had wanted to give him something for all he had given me; otherwise, it would have been rude, I would have been seen as ungrateful. Never mind that I must answer to it now, never mind that I might well receive fifteen years in hard labor, the main thing, the important thing is that I be polite, that I reciprocate in like manner the good deeds that have been performed on my behalf. How everybody must be laughing behind me, how they must be trying unsuccessfully to stifle their laughter, to erase the mirth, the disbelief, from their faces.

My answer is an embarrassment, even to myself, though I am truly ignorant of all the little nuances which come into play. I mumble reluctantly something about my lack of knowledge of Yugoslav law, that I figured everybody killed everybody else during the war, that I wasn't sure who killed whom, and didn't care, either. And added that in my country it was not illegal to distribute leaflets of any content. Eyes down again, this is a mistake. The first one.

The torture continues. The comedy continues. Witnesses are called, the first is Jagica Tonkovich, the landlady with whom we stayed the first day before our arrest. She has been grievously wronged, I see the indignation in her eyes, she, a respectable wife and mother, called in on a criminal trial because of some hoodlums who, by an unlucky stroke of fate, came to hatch their nefarious plot under her roof. She sputters, she expostulates, she indicts, or would if she could. But never once looks at me, refuses to acknowledge me sitting in front of her, hands folded, legs too. She says her piece, waits for applause which never comes, and leaves in a huff, her purse hanging like a dead animal from her lower arm. She shoots me a look on her way out, though, which thoroughly disconcerts me, it is one of solidarity, something in the eyes, the set of the mouth.

Perhaps I am mistaken, perhaps everybody in in silent support, could this possibly be the truth?

A second witness is called, a man who was on the terrace with his children shortly before the leaflets were thrown, who says he saw us there, and nobody else, just as the leaflets went floating down to the street below. Perhaps he threw the leaflets himself! Why has he not been charged, or interrogated, or locked up in Petrinjska, as I have been? There is as much circumstantial evidence against him as there is and was against me. He has dark, curly hair and a snotty look about him. He is doing his duty as a citizen of Yugoslavia, helping to protect the "brotherhood and unity" I am accused of attacking. He, unlike Jagica Tonkovich, looks at me while testifying, looks at me as he would an aberration of nature. What else could I be, attacking a concept as worthy as "brotherhood and unity"? His name is Milicevic and he is definitely not in silent support.

Who is Taik? This question again. It's a shame Marica the gypsy cannot be here for the answer, she who would have given anything to know who put me up to this. But she would be disappointed. He is a spectre, without content, without identity. Just a nickname. I have given them enough, I won't give them any more. Oh, Taik is just a nickname, I say, I met him in Vienna one rainy afternoon. I don't know anything more about him, that's the truth. And it really is, I know this now.

The trial is finally over. Both the prosecutor and my attorney have given their closing arguments, delivered with a flourish, sprinkled liberally with flamboyant arm-waving and head-shaking. But Dr. Dukat is the more impressive of the two, he takes this more seriously, his reputation is at stake here, perhaps even his liberty, as I have been told by Taik that often, the attorneys defending political detainees, because of a too-impassioned defense, find themselves in jail along with their clients. While the arguments are being delivered, I sit meekly in my chair. From time to time, the judges peer at me closely and I wonder what has just been said, whether it will ultimately determine the course of my life, how persuasive it is, what I can do to counteract it. I can do little but sit and look contrite, which is not difficult under the circumstances. But a rebellion is brewing within me as well, whether I am convicted or set free.

Outside the snow is falling, I can see a white blanket of velvet draped across the small windows of the courtroom, all the flakes have melted into one and continue to melt, continue to fall. The voices recede into another room, another building, and I lose myself in the stark white of the windows, I make myself an object, a part of the chair. The windows, the light overhead, the hissing of the radiator, they all seem more human than the spectators, more accessible, affectionate. I would like to cup my hand around the warm bulb above me, rub my palm against the coolness of the white window, lean my calves against the radiator.

Instead, I am taken by the elbow by a guard, one I have not seen before. It is over! I am going back to my cell, my refuge. Slavica and I can play cards, I can joke with the gypsies, give Nada dirty looks, make Kata mad—the possibilities are endless. Such a rich and varied life in the cell, and in such a small area, too. Dr. Dukat tells me it went well, that I will wait in my cell until I am called back to the courtroom. How long will that be? I ask. He doesn't know or doesn't want to make predictions. He is still unsure about his own fate, and while we talk, he looks over his shoulder in alarm at any noise not immediately identifiable.

Back in the cell, nobody seems to recognize me. Everyone is busy, what have they all been doing in my absence, have they forgotten me already, what have I missed, who got into a fight, who said and did what? I feel at a disadvantage, feel deprived, neglected, resentful of the judges, Dr. Dukat, everybody responsible for having made me leave my cell, my little home. Finally Milica the wronged asks me how it went. She doesn't want to, but feels it is the least she can do. All right, I tell her. Just all right. As I feel it is the proper thing to do under the circumstances, I pace back and forth from one end of the cell to the other. Everybody stays out of my way, even the gypsies, everyone gives me my space, my respect. It is so quiet in the cell, everyone is in a state of high tension, reluctant to break the silence with an ill-timed remark. Prisoners have such a highly-developed sense of the appropriate. In no other milieu I know is this sense so refined, so over-developed. Perhaps because all the other senses are repressed, stunted, flattened and squeezed by the weight of imposed mediocrity . I wait for the verdict. Everyone stays out of my way.

And then the door of the cell opens once more and I am taken back to the courtroom. I am led to my throne in the center of the room and seated. Some statements are made by the judges, one by one. After the last judge has spoken, before he finishes, actually, I hear a loud sigh from Dr. Dukat. I look over at him, horrified, but he is shaking his head up and down, he is pounding his right fist into the open palm of his left hand and talking to himself, he has lost his mind! But he hasn't really, he has simply won the case, I am free, I can go! So can he, apparently. He comes over to me, I am bathed in his sweet words, they wash over me like a swollen river. Guilty, suspended, expelled for three years. Yes, yes, yes, I say. Oh, God, I can go! I can go. I'm going.

I literally run up the stairs, the guard is trying to keep up, telling me to wait, wait, I must wait for him. But I don't have to wait for him, it's his job to watch me, and, besides, now his job is over. Dr. Dukat is waiting for me downstairs, he is taking me out for tea, just the two of us. I am not thinking about Slavica or Milica, or the red signal flashes the gypsies' families send them from rooftops near the prison every night, not giving a single thought to Nada's unfaithful husband or the bruises she wears like a second face. But this is not true. I am consumed with such thoughts, I wish never to have to return to my cell, to leave behind all my meager belongings, leave as much as possible of myself to remind them that I am gone, that they, too, will someday be gone. It will break some hearts to see me go, even Nada will be temporarily at a loss. Perhaps she will receive fewer beatings for awhile. Milica the Disenfranchised will be too depressed to lift a finger against her.

When we arrive, the guard opens the cell door with a flourish. I rush in and see immediately that words are not necessary. They know. As it is in every prison, news travels fast, reaching every cell almost immediately after the event has taken place. Nobody moves, either, they are all sitting down, even the gypsies. Nobody wants to look at me, not even Kata, who always has something smart to say. I slow down, move with greater precision, as though anything, anyone, I touch will shatter. And they continue to sit, afraid to move, to get in the way of a force that cannot any longer be stopped, be related to. All that remains for them is hatred and hope.

Slavica finally breaks the heavy silence, comes over to me and holds me tightly. My nose is imbedded in her hair, which smells of stale tobacco and moldy cloth, but she has me, I cannot free myself, nor do I really want to. Slavica begins to wail, lets me go, curses, gives Nada, who is sitting expectantly on her bed, knees drawn to her chest, a warning look, and throws herself on her bed, unable to sort anything out.

The guard tells me to hurry, to get my box, to say my goodbyes, and I hate him at this moment, one would think he was locking me up instead of freeing me. Goodbye, Milica, goodbye everyone, don't worry, you'll all be out soon, I hope. Be strong! I run around the cell, give everyone a hug, tell Milica the Innocent I will send President Tito her letter as soon as I reach Vienna, and she rewards me with a tepid smile.

And then it is done, they are left behind, and already my sadness is flowing out like blood from an open vein. I am free. I see the guard that first brought me to my cell. Idem doma! I yell to him, I'm going home! Good, good, he says, and I can see that he means it, this enemy of Taik. Where is my Mister Madirazza now, I want, I need to see him, to tell him I forgive him for doing his job so well, but that there is much more I will not forgive or forget from so many others. Dr. Dukat, here I am! He turns to me, all smiles. Come on, let's go out the back door, there are too many reporters out front! We race through a door where there is already a car waiting, we jump in, take off, like two bank robbers, heads together, laughing, proud of ourselves for being so clever. The car races away, cutting the world into ragged strips before my eyes.

We go directly to a small cafe, where we have a cup of tea. I have ordered mine with a slice of lemon, which is brought to me by a smiling waitress in a crisp white apron. The room is crowded, everybody is well-dressed and speaking pleasantly with one another. I also am speaking pleasantly with Dr. Dukat. I wipe my mouth politely, using economical motions. The serviette is soft and cool against my skin and the tea goes down my throat like a river of velvet. I marvel at the yellow of the lemon, the color is so rich that it makes my heart ache.

Beautiful Tuskanac, high on a hill over Zagreb, is dotted with mansions, like a piece of sky full of stars would look in the daytime. All the foreign diplomats live here, and here is where I must wait, until the prosecutor decides whether to appeal my case or not. Wilson Orren has volunteered to have me stay with him and his family until the decision is announced, we are driving there now, with his chauffeur, who is chatting with him in Croatian, something about houses, I recognize the word "doma". I sit benignly in the back seat, neither smiling nor reacting in any other way to what is happening around me. I look out the window, accept this instant luxury as a natural thing, something I have deserved or at least know how to appreciate. I can communicate with both diplomats and whores; there is in the opinion of many no great difference between the two.

You'll be happy to have a nice bed and bath, won't you? I am asked. Oh, yes. It's almost too much to imagine, I tell Wilson Orren, and he sits back contentedly, but not overplaying anything. He is suave, he can be taken anywhere and will always behave properly, will never allow a situation to escape him, to spin out of control.

Here we are, he says, and the car stops, at the end of a winding drive. I smell bad, it is obvious to all three of us, and it is with relief, barely disguised, that we climb out of the car.

There is no weather, I suddenly realize as I stand in front of the house. No weather, nothing to describe, as though everything belonging to the concept has been sucked out through some hole in the sky, leaving only a weak memory of what was, had been. A leaf blown to the ground, a small puddle at the foot of the porch stairs—they are clues to a mystery that eludes me, I understand only the atmospheric pressure of my little cell home, where nothing ever comes to rest.

My apartment is in the basement and has three rooms, a bedroom, bathroom and sitting room. The first thing I do is turn on the water for a bath. I tear my clothes off, they smell as though they had been stolen from an old grave, and I wonder if I can hide them somewhere so that they can be thrown away with the other garbage. It is impossible for me to wait until the tub is full, so I lower myself into the hot water, little by little, until I am sitting. I feel instantly purified, sanctified, cleansed of all conceivable sins as the clean, pale blue water rises over me. I scrub, I rub, I luxuriate in this pool of velvet which surrounds me, until a layer of scum rises to the surface of the water, a brown, frothy layer, too thick to imagine it has all come from my body. The more I scrub, the thicker the layer becomes, it looks like lava issuing from some ancient volcano, so I let the water out, clean the tub, and start all over again. With each bath, I change, become more and more the same person, and finally the merging is complete. When I have dried myself on a snowy towel as soft as a sigh, I go into the bedroom, pull back the clean sheets. But clean is not nearly enough, the sheets are beyond that, they have attained a holy state, so above reproach are these pieces of white cloth. I lay myself down on them, they speak to my bare skin, rock me to sleep. I am back in the womb, flowing in some primeval vein back to my source, drifting, floating, a part of the universe, which has seldom been the case with me, and this is my last thought before I am gone, this has seldom been the case, the case, the case.

What is it, being free? I am now free to subject my life to further tribulations. At least in my cell, those decisions were taken out of my hands.

I am allowed to go into town while waiting for the prosecutor's decision, so I set off to the bus stop, which is only steps from the house. Snow lies deep on the ground, and when I breath, small frosty puffs issue from my mouth. My fingers and toes are warm as toast, I am bundled up in a thick coat and leotards. But the contentment I feel is only physical. As I walk down the street, I feel exposed, vulnerable, as though the trees heavy with snow, the birds hunched together on a wire, are conspiring against me, have been diabolically retained to provide a sense of false security, so that I will say oh! we have the same type of trees, the same birds in America, we are all part of a universal scheme. But I do not feel this at all, I am an alien, twice and maybe even three times over. No sooner do I peel back a layer than I discover another between it: a convicted criminal, a foreign dissident, and an enemy of the state, a girl in love. There is no end to it.

The bus deposits me like a pellet in the main square of Zagreb, and I stand uncertainly in the middle of the sidewalk. There is too much movement, I am pulled in many directions by disembodied sounds, a flash of color, faces I do not recognize, their eyes opaque, like small, cold marbles set in clay. I study them as they pass by, take notes. They are different. No, I am different. I cannot decide.

A large coffeehouse is within view, I have heard of it from Taik, it is where he used to go in his student days! I go in, sit down at a large wooden table. A newspaper has been left behind, the Vecernji List, which I pick up and begin to scan, looking for familiar words. A waiter comes, takes my order for coffee. But I am suddenly and strangely frightened; I look up, look around. A man leers at me from another table. He recognizes me from the papers, no doubt, and wants to make conversation in order to have an interesting story to tell his friends, about the American who threw those leaflets, yes, he just happened to spot her in the coffeehouse, the one all the papers have been writing about. But there is something more to him, and suddenly I have it, suddenly I realize with desperation that all is lost. I retrieve from distant memories a face in a Viennese cafe. I am with Ivo, the guitar player, who has brought along a friend. My face is flushed, I have been arguing, but what about, what was the topic? The friend and I do not get along, we do not see eye to eye, and I am disgusted both with him and with Ivo for bringing him along. And then I remember, the words are too clear for me at this moment, too true. Tito is a traitor to his people, I had said, or something to that effect, and there were no doubt other things as well, but this was already enough.

The man continues to leer at me, he has not yet recognized me, but I know him, I even remember what he was wearing that night, he had on a shiny brown shirt with yellow and black diamonds across the front, and his nails were dirty even though they were bitten to the quick. I am sick, horrendously so, and cannot get up quickly enough.

I make it back to Tuskanac, to my apartment downstairs. There is a metal taste in my mouth, as though I have been forced to chew tinfoil. I get into bed with my clothes on and pull the covers over my head. Now nothing can happen to me, it would present the Yugoslavs in too ludicrous a light, to burst in on the American consul and drag a young girl from a bed screaming. I will make myself invisible. I lie in bed and wait for the inevitable. After what seems like hours, I am called upstairs for dinner, and I go, reluctantly, only to embarrass myself by putting the vegetable on the bread plate. Wilson Orren does the same, and it is for this reason he is the diplomat and not I.

The following day, I learn with immense relief that the prosecutor has decided not to appeal, to return my passport to me, and I will be leaving for Vienna the next day. This information is given by Wilson Orren as I sit with his wife, helping her wrap fifths of whiskey in colored paper for Embassy friends and for the natives with whom they work and socialize. They are having a Christmas party, later in the evening, but I must stay downstairs so as not to antagonize the Serbs who will be there. The decision is communicated, as usual, very diplomatically. They would of course prefer my company but it wouldn't be good for "relations".

So I will remain in my room, reading an old paperback book of short stories by Alfred Hitchcock I have found in the dresser next to the bed.

Safe in bed, in the bowels of the Embassy mansion, while overhead the possible murderers of Croatians and other dissidents chat politely, raise glasses, make toasts to friendship, brotherhood and unity, ignoring all the contradictions contained in their mutual amiability, oblivious to the warm presence beneath them of an accused enemy of the state".

I think about my homecoming in Vienna, the explanations that will be asked of me, but I think mostly about calling Cleveland, Ohio, to tell Taik I am free, to bask in his love and appreciation for the sacrifices I feel I have made for him. I will call home as well, prepared to explain to my family how it is impossible that I return home, as I know they will suggest, perhaps even demand. Life is elsewhere now.

Declaration of the Croatian Liberation Forces

National self-determination is a basic human right, universal and fundamental, recognized by all members of the United Nations, a right which may not be denied or withheld any nation regardless of its territorial size or number of inhabitants. Only the inhabitants of an historically determined and delineated territory can objectively and competently prescribe its future trends and its own fate. Any force imposing itself against the desires of a nation are nothing if not occupiers, and, as is widely recognized, occupation can be maintained only by brutal force.

This universal, natural and human right is denied many nations, even from members of the United Nations, or, more appropriately, United Countries, which are obligated by their signatures to support and honor the principle of national self-determination. Croatia finds herself among these nations which are refused the right of self-determination.

Small nations know they are small, but rise up against the unjust consequences of this fact: Small nations affirm their national independence through struggles for freedom, even by means of abductions, bombs, and murders. The necessity for freedom is strong and more just than the legality which powerful nations preach to support their arguments for ruthless force and lethal weapons.

- After a full thirteen centuries of continuity as a legitimate state, Croatian state sovereignty was abolished. Through the artificial and forced Yugoslav-created state, the Croatian nation was subjected to the fascist-monarchical dictatorship of the Serbian kings. After the end of the Second World War, unparalleled and unprecedented genocide was perpetrated upon the Croatian nation, under the banner of 'brotherhood and unity' and in the name of integrationalist Yugoslavism and grim, inhuman internationalism of the Hitler-Stalinistic type. The terror of the Serbian occupation subsided in 1966, only to be renewed in 1971 in an even more brutal manner.
- Croatians are oppressed, humiliated and degraded in their national pride and dignity. In their homes as well as in their homeland, they have no rights whatsoever but are burdened by difficult, unparalleled obligations. The Croatian moral and material possessions are disposed of in any way Belgrade deems appropriate. Through taxes and all resources from the land, Croatians must support the very system for which they are being sacrificed.
- In addition to the moral and historical obligations imposed, it is significant that not a single powerful country respects the recommendation of the General Committee of the United Nations to set apart 0.5% of its national income for use in underdeveloped countries. However, from 1945 until today, 8% of the Croatian national income is extracted. According to U.N. evaluations, the biological and cultural growth of a nation from which 4% of the national income is systematically stripped is severely endangered.
- By the use of sheer force applied inside Yugoslav borders, and through material, military and intelligence support by the Big Powers of East and West, mismatched nations are held together in contradiction, coerced into a Serbian-dominated union, where mentalities, cultures and systems are hostile to one another. Having already lived centuries of their distinct existences inside

totally dissimilar states and cultural compounds, these nations have formulated their own unique world views. Although they may utilize the same dictionary, the origin and basis of their intellectual expression renders these ideas incomprehensible to the other nations with which they live.

- The total command staff of the Yugoslav military forces serving inside Croatian national territory is composed of members of the Serbian nation. Serbians constitute the wide majority of the police force in Croatia. Key positions in judicial bodies, administration, law, the Party, and the economy are likewise occupied by Serbs. Croatians who serve in these bodies are generally statistics without power, potency or influence. This unnatural and inhuman situation is maintained by force and cloaked in one motto: People's Unity. This motto, which is continually repeated, is believed by nobody, not by the occupiers or the few quislings, regardless of how brazen their crimes and treason.

- Croatians are excluded from every decision; decisions are merely relayed to them 'after the fact'.

- Today, when dialects of recently primitive tribes are being developed into new, modern languages, the Croatian grammar and orthography, which has been preserved on a monument dating from the year 1100, written in Croatian letters and language, is prohibited and burned.

- The bearing of the Croatian coat of arms, which was engraved on a Croatian stone monument dating from the ninth century, is equated with evil.

- The singing of old patriotic and even sentimental Croatian songs is considered a conspiratorial, terroristic act, directed against the Yugoslav 'brotherhood of nations'.

- In a contrived manner, the natural growth of the Croatian population is being systematically reduced. At the same time, the most vital part of the Croatian population is being compelled to emigrate by means of economic exploitation, political pressure and police terror. This new form of genocide represents a sustained and intentional extermination of the Croatian nation.

- According to Amnesty International, the most well-known monitoring organization concerned with political prisoners, there are more political prisoners in Yugoslavia, or more accurately, in Croatia and Albanian Kosovo, than in any other Central European country, excluding the Soviet Union, whose population numbers 250 million. This statistic was openly confirmed in a TV interview by the Yugoslav dictator, Josip Broz Tito, at the occasion of his state visit to Sweden this year. Sentences of hard labor extend to twenty years and are often even amended later to death sentences. Sophisticated, diverse and bloody forms of torture are habitually the means by which prisoners are terrorized and 'confessions' extracted. When necessary, the arrested are simply killed.

- It must also be emphasized that, since the 1918 creation of imperialistic Yugoslavia in Versailles, Croatians were and remain an undesirable element in Yugoslav diplomacy. As an illustration, let us consider the national composition of the Yugoslav Embassy in Washington, DC, where the largest Yugoslav delegation in the world is stationed: of the twelve accredited Yugoslav ambassadors to Washington-from 1970 until today—eight are Serbian, two Slovenian, one Jewish and one a Montenegrin. Not one was Croatian. Of the nineteen Washington Embassy employees in 1970, fifteen were Serbian, one Montenegrin, one without stated nationality, and two Croatian (one of which was the chambermaid of the ambassador's wife. Choosing Croatian chambermaids from members of the occupied Croatian nation is not coincidental).

- Yugoslavia is impossible to defend with any generally recognized contemporary legal or socio-philosophical standpoint. Besides the fact that inside Yugoslavia, a sustained genocidal politic is being perpetrated upon the Croatian nation, the Albanian nation is likewise biologically threatened. Belgrade holds under its occupation a large portion of Albanian national territory upon which virtually half of the Albanian population is settled.

- We present the Croatian issue as the issue of freedom. Croatia must be a state of free people and a just society, outside all ideological political, economic and military blocs...Croatia is not up for bids in an international auction block, but plays an integral part in the destiny of the world.

–excerpts from the leaflets dropped during the hijacking over Montreal, Chicago, London and Paris, and which also appeared in major U.S. newspapers (New York Times, Chicago Tribune, International Herald Tribune) on September 10, 1976

Part Two

10

"What is essential is that there should be obedience over a long period of time and in a single direction: given that, something always develops for whose sake it is worthwhile to live on earth."
Nietzsche

Vienna, Austria, 1971–The train ride to Vienna is lost to me, I am back before I realize it, at the station near our apartment. Everything is so clean, so antiseptic, even the German words have a quality of cleanliness and orderliness about them, as though they have been lying like smooth pebbles on the bed of a racing stream for the past ten or fifteen years, until there is little left of them or anything else that has had a connection to them. I am clean, too, the last water I have used on my body is Croatian water, perhaps even water reconstituted and used by Taik in years past, to wash his body, his feet after a day planting tobacco in the fields of Gorica, in the heart of Hercegovina.

A taxi takes me immediately to the main Post Office, where I put a call through to Cleveland, Ohio, to Zdravka's house, as I am convinced the news of my freedom, my success, has somehow reached Taik already. He answers the phone himself. His voice is calm, betrays no emotion. How are you? he asks solicitously. What do you mean, how am I? I want to yell at him. Instead, I tell him I am fine and that it's good to hear his voice, to be back in Vienna. Taik does not approve of hysteria. After all, I have deferred to him so far. There is no reason to change things yet.

As I knock on the apartment door, I call out Melody's name at the same time, so that she will not be in suspense any longer than necessary, or perhaps because I feel like screaming, like releasing all the compacted energy within me. I can hear footsteps running down the hall, a screech, and then the door is open, I am in her arms, she picks me up first and then I pick her up, we swing around wildly, yelling, shrieking, and then, finally, letting the tears come. She has on a new outfit, bought with the money her parents think was used for the attorney fee, a burgundy and black knit dress, long, below her knees, and high black boots. Wait till you see the shoes I got, I'm going to give them to you, they don't fit! she tell me in one long breath, and pulls me down the hall.

Everyone is freaked, she says, they've been coming over every day practically asking about you. They can't believe it. Who's been coming over? I want to know. Oh, Rudy, Ortwin, you know. No Croatians, though? I ask. No, no Croatians, please, she beseeches me, no Croatians!

She pulls out a "Stern" magazine, a seedy German equivalent of "Life" or "Look". See, here you are in the international news section, between Ivan Rebroff and Lyndon Johnson, one a famous singer and the other, at the very least, the President of the United States. But it is indeed my name, with a short description of the activities which have landed me between the two, given me a strange notoriety validated by the mass media. What I have done is suddenly as legitimate as Ivan Rebroff singing to a sold-out concert in Bonn or Lyndon Johnson announcing a cease-fire in Vietnam. I count the lines in each of our paragraphs. Ivan has fewer lines than I, three, to be exact. Johnson has eight more than I, which is to be expected, as Presidents and their activities are more important, in the universal scheme of things, than those of a singer. But what of an American enemy of the state, a former political prisoner, an attacker of the Yugoslav "brotherhood and unity", a girl in love? I realize I have a new responsibility, towards myself and my knowledge, I feel larger than before, as though I have filled out in some intangible way, become more substantial, more to be reckoned with. I have become a force.

But, honey, we think you should come home, you need to be with your family after this horrible experience, my mother tells me when I call. Such a thought has not occurred to me. I have no intentions whatsoever of returning home. What a ludicrous thought, returning home, as though my life had become too much for me to live, as though I were unequal to it! I love you all very much, I say, but I'm not coming home. She is silent, doesn't understand and wants to. But I cannot explain what I do not understand, so we hang up, both loving the other.

When I return home from shopping the next day, I see as soon as I walk in the door that something is horribly wrong. First, Frau Kus is waiting for me in the hallway, something she is not known to do except in cases of extreme emergency. And she is holding a yellow envelope in her hand, as though it were a small, dead animal. Her lips are pressed tightly together, so tightly that even the small lines crisscrossing them are erased. I ask her immediately what has happened, what the yellow paper is, is it about me?

It certainly is, she says, but she is more upset than angry, looks at me with a new sense of awe, even or protectiveness, as though I were her discovery, something she had for years in the attic and just discovered to be a treasure, a collector's item.

I take the envelope, go over to a chair and sit down. She stands over me, in case she is needed for translation purposes, hoping she will be, at any rate, as her curiosity is hopelessly tickled and she cannot for any price bring herself to ask me anything. She is Viennese, after all, and well aware of the dictates of social decorum.

The envelope, from the Austrian Criminal Police Headquarters, is sealed loosely and I am able to open it with one quick movement of the index finger. Inside is a thin piece of blue paper, folded over once, so insubstantial, so fragile, that it is hard to conceive of it containing anything of consequence. Yet it does, it contains at the very least the possibility of something of consequence developing. My presence is required, the next day, at two in the afternoon, regarding Austrian national security. The Headquarters has been so kind as to provide a small, convenient map so that I will be able to find the office more easily.

Frau Kus is simmering slowly, like a barely blanched turnip of something equally pale and bloodless. I am loath to show her this paper, I cannot predict her reaction, but she does not move, does not acknowledge my discomfort, indecision. She simply prevails, a sturdy mountain in whose shadow I am momentarily forced to take refuge. Reluctantly, I hand her the paper, tell her to read it. She does, avidly, though, to her credit, her hands do not shake, and when he has finished, she folds it up again and looks off into some far distant place where birds are singing gaily and the edelweiss bloom. And then she says, well, have you ever heard of such a thing?, more to herself than to me, and simply walks into her sitting room and closes the door quietly. I listen for a moment, to determine what she might be doing, whether she is dialing the phone, lying down with the back of her hand on her forehead, or taking one of the tiny yellow pills she keeps on the top of her dresser. But I hear nothing, no rustle behind the door, no squeaking of the couch springs. It is as though she has gone through the door into a vast nothingness, has suddenly lost her physical presence, evaporated, like a plume of smoke as it travels upwards, closer and closer to the sun.

My head begins to pound, but only on the right side. I can feel a single vein engorging itself with blood, sending bolts of pain from my eye all the way down to the base of my neck. National security, the paper says. What possible connection can I have to Austrian national security? I wonder, yet I accept this proposition as entirely natural, as a legitimate concern of the Austrian government. Again I am suffused with a feeling of substantialness, of wholeness, and I think suddenly of my mother, her words on the phone. Come home, where you belong, she had told me. But I am only just beginning to understand where I belong, where I truly belong, and it is not in some sleepy seagull town like Gearhart, or in Portland, suffering the white afternoons of August from a broiling curb or the hot shade of a sagging dogwood. In a Yugoslav prison, I can forget for awhile that I am American, in an antique-cluttered Viennese fin de siecle apartment I can forget for a moment, I can read the "Kurier" or "Tagespost", hear the Austrian version of what's happening in Vietnam or Watts, but I always come back to it, expose myself, I hang my legs out the windows, I walk barefoot down the hot streets, step on the grass, pick a little flower, neglect to iron my sheets, towels, underwear, commit any number of American crimes against Austrian sensibilities. But I want to be cured of America. Dear Mom and Dad, I write arrogantly in my head, I am never coming home. I am involved in something you may or may not understand. It is called Life. Love, Julie.

11

"The consequences of our actions take hold of us, quite indifferent to our claim that meanwhile we have 'improved.'" Nietzsche

I report to the Austrian Criminal Police Headquarters punctually and am kept waiting in the outer office. I have dressed conservatively, in a jumper and navy blue tights. Outside, the sun is shining, but the air has a heavy chill to it which numbs the cheeks. A day like a false smile, one which does not fit the face on which it has appeared.

Please come in, I am told suddenly by a jolly-looking man, but I know now that this is a trick, and I am not taken in by the hearty smile, the firm handshake, the cool intelligence in his eyes. I sit down across from him at an old, scarred desk, as though we are teacher and student, going over an exam, perhaps, or discussing a term paper. I cross my legs, scoot closer to the edge of the desk, as he has taken out some papers which I assume he will ask me, like my Mister Madirazza, to examine, or names he wants me to identify. I know the moves now, and I know my own moves as well, what is expected of me, what I will give and what I will hold secret. My information belongs to me and to me alone.

You know a certain Zvonko Busic am I right? he asks. Yes, I do. This is common knowledge, I tell myself, no sense in denying it. Do you know where he is now? he wants to know, and very much, because he looks at me intently, even a bit threateningly, daring me to lie about something they know already to be a fact.

I sit and think about this for a few minutes. I think of the call I had gotten from Taik just the night before, from the East train station, telling me he was back, to take a taxi to him right away, he had a train to catch in an hour. No time to ask him anything, no time to cry or become excited. The taxi I had hailed takes forever, I am half asleep from working the graveyard shift the night before, noises around me are too loud, they hurt my ears, make me jump in my seat, even the sound of the driver striking a match. I tell the driver to stop before we are there, I can run faster than he is driving, I throw him the money, keep the change, big deal, he says, it's only two shillings, and I run, up the street, into the big cavern of the station, into the restaurant where he said to meet him, and there he is, smoking a cigarette, laughing at my excitement, I am always too excited for him, he always wants me to calm down, take things easy. Here you are! Yes, I say, and hug him with crushing strength, here I am. My face is wet all over, it happened so fast.

And then he is gone, we have finished a coffee and a tea, I am standing alone in the station, confused, forgetting already what was said and in what tone. But he has left something with me, a heavy presence that accompanies me out of the station, holds my arm as I run for the streetcar, gives me a shove up the stairs and keeps me warm when I arrive back at the apartment and climb back into my bed. But this is not the question. The question I am being asked is: Do I know where he is now? And I do not, he has gone somewhere and will be back for me around the first of October. He has "business". I have learned not to volunteer information. This man across from me does not know if he is coming, apparently, wants to cut him off. I don't know where he is, I tell him, in all honesty.

Are you in touch with him, has he called, written? This is touchier, but I admit I am in touch, though I say that Taik is a very haphazard letter writer, one never knows when one will get a letter, if at all.

You take taxis everywhere, don't you, he says out of the blue, and I am taken aback for a moment, for a long moment. What do you mean, I take taxis everywhere? I ask. What do you do, follow me around? I am filled with horror suddenly. Of course they do, they follow me around, they know everything I do, and my face begins to burn as I think about some of the things they know, have probably written down somewhere, perhaps even on the pieces of paper he has in front of him right now. I try to read what the top one says, upside down, whether it has taken note of the fact that I spent the night at a strange apartment two nights ago, or that I argued with the proprietor of the "Black Spaniard" again the week before, and got expelled from the premises? Do they know what I told the Slovenian, about how I would die for Croatia?

Did you ever say you would die for Croatia? he asks me. My mouth is open, I am stupefied, at a loss for words. Oh, sure, I would die for Croatia. Why would I want to do that? I tell him. I'm American, you know. But you did say it, didn't you? he persists. He doesn't say that it is written on the paper in front of him but I somehow know it is, I know that Slovenian has filed a report about me, that rat who invited himself to our table one night and started buying everyone beers and talking about politics. Of course, I was the only one interested in Yugoslavia, so he devoted all his attention to me, how natural. Even got me to say I would die for Croatia, and I thought it was exhilarating at the time, enjoyed showing the passion, the commitment to die for something, for an idea. And now I can say it was just a joke, an experiment, can't I? But who would believe it of me, after my release from a Yugoslav jail, a convicted political prisoner? So easy to be someone I am not, I think. He forces me to take myself seriously, he even takes me seriously. And I am not what he thinks, not what I seem. It is all a farce, a masquerade. But I am too deeply entrenched, I cannot extricate myself.

Did you say you were an Croatian fighter for independence? he asks me. Oh, now I'm that, too? I vaguely recall telling Ivo the guitar player that I was, one of the few phrases I had learned in Croatian, the one I got the most laughs about among the Croatians. I said I was a witch, too, I recall, but I'll bet that's not on the paper. Does it say I said I was a witch, too? I ask him, and he ignores me, waits for my answer to his questions. So, Ivo was a spy, too, though I am not surprised. After all, didn't his friend, the one I argued with in the seedy cafe, show up in Zagreb, didn't he almost expose me to the authorities before I could leave the country? The both of them are spies or traitors. And who else, who else, I ask myself? Not Milan, that's impossible. Not any of Taik's friends. And now I suspect everybody, even the ones who, to my knowledge, don't even speak Croatian. They could be plants, they could be trying to elicit incriminating statements from me, find out damaging information about exiled Croatians, about Taik, who knows? How about Clive, the alleged Swedish medical student? Or Ralf, the alleged Norwegian oboe player? Or Tony, the alleged headwaiter at "Leopold's"?

How much do you earn at the hospital? I am asked. Why? I say. I am belligerent now, insulted, mortified, appalled at the enormity of the crimes that have been committed against me. You ought to have that in your reports, too! But my interrogator is patient, gives me time to reconsider. And I am not, I ramble on, unable to sit coolly, to wait for his next move. I earn more than enough to take taxis whenever I want. What's so strange about that? I want to know. Taxis don't cost very much, they're cheap compared to America. You don't get money from any outside sources? he asks. From where? Where would I get money from? He shakes his head. How does he know? He wants me to tell him. Oh yeah, now I am bankrolled by some Croatian exile movement, I suppose, but I don't say this, it just occurs to me, it follows in the natural order of things.

While you were in Zagreb, were you supposed to bury the leaflets in a tree in the old graveyard? This is too much for me to bear. Who said that,

that's the craziest thing I have ever heard! But what's the use, he believes nothing I say, nothing whatsoever, he has it all written down by his confidential informants, in whom he has the utmost trust. But I am thinking back, trying to remember something about a graveyard, a hollowed-out tree. The strange thing is, I suppose I could have said that, too, who can remember all the things one says and is supposed to have said? Anything is possible. It sounds like it would have been a good idea, actually, to bury them in a tree to be picked up later. But whether I have said this or anything similar I do not know. I just don't know, I am taken aback.

You know Milan Busic don't you? It was only a matter of time before he brought up Milan's name, I suppose. You know I do, I tell him, so why ask? And because I have not yet admitted anything and long to expel at least a small part of the knowledge impacted in my head, I add that he is the number one wanted man in Yugoslavia. Oh, he is? My interrogator is very interested in this. I shut up. I won't make that mistake again.

In case you are wondering, and I am sure you are, we have received information from the United States that Zvonko Busic is on his way here, and we would like to speak to him about certain issues of concern to Austria, a country very proud of her neutrality, I might add, he says very pointedly. If he should get in contact with you, we would appreciate your letting us know. You are not in the most secure of positions yourself, young lady. Think about that.

I get up, he shakes my hand, though I have given him little satisfaction. Wait till I see Ivo, wait till I see that Slovenian, to find the ones who have committed this treachery against me. I run to the curb, hail a taxi, look up at the window to see if my interrogator is watching. Yes, I am taking a taxi, write that down in your reports, you ass. And I feel that I cannot ever trust anyone again and that my illusions are shattered, I am in a state of rebellion, a state of disgrace as well. I am an freedom fighter, I would die for Croatia. I won't say it again, once is enough. From now on, I will have to pay for it, already I am becoming something different, something I do not yet fully recognize.

When I get home, nobody is waiting for me. There is a feeling of abandonment about the apartment, as though everyone has packed up and left. Even the furniture seems bereft, forlorn. I sit down in one of the chairs, just to have some company. Where is Frau Kus and where is Melody? Outside, I hear a car sputtering down the street and then the screech of brakes. In this apartment, there is no sound whatsoever, not even the ticking of the hall clock. And yet the hands move, time goes on, and I sit watching and waiting, unable to move.

Frau Kus has found two Swedish girls to rent the apartment, since I have informed her I am leaving in a day or two and Melody has already gone home, back to her house over the ocean, to her Paul McCartney posters and old red station wagon. Frau Kus has not asked me specifically where I am going, she is perhaps afraid to know, suspects there is more to it than meets the eye. It is already the last day of September, and I have to move out so that the Swedish girls can move in. But I have nowhere to go, I am waiting for Taik, who told me he will be back to get me on October 1st. Frau Kus says I can sleep on her couch in the sitting room, so I do, for one night, and feel disenfranchised, usurped of my position in the household. I cannot sleep, worrying about whether Taik will be back to get me, whether I have been tricked. But I can't have been that mistaken about him, I can't have misjudged him so totally. But where is he? I am awake all night, I hear every groan the Swedish girls make in their sleep, in their new beds, my bed. I have nowhere to go.

In the morning, I take all my possessions to Milan's room, tell him I need a place to stay until Taik comes for me. He is amiable about it, shows me where to put my things, and then leaves for work. I sit in the room all day long, in case Taik comes, listen to the fancy stereo, make Turkish coffee, stare out the grimy window into the grim courtyard below, where two dirty children are beating each other up off and on for most of the day. I wonder if I should cook Milan's dinner, but first of all,

I don't know how to cook, and, besides, if I leave to buy something to eat, Taik is liable to come. Milan comes home around six, with a big bag of groceries, veal cutlets, eggs, a loaf of pumpernickel bread and some wine. He proceeds to cook dinner while I sit at the table in an oversized white T-shirt and some green cords, making desultory conversation, pretending I am not worried about Taik, pretending I don't even know him, changing the subject when his name is brought up. But Milan is not stupid, knows the dangers of depending on Taik, gives me a knowing smile.

We go to bed early, sleeping almost side by side in his big king-sized bed. It is like sleeping with one of my brothers, nothing sexual about it at all, though we are a man and a woman, both in a strange emotional and psychological exile. When he turns over on his side to face me, I open my eyes. His eyes are open, too. I laugh to cover my embarrassment and close my eyes tightly. And as soon as it is discreet to do so, I turn my back to him and promptly fall into a deep sleep.

When I wake in the morning, Milan is gone. I have not heard him get up, dress, make his breakfast or go out the door. The one indication that he has been in the room are the rumpled covers next to me and the strong male odor they exude. I sit up and rub my fists in my eyes, like a small child. My hair is matted and I have a metallic taste in my mouth. On my way to the sink, just as I pass the door, I hear a noise in the hallway. Then a loud knock on the door. Before I can think, before I can remember not to open doors until I ask who it is, I throw it open and there stands Taik, looking very pleased with himself, very fresh, in a brown corduroy jacket and blue jeans, a cigarette in his left hand, dangling at his side.

Oh, Taik! I say at least three or four times, it is all I can think of to say, and throw my arms around him. He pushes me inside and the next thing I know is that we are on a train to Salzburg, have left a note for Milan, saying we are gone and will write when we are settled somewhere. How we get to the train station, who packs the bags and carries them down the many flights of stairs, when I wash my face and comb

my hair—I have no recollection of any of this. All I remember for certain is that my place in the universe has been reclaimed.

Salzburg, Austria, 1971—We have settled into a small room in a private
house, overlooking one of the main streets of inner Salzburg, with a
view of the mountains in the distance and the castle perched on top of
one of them. There are only four pieces of furniture in our room, a large
bed in the middle which takes up at least half of the space, a wooden
table, and two chairs. We have a sink, next to the door, and the toilet and
bath are down the hall. I put our suitcases on the bed and open them,
trying to arrange our few belongings in some kind of order, or perhaps
I am doing this to look as though I have a purpose in life, as though I
am not at a loss, in this small room with Taik, who always has a purpose,
an action he is either beginning or following through to the end, who
never makes an unnecessary move or gesture, who can look decisive
even as he sits and smokes languidly one of his American cigarettes. But
I have no place to put our clothes, so I stack them on the closet shelf,
Taik's on top and mine underneath, so it is more convenient for him. He
is at the sink, washing some socks. A knock in the door. He steps back,
against the wall, asks who it is. The Austrian Criminal Police, a disembodied voice answers. He tells the voice to slip some identification
under the door, which he does, and which Taik examines in great detail
before opening up.

Taik is given a summons to report to an office the next day. The man
leaves, Taik comes back into the room, sits on the bed, then gets up and
finishes washing his socks. But I cannot ignore this intrusion, I begin to
cry, which causes him to turn on me, to ask me what I am crying about.
Well, I'm scared, I tell him, I wonder what they want! What difference does
it make? he asks. I'll find out tomorrow, what good does it do to worry or
cry about it? It makes sense, but the tears continue to flow silently.

So we go for a walk, along the narrow streets festooned with people
strolling, hanging out windows, riding bicycles in and out of the crawling traffic, or simply standing, looking around in wonder at this jewel of

a city. The day is clear but cold, the sky a mindless blue, as though it has forgotten everything it has ever known. We walk hand in hand, weaving through the people, gently bumping into one or the other from time to time as we pass. The summons is forgotten for the moment. All we know is that we are side by side in the middle of Europe, far from Zagreb, far from Gearhart. We feel somehow omnipotent, I can sense it without words. We know something nobody else knows, and this knowledge will protect us from all evil. But what is it that we know, that gives us such confidence? Perhaps it is a belief in the transcendent power of love. As I think about this, I press Taik's hand more tightly, guide him through the crowd, sneak a look at his face when he isn't paying attention. An inhuman face in a way, because of its refusal to assimilate, to melt into the crowd of faces around us. The black eyes, the sharp angles of cheek and brow—too many extremes. We cut through the soft flesh of the masses like a knife.

The next morning, Taik takes a train to visit his uncle in Linz, the one who was a renowned Croatian soldier during the few short years of Croatian independence in the 1940s, and will return in time for his summons to the offices of the Austrian Criminal Police. I go to an English movie house, where "Love Story" is playing, take melodramatic pleasure in contemplating the tragic nature of love, cry at every opportunity, and emerge, two hours late, cleansed and catharsized, feeling the desire to cry has been purged from me for the rest of my life, thinking how pleased Taik will be.

I am cleaning bits of salami from the dull switchblade Taik carries with him when he returns from his meeting with the Austrian Criminal Police the next day. The remains of my lunch lie on a newspaper on the table, crumbs of pumpernickel bread, shards of Emmentaler, the rind of a spicy salami. When I have finished with the knife, I go to the table, fold the corners of the newspaper together diagonally and throw the bundle into the wastepaper basket as Taik has taught me. Then I sit quietly, waiting for his report, also as he has taught me.

But he is thoughtful, does not want to talk right now, sits on the bed, then lies back, hands folded under his head. It is very quiet in the room, I do not even change the position of my legs, though the left one is going to sleep, I fear any noise will distract him, that he will lock himself away from me in one of his small rooms.

They want me to spy for them, he says finally. Give them information on my own people. Or else? Or else what? This is what I want to ask him. What will happen if you don't help them? But perhaps he will help them, can this be possible in the world he inhabits? Can there be an acceptable reason for this, a political one, an opportunistic one? But I do not ask this, either, because I am afraid of being unmasked as a hopeless idiot. The quieter I am, the less chance of exposing my ignorance, my naivete.

Of course I refused, he adds, and sits up, looks at me intently. Of course you did, I say with vehemence, and everything becomes clear to me, my doubts are dispelled, truth revealed in one quick stroke. This is never acceptable, never excusable. It feels right, too. I go over to him, lie at his side, my head on his chest. Within minutes, we are sound asleep, secure in the belief that it is our world that is correct, our world that is just; all else is artiface.

Taik has decided to enroll at the University of Salzburg, and I go with him to fill out the papers. It is a lovely university, connected by a series of courtyards with high arched entrances.

After he completes the myriad forms he is given, we walk slowly back to our room, stopping in front of almost every window we pass, not so much to look but to feel as though we are unhurried, have all the time in the world to do as we please. It has begun to snow, at first very lightly and then the flakes are swirling in all directions, contradicting gravity in a series of spirals. We pull our collars up, huddle closer together as we walk, blinking away the snow trapped in our lashes.

Back in our room, which is too warm in spite of the freezing wind outside, we laugh as we pull off our clothes, our wet shoes, rub our hands together, wiggle our toes to speed our circulation. And then there is a knock at the door, so Taik goes to it, stands to the side, asks who is there, his usual routine, which nobody does as well as he. It is the Austrian Criminal Police once again, they slide their identification under the door. When he opens it, four men rush in and close the door behind them. They hand him a paper, an expulsion order, I see, as we read it together. We are expelled from Austria, we are a danger to Austrian neutrality, at least Taik is, as he is allegedly plotting to foment civil war in Yugoslavia from within Austrian borders. The men are professionals, they search our room thoroughly, go through the mattresses, each article of clothing, look behind the mirror, out the window, in case anything is hanging down below, hidden from view. But they are not that smart, they miss completely the just-cleaned switchblade lying on the table in front of their noses. And they neglect to search us, except to pat us down cursorily.

Taik is not saying much, he has a look of contempt on his face, but mixed at the same time with wry humor, as though he were not surprised by any of this, had expected it, actually, given the lack of imagination of most of the world's population.

We want to call an attorney, he tells them. We want to fight this ridiculous charge. But they shake their heads, tell us we have fifteen minutes to pack, we are leaving the country. I am appalled, look to Taik for an explanation of what is happening to us, but he won't say anything, to anybody, he simply moves over to his suitcase and starts packing. So I do the same. The men leave us alone while we pack, warn us there are more of them waiting on the street below, that it is pointless to try to escape through the window.

It is impossible to decide what to take, what to leave behind, because I have no conception of where I will be in two days, in two weeks, with whom I will be, for how long. Am I really going somewhere? But I am carried along in Taik's wake. He is packing, so I must pack. We have fifteen minutes only, no time to lose. I leave my electric hair curlers. I leave a robe, two pairs of shoes, books, old letters from home. When I finish, I have filled one small suitcase, all my belongings stuffed into this tiny space. The large suitcase I leave behind, the one my aunt and uncle gave me for graduation. We have to travel light, he tells me, we can't be hauling heavy suitcases around wherever we go. Of course, I know, I say, you see I only have this one, I'm leaving everything else behind.

Our time is up. The men come back in their room. All finished? they ask benignly. We are too well brought-up to be impolite, so we answer yes, as though we had been asked to join them for lunch or go for a drive in the country. Here is what we will do, the older of the four tells us, in a strangely confiding manner, we will drive you to the train station in a taxi, escorted in front and in back by the officers on the street below, in their cars, so it would be fruitless to jump out, to try to escape. And you might get hurt, so don't do it.

I almost feel grateful for the warning, feel an affinity towards this man so concerned about our welfare, who doesn't want to shoot us, until I remember that we are being kicked out of Austria forever, without even so much as a phone call to an attorney, without any evidence to support the charges. It's not merely unjust, it's obscene, an act I would never have expected from the government of the country I consider my second home. So I attempt to harden my heart against Austria, the streets as we drive along look dirty to me, the people smug, the storefront facades just that, facades, meant to lull one into a false feeling of comfort, confidence in the correctness of all things Austrian.

When we reach the station, I jump out first, I am next to the door. One of the police officials jumps out after me, hand in pocket, followed slowly by Taik, who is in no hurry whatsoever. We are walked into the large room where the ticket counters are located, and Taik is told to go buy our tickets, that we will be right behind him. You know, you don't have to go if you don't want to, our escort tells me. He's the one we want to get rid of. I am indignant at the thought of simply leaving Taik, or staying safely in Austria, like a good girl, a good, respectable American.

I'm going with him, I say coldly. Where is he buying tickets to? I am asked. How would I know that, I answer. It could be anywhere! Our escort looks at me sadly, as though to say I am making a big mistake, but he doesn't understand, he couldn't be in love with anybody, he would leave his love at the first sign of trouble if he were, make things comfortable for himself.

Taik returns from the window with two tickets. Where are we going? I ask him, just to prove to the policeman that I really didn't know, that I was willing, am willing, to go wherever he is going, in spite of all obstacles. It seems we're going to Berlin, West Berlin, that strange island in the middle of East Germany, the divided city.

Let's get moving, our escort says, and we are taken to the appropriate train by him and the others. We all sit together in the same compartment, and when the conductor comes to check our tickets, they pull out their official identification, take the conductor aside for a whispered conversation, after which he stares at us intently. Yes, we are the outcasts, the outsiders, the undesirables! This is a new identity for me as I have never felt undesired by any individual or institution, to the contrary. But Taik, he is used to being one, he who was expelled from university for insisting the Croatian language be used instead of the Serbian, which he did not want to speak or learn. Kicked out of his own country, too, it was either that or prison. So Taik left, to become educated, and, no doubt, to avoid being arrested one day for singing old Croatian songs or displaying the Croatian coat-of-arms, which is paradoxically sold in stores all over Croatia.

But he is enjoying the adventure of our expulsion, looking out the window, making pleasant conversation with our Austrian consciences, who surround us and who seem to feel uncomfortable now with the whole scenario. What will you do in Berlin? he is asked by one of them. Oh, we'll survive, he answers cheerfully. Won't we? he asks me, and I am glad to confirm this. And then I refuse to speak anymore, though Taik continues to ask questions, about the landscape, about their families, how long they have had their jobs, commonplace questions had they been asked in any other social setting. As it is, they are not only ludicrous but obscene, and we all know it. Yet he continues and they continue also to answer, until we reach the Austro-German border, finally, and they are allowed to leave, having dispatched us safely to the other side. Now we are Germany's responsibility.

I am facing Taik, we are both sitting by the window. He looks at me and says with a sense of wonder, of awe, that he can't believe it. What can't you believe? I ask him. He shakes his head, he is convinced he is seeing things. I can't believe you came with me! You could have stayed in Austria, but you didn't. He is baffled, he smiles and then is lost in thought, then he smiles again, begins to laugh. I laugh, too, I am thrilled, feel so wise, so good, the best human being in the world, actually, the most loyal, the most faithful. What did you think I would do, just leave you? I ask him. What kind of person do you think I am? We look at each other with delight, so happy is each with the other, and we are not even touching, not holding hands or anything at all, but we are one nonetheless, we can survive any catastrophe, any tragedy, we feel invincible as long as we are together.

This feeling of unity is so new to me, I cannot assimilate it completely. And it is most certainly new to him, he who has never really trusted anybody, least of all a foreigner, a non-Croatian, an American girl who just happened to appear from nowhere in his life and knows nothing about what he lives for. But it is somehow of critical importance that I not be separated from Taik. I cannot dissect this belief, cannot break it down into its component parts. So I accept it; it is like a religion, sustained by acts of faith.

12

"There is an innocence in admiration; it is found in those to whom it has never yet occurred that they, too, might be admired some day." Nietzsche

Berlin, 1971–When we arrive in Berlin, Taik decides to call the head of one of the most popular Croatian exile movements in Europe, Dr. Branko Jelic, whom he had met and admired the previous year in America. We go to a telephone booth across the street from the cavernous train station. Around us, there are brightly lit stores, restaurants, shops, strung on the wide boulevard like stones on a golden chain, people issuing in and out of every door. As he talks on the phone, I look around, I am feeling strangely special, in the middle of East Germany, on this eerie, divided island called West Berlin. The German I hear is rough compared to Viennese, more guttural, like something not completely coughed up. The soft "ch" sounds I am accustomed to are replaced by harsh "k"s, the lazy, stretched vowels clipped, shorter. They remind me of an interrupted smile, something which does not live up to its potential.

I lean against the booth in order to feel connected to something, shift from one leg to the other. Taik talks and talks, he has always loved the telephone, it is his favorite modern convenience. He has forgotten me, forgotten how cold it is outside, that snow has begun to fall, but I don't dare knock, don't dare interrupt him in the middle of his conversation with Croatian hero and exile leader, Dr. Branko Jelic. I put my hands over my mouth, blow hot breath into them, short, hot bursts of air which dissipate as soon as they are separated from their source.

Down the street, I see the ruins of the Gedächtnis Church, standing like a charred piece of wood against the sky, one of the few buildings to survive the American bombing of Berlin in the war. I recognize it from picture postcards I have seen in the past, from German conversation books in high school. It is like a black hole, a collapsed star set in the sparkling constellation of the Kurfürstendamm.

Taik has finally ended his conversation. He opens the door of the booth, seems startled for a moment to see me outside, as though he had suddenly realized he is not alone in the world. Come on, he says, we're going to be staying with Dr. Jelic until we find a place to live. He grabs my hand and pulls me down the street; in spite of the fact he has never in his life been in Berlin, he already knows here he is going, has a gift for divining directions. Here it is, he tells me, Uhland Street. We go down a narrow sidewalk which leads, a few hundred feet farther along, to Dr. Jelic's practice.

The offices are on the second floor of a nondescript but well-maintained building flanked on both sides by what appear to be private apartment houses. In order to get in, we press a red button next to his name, and then there is a loud buzz, allowing the door to open. Taik has let go of my hand, probably because we are going to Dr. Jelic's, and, in the political arena, there is little room for sentiment or romance, but this I have intuited already, I do not take offense.

Dr. Jelic opens the door himself, grabs Taik and hugs him. He is a big bear of a man, thin-lipped, nose out of all proportion to the rest of his

rather fine features. He is around sixty, but has the exuberance of someone much younger, in spite of the fact that he has already survived two
assassination attempts and carries scars over most of his body, according to Taik, who should know.

And who is this? he asks Taik as he looks at me. Dr. Jelic, Julie Schultz,
Taik says. We shake hands solemnly. Taik feels no need to explain me, it
is clear that I am with him, have come the distance with him.

I am accepted immediately, given the same respect, admiration and
regard as Taik, who has had to suffer many years for this. Dr. Jelic calls his
retainer of sorts, old Nikola, in to meet us. Then he calls his receptionist,
as well as one of the nurses, who is German-Croatian, and a few of his
Croatian patients, all of whom, I suspect, are political dissidents living in
exile on this strange island. We are barraged with questions, slapped on
the back, made to sit down, to stand up again, to drink one thing and eat
another. And then, many hours later, we are suddenly alone, everyone
has left or gone to bed and we are in the darkness of the examining
room, which contains six small cubicles behind whose curtains are long,
narrow beds.

Here's where we sleep tonight, Taik tells me. On the examining
tables? I ask him in amazement. These are examining tables, aren't they?
I refuse to let this bizarre proposition simply drop, I insist on pursuing
it a bit further. Taik begins to laugh. He puts his hand on his forehead,
leans against the wall. Well, which one do you want? he asks me. You can
have first choice. I walk down the row of cubicles, throw the curtains
back. I'll take this one, I say, it's closest to the kitchen! And we laugh
again, grateful for the experience of sleeping on examining tables.

Dr. Jelic has not so much medical offices as gathering places for
exiled Croatians of every age and political persuasion. They sit in the
waiting room chattering back and forth, pushing aside the merely phys-
iological sufferers, and when the examination hours are over, they filter
out into the night to continue their fevered expostulations over small

glasses of slivovitz at the nearby "Macedonia" or "Dalmatia" restaurants down the street.

After about a week, we still have not found a place to live, so we continue to inhabit the strange recesses of the medical offices, sleeping either on the narrow couch or the insectile examining tables, haunting the waiting room corridors by day, cooking in the small kitchen in which we gather at specified times of the day. Taik is better than I am at almost everything, even cooking and cleaning. When I wash the dishes, he often rejects a plate or a spoon and rewashes it himself. He tells me when he was young he once forced his sister, Zdravka, to reclean the house because she hadn't cleaned it to his satisfaction. She refused but ultimately succumbed to his superior strength, so he suggested that, as long as she had to do it, anyway, she may as well sing as she cleaned, which she did, at first resentfully, and then with a disbelieving laugh. I wouldn't have sung, I tell him. I wouldn't have cleaned, either. He smiles shyly, as though to belie the image of benevolent tyrant he has just created. I would, in fact, do practically anything for him.

We have finally found a place to live. New Christ Street is the street on which our new apartment is located. It is narrow, short and dingy, it reminds me of a stiff leg covered with rags; the buildings are squat, their windows opaque, clouded with a streaked, yellow dust. Our building entrance is a huge and heavy metal door, always locked after nine at night. It opens into a square courtyard, three sides apartments and the fourth, a small, grassy field littered with old pieces of newspaper. From both of our rooms, we can see the courtyard and the garbage cans placed strategically around it. Our rooms are virtually empty and have more in common with abandoned warehouses or condemned flats. There is no heat, no hot water. A single hot plate, a table, a chair in the kitchen. In the bed/living room, an old office desk and chair, a bed. I try to move the desk but Taik stops me. Why not? I ask. If you put it there, he says, someone has a clear shot at me through the window. Of course,

I tell myself. Someone would have a clear shot. I sit down at the edge of the bed, try to forget what I have heard.

We have a bathroom as well, a tiny cubicle off the long hallway dividing our one room and the kitchen, but the remains of the toilet resemble a large, decayed wisdom tooth which has been only partially extracted. The door to this wisdom tooth, like a stubborn mouth, is opened by us only once, and remains closed forever thereafter.

What are we having for dinner? Taik asks one night. Your favorite, I tell him. Pasta asciutta, at one mark, fifty a package. It is the only thing we can afford which gives our stomachs the illusion of being full. Another night I try to make soup, but I am unsure if it is acceptable to put noodles and potatoes in the same broth. Taik is reading in the other room, buried in blankets to keep warm, so he is not witness to my anxiety. I decide to throw them both in; after all, what possible objection can be found in that? I take Taik a steaming bowl, serve it to him in bed. He fills a spoon and sips down the liquid. I look away, but it is no good. Why did you put noodles and potatoes both in this soup? he asks. Because I'm a moron, I tell him, and leave the room, slamming the door behind me. But he comes after me, tells me I am an original. It's what a best friend would say.

We manage to meet most of the Croatian exiles in West Berlin, so we always have a warm place to go and a warm meal when we are broke. It is a new experience for me, being poor. But I don't feel poor, I see it all as a grand adventure with love in the center of it all. In fact, we sometimes cannot even afford to pay for the public restrooms, so we are forced to hunt all over town for restaurants whose facilities we can surreptitiously use, though this is not at all easy, the Germans are adamant about such things, demand that one must first be a paying customer.

One rainy evening I am chased out of a local restaurant, but I deserve it, because this is the second time I have used their bathroom, they have already warned me once, and I know they are on the lookout for me and consider it a matter of honor to prevent my using it again. But I am in pain, so I take the chance. When I go in, the proprietor is serving a beer behind the counter and doesn't see me, but a table of four does, a table of regulars, friends of the owners, who pass every evening here nursing an orange soda all night long or a small glass of bitters. One of them gets up and goes over to the counter, but I am already across the room and in the bathroom, pulling down my pants as quickly as I can, releasing everything which has built up inside me, spilling my guts recklessly. I am rushing, can't get my pants zipped up fast enough, don't even try to button them. I open the door, head for the exit without looking either to the left or right.

There she is! someone yells. I ignore this, keep on going. That's the one! I keep on going, hands in pockets, head erect. Don't you ever come in here again, you hear me? Everyone is yelling and pointing, but nobody dares to come after me, to touch or grab me. They hate me but they are afraid as well. They think only a lunatic could do what I have done. When I get out to the street, I turn around to face them. Nanernanernaner! I tell them, flip them off and run away.

Sometimes I sit and wonder how my life has come to this, how I could ever explain to my parents that I don't have any of the comforts I grew up with, don't even have any shoes, except for the old brown ones with the toes that will never bend again. And then I look up and around the one big room where everything happens, and I see Taik at his desk, so strategically placed, and I am curiously happy and content, feel I lack nothing, feel sorry for others who have the sparkling toilets and bathtubs, the scalding water whenever they want it, whose clothes are bulging out of their closets, whose shoes are not a part of them like mine are but merely dead pieces of animal without life or meaning. My wealth is measured by the things I can live without. Thoreau. And Taik is my Walden Pond, we can drown ourselves in each other.

13

"Whoever does not know how to find the way to his ideal lives more frivolously and impudently than the man without an ideal."
Nietzsche

Christmas in Berlin is in some ways like Christmas in America. On every corner stands a group of Christmas trees, prices hanging from the top branch. They are generally scrawny and remind me of embarrassed schoolboys leaning together, one foot on top of the other. I take five marks, all I have been able to scrape together, and go out looking for our tree. Taik does not come with me, because, a day earlier, he has suddenly taken off on the train for somewhere else, to meet somebody from America or Australia, it is not completely clear to me.

When will you be back? I ask him nonchalantly. He tells me it depends, and when I ask him on what, he says I don't need to know, says it is better that I don't know. Meanwhile, he is methodically packing odds and ends in a small canvas bag.

But it's Christmas tomorrow! I blurt out. Tears form in my eyes, stubborn pools that, in spite of feverish blinking, lie stagnant and accusing. I turn a page of the magazine I have been pretending to read. A caption says: Of Course You Can live Without Chivas Regal. The Question Is, How Well? I don't dare look up, but know that Taik is silent and watching me intently. Julie, I have to go. It's very important, he tells me gently. Sometimes there are more important things in the world than Christmas. I'm sorry. I feel ashamed, but not completely. Not to me, I tell myself sullenly. So I take a deep breath and go to him. See you when I see you then, I say, as I hug him with all my strength, realizing suddenly this could be the last time I will feel him against me.

He gives me a wide smile to show me how much he approves of my attitude. I give him a smile back designed to show him that I, in fact, hold this attitude, which I do not, and before I know it, he is gone and I am left sitting on the bed. "Bye Bye Miss American Pie" plays menacingly on the U.S. Armed Forces station, and all the nameless assassins I have been warned against by Taik lie huddled outside in wait for me. Snow begins to fall and so does dusk, tucking Berlin and me in for the night.

There are three presents for Taik under our tree: a pair of slippers costing five marks, a Georges Simenon mystery translated into "Serbo-Croatian", and a magnetized chess set. On our Christmas tree remain only three of the cookies with which it was bedecked, the others having fallen prey to my nervous munching. It is intolerably quiet in the room where I sit with our tree and the three presents. The radio I do not dare turn on. The sound of American Christmas carols would annihilate me. So I go out to our New Christ Street neighborhood Gasthaus to buy a bottle of wine. Otto is already there, drinking a glass of Christmas cheer, an orange Fanta cola he will nurse the entire evening unless he is stood a drink or wins at dominoes, and when he sees me, he raises his glass in salute.

Otto, a wizened old raisin with deep-set blue eyes that sparkle out of a constellation of wrinkles that threaten at any moment to suck them in and bury them, has weathered many a personal crisis in his long and illustrious eighty-nine years. He is a refugee from East Berlin, and steadfastly refuses to reveal his method of escape for fear of "compromising others". After Taik and I get to know him, first by beating him soundly at dominoes, his only apparent area of expertise, then by standing him a drink regardless of his defeat, he deigns to show me privately what is doubtless one of his most prized possessions. Taik, for obvious reasons, is excluded from this confidence. Otto is a gentleman and would not intentionally wound another man's pride.

Otto pulls our a worn, albeit virtually empty, billfold he carries with him always. In it are two pictures, one of a sweet-faced woman around thirty-five years of age, whom he claims as a sister, and the other of Otto, standing in front of a window wearing only a dark brown shirt. He is leering into the camera, hands on his bony hips, and his spindly legs are buckled as though he could at any moment collapse. The eye travels almost immediately, however, to the exact center of the photo, where a huge, veined penis dangles dangerously down between his legs like a giant knackwurst. I look at the photo, then at Otto, seeking in his face some hint as to what he expects my reaction to be. He looks smug; there is no other word for it.

Not bad, Otto, not bad at all, I say seriously. I return the photo to him, taking on last, lingering look just to show my sincerity. He replaces it casually in his billfold and sits back in his chair in a decidedly supercilious manner. I shake my head and my finger at him. You ought to be ashamed of yourself! I tell him. Bet you never saw one like that before, did you? he asks. No, I never did, I answer solemnly. Thank God, I think, as I press my knees tightly together until they throb.

When I return later to the apartment, not a soul is to be seen either walking on the street or looking out of shop or apartment windows. During all the time we have lived on the street, we have rarely met passersby, regardless of the time of day or night, so I am not disconcerted, therefore, that I find myself walking back completely alone. Since the only cars that utilize our street are those whose drivers have lost their way, the snow is pale and smooth, both on the sidewalk and street, and the air is crisp. The moon, almost full, sheds an eerie light, like sun penetrating a murky pool, on the dark, squat buildings that line our street. I walk down the center instead of on the sidewalk, dragging my feet along in the snow. Assassins are far from my mind, although, to be sure, they are no doubt just as active during the holiday season as any other time of the year. This indoctrination has been insidiously subtle. One day I simply wake up and the consciousness of death is present in the very depths of my being. I recognize myself still, but I am not the same, I have a different walk, a different way of looking over my shoulder.

As I walk in the door, I hear a noise from the main room. I run down the hall, burst into the room, and there is Taik, sitting at the desk. All his presents have been torn open. He is wearing his new slippers and leafing through the book. All the criticism I want to make about the impropriety of opening one's presents in the absence of the presenter are immediately forgotten as I rush to him. You're back, I say, and all the tears I had so zealously guarded pour forth. I hold him for a very long time. Suddenly I remember to wish him a merry Christmas.

And you aren't supposed to open your presents without me, you know, I tell him. Why not, he asks, they have my name on them! and laughs. Who else's name would be on them, I say, since you obviously don't have anything for me! Yes, I do, he tells me triumphantly. Me! I burst out laughing. But I never find out where he has been, what he has done and with whom. All I know is that he is back, but for how long?

Taik bursts in one night in a strange state of excitement, turns on the radio immediately, puts his ear very close to it, though he has turned it up quite a bit already. I know better than to ask him anything, so I wait, listening. After a few minutes, the news comes on, we sit impatiently, through this and that, and finally we hear it. An mass uprising has begun in Croatia and it is being called the Croatian Spring. Students and intellectuals are speaking out, demanding the right to keep Croatian resources in Croatia, the right to use the Croatian language in schools and elsewhere. Hundreds have been imprisoned and the Croatian leadership is being purged. Suddenly he turns off the radio, gets up and leaves, straight out the door, without a word to me, without a word at all. And I am left behind to wonder what this means, whether I should pack my things, whether Taik will return in an hour or never at all.

Oh, goodby! I yell after him, trying to contain my sarcasm. I am so upset, yet can't bring myself to admit this, it is shameful to me somehow that I can't just rise to the occasion. But the fact remains that we are bound together and that he is coming to recognize my importance in his physical as well as his emotional life. I change the radio to the Armed Forces station. "Bye Bye Miss American Pie" is playing. It always seems to be playing, it must mean something. So I sing along, it's not a song to dance to, I sing loudly, at the top of lungs, the thumb of my right hand hooked in my belt loop. I don't need you, I tell Taik, wherever he is. I don't need you or anyone else. But I need to talk to somebody, so I go to our neighborhood bar and tell Otto the story of my life. After five minutes, he is sound asleep and I realize for the first time as I watch his sagging jaw that he doesn't have a single tooth in his head. He's got a big dick, though, I remind myself, and laugh and laugh until I am completely empty, until there are no colors or sounds anywhere, until I wake up hours later in bed with Taik at my side.

We sometimes use the public restroom at the Castle Street subway, we penetrate deep into the bowels of Berlin, down two long, almost interminable flights of stairs, until we reach the doors, marked "Damen" and "Herren". But the doors to our deliverance are locked, and I am beside myself, as they are generally known to be open 24 hours a day. I look around at the scattered fragments of the Berlin subway society, an old woman wrapped in newspapers, sleeping noisily under a brightly-lit display window; two boys milling around, smoking cigarettes as they studiously avoid looking our way; another dark form at the end of the station, a hunched figure, a black question mark.

Now what should we do? I ask Taik snottily. Sometimes I am unwilling to take the responsibility of having chosen to live this life, and this is one of those moments. Let's go! Taik grabs my hand and we run back up the stairs. Suddenly I feel a malignant presence, like a lion turning over in its sleep. Once out on the street again, we hurry back towards home. The wind is up now and it whips around and through us until our teeth chatter. As we rush along, heads tucked down on our chests and collars up, I consider whether we can manage to sneak behind one of the hedges lining Castle Street, but before I go any further, I hear a sharp crack. A branch breaking, a whip snapping somewhere, what is this strange sound? I am thinking, as I find myself yanked viciously to the ground by Taik, who covers my head with his arms. "Lie still" he orders me as he struggles to pull from under his belt his old gun, the relic I make fun of whenever I open the desk drawer for a pencil or a scrap of paper.

My nose is pressed into the snow and becomes immediately numb. My mouth is twisted back so that my teeth are exposed and when I try to lick the snow from them, I get small particles of grit all over my tongue.

Time beats around us like an excited heart, we wait and wait until the beat slows down, until it stops, and then we slowly get up. I desperately want to cry, but know it would be a major distraction, so I merely wipe my mouth on the sleeve of my coat and stand mutely until I am told what we are to do next.

Keep your head down and walk fast, he tells me. He grips my right arm so tightly that it begins to ache. I watch our feet taking each step in the snow and, after awhile, they begin to look unattached, moving of their own volition, the rest of me is somewhere else, my head, my heart, off in some unknown region where sounds are not dangerous, where black prints in the snow have no hidden meaning.

Once back home, Taik checks the entire apartment for anything suspicious. I lie on the bed, watching. Finally I sit up, prop myself with one hand. He stops what he is doing, looks at me in a strange way, as though surprised to find that he is not alone. You always seem to forget I'm here, I tell him, have you ever noticed that? Things aren't always as they seem, he says, and comes over to me, holds me in a warm cocoon. I want to know if he has done something I don't know about, something serious. Nothing I deserve to be killed for, he tells me. Do you know who it could have been? I ask. But he doesn't, says it could have been any number of people, it could have been his friend Jozo or even Stipe, Jelic's bodyguard. But aren't they your friends, you don't even trust them? I don't trust anybody but you, I can't afford to, he says. And then he gets up and pours us each a cognac. They only want to scare me. They could have killed me, you know, he says reasonably.

So I should feel happy, but I don't feel anything at all, it is too dangerous for relief, gratitude, even anger, too dangerous to be vulnerable. I'm not changing my mind about staying with you, you know, I tell Taik. Yes, I know, he says. Because I want a real life! But I don't say this, it is my secret.

Taik has had some kind of disagreement with Dr. Jelic, they don't see eye-to-eye anymore. The papers here write constantly of the mass arrests taking place in Croatia, the demands for liberalization, the purging of the Croatian Communist leadership. How many people have been arrested? I ask Taik, because I know the figures in the newspapers are always underreported. He tells me around thirty thousand: students, workers, intellectuals, many of them Communists who are demanding their rights under the Yugoslav constitution. The journalist and statistician, Bruno Busic a childhood friend from his village, is one of them, as well as many others he knows from home or the University of Zagreb or through friends.

He is so unhappy, so restless, he walks around the room aimlessly as he tells me all this, as though he is looking for something but can't quite remember what, and here he is, in exile in Berlin with a chubby and clueless American who feels she has no words to comfort him. But my actions have shown him, I have given up all I have ever known or cared about so that I can be chased out of bathrooms, shot at and left alone on

Christmas day. But we love and are loved! Is that not the supreme human achievement?

By distancing himself from Dr. Jelic, Taik has become a double outcast, he is now under suspicion of being a spy, an infiltrator, one of the paid Yugoslav agent provocateurs he himself is always on the lookout for. And, by extension, I am the woman of such a person, subject to the same dangers, the same suspicions. When we go visiting, we are heartily welcomed, the drinks are brought out immediately, the table stacked with food. But I sense a change, a shift in perspective. Watching these people is like watching an actor acting. I believe what I see and hear, but at the same time I am aware that a method intended to persuade and seduce me is being utilized. There are no more simple gestures of friendship, the smiles I see are spooky, like the smiles one sometimes sees on an animal, a dog perhaps, and knowing such creatures lack the necessary intent, the capability for warmth and friendship, the smiles alarm and frighten me, I pull back as though stung. But Taik tells me to relax, it has always been like this, only the characters change; it is typically East European, from day to day history is effaced, altered, faces are airbrushed from history book photographs, painted back in a year later.

So the list of those wanting Taik dead or, at the very least, frightened into inactivity, passivity, has expanded now to include not only the Yugoslav government, but potentially all Croatians, at least those who believe the rumors.

One of the exile Croatians, Velimir Tomulic, is supposed to be working for the C.I.A. and the K.G.B., Taik tells me, to make me feel better, I assume, though it doesn't, it only reinforces the insidious nature of the situation, the hypocrisy and fear inundating the exile community. Yet Dr. Jelic meets with him all the time, even has him write articles for his paper, I remind Taik. I know, he says, they're using each other, but they both know it, they're using me as well, for their own ends, just as I am using them for mine.

I draw more and more into myself. I have no friends, this is not possible for me. I never speak English, rarely even hear it spoken by anyone else, as the areas of Berlin we frequent are areas the tour guides and the travel books warn against, if they have even heard of them at all. My only link with America is the Armed Forces radio station, whose music and comments seem so irrelevant to what my life has become that I find myself switching stations, moving the dial back and forth until I find something Slavic.

We have a post office box about half a mile from our apartment, but it is almost always empty. We observe the ritual, though, of going there at least once a week to check for the mail. On some occasions, Taik suspects we are being followed, he points out a man with a newspaper, a woman with a dog. I have given up asking him why, there is always an answer, a reasonable though not necessarily a correct one. He tells me what I need to know. If you don't know anything, nobody can force information from you, he says. Are you talking about torture? You mean if I'm tortured, I won't be able to harm anybody else? Yes, he says, a lot of people have been unnecessarily killed because others knew things they didn't need to know.

I don't ask any more questions. What I am curious about, I imagine on my own, my understanding of this underworld grows with each day, and with it comes also the realization that many of my illusions have been shattered, that ego and pride, not commitment, are often the foundation for much of the tragedy I have seen in the exile world, that a search for identity is the driving force behind the subterfuge, the violence, the constant manipulation of events and people. The Croatians have lost their identity, without which they have no personal value. Stipe and his shoulder holster, Dr. Jelic holding court in his waiting room—this is not merely commitment to a cause but the simple search for an identity which has been taken from them by political means.

I am growing up. When I think about Vienna, about the reckless things I did to feel alive, I see another girl, one who had no understanding of cause and effect. Everything I do, everything I say now has potential deadly consequences. But, strangely, I feel equal to the situation. What is the origin of this strength and confidence? Perhaps it has been with me all along, like a rich, dark oil flowing just beneath the ground.

Taik has asked me to marry him and, even though I have often imagined this moment, when it comes I react violently, as though a giant jolt of electricity has surged through my body. We are lying in bed, late at night. I don't know why he decides all of a sudden that we should marry, perhaps it is the moment of logical culmination. We should get married, he says. And my stomach turns over slowly, like a bad motor. We could, I say. There is no flood of emotion, there are no stars, the room does not begin to spin, but, rather, a sense of completion overwhelms me, as final as death.

My stomach started to ache when you said that, I tell him. He takes this personally, says we don't have to get married, but we know we will, there is no way around it. I need my papers from Croatia, though, he tells me. That may take awhile. But we have all the time in the world. I lie back in his arms. My stomach is at rest, it has transformed itself from a coiled ball of barbed wire into long, smooth strands of satin ribbon entwined throughout my body.

Meanwhile, our life goes on. Whenever we manage to scrape together some extra marks, the first thing we do is go to the movies. One Tuesday night, we come out of a theater on the Kurfurstendamm and discover that snow is falling lightly and the streets are filled with strollers. We run hand in hand against the traffic lights but before we have crossed to the other side of the street, we slip on the slick pavement, fall as one body, in perfect harmony, our legs slide out from under us and we coast on our behinds the rest of the way. When we get up, we are laughing crazily and so are all the people who have watched our trip across. We are delighted with ourselves, and I immediately lock this feeling of unadulterated happiness and sense of unity away in my mind, it is only the second time in my life I have felt a part of the universe. And thus my bond to

Taik grows stronger, though with it comes a feeling of separateness, alienation from the rest of the world, a strange contradiction I am as yet unable to resolve.

Tomulic has asked us to come to his antique shop in order for me to translate something into English. When we arrive, he hands me some long sheets and when I look them over, I find they are addressed to members of the "Sinn Fein". Who are the "Sinn Fein"? I ask them both, but Taik lets Tomulic talk, I have the feeling it is his production. You know, the Irish, he says. We want to do some interviews with them for the Croatian press. I sit down and get to work. It seems a normal thing for me to do.

So now we're going to Ireland. It's a good thing I have nothing, because I can pack fast, I don't need more than ten or fifteen minutes, my whole life can be carried around in a small canvas suitcase, I have nothing to be sentimental about, nothing to long for or leave behind, nothing that doesn't fit. I have no letters to save, no photographs in frames or stuffed dogs; in fact, if I were to get hit by a train or a bus, if my suitcase were to go flying through the air and land sprung open at some stranger's feet, the paucity of information provided by its contents would lead one to believe it to be a stage prop of some sort, filled with any old thing simply to give the semblance of weight as it is carried across a stage and then thrown in a back room until the next night's performance. My identity is not contained in a suitcase or a room, it can't be forced anymore into such small spaces. And tomorrow I'll be in Ireland. I belong everywhere now.

14

"The great epochs of our life come when we gain the courage to
rechristen our evil as what is best in us." Nietzsche

We make our way from Berlin the next morning in the wee, dark hours
before dawn, we leave like thieves, dressed in shapeless clothing and
hunched over against the wind and snow. There is that quality to our
departure, though we have done nothing wrong, have nothing to hide;
we are free to go almost anywhere we please. No goodbyes, no
embraces, we leave Otto with his Fanta, Jelic with his band of syco-
phants decorating his waiting room in shades of plum and gray. We are
moving on, just ahead of the next assassin, we have outgrown Berlin.

The flight to Ireland is quick and uneventful. When we land and go
through customs, and since Taik does not understand English, it is left
to me to answer all their questions without checking with him first.
After all, I should know what we're doing in Ireland. We're tourists, I
say, and they finally, reluctantly, let us through. Taik is unhappy that his
English is not better, he is unaccustomed to depending on others, on
the judgement of others. What did he say? he asks, what is written on

that sign, he wants to know, as though he can absorb this language immediately if only he asks enough questions. I savor his dependency, it is an entirely new role for me. What does this say? he asks as he points to a newspaper headline. Wait a minute, I tell him, I'm trying to figure out where the buses to Dublin are. And he has to wait, he has no choice, I am in control now.

We find a room in a bed and breakfast right in downtown Dublin, on Mary Street, one of the arteries branching off from the main organ of the city, O'Connell Street. The house is run by the very English Mr. Butler, and his Irish wife, Megan, who obviously adore each other, and their dog, Sandy, whose little nails can be heard constantly skittering across the tiled floors. They show us our room, which is large and over-stuffed and looks out onto the narrow street. Breakfast is from seven until eight, they tell us, the bathtub is down the hall, the bookshelf is up a floor, they go on and on, trying to make us feel at home, and we do, we feel we could live the rest of our lives in Dublin with the Butlers and Sandy, we could forget everything that went before.

Taik asks me if I remember the translating I did for Tomulic in Berlin. I remember, I tell him. So he explains that the papers are meant as letters of introduction to the two main political parties in Ireland, the official wing of the Sinn Fein and the Provisional wing, or the Provos. He is to do interviews with both of them for Croatian exile newspapers. You mean I am, I point out. You don't speak English well enough. He is unconcerned about this minor point. He will give me the questions and I will translate back and forth. But first we need the addresses of their offices, so I do the reasonable thing, I look them us in the telephone book, write them down and check a small map we have found in our room.

The first contact we make is with the Provos, as they are called, because the official wing is associated with the Marxists and this is anathema to Taik and most other Croatians. We find the Provo office not far from downtown Dublin, on the second floor of a shabby build-ing. As we climb the stairs, we look at all the posters plastered over the walls, of the heroes of the 1916 uprising and the recent victims of the British occupation, slogans, fighting words. The building appears to be deserted, there is no sound except for the cars passing by on the street below, our breathing.

When we reach the office, we find the door open, so we go in, say hello, hello, is anybody here? There is a long wooden table around which heavy chairs are arranged. A small curtained window looks out onto the street like a little lidded eye. And then the door to an adjoining room opens and a man and a woman come out.

What can we do for you? the man asks us, accustomed, it seems, to finding strange people in the office, not the least bit suspicious or disconcerted. I tell him who we are, or, more accurately, what we are and what we want. I pull out one of the letters of introduction, which they both scan quickly. This is addressed to the people of the official wing of the Sinn Fein, the man says, and returns it to me apologetically, as though sorry he is not the one we want, cannot be of any help to us.

What did he say? Taik asks, but how can I admit my horrible blunder, I am the one who speaks English, upon whom the success of the assignment depends! He said thank you for the letter, I tell Taik, as I pull out the other, the correct paper, and hand it to the man. This is the one intended for you, I say. I'm so sorry. We are planning on interviewing both groups, you see. Why are you giving him the other letter? Taik asks. I refuse to tell him the truth, I am too embarrassed. He wants to see it, I say, he wants to check our story. Taik is talking now, telling me to say this, say that, he is totally dissatisfied with the state of affairs, feels powerless and ineffectual, suspects rightly that he is not being told everything.

Why don't we sit down? the man says. But first he introduces himself as Paddy O'Ryan. We give him our names and shake hands. The woman sits silently, does not give her name or hand, perhaps she is on the run, wanted by the police, or maybe working here without the knowledge of her family. My imagination allows her any number or roles.

For about an hour, I translate back and forth between Paddy O'Ryan and Taik, explaining Croatian issues, their interest in Ireland, the similarities, the differences, and our desire to do interviews for the Croatian press. Paddy O'Ryan nods his big, sandy head, a gigantic head topped with a wild thatch of straight, thick hair. The hands he has folded in front of him on the table are like sides of beef; it is hard to imagine Paddy O'Ryan without a shovel or a gun in his hands.

Suddenly he gets up and goes over to the window. Come over here, he tells us, as he draws the curtain aside. See that car down there? We look out to see a black car just sitting on the side of the road. What did he say? Taik wants to know. If we see that car, I tell him impatiently, and he shoots me a murderous look which makes me shrivel inside. Sorry, I murmur, but it is not enough. That car is always watching us, it doesn't even try to hide, Paddy O'Ryan tells us.

So what? I would like to ask. If you know that, then be especially careful. I am unsure of the point he is trying to make and finally conclude he simply wants to impress two naive foreigners of his and his group's importance. Image seems to occupy top priority to them, just as it does with the Croatians. Both have lost their identity; all they have is the image they project to the rest of the world, they no longer die for what they are but what they would like to be.

We make arrangements to meet again, shake hands, go down the stairs and onto the street, where a taxi materializes immediately, screeches to a halt in front of us, and even though we suspect that we are being spied upon, we are no different than most people who believe that the awareness of danger is synonymous with mastery over it. So we climb into the back seat and give our address, Mary Street. We want to go back to the Butlers, to Sandy, who greets us whenever we return with an amazing leap through the air; he doesn't even need a running start, but merely pops up into the air as if ejected by some unseen force below him.

Taik is silent during the ride back, though both the taxi driver and I try to engage him in conversation. He is interested neither in my attempt to get back into his good graces nor in the possibilities for intrigue and diversion the theory of taxi driver as spy represents. He simply doesn't like my being in control, realizes there is nothing he can do about it, must accept it or drag me back to the continent. You say that you trust me, I tell him, so what is the matter? He thinks about this for a minute, this novel question, and then he seems to remember that he can and does, that he has somehow insulted me and himself. I do, he says, but it's more than a simple I do, it is an affirmation of total faith, a willingness to be totally exposed and vulnerable, a new feeling for him. After all, don't I deserve this trust, haven't I proven myself many times over?

He takes my hand, tells me in German that we are too intelligent for the oaf of a taxi driver, who continues to ask us the silliest questions. Maybe he speaks German, I say. Why do you think I called him an oaf? And we laugh at our cleverness, all the way to Mary Street.

We find it hard to sleep in our cosy room, because around three every morning, a band of small children pours out into the street below our window, little ragamuffins, some in shirtsleeves, though it is the middle of winter, others on bicycles followed by a snake of four or five others on foot. There is much laughing and crying, but in eerie, muted tones; the sounds remind one of a horror film, where spooky impostors are masquerading as children, but have spent too little time watching the real ones, haven't quite gotten the hang of it. They play and run, even fight, though they seem to barely have the energy to lift their wrinkled nuts of a fist.

I watch transfixed at the window until they disappear, scatter in all directions, into little cracks and crevices, over walls, around corners. And after they are gone, I still can't sleep, I hear their thin laughter, their weak cries, they echo in my memory like the opening and closing of a cage of dying animals.

We still have the other letter to present, to the official wing of the Sinn Fein, so we get out the map and figure out where the office is. We decide to walk there, which is a mistake because we end up stopping everywhere along the way, first in a small shop selling socks and ties, so small that we have to walk single file down the aisles and still are crowded and have to pull our elbows close together. We both buy a pair of socks, socks from Dublin, mine are brown and Taik's black and stretchy. We stop next in a stationery shop and buy writing paper, several postcards. We look in every window, down every side street. Finally we arrive at the office, which is on the ground floor of a huge, sparsely furnished building.

There is a young man at the counter, so we approach him, give him the letter and ask to speak to the head of the organization. The letter disappears into a back room, there is much whispering and activity. The man returns, tells us to go to a pub across the street and wait to be paged for a phone call. But you don't know our names, I say. Jackie Johnson, he tells me.

So we go across the street and, five minutes later, Jackie Johnson is paged for a phone call. That's me, I tell the bartender. Hello, hello, this is Jackie Johnson. The voice on the other end gives me an address of another pub and tells us to meet him there in an hour, to take a taxi and to sit in one of the far booths when we get there, he'll find us, don't worry.

A taxi just happens to be cruising by when we come out, but we let it pass, wait for the next one. Fifteen minutes later, we are deposited in front of a low, dark building, and inside, it is just as dark, there are only a few dim lamps over the corner booths, a faint bulb over the counter of the bar. We look around, find a far booth, sit down, order a beer. Nobody else comes through the door, we look up every time the door opens, but it is only people leaving, the place is slowly emptying and soon we too will have to go. Then a lone man walks in, who looks like a poet in his patched corduroy jacket, pipe and heavy boots.

He comes directly over to us and says we have to leave, so we follow him into the street, climb into his small car, our knees jackknifed almost to our chins. This man drives like a maniac, a man possessed, constantly checking the rearview mirror as he careens around this corner, that corner. He gives us his name, but not his hand, luckily, asks us ours, though I can tell he will not remember them five minutes from now. Suddenly he slams on the brakes in front of a tidy, brick duplex, in front of which is a neat lawn and flower garden surrounded by a low picket fence. Lace curtains hang in the windows. The few steps leading to the front door are painted green. He opens the door without knocking, calls out to somebody in a language I've never heard before, which must be Gaelic. A woman hurries down the stairs, wiping her hands on a rag, sees him, us, waits patiently for him to finish his explanation, after which she smiles and heads for the kitchen.

Come with me, he tells us, and we follow him into a small sitting room. That's the widow of—, he says, and names a famous, a notorious Irish writer and playwright. He and I used to paint houses together, he says.

I experience a great thrill over this information, imagine the reaction of my family and more literate friends to the fact that I am sitting in the home of the late, great—, that I am eating cookies, drinking tea served by his loyal wife and chatting with his best friend, who nonetheless drives like a lunatic, who will die not because of sectarian violence or political intrigue, but by crashing into a tree or going off a cliff into the sea.

He is proud of the fact that he can walk into this house as if it were his own, bring friends, even strangers, I can tell he has brought many others to this place, confided to each one that this is the house of the late, great Irish writer—. It seems the only reason we have come here is to provide him this opportunity, because as soon as we have finished our tea, we climb back into the car and zoom off to another destination, to another brick house, but a larger one, with a lush, sprawling lawn, a higher picket fence.

We are ushered into a quiet den overlooking the garden by a trim, business-like woman in her forties. The four of us take a seat, form a semicircle in front of a fireplace. There is no Gaelic spoken here, only the Irish English my ears have slowly become attuned to. I explain as best I can what our interests are, I give a short history of the Croatian nation, hand him the letter of introduction. He reads it, wants to know why we don't talk to the Provos. We have, I say, we want to talk to both groups.

I translate back and forth and, after every conceivable question has been asked, we take a break, sit back and look at each other. I like this man, he is a professional, or at least fits my idea of one. I'm part Irish, too, I tell him. My great grandmother's name was Mary Kelley, with an "e". I say this because I want desperately to belong here, among these strange people, so full of contradictions. Taik already has somewhere to belong. He is 100% Croatian, he has a country, an identity, a culture, religion, language. But I have none of these totally, only bits and pieces gleaned from casual contacts, forced inculcation, osmosis, haphazard experimentation. It must be a wonderful feeling being something, I had once told Taik. And ever since then, he had understood something about me that neither had understood before.

We arrange to meet again, I am to call this trim, neat woman in three days to arrange a time and place. But don't give your real name on the phone, she says. What should we call you? She ponders for a moment.

Jackie, she tells me brightly, as in Kennedy. It seems Jackie is quite the popular name here. We are driven at breakneck speed back to the center of town, where we are deposited like pellets on a street corner. As soon as we get out, it begins to rain, so we return to our home with the Butlers and Sandy, who greets us with the highest standing leap so far, setting a new record.

The day has come for "Jackie" to make her call arranging a further meeting with the head of the Officials. We take a long walk down one of the side streets leading to the river Liffey. Outside a pub facing the water, there is an enclosed phone booth. I pull out the folded piece of paper with the number on it, put my money in and dial. Hello? Yes, this is Jackie calling, I say. The woman in the other end tells me to hold on. When she comes back, she tells me our friend has been arrested, nobody knows where he's being held, for how long, even why. She advises us to leave the country as quickly as possible.

But we haven't done anything wrong! I protest to Taik. I don't want to leave, I would be perfectly happy spending the rest of my life in Dublin with the Butlers and Sandy. Taik could learn English, we could study at Trinity College, be fishermen in Howth, run a school for truant boys, any number of things.

We are here to do interviews and if we can't do them, we have to leave. We can't just spend the money on ourselves, Taik tells me. Besides, I don't understand this country. They can probably arrest us here for no reason, just like in Yugoslavia. He is more or less convinced that people can be arrested wherever they are for no reason, this belief is firmly entrenched in his nature, it is almost a genetic trait. But we haven't done anything wrong! I begin to protest, I don't want to leave, as we have had to leave Salzburg, Berlin. Where are we going? I ask. Where are we going this time? But it is a premature question, Taik doesn't even know yet.

When I figure it out, I'll tell you, he says. And I have to be satisfied with this, I have no other choice. I think of Sandy defying the laws of gravity, of his little nails clicking on the tile and begin to protest again. We have to leave.

Frankfurt is our next destination, though there is just as good a reason to go to Geneva, Madrid or Copenhagen. I pack silently, taking great care as I fold my few items of clothing, place them in my suitcase. Perhaps if I am slow, there will be time for something unexpected to happen, something that will allow us to stay. It occurs to me to call home, to find out where the ancestors of my great-grandmother, Mary Kelley, now live, if they are living. Perhaps they are just down the street, my own flesh and blood, or in Howth, fixing a net that has become frayed, or any number of things. If I can find them, I can stay, this I know with calm certainty. Taik understands the bond to one's country, one's own blood.

But it is too late for all this conjecture, my bags and Taik's are already packed and the Butlers have been told we are leaving, though Sandy has not yet sensed the imminence of our departure, he is lying on the floor, all four feet splayed out as though he is a butterfly or an insect pinned to a piece of paper. As we go out the door, a look of tardy and surprised comprehension comes across his whiskery face, he begins to howl, to scrabble across the floor to us, but we are gone, the door is closed, my heart is closed.

Taik makes a steeple out of his fingers, gently puts the tips on the tips of mine, which is one of the ways he has of showing me he is sorry, he loves me, a reminder, in the middle of Dublin, or wherever else we might be, that we have each other, that our bond is immutable, indestructible, that it not only survives but thrives on adversity.

15

"As in the realm of stars the orbit of a planet is in some cases determined by two suns." Nietzsche

Frankfurt, Germany, 1971–Compared to the cozy, small-town ambience
of Dublin, Frankfurt has a frantic quality to it, like a huge and efficient
machine working twenty four hours a day. There is an excess of activity
here, too much steel, too much glass, too many cars continually howling
and screeching on the brakes; the cars remind me of flocks of geese who
have lost their way and are trying to extricate themselves as quickly as
possible from the lethal maelstrom of Frankfurt. Already I am depressed,
feel I have been torn by the roots from the warm and fertile soil of Dublin
and thrown like an old brown weed on the cold asphalt of Frankfurt.

On every street corner there are wanted posters, this I notice immediately, gaunt faces with stringy hair stare out at us, feebly smiling in
some of the pictures, as though to persuade the public that there are
worse tragedies than having one's face plastered on every pole and bill-
board in the city. Holger Meins, Andreas Baader, Gudrun Ensslin—
these are the principals of the Baader-Meinhof group, the ones who

have been bombing not only U.S. armed forces installations, but German department stores as well, in the fight against any number of things. They call themselves the Red Army Faction, this much I remember from the newspapers. I notice a resemblance between Taik and Holger Meins.

We have very little baggage, even less than when we arrived in Dublin, as we have left some behind there, just as we have left parts of ourselves behind in Salzburg and Berlin. We are spread out all over the continent. Taik has a number to call. I can always depend on his having a number, in my waiting patiently outside a telephone booth to find out where we will sleep, on whose couch or floor. Nobody answers, though, and it is getting late, we are exhausted from our literal and figurative flight, so we pick up our suitcases and start walking, down a narrow street lined with bars and porn shops. Next to the entrance of one such bar, there is a "Rooms for Rent" sign. This can't be too expensive, Taik tells me. Let's go ask. So we go in and find a man behind a wooden counter, who reluctantly gives us a key, takes our money, leads us up the stairs. All night? he asks, but already he knows the answer, we have suitcases, we aren't going up for a quick hour of sex, we are in love, we just want to sleep.

The room is very large and dark; even when he turns on the light, it is dark. There are two single beds, on opposite ends of the room, a sink, a window looking out onto a solid cement wall. We are left alone to contemplate our misfortune, but Taik, as usual, is amused by the room, the city, the existential drama presented by our situation. Beneath us, there is a steady wave of music and laughter from the bar; in comparison, our room is like a crypt, we are shut off from the world of light, laughter, color; it is even a bit like a laboratory, there is a sense that some strange experiment is being conducted on the two of us, that our responses are being noted, our reaction written down on a graph somewhere.

Taik is sitting and smoking, contemplating the nature of things, taking obvious pleasure in the fact that we have found ourselves living in this room. He wants to talk about it, discuss the possible philosophical issues, the role of Fate and destiny, but his voice puts me to sleep, I fall asleep on top of the covers with my clothes on. In the morning, I am cold and grouchy and Taik is sleeping soundly, snuggled in the covers, which I am surprised to find clean and even aromatic, and I am only able to awaken him from his innocent sleep with great difficulty. Where are we? he asks. Even though I am awake, this seems an eminently reasonable question.

We can't just walk around the city with our suitcases and we can't leave them in the room, so we check them at the train station just down the street. Without them, I feel suddenly unencumbered and lighthearted. I begin to like certain parts of Frankfurt, the cobbled side streets, the little ice cream parlors, the gingerbread facades of certain narrow buildings. Taik makes another phone call while I wait outside. There are so many movie theaters, lucky Taik, two or three on every street. And the department stores are immense, more advertisements for German prosperity than anything else, the German ability to spend, to want to spend.

Taik is talking, laughing, talking some more, and then he hangs up, comes out. A friend of Tomulic's, he explains. The one who gave the money for Ireland. So do we have a place to sleep tonight? I ask him. Of course we have a place to sleep! he laughs. Have we ever not had a place to sleep? As a matter of fact, he is right, as usual. We have always had a place to sleep, we have slept stacked on narrow couches and train seats, spread out in oversized beds covered with thick Austrian coverlets or Irish linens, we have slept chaste and alone on medical examination tables, hard cots in worker's barracks and above porno bars. Just leave it to me, he says, and so I do, I do. Taik is the only person I have ever trusted more than I trust myself.

Tomo, this friend of Tomulic's, lives near the Frankfurt zoo, in a luxurious apartment above an Arab travel agency, Nabhan Tours. He has a German wife, who is big and boisterous, and two children. He greets us effusively, calls for food and drinks, ushers us into the living room. Tomo is good-looking in a cunning sort of way, but his eyes are too close together, like a ferret's or a weasel's, I can tell already he considers himself a heartbreaker and feel sorry for the big hearty wife in the kitchen, whom he undoubtedly leaves at home a large part of the time, cooking, cleaning, and answering the phone, which rings at least once every five minutes.

Taik discusses the events in Dublin, this much I understand, though I can't get most of the details. Tomo seems amused by it all and is not the least bit concerned about the money. Taik has told me a little about him, that he and Tomulic have founded a Croatian Communist Party, for propaganda purposes, because the press and Yugoslav government are always trying to slander Croatian dissidents with the label "fascist". But Tomo is no more Communist than we are, he simply enjoys the intrigue, the scandalousness of being the founder of this party, and he also likes being the center of attention, of being written and talked about. He doesn't work, he spends his days in town, going from one restaurant to the other, one cafe to the other, taking walks, flirting with women. Taik says he's probably an agent, but it seems that everybody is either an agent or suspected of being one. It is something I have gotten used to. You know a lot about him, I had told Taik on our way over. He's notorious in his own way, he had said.

Let's go into town, Tomo tells us, to a restaurant that belongs to a friend of mine. We agree, but first Taik suggests I go apply for a job at Nabhan Tours, where a bi-lingual employee is always needed. I say OK, but with a sinking feeling, knowing I will undoubtedly get a job, I always do, I am the type that gets hired on the spot, and Taik will not, of course, be able to find one, he has no papers, he will be forced to spend his days, like Tomo, in the cafes and restaurants, waiting for me to get off work. And naturally Mr. Nabhan does hire me, I am to answer the phones in his old office, transfer them to the new office. This is all I have to do? I ask. The office is closed for business, he says, all I need is for you to transfer the calls, maybe four or five a day. He gives me keys and the address. I start the next day; even though we have no place to live, I have a job. It's just my luck.

The restaurant "Zagreb" is right in the middle of town, and even though it is the middle of the day, it is packed with people, both Germans and Croatians. We take a large table in the back, where we are joined immediately by the owner and various others. Food and drinks are brought and consumed and, hours later, we find ourselves with a room to live in, it belongs to the owner of the "Zagreb", who keeps it for the guest workers he employs, but one has just recently left for Croatia so it is ours. See, we already have an apartment and a job, Taik tells me. I have a job, I remind him. He forgets these small details.

Our new home is small and cramped and doesn't even have a bed, but couches pushed together; there is a monstrous wooden armoire with a mirror for a door, a long counter whose function escapes me, a small round table and one chair. The bathroom is down the hallway, in a room so tiny that one must almost back onto the toilet; there is no room to turn around. But there is a communal kitchen, a stove, a refrigerator, a kitchen table, though we do not yet know with whom we are to commune. The apartment is on the fifth floor, and there is no elevator, so by the time we climb the stairs, we are completely winded. One, two, three, four, five—there are six tiny rooms on our floor, we have six neighbors, all of whom are either holed up behind their closed doors or out working, cleaning office buildings perhaps, or carrying hod on some construction site; whoever lives here cannot afford much, works to live instead of the other way around.

But the view from the single window of our new house is spectacular, at odds completely with the shabbiness and poverty of the room itself. Before us, just feet from our apartment building, is the Main River, along whose banks are moored dozens of boats, tiny rental rowboats in bright colors, treadle boats for hire, as well as the largest and most lavish of cruise ships, which take daily trips all along the river. There are floating restaurants and sidewalk cafes with umbrellas sticking from the middle of each table, and on each side of the river is a wide boulevard, full of people strolling or sitting on wooden benches facing the water. From time to time, freighters pass by, scattering all the tiny boats like a whale scattering a school of minnows. From their decks can often be seen a woman hanging clothes to flap dry in the wind, children chasing each other from one end of the boat to the other, little water babies who feel beached on solid ground.

A wide, cobbled footbridge stretches over the river, and on the other side is a courtyard containing the city hall, an open air market, several Italian ice cream parlors, even a McDonald's. But when we go for a walk later, I am chilled by the omnipresent wanted posters and the atmosphere of tense expectation in this city.

My office is expansive and expensively furnished and it even has a small kitchen. There is also a conference room, as well as two large desks and wide windows overlooking Kaiser Street, which is just steps away from both our apartment and the train station. During the first three hours, I receive just one telephone call, which I competently transfer to the other office. I have absolutely nothing else to do but look out the windows and watch the string of prostitutes on the street below, take note of their modus operandi, their individual quirks and idiosyncracies. I often see American soldiers passed out in doorways or hanging around in groups on the corner, white-faced boys with cowlicks and shoes which always look a few sizes too big. Du schlafen, ich zahlen, you sleep, I pay. This is all the German they seem to know.

My first day at work, the phone rings three times, once in the morning and twice in the afternoon. When I return to our new home, Taik asks me how I like my job. It's hard to describe, I say. It's too absurd.

During my lunch hour, I often go to the Amerika Haus to check out some books in English. It is only minutes away, near a huge and lush park threaded with narrow walking paths. I browse through the stacks, taking my time, picking up books and putting them back, savoring the quiet atmosphere, the feeling of belonging—the Amerika Haus, for the expatriate Americans, to soothe them, remind them of who and what they are. But others are reminded as well. A bomb goes off in the Amerika Haus and the Red Army Faction takes responsibility. They are attacking the forces of imperialism at their very heart, but they are also preventing me from checking out a Dos Passos I have not yet read, a Henry James. So I sit in my office and listen for the sound of bombs, watch the soldiers in the doorways for any signs of movement or concern, but they are thinking of other things, Susan back home, who hasn't written for a month and a half, the Chevy that younger brother crashed into a telephone pole, even though he knew he wasn't supposed to touch that car. They break my heart a little, these skinny kids with shiny ears, but I am not American the way they are, I have become more, an anomaly, a seed sprouted from stone. There are no limitations anymore, I have such a feeling of power.

16

"One does not punish a rebel; one suppresses him." Nietzsche

Taik has left me again and I am stuck alone in the apartment. There are noises coming from some of the other rooms, but nobody ever seems to emerge, we are like little animals in boxes who hear each other across the walls, who long to see and touch each other, to convince ourselves we are alive, but this never happens, we must convince ourselves by other means by suffering what we suffer, by going without what we need. These are the kinds of things that underline human existence; when one is happy, one forgets one is alive.

We finally come face to face with one of our mysterious neighbors, we literally run into her as we return one night from the "Dubrovnik", she is coming out the door as we are going in, there is a collision, embarrassed apologies are received and given, and then we stand back, regard each other solemnly. She is tiny and frail, with a head like a little nut, all wrinkly and bleached-looking, as though it has just emerged from a warm-water blanch. Her eyes are set very closely together; in fact, all her features are congregated around her long nose, as though it is the focal point of all that is happening on her face, it is the sun around which all her little planets rotate. How do you do? she asks us. I'm Ruth. We introduce ourselves, tell where we are from, though little else. She herself is quite talkative, gives a long history both of her exciting flight from East Germany to the free West, and her subsequent life in poverty cleaning office buildings like a slave from late at night until the early hours of the morning. Her fingers are stained a mahogany brown, and not just the usual smoking fingers but all ten of them, as though she alternates the cigarettes, thinks the color won't be noticed if it covers everything evenly. Her teeth are the same mahogany, but their length distracts one from thinking of anything else, they are like a huge hare's, perfectly formed, perfectly symmetrical, designed for chewing and gnawing and tearing things apart.

She is going downstairs for a bottle of apple wine, which is sold at the little stand just below our windows. It is the cheapest alcohol one can buy in Frankfurt, and it is not bad—fruity, tart, a little carbonation to speed it through the system. Will we join her for a glass? she wants to know. But we are tired, we tell her some other time, leave her flurrying down the stairs. She has already forgotten us in favor of the first long drink.

Before we reach our little sanctuary, we meet another neighbor, who simply appears from the stream-filled kitchen, emerges from this cloud of vapor like a little round apparition, sweat running down both sides of his flushed cheeks. Oh, excuse me, excuse me, he says to us in a heavily-accented German. He smiles, such a beatific smile, so out-of-place for this particular time and moment, for this encounter. I am cooking artichokes, he tells us, as though this explains everything, the heat, the sweat, his sudden appearance before us. I cook artichokes every day, very healthy, at least one very day. Would you care to join me? He waves us into the kitchen, opens one of the tiny windows. I am Habib, he says, from Tunisia. We introduce ourselves once again, I am Julie, he is Taik, we don't care for artichokes right now, maybe later. But Habib is unwilling to accept this, we can tell he finds it inhospitable that we decline to share his meal, gives us a sour look, not completely sour, he retains a bit of good-will in his expression in case we change our minds, but we refuse to be bullied. I have a television, he offers. Would you like to watch it sometime? Now this is a different story. In the absence of money for movies, Taik is enthralled with the television. Yes, we would, Taik says. How about right now? Habib is unprepared for this, but accedes graciously, takes his artichoke, his melted butter and mayonnaise on a tray into his room, waves us along.

So we watch television with Habib for at least two hours, we watch American crime dramas, educational programs, debates, we switch the channel every five or ten minutes. I finally get up, go to bed, leave Taik transfixed before the screen, ignoring Habib, who is munching contentedly on his moist leaves of artichokes. He doesn't need Taik, either.

One morning Taik tells me he has to go away for a few days, he doesn't say where he is going, or how far away, only that he has somebody to meet and that he will be back soon. It doesn't occur to me to ask him any questions at all, my inquisitive nature has receded so deep inside me that I barely even notice it anymore, it is as though I do not need to be given answers or explanations for anything, I am satisfied and content with so little, take such strange pride in my refusal to know or want to know.

We walk to my office together, and Taik continues down Kaiser Street to the main train station to check the schedules. I watch him for awhile before I go up the stairs, I see him stop, light a cigarette, continue slowly until he reaches the entrance. Then he turns around for just a second, takes a quick look behind him, whether for me, the sight of me, or somebody else he suspects of following him, I don't know, I only know I see a short flash of white face and skin and then he is gone. I don't even wave, we aren't like a married couple whose wife is seeing her husband off at the station, we aren't like that at all.

After work I stop along the way at a little deli and buy some white rolls, a bit of salami, some Camembert. Crossing the footbridge to our apartment, I look up at our window, but it is blank, like a glass eye.

Behind Ruth's window, though, there is movement, furtive, quick, as though a bird is caught in the curtain and is trying frantically to free itself. I decide to buy some apple wine, both for Ruth and myself. We'll spend the evening together, I won't worry so much about Taik that way. And maybe Habib will let us all watch his television together. A flood of relief pours over me, I find my eyes filling with tears at the sweet thought of spending the evening with my little outcast family, with rabbity Ruth and sweating Habib. Anything but being alone.

But I have imagined things, Ruth is not in her room, does not answer my knocks on her door. I press my ear against the door, strain to hear even the smallest of sounds, a rustling, a turning over on the bed, a groan or sigh. Perhaps she has passed out or fallen into a drunken sleep. No matter, I cannot rouse her if she has. And Habib, he also is not at home, nor in the kitchen cooking artichokes. But he has a car, he can move around the city at will, by himself, take himself here and there, stop where he wants, lock himself in and just drive and drive for hours if he likes. I open our door, close and lock it behind me, go over to our window without turning on the light. Below me is the Main, all shiny and smooth, the sun is just setting, all the colored lights along the promenade are being turned on, people are arriving at the outside restaurant in little bunches, like tiny bouquets of vivid flowers. And I watch the street, the water below, every movement that catches my eye, watch for a familiar shape coming across the footbridge, watch for hours, and as I watch, I drink the apple wine, as quickly as I can, and then I go down to buy some more. Up again at the window, I feel like singing, an old folk song, about a boy who dies too young, the green grass that covers his grave. And then I am crying, because I am alone and lonely, because my mother and father, my three brothers, my grandmas Mimi and Frances are so far from me, my friends, Melody, Joanne, my old boyfriends, my enemies from high school, all so far away, and all I have is Taik, and not even him at this moment, all I have right now is Ruth and Habib, who aren't even home, and I have these empty bottles of apple wine, and that is all.

So I give up watching the footbridge. Besides, it is too dark to see anything. I stumble to the bed, pull off my clothes and get under the top cover, making sure I am completely covered in case Taik should arrive late with a friend. But in the morning, I lie alone in the narrow bed, nothing has changed, the Main is still shiny and smooth and I am still alone. Ruth has left for work hours before and Habib as well. I pull myself up, sit rubbing my eyes. There is nothing as bleak as Frankfurt in the early hours of the morning.

When Taik comes back, he doesn't say anything at all, he comes in and lies down on the bed, hands behind his head. What's wrong? I ask him, but he won't talk to me, he just shakes his head. But I know if I wait long enough, wait quietly, read a book, cut some vegetables for a soup or wash a big pan of socks, he will tell me, he can't hold things in for too long. So I get a book, sit down next to him, leave him to his thoughts. After about ten minutes, he sighs, rolls over, looks at me. What are you reading? he wants to know. "Portrait of a Lady". I tell him, by Henry James. Is it good? I think it will be, I say.

I was on the train, you know, on my way to visit Senic, he begins. Who's Senic? I ask. He is assuming too much, he has never told me about any Senic. He is the head of a Croatian organization opposing the Yugoslav government, he tells me. Yes, I remember now, I tell him, although I don't, there are so many opposing the government, they are everywhere So you were going to visit him? Yes, but I was on the train, I had a newspaper I had bought at the station before I left, and I was sitting in the compartment reading it, and there on the front page was an article about Senic, that he had been murdered the day before, shot in the head in his bed. Oh Jesus, I say, but I don't touch him or move towards him, it would interrupt his story. So I just got off at the next stop and came back, he says. I wait and wait but that is the end of the story. I don't bother to ask who killed him because it is obvious that it was the Yugoslav secret police.

One day we agree to meet at a supermarket near my office to do our grocery shopping, after which we will carry the bags home together. I arrive on time and wait by the entrance for Taik. I wait and wait, becoming more irritated as time goes on, assuming he has run into somebody and gotten involved in some political discussion as so often happens. After about forty five minutes, I walk home. When I arrive at the apartment, Taik is standing there, smoking furiously, surrounded by brown paper bags, some of which have broken open at the bottom. Isolated cans and packages lie hostilely on the floor. What happened to you? he asks. You see how many bags I had to carry home, up five flights of stairs? I am incensed that I have been unjustly accused. Where were you? I counter angrily. I waited for almost an hour. We go back and forth until his face gets red, he loses his temper and punches the armoire. It promptly collapses, falls flat to the ground like a flimsy house of cards. The mirror shatters as well, sending shards of glass across our clothes, which have spilled out. That's it, I say. I am going home to America. I refuse to put up with this. I take my battered suit-case and begin to stuff my clothes into it. I grab this and that with an intensity of rage that makes me proud. Taik watches me for a moment and then begins to hand me clothes, to help me pack. I am outraged that he should attempt to help me pack instead of beg me to stay, I throw back in his face everything he tries to hand me, frustrated that a harder, more lethal ball cannot be fashioned from a wadded piece of cloth. I'm just trying to help, he says. I'd never force anybody to stay with me. If they stay it has to be their choice. I stand motionless for a minute or two, seething, contemplating the situation. That's how much I mean to you, huh, that you would let me go so easily? I say as I pick up my purse, wind up, and hit him as hard as I possibly can on the back of the head. I actually imagine that I see scores of twinkling stars rotating around his head, just like in a comic strip. He shakes his head for a moment before turning to me in shock. What did you do that for? I loathe you right now, I say. But I love you, he tells with a sheepish smile, and holds me in his arms. I would be so unhappy if you were to go. Then we start laughing until tears come to our eyes. We belong together, I say finally. Nobody else could possibly put up with us.

Taik has gotten his papers from Croatia, his birth certificate, his baptismal documents. A friend from his village has gone home and brought them back with him. This means we can get married, he tells me. We haven't changed our minds. Of course, there was really no danger in that. The sun would sooner fall from the sky.

"One does not credit people with their follies: what a loss of human rights!" Nietzsche

The night before we get married, we have another big fight, and I run off and drink apple wine in a pub not far from our apartment, with a South African who picks me up on the street. He's a big, friendly guy who doesn't speak German and wants some company, so I oblige him, even so far as returning to his hotel room with him, which happens to be just on the other side of the footbridge, two minutes from our apartment, but only for a nightcap, I tell him, I'm getting married tomorrow. But after he drinks a few double whiskeys, he doesn't care about my marriage, he gropes for me, tells me he needs me. That's too bad, I say, and push him away. He is too drunk to pursue me, so he falls on the couch and passes out. I get up, go out the door, down the stairs, run across the footbridge, home to Taik. But it is four in the morning, he is out looking for me, the apartment is empty. When he returns, he is in a formidable rage, but it appears that he still wants to marry me because I have had the consummate nerve to do such a thing the night before my wedding. This he admires in a strange way. I tell him I'm sorry, that nothing happened, I tell him almost everything, except for the groping part. He says that in the morning I must go and say hello to this guy in the broad daylight, go visit him in the hotel room; otherwise, he won't forgive me. I am horrified at this humiliating ultimatum, but I go, because otherwise I will not be Mrs. Zvonko Busic. I ring the bell, but nobody answers. Taik is satisfied. I tried. He will marry me now.

For our wedding at the City Hall, which is in the square on the other side of the footbridge, I have chosen a black dress with pink flowers and a black pair of shoes I bought in West Berlin. It's not that I feel morbid; I simply don't have anything else to wear. Taik is wearing his only suit and a thin, red tie. His hair is wet and his nails are freshly clipped. He doesn't mention the South African, except to say with a sneer: "Neue Kräme", which is the name of the street his hotel is on, only steps from the City Hall. He still finds it hard to believe that a girl would drink apple wine with a stranger and end up in his hotel room the night before her marriage. A Croatian girl would never do such a thing, but then, if he wanted a Croatian girl, he would be marrying one today.

We have asked Tomo and his wife to be our witnesses, mainly because we don't have any friends in Frankfurt, we only have each other. We wanted to take two strangers right off the street and give them each ten marks to stand with us, but the solemnity of the occasion prevented us from doing this. So we settle for Tomo and his wife, even though Tomo is the President of the Croatian Communist Party, or maybe because he is. The motives for much of what we do are unclear, open to many interpretations.

As we cross the footbridge, we look down onto the water. It's a nice day to get married, Taik says. Yes, it is. We don't say anything more, there is nothing left to say, everything is understood. We just look down onto the water, look how it changes colors when the wind ruffles the surface.

Our witnesses are waiting in front of the City Hall already by the time we arrive. Tomo has a bouquet of flowers in his hand, which he gives me with a flourish. We only have five minutes until the ceremony, so we go upstairs, to a plush waiting room which reminds me of a confessional, all velvet and blood red. Another couple is inside saying the vows. After a few moments, they emerge, cheeks flushed, smiling, laughing, hanging from each other like ripe fruits. An official emerges behind them, looks around, sees the four of us, and asks hopefully if we are Mister Busic and Miss Schultz. Yes we are, we tell him. Please follow me, he says, so we do, we follow him obediently, seriously, one by one, into the chambers where we will become, in a matter of minutes, man and wife.

We stand before him, answer a number of questions having to do with our free will and desire to do certain things for one another, I don't remember one of the questions in its entirety, and when we are finished, we sign our names to a paper and are pronounced man and wife. I kiss Taik and Tomo, who holds me longer than necessary, so I give him a little shove, and his wife kisses Taik, but not me, maybe it's not the custom. Then we go out, where a photographer is waiting to take our pictures. We tell him to take a dozen or so, which he does, ordering us around, telling us where to stand and whose shoulder to rest our arm on. And then we are finished, we are Mr. and Mrs. Zvonko Busic. I don't feel any different, there are no metamorphoses, no transformations. I only feel a sense of completion, a sense that events have culminated logically.

Tomo takes us to a restaurant for a late lunch. We are the only four people there and are waited upon by the owner, who has graciously allowed Tomo to rent the room. But we are impatient and we don't want to sit around with Tomo and his wife. We are married now, we want to go somewhere as Mr. and Mrs. Busic. We excuse ourselves as soon as we can, catch the first streetcar that comes along. Where should we go? Taik asks me. Let's go to the circus! So we go to a tiny traveling circus set up on a the outskirts of town. There are two skinny elephants, a sad clown and a menagerie of other animals who look as though they haven't slept in a month. The tent smells like decay, the spectators are falling asleep, but we are together in the stands, we like the smells, the jaundiced elephants, the tired festivity the performers try so hard to communicate to us.

As we ride the streetcar back to town, I lean my head on Taik's shoulder, I lean my head on my husband's shoulder. This is my husband's shoulder, I tell him, and poke it with my finger. He is so serious as he looks at me, he doesn't answer for a long while. When he does, all he can say, all he is capable of saying in response is that, yes, it is indeed my husband's shoulder. When we get home, we climb the stairs wearily; we fall into bed wearily, too, are asleep almost as soon as we close our eyes. Taik's leg is draped over my waist, he likes it there, and it is with the thought of this weight on me, his weight, that I drift off.

We discover a club we like not far from our apartment, the "Club Voltaire". I am attracted to it by its name. I have always been impressed by Voltaire and his "Candide", I remember reading it at the age of thirteen, finding it on one of my father's voluminous bookshelves, going into the backyard and sitting under the one scrawny tree we had, the one that never seemed to blossom, finishing it the same afternoon and thinking I had understood something about it nobody else had, something about the monkey. The club is all old wood, not the aged wood with the rich veneer, but old wood, scratched and dull, the kind one finds in workingmen's clubs or ramshackle barns, Texaco stations in Missoula, Montana. On its walls are revolutionary posters, posters of Che Guevara, the one everyone has seen, even those who don't even know who Che Guevara is, Angela Davis, Castro.

We go into the main room, which is set up with long tables where everybody seems to be playing chess or watching others play. Taik loves chess and finds a game immediately. I go for the drinks, a carafe of house wine, two glasses. I sit and watch, watch some more, and before I know it, three hours have gone by. But Taik is not finished, he likes to take things to extremes, like going to movies, talking on the telephone, playing chess. So I tell him I'm leaving, going home to bed. I have to work the next morning, I'm the one with the regular job. He looks up, nods, tells me he won't be too much longer, but he doesn't know this, anything can happen and usually does, especially to him. I trudge out, wishing he were with me. Something always happens to the two of us. Alone, it is infinitely more difficult to attach the proper significance to what I see and hear. And as I expect, absolutely nothing happens on my way home, nothing strikes me as strange or unusual, even faintly interesting. I climb the five floors to our little home, change my clothes, fall into bed. But before I am asleep, I hear the rustle of paper under the door. I pull myself out of bed, pad over to the door and bend over for the little piece of yellow paper I find there. It is folded once and when I open it, I find a humbly-worded request from Ruth for five marks so that she can go down and buy some apple wine. I take a five mark piece from my coat pocket, put it on the piece of paper, and slide the paper back underneath the door, where I am certain Ruth is waiting on her knees to retrieve it. And she is there, I hear her breathing, her intake of breath as she sees the money coming out like a slot machine payoff, this is her lucky day, she can't believe she has finally won, after all this time, all these years! She scurries away, goes to her room for her coat, trips down the stairs, at least the first flight, I hear her swear. And then I am asleep.

Suddenly the door is thrown open. I jump up, confused. Where am I? It is Taik, he is on his hands and knees, crawling towards me. What happened to you, what are you doing? I ask him as I get out of bed, run to him. Go back to bed, hurry up, he tells me. But what are you doing, what's the matter, tell me! Can you see out the window? he wants to know. Yes, if I scoot over, I say. Then scoot over there, he says, but don't stick your head up, see if there's anyone on the footbridge or standing underneath our apartment. I scoot over to the window, peek out cautiously, but I don't see anybody at all, everything is shut up, everyone is sleeping. Are you sure you don't see anybody? he asks. Look really well. So I look again, but there is nobody. Taik sighs, pulls himself into bed. His watch is broken, his wrist is scratched and bloody, and he holds it up for me to see. You won't believe what happened, he says. First I got pulled over by the police. They thought I was one of the Baader-Meinhof people. And then on my way home, two men jumped me just before the footbridge, I don't know who they were, but I managed to get away. He is close to shaking, the first time I have ever seen him like this, and I feel a cold fear sweep over me. If Taik is scared, it must be very serious. But what is more serious than death, of which he has never before been afraid?

He doesn't say anything more and neither do I. I figure if he wants to do something, he will know what to do. All I have to offer is my warmth next to him and my presence, upon which he depends so much. We lie entwined until he falls off to sleep, but I cannot turn off the crooked thoughts that twist through my mind. And in the morning I am afraid to leave him sleeping, afraid he will not survive the day. But he picks me up after work, everything is forgotten, it was all a bad dream.

Sometimes we visit Habib at work. He is a bartender in a hotel just minutes away from the train station. We are barely able to recognize him in his work ambience, as he is dressed so neatly, his clothes are spotless, ironed meticulously, his shoes shined, his wiry hair brushed back on his head like a close-fitting cap. He smiles at one and all, a wide, obsequious smile designed to dispel before it is able to form the contempt his customers will feel towards him as soon as they hear his accent, figure out what part of the world he is from. As we watch him and marvel over his grooming, we picture his tiny room down the hall from ours, the bed piled high with dirty clothes, the television covered with a heavy film of dust, the wilting artichoke leaves which have been lying under the chair for at least two weeks, lying where they fell from his plate as he watched an American crime drama, our Habib, from Tunisia, who pads around in his bare feet at home, across the kitchen floor, which, to my knowledge, has never been swept or mopped by anybody since we have lived in the building, down the hall to the bathroom, where he picks up another layer of old urine and dust mixed together, back to his room, where he dresses, puts on immediately his socks and shoes and gets ready for work. I have watched him do this. And here he stand before us, so shining and creased, so brushed and lacquered and buffed, our Habib.

But soon the whores will come in, they are accustomed to having a drink with Habib when their shift is finished, relaxing for an hour or so before going home to bed. The management does not discourage them, as they are not the stereotypical whores who look as though they have just come from a heavy debauch, but, rather, resemble career girls, who dress well and have good manners. Since the customers in the bar do not recognize them for what they are, why not take their money for the drinks they buy? By the time they come in, they are not interested in propositioning anybody, they are beat, only want a quiet drink and, after that, a soft bed, alone.

One of them, a stocky blonde who chain-smokes furiously from the moment she comes in, sits down next to us after asking if we mind. We do not mind, at least Taik doesn't, and says so, so she lowers herself onto a stool at the bar. She is in the mood to talk, to Habib, to anybody who will listen. Taik, who collects stories with a passionate dedication, invites her to our apartment to sample his home-cooked bean soup. Ilse, this is her name, accepts readily, would love to come to our home for bean soup, doesn't care that it is almost two in the morning, or that I greet the suggestion with a decided lack of enthusiasm. Taik is excited. He ushers us both out by the elbow and into the street, points her in the right direction, even forgets and points me, as if I don't know where we live. We'll walk, he says, it's not far. And the air is fresh.

Ilse is game for anything. Except that she is having trouble walking, and must grab on to Taik for support as she weaves down the street. We arrive at our apartment after what seems like hours, and then after what seems like several more, we arrive at the top of the five flights of stairs. Oh, are we finally here? she asks. We're here! Taik tells her. He unlocks the outer door and then leads the way to our apartment. Here we are, he tells her and pulls her into the room, sits her down on the chair, turns on the hot plate, upon which a large pot of bean soup is resting. This is the bean soup, he explains. She has the nerve to ask how long it has been sitting there. For two days, he says, but bean soup is always better the second or third day. She nods her head sagely, makes a mental note of this.

While we wait for the soup to heat, she tells us the story of her life. She tells us about her daughter in private school in Switzerland, how her daughter would die if she found out her mother was a whore, but she could never afford to educate her daughter properly if she wasn't one, and so on, predictable stuff that fails to excite the imagination, fails to stir the Muses. Taik, however, is enthralled, wants to know more and more, asks this and that question, listens reverently to her answers, watches her gestures, treats her like a queen. I yawn and lean against my pillow, where my body gradually moves from a forty-five degree angle in relation to the bed to a ten, a five degree angle, and before I know it, I am prone, I am beneath the voices that drone on across the room. And when I wake in the morning, I see traces of Ilse—the bean-encrusted bowls still sitting on the table, the spoons lying together next to them, Taik lying next to me. Soon he will be ready for another adventure.

Every Sunday afternoon, after Croatian mass has ended, a sad ritual takes place in the main train station, the one just minutes away from both my office and Habib's hotel. From the church, a stream of Croatian men heads for the station like lemmings to the sea, unable to help themselves, this is what they do and want to do, although the ritual causes them much pain and suffering. There must be a bit of joy, of cathartic relief as well, as I find it impossible to imagine that Croatians actively seek unmitigated suffering, though they do take great pleasure in recounting the indignities and gross injustices to which they have been subjected: this is part of their heritage, they would not be Croatians otherwise.

When this determined stream of good Croatians reaches the train station, its first stop is at a small wurst counter just steps from the tracks. There one finds the best frankfurters in all of Frankfurt, the pale gray ones with little red and spicy specks, which are served along with a large dollop of incomparable mustard and a thick slab of brown bread. It all comes on a flimsy paper plate that groans under all this weight, and it is difficult to navigate this plate safely to another counter without the whole affair toppling to the ground. But they manage, just as we manage; we all have plenty of practice, we have spent many Sundays on this procedure, made all the more difficult as afternoon becomes evening and we have all had a number of beers as well.

But this ritual, this instinct—this irresistible impulse shared by the Croatians, and not just the men, though they are the only ones who make the weekly journey to the station, the women having to go home in order to be ready with dinner when the husbands stagger in—this impulse to be near the trains that are coming from their homeland, in most cases their forbidden homeland, this urge to see the names of their cities written on the big white signs on the side of the cars, exotic names such as Dubrovnik, Split, Sibenik, Banja Luka, Sarajevo, to watch as the people disembark, check the design of the women's handwoven purses, which tell the region from which they have come, look for those they might possibly recognize from years past, perhaps as children who played together in the woods—it is an uncontrollable urge, it simply takes over, moves them in a certain direction, leaves them there as long as they can endure, after which they return to the wurst stand, order another beer, perhaps a last frankfurter and, as hot tears form in their eyes, sing nationalist songs until they are ejected from the premises. The Germans don't like singing unless they can understand what is being sung or are singing themselves. Get out, the proprietor yells at the weaving Croatians, who have formed a circle and draped their arms around those on each side of them, out, out out! They do not protest, they leave quietly, heads down, they have ceased to sing, the singing was a masquerade, anyway, a sad farce. But they cannot resist one last walk to the tracks, to retrace the steps of those whose feet have traveled perhaps over the stone roads of the exiles' home villages only the day before, or across the market square in Zagreb, or some narrow road leading down to the shockingly blue Adriatic, a blue that is not simply a color but a way of thinking as well, so many things does it suggest and connote. They walk in small groups most of them, as it is too hard for them to be alone with their thoughts and feelings. Sometimes Taik and I walk behind them, follow them out to the tracks as well, and once in a while, the right train comes roaring in as if by plan or divine intervention, the train from Banja Luka, or from the coast, and everybody stops, everybody freezes. Cigarettes burn down, unheeded, unsmoked, eyes don't blink for the longest time, so afraid is each man that he might miss something.

Look, she's from Imotski! one of them says as an older woman disembarks from one of the cars; she is dressed in a distinctively patterned skirt and carrying a hand-woven purse. Imotski is only minutes from his village and he is in extreme pain, can hardly bear the thought that this unsuspecting woman has just left a village minutes from his own. He wants to hate her but cannot, it isn't her fault he can't go home, he may be a peasant but he's not that unfair, not that unreasonable. He can't watch any longer, though, he can't stay, he turns around, heads back into the station proper. I watch him go, watch for Taik's reaction, but there is none. Taik is standing very straight, smoking slowly, as though it were for the most part an afterthought. I have had enough, I am affected, I want to go home, now, not sometime in the future, and I can go home, nobody can stop me. I want to go home, too, I tell Taik. He turns to me, I can tell he has forgotten I am next to him. Think how it would feel if you couldn't, he says. I try to imagine this, but cannot. How could it be that somebody can't ever go home?

But we often do things normal people do, it's not as though we are living a totally unnatural and abnormal life. We play mini-golf at a little course along the river; I am a good sport, I go because Taik takes such childish pleasure in the tiny castles, the intricate obstacles he must overcome with his club and ball. We rent rowboats and row for hours along the river, and then we walk up the stairs to our apartment and cook dinner, just like everybody else when it is time to eat. We eat and sleep and make love. We are sometimes worried, angry, frustrated, happy, content and optimistic. Yet there is something wrong with my life, something I am not yet wise enough to identify. I am like a plant growing wild, one which quickly gets out of hand and must be clipped back. And Taik, it seems, is the one whom I have entrusted with this responsibility. I have given him this power, he has not asked for it. Who would not be tempted to exercise it? He is, after all, a person affected like any other by the seductive qualities of power.

18

"Every prohibition worsens the character of those who do not
submit to it willingly, but only because they are compelled."
Nietzsche

I have decided the time has come to leave Frankfurt. There is no single
event which has precipitated this decision, but, rather, a general sense of
oppression, that, just as in Vienna, Salzburg and Berlin, we are under
perpetual observation, by the Yugoslav Secret Police or their allies in
Western Europe.

I want to go home, I tell Taik. I look up to see his response, which is
noncommittal. I want to see my mom and dad, my brothers, Gearhart,
I want to escape this consciousness of perpetual danger. He is fiddling
around with his cigarette lighter, which refuses to spark. You need more
lighting fluid, I say. Oh, do you think so? he says, but not snidely. He
thinks it is something more complicated and is looking forward to the
challenge of unraveling the problem.

Let's go then, if you want to, he says. I am not surprised that he is so
agreeable, he is very adaptable to sudden change, enjoys it, in fact. I still

have a ticket from Luxembourg to New York, which is good for another week, part of a roundtrip ticket I used to return to Europe the previous time. All we have to do is buy you a ticket, I tell him, and we can use some of our wedding money for that. So it is decided. When should we leave? I ask him, hardly daring to think that in a week's time I could be home, I could be sitting safely in my own living room, on our old couch, laughing and talking with my parents, entertaining them with stories of Europe, which will seem so far, far away. And Taik, how will he look on our old couch, reclining with a beer in one hand, how will he fit in with the scheme of our home, our life, our universe?

But I have another life and another universe now, with Taik, another world removed from anything I knew before. Where do I belong now? I am drawn to the aura of security and comfort my family offers, but I am drawn more strongly to Taik, to what he represents: love and passion, commitment to a cause for which he would sacrifice everything, perhaps even me. The thought thrills and chills me. I guess we could go as soon as our suitcases are packed and we have my ticket, he says. Then we can go tomorrow, I tell him, because I'm going to buy the ticket right now. Within an hour, I have returned with the tickets.

Here's your ticket, I say, and hand it to him. He takes it, puts it on the table. I'm trying to fix my lighter, can't you see? he tells me. But I excuse him, he can fix his lighter all night long and all the next day, because I am going home. That is all that matters now, that and packing our bags.

As I fold our few possessions and place them in the suitcases, I sing about somebody named Joe who is going somewhere with money in his hand, an old song we used to play on the guitar back home. I sing and sing, until I am tired of my own voice, until I am finished packing. Then I go to bed, leaving Taik alone with his lighter. When I wake up, he is still sitting at the table, thinking, and he has put his lighter to the side. Is it fixed? I ask him. No, it's not, he says, but it doesn't matter, does it? I feel he is asking me something which has nothing at all to do with the lighter, so I am careful with my answer. Yes, it does, it always matters.

And I give him a hug, and it is a very long one, because he holds me tightly and does not release me until I complain. I'm going home, I tell him softly. I'm going home!

We leave the next morning before the sun comes up, on a cool, cloudy morning. There are a few cars inching down the street, they remind me of giant bugs making their way through unfriendly territory. And we are cozily arranged in one of these bugs, which is whisking us to the train station, where we will travel on to Luxembourg. Our taxi driver does not pretend a friendliness, he is tired, his eyes are like poached eggs, so we, too, are silent, thoughtful. I feel no sadness at our departure. Frankfurt has not captured a part of my heart, as Berlin and Ireland have done. It has held no mystery, no allure for me, has presented no riddles or enigmas. I was married there, I worked, I drank, I spent a lot of time alone and was very frightened. That is all I will be able to say about Frankfurt in the years to come. It is more than enough.

The Loftleidir plane is crowded, the aisles narrow, the seats close together, with little space for our legs. We are sitting like insects, legs drawn back to our chins, elbows pressed against our ribs. The flight is very long, it is as though we are in modern-day steerage heading for Ellis Island. Around us are families with small children, there is a dirty diaper in the aisle, which all pretend not to see. When the ruddy-faced stewardesses wheel their trays down the aisle, they must stop again and again to kick something out of the way, a shoe, an empty plastic cup.

After hours of trying to arrange ourselves comfortably for sleep, we are finally able to drift off. My dreams are confused, my sleep uneasy. When I awake, I see the sun, which is traveling with us to America, maintaining the illusion of perpetual light and illumination. I let Taik sleep, it is his escape, he loathes being awakened unless it happens on its own. But when we approach the airport in New York, I gently nudge him with my elbow. We're here! I tell him. He is groggy, forgets we are in the air. Are we in Cologne? he asks. I play with him, tell him yes. When he finally opens his eyes and looks around, he gives me a dirty look. But

I am laughing at him, so he humors me, laughs along with me. Wake up, wake up, I tell him, we are almost back in the United States of America. And an excitement overcomes me, which is a surprise. Am I home? Can this be the source of this strange sensation?

Cleveland, Ohio, 1972–Home is something other than Cleveland, where we are staying temporarily with Taik's sister, Zdravka, who is now married and living in a new apartment not far from the other house they had rented the previous year, between St. Clair and Superior, the bowels of Cleveland, the wasteland. But their little place is spotless, their little yard well-tended and green, fringed with bright flowers and healthy shrubs. We go out every day and look for work, but not in factories, though we have no skills or talents for anything else. Unless we earn some money, we cannot travel to Oregon, I cannot go home, so each day that we are without jobs, I become more despondent. Finally we are hired as assistant caretakers in a high-rise on Lake Shore Drive.

Our bosses are Dodie and Fred. Dodie is a fat and pasty bleached blonde who smokes continually and rarely gets out of her chair. Fred pretends to us that he is the boss of both the operation and the marriage, but he looks down when she speaks to him. We don't want to go running around looking for you, we want you to be in the building at all times unless you're off, she warns us. Our apartment is across the hall from theirs, it looks exactly like a motel room. I am in charge of dusting the washing machines on each floor and emptying the garbage. Taik is to handle any small maintenance jobs, day or night. Our pay is three hundred dollars a month. I am appalled, but each dollar brings us closer to Oregon, so I hide my discontent, my indignation. After all, we don't pay rent. We can save at least one hundred fifty dollars a month.

But after two months, we are fired. Dodie doesn't give us a good reason, but I suspect it is because of the squid we fried one weekend and the stench that lingered for days afterwards in the lobby. We apply for another similar job, with a Mr. Johnson, in Mayfield Heights, in the Cleveland suburbs. He likes us, we are hired. He's an alcoholic and has a wife and six kids. His wife often comes to me with her marital problems, asks me if she should leave him. I am torn, though I agree that he is incorrigible. You have to decide for yourself, I tell her solemnly.

My duties are to sweep the stairs and mop the lobby of my building and the adjacent one. Taik is to be shoveling snow day and night, for it is winter and there is always snow on the ground. I have no friends, we have no car, and cannot go into the city, to a museum, a library, there is nothing to do but sit in the apartment and watch television, cook or read. I find myself poring over cookbooks, I try stuffed meatloaf, rice and almonds, I bake one thing after another, anything to distract me from the thought that my life is empty, has no meaning. I get fatter and fatter, Taik is gone for days on end, I sit alone, I have no friends, nobody to talk to, I break out in a horrible red, scaly rash underneath my wedding band, which then spreads all over my arm and especially in the crook of my elbow, where I pick it constantly until it bleeds. Little water blisters appear on my fingers, which I poke with pins and squeeze.

I decide to go on a diet and begin jogging each night after dinner, round and round the apartment complex, ten laps to a mile. One night Taik and I have a fight over whether a tomato is a fruit or a vegetable. Botanically speaking, it is a fruit, I tell him, but he refuses to give in. I leave him to his ignorance of fruits and vegetables and go outside to begin my run. When I return and unlock the door, I see that he has chained it from the inside and that I cannot get in. He probably thinks he is being funny, but I am not amused, covered as I am not only in sweat but bleeding sores and blisters whose origin is still a mystery. I back up from the door before he even has a chance to get up from the couch, raise my right knee to my chest and propel all my strength and weight against the door in a surge of pure and directed will. The door flies from its hinges and falls forward with a whoosh. Taik's eyes are huge as he watches the door fall before him like a side of beef. I feign nonchalance as I walk into the room, though my heart is racing. The door is destroyed. Taik is respectful.

A neighbor with a truck takes me shopping once a week, but I find myself panicky being alone with her in the truck. My confidence has again deserted me and I find I am incapable of acting normally, speaking normally, I am afraid I am losing my mind, losing my self. I rehearse snippets of conversation alone in the apartment, so that I will not be at a loss when we go out, but when the time comes, I freeze, I cannot act, cannot speak, a nameless terror overcomes me, a fear of nothingness, that I am nothing, that I do not exist, do not deserve to exist. I cook, I clean, I iron, I am the perfect Croatian wife. I watch "Jeopardy", I read books I once would have understood, such as "The Trial" and "An American Tragedy".

Melody, who is now a stewardess, comes to visit during a stopover in Cleveland. She doesn't see that I have changed, she is like a temporary nurse in a hospital for the terminally ill, comes in for a day and goes home, forgets everything, is not touched, not tainted. I don't know what I need or what I want, I am not even clear about the most fundamental issues in my life. I cannot escape, I need to be rescued. It is as though I have given up life, have stopped fighting; I lie back, passively surrendering myself to the forces around me. And Taik? What does he understand of my anguish? I am a good little actress, I cook, I clean, I iron, I am a good Croatian wife. Has he forgotten who it is he married? There is a stranger in his house, he sleeps with her and eats with her and talks with her, but she is not there. And his failure to find me, to recognize my terror, increases my sense of alienation until it is barely tolerable. Still my rash persists. I scratch it feverishly, with my nails, with a hairbrush, a piece of scouring pad, some sandpaper. If I keep on scratching, I think to myself, I will scratch myself away. The thought comforts me. The less the better.

Each day in Mayfield Heights is like a month, a year, in the prison of one's worst imaginings. The colors all look the same, as though their life, their freshness, had been drained out of them, as though all the leaves and flowers, the grass, the earth, had been rolled up in a giant ball and then flattened by a huge steamroller or squeezed by a monstrous fist until everything that meant anything had been bled out. My rash persists, I continue to feel apart from the rest of the universe, even from Taik, who is still unaware of my alienation. Sometimes I think of killing myself, though it is only a way to distract myself from the very real task of living.

When I awaken each morning, I see before me an endless expanse of nothingness, unrelieved by beauty, joy, tenderness, meaning. I see nothing but emptiness, a huge void into which I feel myself floating, sinking, losing control. I sit and stare at nothing, try to discover my place in the world, but I have no answers, there is something amiss, something which eludes me. I cook, I iron, I mix cornstarch and water to make Taik's collars stand up, I invite friends for dinner, I mop the halls, vacuum the wall-to-wall carpeting, which is olive green, a color I loathe and which I am forced to look at for at least sixteen hours every day, I spray the oven and clean, scrape the black scabs of dinners past from the burners with a knife, and then another day is over, I fall into bed, alone, because Taik is talking politics in Cleveland or Chicago or Akron or Cincinnati.

We are finally able to leave for Oregon, some months later, but I feel barely capable of grasping the idea, so alien does it seem to me. We will drive across America with our friend, Peter, in his new maroon convertible, it will take us five or six days, depending upon how often we stop along the way. I have nothing but bright pictures of home in my mind, of my mom on the porch, my brothers rolling around on the ground and yelling, my dad holding court in the living room, book in hand, glasses perched on the tip of his nose.

Other people have homes, too, I want to tell Taik. I feel I would kill him, Peter, anyone who stands in my way of getting home. Just don't try anything, I say, unsure myself of what I mean by this. Taik is puzzled, but remains silent. When the car is loaded with all our belongings, we drive off ceremoniously, and when we have left Mayfield Heights, left

Cleveland, left Ohio behind, I begin to cry, as though a monstrous weight has been lifted from me. I can talk again, I am convivial, animated, my face is flushed, I have begun to live again. The farther west we go, the more my rash disappears, and when we finally reach the Oregon border, it is almost imperceptible, it has faded to a rosy pink, the scabs are gone, the skin is smooth. And it is raining in Oregon. I am really home!

Portland, Oregon, 1972–As we approach my street, I am almost too excited to give directions. Rain is running down the windshield in rivers, we can hardly see to drive. I am sitting forward on the seat, barely able to contain my excitement.

Here it is, I tell Peter, the next house on the right! He pulls over to the curb and, before the car stops, I crawl over Taik's lap, open the door and spill out. I run to the porch, try the front door, which is open. Somebody is home, who is home, I go into the living room, my living room, which is dark because of the dark sky outside and because there is only one small lamp on in the corner by the fireplace. Mom? Dad? I call out. Before I know it, my dad appears from nowhere, followed by my two youngest brothers, Stewart and Todd. I'm here! I tell them unnecessarily. My dad is laughing his contained laugh, as though afraid it may become a bit too much for him to handle if it is allowed full rein, and my brothers are screeching, hugging me and running around in circles.

Where's mom? I ask. She is still at work, it seems, so we will wait in the living room while my dad goes to pick her up. It will be a surprise. But where is Taik? they ask me. I have forgotten about Taik, about Peter, in my excitement. I look out the window and see them standing in the yard, smoking cigarettes and talking, biding their time, though it is still sprinkling and they are surely getting wet. I call them inside, make the introductions. My father tells me to get some beer or wine, make some crackers and cheese; he will go for my mother while we wait.

Stewart and Todd are suddenly quiet in front of these two strangers, who do not speak proper English and do not look American. Taik sits for a few minutes, then goes out into the back yard, perhaps to smoke a cigarette. Suddenly my mother comes through the door. Oh my God, she says when she sees me, oh my God! And we are in each other's arms, I am crying, she feels so good, I am safe in her arms, nothing can hurt me, my mother, my mother.

And then she sees Peter sitting on the couch. Taik! she says, and runs to him, enfolds him in her arms. Peter is laughing, taking it good-naturedly. Mom, that's not Taik! That's Peter! I say, but she is not embarrassed, she is too happy and surprised to feel bad about anything. Where is he then? she asks. But I have gone to get him, I bring him in proudly, as though I were presenting her with a bouquet of flowers or a beautiful plant in bloom. Here he is! I tell her. And she enfolds him in her arms, laughing, flushed. We all tease her for thinking Peter was Taik, we make jokes, comment on how well each of us looks, simply get used to being a family again. Europe is far away, the danger, the loneliness, the feeling of alienation. I am sure of myself now. I have returned.

It is important to me to share with Taik the place I love best of all, the scene of my childhood fantasies, hopes, the town I longed for those muggy nights in Frankfurt as I looked out onto the river, wondering if Taik were coming home soon, wondering if he were ever coming home. Gearhart, which should be called by a more romantic, a more evocative name, such as Sandstone or Seafoam, Gearhart is where I want to go, immediately, I do not want to stay a minute longer in Portland, my nostalgia for my street, our house, has vanished, has been replaced with that wild longing I have and always have had for Gearhart, where my life began, where waking up in Gearhart each morning was all one needed from life. Taik is also anxious to know Gearhart, for knowing Gearhart will lead to a deeper knowledge of me, or so he believes, just as he feels I will never understand who he is, how he became the man he is, the depth of his commitment to his country unless I make the journey to Gorica, the village of his birth.

So we get into Peter's car the next morning and drive to Gearhart. We have left Peter in downtown Portland to look for a job, to find an apartment. As we drive off, I turn around to wave, but he has already taken off down the street at a fast clip, as though he knows exactly where he is going and whom he will meet. The drive to Gearhart is very quick. Taik has never driven with me before and tells me what to do, when to turn, when to speed up and slow down. You don't know how to drive, I tell him, so why don't you be quiet? I can't paint, but I can still tell the difference between a good and a bad painting, he says. But I ignore him, he can say whatever he likes, because I am on my way to Gearhart, where I know everything and he knows nothing. I push down on the accelerator, feel the surge of movement underneath me. Slow down! Taik yells. Are you crazy? I laugh, hang my arm out the window. I am in control now. It feels good.

Before we come to Gearhart, we must go through Seaside, which has not changed at all since I was last here. It is a tourist town, designed and operated with tourists in mind; the small amusement park on Broadway, the little colored boats in water for the kids, the bumper cars, the roller rink, the pink cotton candy stuck on tall white cones, the pronto pup stands, hush puppies in any other place, the penny arcade, where, for five cents, anyone can look into a little hole and see pictures of half-naked women shaking their breasts back and forth, the shops that sell the sand dollar ashtrays and the starfish hanging on a string, the wooden plaques upon which tiny, pastel shells are glued, the water glasses with beach scenes painted on the sides and a big SEASIDE, OREGON above and below, the salt water taffy store, before whose window one can always find a group of slack-jawed, sandy children without shoes watching the taffy being pulled out....this is Seaside.

In the winter, when the rain falls sullenly for months on end, the town rolls itself up, the natives go inside and emerge, like moles, only for short bursts to the grocery store, to have a tooth filled, to pick up some dry cleaning. I am not so interested in Taik's feelings about

Seaside, but in what will he think of Gearhart, how it will compare
with his village, Gorica, how will his picture of me change when he
experiences my village, walks down my old roads, my beach, my trails
overgrown with huckleberry bushes. I will show him the spot where I
first was kissed on the lips, by Rick Trucke, behind a big log by the
creek, a kiss witnessed by my best friend, Joyce, and a Mexican named
Danny Estrada, the first Mexican Gearhart and I had ever known, who
had the darkest skin I had ever seen anybody living in Gearhart have,
not counting Mark and Marie, the cooks at the Gearhart Hotel, who
were Negroes, but only lived here in the summer and never emerged
from their kitchen except to drive to Portland once a month to visit a
son or a daughter, I forget which.

But these things Taik will never know or be able to understand, the
creek, the taste of gooseberries after it has rained, digging clams at four
in the morning—he will only see locations, objects, colors, he will not
have the experience, he won't feel the way I have, the way I do. Perhaps I
will be surprised, I think as we turn into Gearhart, perhaps one can have
an instant flash of recognition for things one has never seen, never
heard or smelled or tasted, a primitive consciousness that everything is
connected, that all is one.

Gearhart, Oregon, 1973–This is the main street of Gearhart, I tell
him. We drive past the Cobra Gardens, where snakes of every shape,
size, age, color and disposition have lain on display in foul-smelling
cages surrounded in glass for the last twenty-two years. As a child hoping to be pleasantly frightened and disgusted by the huge coils moving
menacingly behind the thin glass, I had found myself saddened instead
at their grim existences, their dull eyes, the dead husks of skin they regularly shed lying in their cages, which seemed rarely, if ever, to be
cleaned or freshened. Taik wants to know what a cobra is. A big snake, I
say, trying to chase a strange sadness away. We are past the Cobra
Gardens, approaching the only four-way stop in town.

The post office, grocery store, gas station and a little park with a bench occupy the four corners. Randy Curs owns the grocery store, and Jon Blissett has the gas station. His father, Guyon, sits behind the desk at the post office. This is what I remember, anyway. I don't like to think that anything could have changed in my absence, that my world has changed. Taik looks around with great interest, but says little. I point out all the spots of interest, their significance in my life, the lives of my friends. I show him where all the dogs in Gearhart hang out, in front of the store. Every morning they are there, sprawled across the sidewalk, scratching, standing around socializing with other dog friends, growling at strangers as they attempt to buy a newspaper at the stand on the corner.

There's Thurber! I tell him, and pull over to the curb. Thurber, a small and scruffy mutt who looks as though she is smiling, comes trotting over to the car at the sound of my voice. She remembers me, I tell Taik with great delight, as though my place in Gearhart is confirmed by her recognition. And she does. She licks my hand and puts her paw on my knee, all the while sneaking looks at Taik, unsure yet whether he is to be a permanent addition to our community, whether it would pay to gain his favors. She used to visit me when I lived on the second floor of the Ocean House, I tell him. She would walk right through the lobby, up the stairs to my door, and she'd scratch with her nails until I opened up. Then she'd jump up on my bed, visit for a few minutes and go again. I hug Thurber tightly. You sweetheart, I say, you little doll.

But we must find a place to spend the summer. We run into the Mobleys, friends of my parents, who offer their house for the summer, an old beach house, furnished, on a dead end road next to the Ridge Path, the historic path leading through Gearhart all the way to Little Beach. It is perfect, with two stories, a large yard in back and in front, a large kitchen, wood floors. And we need a job. I can work as a waitress at the Crab Broiler, owned by old friends. Taik can find work on a fishing boat, but we will worry about that later. I am home, after all this time. I am where I belong, regardless of all those strange ideas I had in Europe, that I belonged with Taik, wherever he was, that I belonged nowhere, that I belonged in Europe.

What do you think? I ask Taik. He likes Gearhart. He feels an affinity for it, for the small town, the feel of it. We can be happy here, we will be happy here. We are out of danger. It is a funny feeling, it is as though we have survived a deadly and often fatal disease, we have been given a second chance, to do things differently, to live without fear and anxiety. But perhaps we cannot adjust to such a radical change, perhaps we will need more, something to live for, to die for.

All my childhood friends like Taik, with the exception of Katie, who is afraid of the dark looks he gives her when she leaves our refrigerator door open, the milk carton on the counter, her dishes in the sink, unwashed. He can't understand the way she does things, the way she comes into our house, makes herself at home, opening the cupboards, the drawers, taking what she wants, leaving everything in disarray when she is finished. That's Katie, I tell him. There's no other way I can explain her. She's a force of nature, a legend in Gearhart! A legend for what? he wants to know. For being herself, in spite of everything, I say. There is no other way to explain Katie, so I leave it at that.

Hazel likes Taik, and so does John, my high school boyfriend. They are married now, Hazel stole him from me the first time I went to Europe to live with an Austrian family in the Tyrol. The four of us do things together all the time, drink beer in Seaside taverns, ride bikes on the old roads in Gearhart, broil salmon fresh from the ocean, go to garage sales, fruit stands, hang around town, take their dogs for walks. They like him but don't fully understand him, which is fine, for they are not judgmental, do not need to understand everything.

I am able to quickly find a summer waitress job at a friend's restaurant, the "Crab Broiler", where it is possible to make up to twenty, thirty dollars a night in tips. We have no car, so I must either ride my bike the four miles to work, along winding Highway 101, or hitch a ride with someone else who works there. While I am at work, Taik stays home and

sleeps, reads, roams around Gearhart. He cannot find a job on a fishing
boat, mostly because he won't hang around the docks or approach people. He seems to feel that he should not have to sell himself, that his
skills should be recognized, even by those who do not know him.

When I come home at night, he tells me to empty my purse of my
tips. He likes to count them out, stack the quarters in piles of four, lay
the dollar bills together. When he is finished counting, he takes at least
half and puts it in his pocket. I am indulgent with him, as I would be
with a small child. This is my home, my town, country, nation, language, culture. I feel a strong need and desire to take care of him now, to
set his mind at ease, though he has never expressed the least bit of anxiety or trepidation about his position as an alien.

19

"Whatever is profound loves masks." Nietzsche

While I am preparing cole slaw at work one morning, one of the fore-men at the restaurant calls me. There's a man at the back door asking for you, he tells me. Who is it? I want to know. He didn't give his name, he says. So I go to the back door, walk outside. A stocky, dark-haired man in sunglasses is standing uncertainly before me. He is dressed con-spicuously, in a dark suit, white shirt and tie, highly-polished shoes, not the kind of clothing one often sees in our area. He looks suspicious, asks if I am Julie Bušić. Yes, I am, I say, and who are you? He pulls out some type of badge or card, gives his name, which I don't catch, tells me he is from the Secret Service. Are you married to Zvonko Busic? he asks. I tell him I am. He wants to talk to Taik, asks directions to our house. When I want to know what this is all about, he says he isn't at liberty to say.

As soon as he leaves, I go to the phone and call Hazel, tell her to go to the house and wake Taik up, that the Secret Service is on the way. Hazel is excited, has never been involved with the Secret Service before, or the FBI, or any of these agencies. I go back to the cole slaw, thinking,

thinking. If we are not free of such disturbances in Gearhart, Oregon, thousands of miles from Europe, where can we ever be free? The world suddenly seems so small and I feel imprisoned.

When I return home after work, I find Hazel and Taik in the living room. She is red-faced, excited, even though the agent has left hours ago. What was it all about? I ask Taik. He is acting as though the whole thing is amusing, an amusing diversion, but I am not in the mood to be diverted, I am angry, I feel threatened with this intrusion, this disturbance in our lives. Brezhnev is coming to Los Angeles next week, Taik tells me. So? I say. So what? I was on a list of people the U.S. government thought might try to kill Brezhnev, he tells me, so this agent came to interview me, to assess the situation. Taik smiles, tells me the agent came to the conclusion that Taik wasn't much interested in killing Brezhnev.

That's great, I say, that's great. I am outraged, find it hard to believe that Taik's name is on such a list, Taik who never even fights with anyone, at least physically, who couldn't care less about Brezhnev, whether he lives or dies. What are you supposed to have against Brezhnev? I ask him. Don't you know all Croatians are fascists? he says. You mean to say after all this time, you didn't know that? Funny, I say, very funny. But Hazel is excited, wants to tell me every detail, how she came to the house, woke Taik, how they waited together for the man to come, how she made coffee for the two of them while they talked.

And I was just sitting in a chair, she tells me, pretending to read a newspaper the whole time, listening to every word they said. She laughs, can't believe she had been involved in such an adventure in Gearhart, Oregon. I asked if they wanted me to leave, she continues, and Taik said no, so I just stayed and pretended to read a newspaper. I couldn't tell you one word I read on that newspaper, she laughs. She shakes her head at the incomprehensibility of life, at the strange quirks of Fate to which she has unexpectedly been exposed. Taik is composed, as usual, would not get excited if a bomb exploded under his feet. Is this the end of it, then? I ask him. Will this guy be back? He says he doubts it. I don't, though. Anything can happen now that our sanctuary in Gearhart, Oregon, has been violated. But we don't get another visit, we don't hear another word about it. And Brezhnev comes, and Brezhnev goes, and there is not a word about threats to his life in any newspaper or on the radio or television.

Since Taik does not seem to be able to find work in the area, he persuades Peter to drive down to San Pedro, California, with him, to look for a place there on a fishing boat. San Pedro is home to hundreds of Croatian Dalmatian fishermen, immigrants to America who could not bear to live away from the sea, who transplanted their nets, their skills, themselves, from one continent to another. If I find work, I'll only be gone for a few months, Taik tells me. I don't mind that he is leaving, though I doubt he will find a job. I suspect, in fact, that he is restless, needs to move around, see new landscape, new faces, Croatians. Gearhart cannot hold him as it does me. Oregon cannot hold him.

As he drives away with Petar, I feel a strange peace descend upon me, not because I am unburdened of Taik, it is not that; it is because I am finally able to feel completely at one with my surroundings, I am not distracted by any external forces, am not required to explain or elaborate on any of the strange phenomena that are Gearhart. But the days pass quickly, and before I know it, Taik has returned.

As soon as I open the door after coming home from work, I know he is near, just as one senses a chair that has recently been sat upon and one that has been empty for a long time. I call his name, but get no answer. I go to the back yard. He, Petar and some woman are lying in the sun on a big blanket. Look who's here! Taik tells me as he gets up, comes over and hugs me. It's Alice, our friend from Cleveland, Ohio!

I am hardly surprised. It is to be expected that Taik should be driven all the way to San Pedro to find a job on a fishing boat and return, two weeks later, with nothing but a captain's cap on his head and an old friend from Cleveland, Ohio. He looks very handsome in his captain's cap and his tank top, he looks tanned and healthy and proud of himself, as always.

I looked for a job, he tells me, but instead I was on a television show. What? I ask him. He relates the whole improbable story, how he was walking along the dock, past a camera crew who was shooting a scene for a weekly crime drama. He was asked to run along the dock with somebody chasing behind. He agreed, naturally, who wouldn't? It is, after all, more exciting than slinging fish onto the deck of a smelly boat. After the completion of the scene, he received twenty dollars for his cooperation.

When can we look forward to seeing your face on the television screen? I ask him. I didn't do it for that reason, Julie, he patiently explains. I did it for the adventure! So he has had another adventure, he is pursued, wherever he goes, by adventure, as though it were a carnivorous animal and he a sumptuous and fleshy feast. Who could resist the company of someone such as Taik?

Because Taik is so restless in the summer, when everything that can happen in Gearhart is happening, there is no chance that he will be content to remain throughout the winter, that he could survive weeks, months on end of rain, wind, perpetual grayness, isolation. I would like to go back to school, I tell him one night. I want to get my degree, go back to Portland State. He thinks it is a good idea, looks forward to spending time in Portland, where there are other Croatians, more than a handful of cars, stores, and buildings that are higher than two, three stories. Taik is from a tiny village, but he is at heart a cosmopolite, thrives on the movement, ambience of a big city. And I am excited about being a student again, buying lined notebooks in different colors, blue ball-point pens, a book bag. I am ripe for new ideas, new information. I want to think again, think for myself.

Portland, Oregon, 1972-1973—It is very hard for me to leave Gearhart, to go where there is no more scotchbroom, no ocean roar as I lie awake in bed at night, no horse walking down the main street in the middle of the day. But I am a student again, I must concentrate my energies, my will, on academics. It is time to pursue a career, it is time to stop running from country to country as Taik's adjunct, disciple, convert, wife. I have decided to take German, linguistics and political science classes. The first day of school, I am pleased to see familiar faces among the professors I have received. As I sit in class, taking copious notes, the joy of assimilating new ideas overwhelms me, I wish to remain a student for the rest of my life, learning, learning. The other faces in my classes are difficult to interpret. As I look at them, I am certain that I love school more than any of them, that I am the happiest person in the room and could spend the rest of my days going from classroom to classroom, never satisfied with what I know, always wanting more.

Do you understand his notion of "deep structure"? one of the students in my linguistics class asks me. Yes, I tell him, don't you? He shakes his head sadly. I'm a teaching assistant, he says. I'm supposed to know this stuff! And I end up with an A at the end of the course, while he receives only a B. It is because of my love of learning, my concentration, my need to understand and conquer, which he seems to lack. He only wants the class to end. He will forget it all a few months from now.

Taik takes a deep interest in my classes, especially the one on Eastern European politics, which he audits from time to time. My professor, Ladis Kristof, is a sweet and kindly Moldavian with an accent as thick as bricks. He speaks often of the state and how, according to the Marxists, it will soon "wivver away." Taik and I argue with some of the other students who hold views different than ours, who have never been in Europe, let alone Eastern Europe, who know only what they have read in books or seen in movies. American students are so naive, Taik tells me. You can tell them anything and they will believe it. I have to agree with him. It has also been my experience that we are not as curious as Europeans, we lack a comprehension of motivation, nuance, the power of propaganda.

Taik is asked by my German professor, Franz Langhammer, to give a lecture for the Eastern European Affairs Colloquium. He chooses to deliver his talk on the effect of the Yalta agreements on Croatia and Yugoslavia. He naturally procrastinates until the day before the lecture, so that I must stay up all night long translating what he has written. The lecture, read by me, as Taik's English is still poor, is a success, and many probing questions are asked afterwards, which I translate to Taik and then translate back to the audience. We both feel that we are in our element, the world of ideas and academics. When the colloquium has ended, we stand around with some of the students, elaborating on certain statements, exchanging views, accepting compliments, answering questions. It is difficult for Taik to go to his job the next morning as room service waiter at the Benson Hotel, one of the few jobs he can get which does not require fluent English. It hurts me that he must work at such a demeaning job, that he cannot better use his intellect, his talents and curiosity, but it can't be helped. He has never been anything but a student, he has never had more than just a transitory job, has no specialized skills. And because we are only temporarily in Oregon, a fact which is known by both of us but has never been articulated, we see no reason to be alarmed. We have our lives ahead of us, we have plenty of time to do great things, to become known, admired.

The FBI has managed to find us in our apartment on Hall Street, just as the Secret Service found us in Gearhart. The agent who comes over is named William Davis, small and trim, with black, neatly combed hair and closely clipped fingernails. His suit is gray, his tie is gray, he sits down and crosses his legs, places his hands in his lap.

We'd just like to know what you've been doing in Portland, he says conversationally. I stand in the kitchen, boiling water for coffee. Would you like some coffee, I ask him. Oh, no, no thanks, he says, as though he has really considered it and, at the last moment, decided he'd better not. Anyone knows the feds don't accept drinks from suspects, they could be poisoned, I could giving him some kind of lethal knock out drops, after which we would, being the disreputable characters we are, steal his wallet and identification, load him into trunk of our car, if we had one, and dump his insensate body into the muddy Willamette.

What do you mean, what are we doing? You mean illegally, obviously. Nothing, I say. When have we ever done anything illegally in our lives? Special Agent Davis has the grace to be embarrassed. I'm not assuming that, he says apologetically, it's just that we have to check out reports we get, and Zvonko has been involved politically for some time. I've just been asked to interview him. I am so angry that I don't let Taik say a word, I just continue on, telling him that first, we were followed to Gearhart by the Secret Service on the basis of some bogus report about Taik's intentions to assassinate Brezhnev, for God's sake, and now we have to deal with the FBI. Can't we be left alone? Can't we go anywhere and just live in peace? We get kicked out of Austria on the basis of some other ridiculous accusation, that Taik is planning a civil war in Croatia from inside Austrian borders, we get shot at in Berlin and, right after we leave, the German police show up to question us; we have to leave Ireland when our contact is suddenly arrested and held incommunicado, we get attacked again in Frankfurt, Taik gets assaulted, we are under constant surveillance, we don't know who to trust, there are Yugoslav agents running around all over the place, spreading stories that we are spies, that I am one, that Taik is one, that we are undercover agents, infiltrators, you name it. Or else we find out friends we trusted are spies, infiltrators, even murderers. Taik is even accused of having somehow caused Branko Jelic's death by telephone, as though he sent some secret poison through the wires. I'm sick of it, I tell him, my voice rising dangerously. I wish everyone would just leave us alone.

I can sympathize with you, he says. It must be tough. Yeah, yeah, I say under my breath, disgusted with the entire world with its hypocrisies, its lies and deceits. Later, after Taik has been "interviewed", he tells me it is important to present an image of tranquillity and calm, regardless of how I feel. Don't let them know what's on your mind or give them any superfluous information. You have to conserve yourself, conserve, conserve…

Even in Portland, Taik is restless. One day when I come home from school, I find a note on the kitchen table from him, saying he and Petar have gone to Las Vegas for four days. My first reaction is laughter. He knows me, wants to avoid explaining why he has to go to Las Vegas. I can't argue with a note. When I tell my friends what he has done, they are shocked, can't believe a husband can get away with such a thing, that I would tolerate it.

You mean, he just wrote you a note and left? a male friend asks. Yes, that's exactly what he did! I say. He is envious that Taik is able to perpetrate such an outrage, but I feel a certain pride that our marriage can withstand anything, that we are different than others, live by different rules. In fact, I relish the time alone, feel like a young and single girl again, eating when I want, sleeping as long as I like, being quiet and focused on myself for a change. When Taik returns, he is feeling low, he has lost two hundred dollars and hasn't slept in three days. Petar is dragging, tells me he drove non-stop both ways. What about your job? I ask him. I probably lost it, he says. You know Taik can talk anybody into anything! He laughs, we know this is true, that Taik's enthusiasm for any idea is contagious, he infects everybody around him with it, against one's will, one's better instincts. Were you mad at me, Punky? Taik asks. I lay my head on his shoulder, tell him I was a little bit mad. But you're not mad now, are you? I'm home! He is so sure that his return will eradicate any ill feelings, any criticism of his behavior that I, too, become sure. I'm not mad now, I tell him. And it is the truth. He is home, my batteries have been re-charged and we are poorer by two hundred dollars. I don't mention the fact that we might be needing that money because I think I'm pregnant.

When I am called into the doctor's office at the Student Health Services, the doctor, who is a woman, is smiling a wide and toothy smile. I have a sinking feeling in my stomach. This can only mean that my pregnancy test is positive. She is certain she is the bearer of good news, asks me to have a seat, folds her hands in her lap, looks at me long and hard, as though trying to determine how good a mother I will be. Congratulations! she says. You are going to have a baby! Oh, great, I say despondently. She is taken aback, does not approve. But I do not want a baby, I had even postponed getting the test. My classes, my books and papers take up all my time, intellectually and emotionally, I don't know what to do with a baby, those things do not come naturally to me, even though I am a woman, I am at a loss, feel helpless, inadequate at the thought of being totally responsible for the life and welfare of a miniature human.

When I go home, I give Taik the news. He responds like the Taik I know, he is cool, unexcited, accepting, contemplative, although there seems to be a strange excitement stirring beneath the surface. I am mad. Right in the middle of school, I tell him, and we have no extra money, we can't have a baby in this apartment, well, what else could go wrong? But my mother is ecstatic, she begins immediately to knit little neutral-colored booties and sweaters, in yellows and greens, to collect odds and ends at the estate sales she frequents on the weekends. My grandmother begins to knit as well. Grandma Mimi can babysit for you while you two are at school or work, she tells me. She would love it, she told me so. Everybody is planning, getting in the mood for a little baby, everybody but the mother of this baby.

I change my eating habits, though, I am not careless or unfeeling. I order tuna sandwiches with alfalfa sprouts, eat bowls of spinach and broccoli in the Student Union. But it doesn't feel real somehow, it doesn't seem possible that I am having a baby. A mistake has been made, a mistake in the orderly running of the universe.

One morning after Taik has gone to work, I wake up doubled over with pain. There is blood all over the bed, dark blood, almost black. I stagger to the bathroom, to the toilet. Blood is everywhere, it is pouring from my loins in rivers and I am overcome with waves of pain in my stomach, I cannot stand up, I am like a crippled insect scooting across the linoleum. I finally reach the phone, call Taik at work and tell him to come home immediately. Then I manage to call the doctor, who tells me to report to the hospital right away, that I am probably having a miscarriage. The pain coursing through my stomach, my entrails, is like no other I have ever suffered, it radiates into every nerve, overshadows all other sensations in my body, forces my entire consciousness to exist for it and it alone.

Taik and Petar burst in the door. They don't know what to do, look to me for instructions, advice, comfort? Help me change my clothes, I tell Taik. We go into the bathroom, I try to wash myself, make myself presentable. Then they each take one of my arms and transport me downstairs to the car. I am in such pain that I am barely aware of the trip to the hospital, of the check-in, the wheelchair, the bed, the bedclothes. A kind nurse holds my hand, then gives me a shot. Within minutes, I am suffused with a sense of well-being, of giddy painlessness. The world is a lovely garden of joy and happiness. I smile woozily at the nurse. I feel so good! I tell her. I was in such pain, such indescribable pain! I know, she says as she strokes my hand, I know. The doctor comes in soon thereafter, does a quick examination. It seems I am having a miscarriage, labor pains, which will necessitate a surgical procedure. We will do the little operation very soon, he tells me, the kindly, dear doctor Hutchinson. Meanwhile, you try to relax.

When I tell Taik what has happened, he has little reaction, he just holds my hand, tells me he will be back in a few hours. Nothing is bothering me, I don't even mind the unpleasant preparation for the operation, the shaving, the alcohol. I feel so good. When I am finally wheeled into the operating room and given the shot, I don't care about much at all, as long as I keep feeling good for the rest of my life. A mask is placed over my face. Bye bye, the nurse says. Bye bye, I say, and then I remember nothing until I regain consciousness in the recovery room. When I realize I have not died, that I am on a stretcher, I try to focus my eyes. I see a form walking by which reminds me of Taik. Taik! I call out through heavy and unmanageable lips, Taik, come here! The form looks my way and hurries past.

Much later, the next morning, I come to again in my hospital room. The nurse is standing by my bed, saying my name. I'm so hungry! I tell her, though I am not hungry at all. I somehow have the idea I should be asking for food, that it is a good sign, a sign of health. She is surprised that I am hungry after the anesthesia. But I am! I insist. Do you want a sandwich? she asks. I want two sandwiches! I tell her.

As I am eating, Taik arrives. I have just been given another shot, so I am as happy as any one person can be. How do you feel, Punky? he asks. Fine, I assure him. I'm so hungry, though! He has to go to work, so I call my father to pick me up later in the day. We can hardly afford another night in the hospital. When my father comes, I feel shy. Why didn't you tell us last night that you were coming to the hospital? he asks me. I didn't want to worry you, I say. We drive to our apartment in near silence. I am relieved to get out of the car, to be back in our apartment. I climb into bed, wait excitedly for Taik to come home, to pamper me, sit by my side, bring me tea or soup. When he arrives, he gets undressed and climbs into bed with me. This is not what I have in mind. Get out of bed! I tell him. I want you to sit with me, not go to sleep. But you're in bed, you're going to sleep! he says. You aren't supposed to, though, I say, you're supposed to be awake, take care of me! I begin to cry without understanding exactly what is bothering me. He gets into bed, takes me in his arms. Sleep, he says. I am angry with him, resist sleep as long as I can. Sleep, sleep, he tells me, and then I sleep.

My mother is upset that she is not to have a new grandchild. She seems to be the only one. Taik does not mention the subject except when I bring it up. The baby had only been an idea to me, not a tangible and living concept, and like any other idea, it had disappeared when replaced by a new one. And the new idea is that we are moving to New York as soon as I graduate. It is as though we have lost whatever might have bound us to this city, that we are once again of the world and not of our city, our home, our family.

When Taik asks me what I think about moving, I am cold and non-committal. On one hand, the images, the fantasies and visions I have of New York City, its decadence and grandeur, draw me, but in an unnerving and not an exhilarating way, as though I were a piece of flotsam being drawn, sucked, into a gutter drain. On the other hand, I am leaving my family and friends and the one place of all others than I can call, with any sense of certainty, my home. What does this mean, leaving home? I'm leaving home, bye bye. The Beatles song goes through my mind with all its implications. Where do I belong? And the answer seems to be: with Taik, at the expense of all else.

I am a college graduate with high honors. Because we are moving to New York a week before graduation, I will miss the ceremony, the pomp and circumstance. It doesn't matter to me. The train ride through Canada to New York City tempts me much more than the graduation festivities. My family has doubts about our moving back east, or perhaps they are simply sad. My mother especially wants us to stay, wants to be able to go shopping with her only daughter, out to lunch, to movies; she just wants me near. But my first allegiance is to the only all-encompassing love I have ever had, which, for a reason yet inexplicable to me, overshadows all else. The nature of my love for Taik is different than the love I feel for my family. For him I must make sacrifices, even though he asks for none, at least not directly. For him I must be ready to leave my home, all that is familiar to me, all that I hold close to my heart. The measure of our bond, its thickness, its invulnerability, is equal to the sacrifice I inflict upon myself in the name of our love. Whether he perceives the psychological implications of my actions is doubtful. I am unclear about them myself, I simply act automatically, as though controlled by primitive instincts bred into me, my entire sex, throughout the centuries.

My mom and dad take us to the station in their car, help us unload our boxes of dishes, our books, pots and pans. After we are settled in our compartment, we come out once again to say our goodbyes. My heart is full of love and sadness for my mother, my father, both standing so straight and stoically on the platform. I embrace them one by one, extricate myself as quickly as I can for fear I will not be able to board the train, leave them, my home, behind.

Call us when you get there and send postcards along the way! my mother tells me. We will, I say. I turn around for the last time, tell them I love them. I am crying but trying to hide it, hold on to Taik for inspiration, hold on to the one for whose sake I leave everything behind. The train pulls out slowly from the station, my parents become smaller and smaller until I can no longer see them at all. This image of my mother, my father, is an analogy for my life, which at queer and rare moments is so vivid before my eyes. And then it fades, becomes more and more indistinct, moves back into my consciousness, as though it, Life, can be replaced by something else!

20

"Dark bodies inferred beside the sun…" Nietzsche

New York City, 1975–When we arrive at the Port Authority Terminal in New York City, I am overwhelmed by the vitality around me. But it is a decadent vitality, like the frenzied activity of lethal cells in replication. One wishes things were not quite so vital. I hug my suitcases, my purse tightly against my ribs, while trying to keep up with Taik, who is enthralled with everything and surges on ahead of me. I avert my eyes from rumpled, ill-smelling figures on the ground who wave limp hands in my direction or call out feebly "ma'am, please, ma'am…"

Where are we going? I ask Taik, who acts as though the terminal is his personal office, one whose every corner and angle he is already person-ally acquainted with. We have to call a friend of mine to pick us up, he tells me. As we sit out in front of the terminal waiting, sitting on our suitcases, I am struck by the security Taik's presence affords me. I feel no evil, no catastrophe, can ever befall me as long as we are together, a unit, both in body and in spirit. I scoot a bit closer to him, so that our arms are touching. Here we are in New York City! he says. His enthusiasm is contagious, as always, and I find myself suddenly fascinated by the dirt, the squalor, the grim rapaciousness of this city.

I find it impossible to be enthusiastic about Jersey City, however, where we will be staying with Croatian friends until we find an apartment and jobs in Manhattan. The apartment building they manage is located high on a hill overlooking a sprawling, foul-smelling dump, below which lies Hoboken, a city about which I had heard, in the past, many unsavory jokes and snide comments, all, in my opinion, based on indisputable fact. It is not so much a city as a depository. People do not live in Hoboken. They wait to die.

Our apartment is unfurnished except for a bed and a table and two chairs. The bathtub is chipped and yellow and lacks a plug. There are no curtains, so the horrifying view of the dump is always before us, obscuring all else that could conceivably serve as a distraction. I am unbelievably depressed about living in Jersey City, even for a week, a month. The people I pass on the streets or see in the markets or laundromats are uniformly ill-dressed, ill-mannered, and just as miserable, it seems, as I at the realization that we are living in Jersey City. There are delinquents running all over the place, at all hours of the day and night, making obscene comments to every woman or girl they pass, grabbing hold of a sleeve, sometimes even a breast; there are sickly dogs everywhere, who growl and scratch, but have too little strength to bite, who have been sapped of their natural instincts living in Jersey City. Their fur is matted, their noses run, their eyes, bleary and streaked, are unable to follow an object for longer than a few feet.

After a week or two, I find a job as a waitress at La Crepe, a franchise with restaurants all over New York City. I am given a black uniform with a white apron, and am expected to do at least a hundred things at once. Most of the other waitresses are not real waitresses, but aspiring actresses, or dancers, or ballerina students. They are temperamental and high-strung, and I must not make them angry or treat them as though I am their equal. One is Djuna, no doubt named after the notorious lesbian writer, Djuna Barnes, by parents who fancied themselves rebels and intellectuals, who hoped their daughter would be the artists they never were. Instead, she is a waitress at La Crepe, and so am I. Sarah is a ballerina student, who lives in a fancy brownstone not far from the restaurant; she works part-time, if only to convince herself her parents are not paying the rent. But she is clumsy, she is forever letting the crepes slide off the plates as she careens around a corner.

During our breaks, we may have, free of charge, a plain crepe with a scoop of ice cream on top. For the fancier crepes we must pay like everyone else. The artists and dancers who surround me must constantly watch their figures, so I eat their crepes. My pride has completely abandoned me. All I want is to eat, to fill up the emptiness. Let Djuna act, let Sarah dance. Let me eat!

When I drag into the apartment after work, the first thing I want to know from Taik is when we are leaving Jersey City. Nothing else holds the slightest interest for me. If he does not know, I ignore him for the rest of the night, go to bed. I work, sleep and eat. This is my life.

New York City is more than I had expected, more decadent, more ostentatious, more flamboyant. Women smoke cigarettes as they walk down the street, a notion I find very strange and rebellious. Such a thing would never happen in Oregon or in Europe. Hippies dressed completely in purple ride their bikes through the streets, distributing leaflets printed in infinitesmal letters, so small that one gets a headache trying to decipher them. And when one does, one is warned against wearing the bodies of animals, not belts, not jackets, not furs, not even shoes.

At Times Square, the streets never empty. They are full, twenty four hours a day, of pimps, drunks, hookers in skirts so short they seem to be all legs. There are men on every corner selling watches, a radio, a TV (in a box behind the frankfurter stand, wanna see?), drugs, whatever they think you might buy. The first day we are in Times Square, we go to the famous Nathan's for a hot dog. While Taik is in line, I sit at a table, looking at the want ads in the New York Times. Suddenly, a tall, black man in a pink, three-piece suit and platform shoes materializes behind me. Lookin' for a job, sugar? he asks. I am appalled, give him a dirty look, turn the page. Still he stands there. New in town? he asks. Don't bother me! I tell him. The people next to me look away, embarrassed or perhaps scared, hoping they will not become involved in something larger than themselves. Before the black man can say anything further, Taik returns with two hot dogs. The black man has not counted on this; however, he cannot afford to lose face. Who knows who might be watching?

You'd better teach your woman how to talk to people or she might get hurt someday, he tells Taik. Taik doesn't understand this English, which sounds like taffy being pulled, so he is unsure how to react. This idiot is bothering me, I tell Taik in German, this asshole. Well, just ignore him, he says. The black man sees that he has salvaged as much of his dignity as possible, that we are foreigners and can't be expected to treat a pimp with respect. He walks off, so cool, lights a cigarette, turns his back to us. That stupid shit! I tell Taik. Who does he think I am? I feel so angry, so violated and shamed. I envision the head of this pimp being blown to bits by a huge gun whose name I don't know but imagine very explicitly. I imagine him never again being able to speak to anybody, especially to young blonde girls new in town, girls looking for a decent job. I have lost my appetite. You eat this hot dog, I tell Taik. Even though it is unfair, I am mad at Taik for not knocking every tooth in the pimp's mouth down his throat.

The beggars in New York are all geniuses. They make more money than corporate heads, they are consummate actors, their sound effects are beyond comparison; they run the gamut of all emotion known to the human animal. I follow one home one night. He lives in a fancy brownstone on the upper West Side. As he climbs the stairs, he looks behind him, just in case, and holds his day's earnings more tightly against his chest. But I see you! I tell him under my breath. I feel so sanctimonious, so self-righteous. When I see him next, I have an over-whelming desire to slap him. It is hot, it is humid, even when it rains. I feel as though I am always dirty, that there is a film of dust and grit on my skin which can never be washed off. And when the sun is out, there is a foul, overripe odor in the air, the smell of decomposition, of decay. Dog shit is everywhere. Is this the odor? But the side of every street is overflowing with garbage, which is collected only sporadically. The combination of the two launches a constant olfactory assault.

We have found a studio apartment on the upper West Side of Manhattan, and even though this is a fairly respectable neighborhood, it does not guarantee dependable garbage collection or removal of the animal feces which lie in mounds up and down every street. There is a shabby girl who stands on the corner of our street, watching the cars go by for hours on end. Her hair is oily and unwashed, her shoes are little more than cardboard. She stands with her hands stiffly at her side, and when somebody passes, she looks the other way. Even when it rains, it does not occur to her to move. She stands, hair hanging in wet ropes around her face, clothes soaked clean through, until a tall, well-dressed and coiffed woman comes out of somewhere and takes her by the arm. Who is this woman? Mother? Nurse? Is the girl insane? Is the mother insane? Day after day, the girl stands on the corner. She begins to anger me. When I walk by, I tell her to go away, to go somewhere else. Her existence disrupts mine, makes me uneasy, angry. But the girl simply ignores me. I do not exist for her, I am like the cars that zip by, one after one, or the leaves that blow past when the wind is up.

There is an ad in the newspaper for an English as a Second Language teacher. When I go to apply, at a private technical school only steps away from Times Square and the Public Library, I am interviewed by a big, gruff, hairy brute of a man with the unlikely name of Steven Sunshine. He seems fascinated with the fact that I am from Oregon, as though it is a foreign country which civilization has not yet reached. I talk funny, too, but he is too polite to mention this. I enumerate my qualifications.

He asks where I live. It so happens we live on the same street as he and his wife, Madeline, or Mady is she is called. This settles it. I am hired. But first I must do a demonstration lesson, which, though it is an utter failure, impresses him. If you think it was a failure, why did you hire me! I ask him later. Because you refused to give up! So I am hired because I am incapable of admitting defeat. It is as good a reason as any, I suppose.

My students are mostly South and Central American, though I have one Basque and one Rumanian. I teach all levels, six days a week. My students are all ages, all shades and sizes. Most are blue-collar workers interested only in learning conversation. A few are serious students, such as Julio from Peru and Martha from Colombia. Lenin from the Dominican Republic is in school because his mother has forced him to come. He is a hopelessly inept student, as is Esperanza from Guatemala, but their good humor excuses them their other failings.

I am an excellent teacher. My students take to me immediately. On holidays, I am always presented with a piece of jewelry, a box of candy. Whenever one of the classes is finished, we have a party, each student bringing a dish from his or her respective country. The men contribute bottles of whisky, camouflaged in brown paper bags, which they pretend to hide under their coats or in one of the desks until the time is right. On one occasion, I am invited to Olga's apartment for a Dominican dinner. She lives with an older sister in the Bronx, in a tenement three stories up, and as we climb the stairs, I am glad I have asked Taik to come along. Olga is not intimidated, however, as we make our way to the apartment. The empty streets, the burned-out carcasses of buildings we pass do not seem to affect her at all. From time to time, a face, a sullen face, appears in a doorway, watching, evaluating us. I feel as though we are in a wild and untamed country, that nothing I have ever learned about survival can help me here. The dangers I have confronted in Europe, the fear, cannot be compared to what I feel about the Bronx. In Europe, there are rules, certain things that simply are not done. There are no rules in the Bronx. It is a place of total anarchy.

We explore New York City and its surrounding areas, just as we had always done in Europe. Taik takes me to a strip joint in Times Square. He is interested in watching the faces of the men in the audience, and I, the only woman in the place, pretend to do the same, pretend I am academically interested, that I am engaged in a research project for a sociology dissertation. But I feel my face growing hot as I sit with Taik, as I watch the pale woman above me shake her breasts in my face. Her skin is sallow, like squeezed-out clay, and her breasts are too large for the rest of her body. She appears to have to prop herself with one foot in front of the other so as to maintain her equilibrium. And she can swing the breasts in a circle. The shiny tassles tied to her nipples catch the light overhead and send out bright flashes of color as she undulates across the narrow stage. I am relieved when we are once again out on the muggy street, away from the noise, the smoke, the leering faces. But the street, too, is pornographic. There is no real escape from it.

On Sundays we go to the Croatian Center, which is a low building attached to the Catholic Church. We plan it so that we arrive just when mass is getting out, ease ourselves into the crowd as it winds its way next door. There is a bar in the basement and, on the ground floor, Croatian wives serve home-baked pastries and coffee. We head for the basement, order cheap red wine in plastic cups, stand around in tight, smoky circles for hours on end. I am the only woman down there. Because I am an American, allowances are always made for my unusual behavior; everything is allowed me, I have no limitations. I have never before known such freedom and often am afraid I might lose control.

Taik is acknowledged by most as a leader. His opinions are constantly solicited, he is forever giving speeches, standing behind the podium in his black suit and neatly-trimmed beard; though his collar is frayed, as well as his cuffs, he cuts a handsome figure, he draws people to him, whether they like him or not. Some here also believe him to be a spy, an infiltrator working for the Yugoslav Secret Police. They cite "evidence" they have accumulated, second and third-hand, they relate stories about alleged conversations he had with an agent provocateur, a former Partisan leader, a double agent. But he is not disturbed by these nasty rumors, not nearly as disturbed as I am. Everyone who is doing important work will sooner or later be a victim of misinformation, he tells me. It's a sign they're afraid, they want to discredit me. Afterwards, I wonder what else they might do because of their fear, how far they are willing to go, how afraid they are.

Taik is sometimes gone for days at a time. He tells me he has to meet somebody from Europe or travel to Connecticut or go to New Jersey to get a phone call from Germany. This is his secret work, work which I am not allowed to share. Remember what happens when people know too much, he reminds me. They end up dead in the Rhein or shot in the head. I don't want to know! Did I ask you anything? I say impatiently. And this is the truth. I don't want to know where he is or with whom. That way I can protect myself from fear and the feeling of powerlessness, the sense of isolation which washes over me at the thought that he might not be coming home, not ever. When he does, though, I feel reborn. We have survived another day. We are still together.

Hi, Punky! I say as he comes in the door. I go to him, wrap my arms around his neck, hold him tightly. He humors me, lets me do whatever I want. After all, what other husband can get away with disappearing for days on end, without explanation, without guilt? I have to leave again tomorrow, he says. Go ahead, I don't care, I tell him. You're here now, aren't you? And we fall onto the bed, laughing, lying close, entwined. This is my best friend, I tell myself. I can't imagine my life without him in it.

But something intangible has changed. There is a feeling of danger in the air, especially when we are in our apartment, alone. Taik stops whatever he is doing when we hear footsteps on the stairs. What's the matter, what are you listening for? I ask him. Nothing, he says, but he is lying and I, well-trained, do not press him.

Sometimes the telephone rings and, when I answer, there is no sound, only a pregnant, ominous emptiness. When Taik answers, he tells me it was a wrong number. He is lying again, but I fear the truth, am relieved he does not burden me with it. We are living two lives, one as soul partners who share everything and one as strangers living a false life by withholding facts and feelings. I don't tell him I am scared, nor does he tell me. We deny the reality of our existence to one another, perhaps to ourselves; on the other hand, we analyze one another, our deepest secrets, our every idiosyncrasy; we discuss philosophy, literature, culture, our parents' effect on our personalities and character, whether a tomato is a fruit or a vegetable. It is a fragmented life and we become fragmented personalities, either too profoundly in touch with our experiences or not in touch at all.

One day, Taik buys a new lock and installs it on the door. We already have two locks, I tell him. Why do we need a third? I feel safer with it, he says. This isn't Gearhart. So it takes five minutes to unlock our door and another five to lock it up again. Whenever we come home, Taik makes a round of the apartment. He puts little things around the room which leave clues about possible intruders—powder on the floor, a tiny piece of paper wedged in the door—but they never appear to have been disturbed. If we have intruders, they are smarter than we are.

As the days go on, Taik begins to jump up when he hears steps on the stairs. It is no longer enough to merely listen. He goes to the door, stealthily, like a robber, presses his ear to the wall. When the steps pass, he waits a few minutes longer. He is not so easily duped, it could be a clever ploy, these people are not stupid.

Come back to bed, I say. It's nothing. And he finally comes, his senses still alert. When I hold him in my arms, I can feel the tension in his body, feel we are not connected to one another, that his attention is focused on something vague and inaccessible to me. Go to sleep, I say, sleep, sleep. It seems we are always on the verge of sleep or comprehension and that both continue to elude us.

Taik has had a report from an old friend from his village, a Croatian priest who has recently been to the homeland. It is a warning from the authorities, who had interrogated him during his visit home. If Taik doesn't discontinue his activities against the Yugoslav government, he will be silenced. It's that simple. Since only death could silence Taik, a fact of which they are well aware, the warning cannot be taken as lightly as Taik seems to take it.

Oh, so they'll kill you just like the others if you don't stop, I say. He doesn't want to discuss the subject. It's not the first time he has thought about death at the hands of the Serbs. He has been thinking about it ever since he was small, ever since he saw or heard of friends and relatives hanging from trees, cut open, shot, both during the war and years later in Western Europe. His attitude is that there is no reason he should be exempted from these slaughters. So you won't stop? I ask, knowing his answer but wanting to force him to say it, to dispel any possible doubts I could be harboring in the back of my consciousness. I should stop thinking and talking? he says. Why don't I stop living, too? It is the answer I expect from him. And I am prepared to be by his side, to suffer with and for him, as I have always done, always will do.

21

"One has watched life badly if one has not also seen the hand that considerately—kills." Nietzsche

It is easier to feel nothing than to feel fear, anxiety, tension, frustration, hot anger. So I don't allow myself the luxury, I pretend our life is a sea of calm and harmony, that we will live safely and happily ever after. When Taik doesn't come home at night, doesn't call, I tell myself he is playing cards with his friends, or having some beers in a bar somewhere. I take out a book, read twenty or thirty pages, until my lids are heavy, so heavy. I must sleep. I put down the book and turn out the light, but sleep does not come, there are too many noises which say too much—a key in another door, steps belonging to someone else's man and not my own. I feel so utterly alone and powerless. My life is a sea of calm and harmony. Repeat it, repeat it until you have lost consciousness. And then I awaken, there is a scraping at the door, a sound of metal. It is Taik, he is alive, he is home! I have failed myself. I feel relief, love, an overpowering sense of having escaped or been saved.

Where have you been? I demand. I didn't want to wake you up, so I didn't call, he says. I was playing cards. Nothing changes because I suffer or lie awake and trembling at the thought of his death, his excision from my life. So, since it doesn't matter, I won't feel, I will press it all down into my guts, where it can stay and fester forever.

In the early seventies, two young Croatians assassinated the Yugoslav consul, a certain Vladimir Rolovic, in Sweden. Croatian supporters later hijacked a plane and demanded and forced the release of the two, who had been sentenced to life in prison. They all fled to Spain, where they were given political asylum, and from there, went in different directions. Rolovic, according to Taik, was a high operative of the Yugoslav secret police and had been responsible for the murders, in Western Europe, of many dissident Croatians. Taik wants me to look up some information on the hijacking. What do you want to know? I ask him. I wonder how they did it, what kind of plane it was, you know? He is vague, doesn't seem to know what he wants, so I forget about his request and, after reminding me halfheartedly one or two times, he also forgets. Or at least he doesn't talk about it. He is still dreamy, contemplative, and I feel excluded from his inner life, find it difficult to reach him, to get his attention. So I withdraw into my own secret world of books. I gorge myself on Frederick Forsyth or Trevanian, tales of spies, espionage, danger and terror, as though I hadn't enough of such things in reality.

I decide I must be an expert on something, I must be an authority on at least one subject, as Taik is, as so many others are. But I find it difficult to choose my subject, my area of expertise. It is not enough that I know something of literature, that I speak foreign languages fluently and have a flair for linguistics, that I am an excellent teacher. It is not enough, I must know more, everything, about one specific subject so that I can feel adequate, knowledgeable, capable, irrefutable. I have visions of debates and discussions I will lead, questions posed that only

I can elaborate upon, insights only I possess. There is no argument I cannot demolish, no ego I cannot shatter if I so desire.

But what is this subject so worthy of my efforts, what is the subject whose value can approximate that of Taik's cause: the liberation of his people. I make trips to the library, stroll down one aisle after another just looking, checking out the titles. After long and careful consideration, I make my choice. I will become an expert on revolution! Whatever is to be known about revolution, I will know. Whatever book has been written on the subject, I will read. My task is staggering, but I irrationally decide that only through the mastery of it can I achieve my value as a thinking and worthy human being. Taik is not a part of my agonies, he is engrossed in his own vicissitudes: Is he being followed? Is his life in danger, and, if so, by whom? Will he live out the year? Does he have enough locks on the door? I bring home armloads of books, but manage to finish only one, a thin and dry account of the life of Che Guevara. My existence is characterized by a state of utter exhaustion, as though my resources have been drained from me by some unknown source, leaving me shrunken and wasted, unable often to summon sufficient energy to walk to the corner for a newspaper. Taik is the only spot of color in my life and I feel connected only when I am in his presence. The rest of the time I wait. For what, I do not know.

It is increasingly difficult to sleep at night. Taik jumps at every noise on the stairway, sits up in bed, rigid, listening to all footsteps, jumps out of his skin if they happen to stop or even hesitate outside our door. When they pass, his entire body deflates like an old tire, leaving him limp, lifeless. Try to sleep, I tell him. Everything is OK. No, it's not, he says, but offers no further information, no clarification other than what I already know: He must stop his political activities or else. This is the warning from Yugoslavia. And because he is not going to stop, not under any circumstances, every sound, every unfamiliar face, gesture, nuance of speech, is a source of tension and fear.

When the phone rings, I react as though a horrific shock has been administered to me. You answer it, I tell Taik, I don't want to hear the silence. And sometimes he does, but more often not. We need to change the number, I say. But I feel that the fear is manageable as long as we are still connected to its source. If the telephone did not ring, something else, something much worse, might happen. We can manage the telephone. It can only do us psychological harm.

Taik has not forgotten about his request regarding airplanes. Even though I am certain there is more than he is telling me, I do not pursue the subject, I simply ask him exactly what he wants to know. How could leaflets be dropped from a plane when it's in the air? he wonders. Did those others drop leaflets? I ask. I do not remember such a thing having taken place, but I know little in general about the case. He says they did drop leaflets, though he doesn't know how or exactly where. And I want to know which planes can fly the longest distances, he adds.

So I take myself dutifully to the main library across from my school and look up books on airplanes in the card catalog. The best source of information seems to be a British publication, "Jane's Around the World Aircraft". It is a huge book, more like an encyclopedia than anything else, and I find it difficult to lift it from the shelf to a table. I read everything about commercial planes, the 727s, the 747s, the DC-10s. I peruse drawings of their insides, note how many miles they can fly without refueling, and then I make copies of what I feel are the pertinent pages. Taik can read them himself. It is all in black and white.

We learn from friends that one of Taik's childhood friends from near his village, Bruno Busic has recently fled Yugoslavia to seek political asylum in Western Europe. Articles by and about him are all over the Croatian exile newspapers. There are many pictures, too, which show a man in his late thirties, with an interesting, kindly face, long and angular, but softened by deep, soft, doe-like eyes. His hair is unruly and white, prematurely so, I am told, due to his many incarcerations at the hands of the Yugoslav government. He is a journalist and statistician and he also writes beautiful poems and short stories, which he has had published since grade school days in magazines throughout the country.

Taik remembers him vividly from his earliest days in the village. He and Taik's oldest brother, Ante, were bosom friends and spent most of their time together in the rocky hills, talking, smoking, eating stolen watermelons and freshly-baked bread grabbed off a windowsill where it had been cooling. He is obviously one of Taik's heroes, for many reasons, for his integrity, his courage in choosing to endure imprisonment at hard labor instead of renouncing his beliefs, for his good humor about his physical disabilities.

What is wrong with him? I ask Taik. I am told he has a severe speech impediment due to early neurological damage. He can hardly be understood when he talks, and only by those who are used to his speech. I marvel that such a person can, ironically, be the most influential spokesman for the Croatian population in exile. His name stays in my mind. Bruno, Bruno....I fantasize meeting him, telling him I, too, have been in prison for Croatia. It is a fact I guard like a brilliant jewel against my heart, it is a fact which allows me to exist with some small measure of value in the universe. Where is he now? I want to know. He's in hiding most of the time, Taik says. They want to find him and kill him, get him out of the way. He has too much influence with Croatians in opposition to the government. They're afraid of him.

I picture Bruno in a one-room flat in London, poring over an elementary English grammar, the dissident who cannot speak. Or perhaps in a small pension in Spain, surrounded by aging Croatians, who get drunk and sing nationalistic songs until one of them pulls out a gun and starts shooting into the air, and Bruno is forced to eject them from his dreary room. These Croatians, the tragic ones, who have no allies, no supporters or lobbyists. They have only themselves on which to depend, only themselves to blame for the future. I must meet Bruno. I feel he has the answers to many of my questions.

We spend a lot of time at a friend's restaurant, A la Chandelle, which is just across Central Park from our apartment, on the east side. To get there, we often walk or, if we can, borrow bikes, even though we have been warned often by native New Yorkers that it is a very dangerous thing to do after dark. I continue to feel that as long as Taik and I are together, we are somehow protected from danger, that even the most sociopathic, desperate, and unscrupulous of criminals can sense our inviolability, the sacredness of our union. And, in fact, this seems to be the case. We are stalked many times by dark figures on foot and in cars, who, when they come close, seem surprised at what they see: a blonde and wholesome girl and a dark, possibly even sinister man who looks directly at them, as though they are exhibits of some sort. It is the directness of his gaze which disconcerts them. They feel their omnipotence is being endangered in a strange, unavoidable way, and they pass by us, drive around our bikes without a sound.

Once we are stopped by a policeman, who tells us we would be wiser to take a taxi or walk the lighted streets. We get into a conversation with him, he asks us where we are from. When he hears that Taik is an Eastern European, he confides that he is a stamp collector. Would Taik have any stamps from that part of the world? Taik promises to send him some, so he gives us his address. The next day, we conscientiously put as many stamps as we can find in an envelope with no return address, and stick them in the mail. We take great pleasure in performing anonymous kindnesses.

I have realized that in order for me to understand Taik on every level, it is necessary for me to experience his village and family, to walk the roads of Hercegovina, where he grew up, suffered, learned what it meant to be Croatian and what he was prepared to sacrifice in order to claim this identity. Can we go to Europe? I ask him one evening as we are sitting in our tiny apartment, both restless, fidgeting. We have enough money saved. We don't need much. He has had this idea himself, but hasn't yet brought up the subject, I can tell by the way he responds. I don't see why not, he tells me with a slow smile. We can't stay that long, though. I don't care how long we stay, I answer. There is a desperation within me, as though I will become unhinged if I cannot get out of New York City, away from the stink, the humidity, the ragged, vaguely human-like creatures who assault my senses and sensibilities each time I leave our building. I need to go to Gorica, where I can be both special and anonymous. I need to understand Taik. In Gorica I will learn how to live. In New York, I learn only how one does not.

Taik begins making phone calls, to the West Coast, to Canada, Europe, even to Australia. Our monthly bills are never less than two hundred dollars. When he awakens each morning, the first thing he does is light a cigarette and the second is reach for the telephone. The silent calls have stopped. At least I have not received any. If Taik has gotten threats on the phone, he has kept this information from me, feeling, and justifiably, that this knowledge can do me no good whatsoever. He is more often gone for days at a time and returns to the apartment wasted and pale. But his sense of humor is intact. He makes me laugh by putting on one of my bras and parading around the room pigeon-toed, talking with a lisp, his lips pursed together, his eyes crossed. Sometimes we wrestle on the floor and I pin him down with my legs, which are almost as strong as his. It's all the horses I jumped when I was a kid, I tell him. It's all the miles I ran on the beach! He measures my calves with his hands circled. They are as big as his, maybe even a little bigger. We have tender moments, moments of giddy laughter and shared consciousness. He is still my best friend, but we are somehow traveling on parallel courses; we look over, recognize each other, but we don't meet. Something is going wrong with our life together, and I feel powerless, unable to discover the source of our despair.

Thoughts of returning to Europe have invigorated me, infused me with new energy. I feel alive again, as though I have awakened from a long and involuntary torporous sleep. There is much to do before we will be ready to leave. The tickets must be bought, so we go to Icelandic

Airlines, which still offers the cheapest flight to Europe and is a sentimental choice as well. Gifts to present to Taik's family must be pur-
chased, items difficult or impossible to find in Croatia, such as real
Levi's, name brand jogging shoes. For Taik's mother I have a gold chain
with a cross, one of the many gifts I have received from the students in
my English classes. The idea of the necklace remaining behind in
Croatia, a continent away from where it was first bought and received
pleases me; it binds me together with my husband's family, it brings all
my students into it somehow, and all the countries they represent. We
are alive, bonded together throughout the world, and all because of the
necklace, which started out in New York City and came to rest in
Croatia. It is strange that we fail to articulate a clear reason for the
necessity of going to Europe. We don't even have an itinerary, don't
know exactly where we are going or whom we will see. I want to meet
Bruno, I tell Taik. Of this I am certain. And I want to go to Gorica, I add.
These are the only two things I require, the only things that matter.
Gorica will explain Taik to me, once and for all, and Bruno will explain
the rest of life.

Even though Taik was brought up in a patriarchal, chauvinistic, society, he seems to have realized that with me the rules do not always apply.
He doesn't allow me to be treated condescendingly by Croatian men, even
though I don't always understand what is being said, don't grasp the
meaning of certain gestures or nuances of movement. Sometimes when
we have guests over to our tiny apartment, he cooks the Turkish coffee
while I sit and talk at our table, enjoy being waited upon and feeling special. But I always feel special with him, he lets me know what I mean to
him in so many ways. He brags about me, how I ran a 26-mile marathon
without stopping, ran and ran for four hours and eighteen minutes. He
stops people in the middle of a conversation and tells them that I am the
best wife in the world, not caring if I hear him or not, just saying what is
on his mind and in his heart. These are the moments that bind me to him
forever. He is incapable of doing anything which would affect my love

and loyalty towards him, he is innocent, blameless, a perfect human being, or at least perfect for me. And he is generous. He always has time for me, sits for hours analyzing every small insecurity I am suffering, every pain and anxiety. There is so much I cannot say, though, so much I feel he would consider a weakness, less than I believe he requires of me. So I remain silent about my alienation. There are many more important issues in the world: torture, national oppression, murders of innocent dissidents, political exile. At night, when Taik stiffens at the sound of a step on the stairs, I am aware of the interrelationships and how they color our life. Relax, I tell him, and snuggle close to him, hold his head in my arms. It's nothing. It's the neighbor upstairs. He wants to believe me, but often doesn't. He knows better. I should, but I still have years of easy living to exorcise from my system.

The subject of hijacking has moved from simple hypothesis to a shady area that defies analysis. The more a word, an idea, is repeated, the more real it becomes, it develops a life of its own, an operational framework, a strange legitimacy, like a tiny nation which has won a war and suddenly finds itself with a government, laws, a right to exist. Taik has never said to me that he wants to hijack a plane, as a political action, that he feels it is the only act that will bring attention to his plight and the plight of his nation. But I know instinctively that all the questions, the research, the comments he has made in the past few months have not been due to idle curiosity. This reality I am loath to confront, so I do not, I go about my business as though am oblivious to his desperation, his determination. If he wants to talk about it, I will make it as hard as I can for him. At times, I believe that he could well forget about the whole idea if the subject is not openly discussed. This though, turns out to be intolerable to Taik. One evening, he asks me out to dinner in a local restaurant, makes a big show of it, as though he is asking my hand in marriage. When we arrive and after we have ordered, he looks around see if any suspicious persons are loitering near our table. Satisfied that we cannot be overheard and have not been followed, he asks me what I think about a hijacking. He explains that his life is in danger, that he firmly believes he will soon be assassinated as so many other Croatian dissidents before him. A highly publicized hijacking could prevent the Yugoslav secret police from continuing such activities, at least on American soil, he says, and give the oppressed Croatian nation sorely-needed media attention to the torture being perpetrated on it by the fascist Yugoslav government. I feel completely out of my element, have dreaded this moment for some time and, now that it has arrived, find myself unable to articulate a single persuasive argument against such an action. What if he is right, what if a hijacking would prevent his assassination and the assassination of other innocent Croatian dissidents? How am I to know, to judge the efficacy, the ethics, of such a thing? What is right, preventing murder in the future by means of a hijacking for publicity or doing nothing, waiting around to be killed? These questions swirl around in my head, I am confused, confused, I feel as though I have no core, no nucleus of philosophical belief to guide me. The thought of frightening innocent people repulses me. How can such a thing be justifiable, regardless of the motives? The end justifies the means. How often have I heard this phrase, this sentiment? What do I believe? My head hurts, there is a pressure building up inside which threatens to split it open. Have some more wine, Taik says, and pours me a glass.

I want to know what he hopes a hijacking will accomplish. Publicity, mostly, he answers. Imagine what people will think when they read that we are willing to sacrifice our freedom just to get the truth about the Serbian-dominated government's oppression and murder of Croatians before the public. They will wonder why they've never read about this before. They can't read about it, because the Yugoslavs fill the papers full of their propaganda. We have no lobby, we have no money or power. The Croatians are forced to such desperate actions because it's the only way they can get the truth out. Although I agree with him and know this is true, the public does not look kindly upon hijacking or hijackers.

Their sympathies are not with them or their arguments. There have been too many hijackings, I tell him, and all with negative publicity. Hijacking has lost its novelty, its ability to command the type of media attention you want. But he has made up his mind. Though he listens to what I say, he gives it little serious consideration. There won't be any weapons on the plane, he says. Nobody could possibly get hurt. I shake my head, unwilling to support or reject his ideas. Nothing I know or have experienced has prepared me to make a decision in this matter. Symbolic acts, sacrifices, the laws of man versus nature—all these concepts are fuzzy in my mind. What do I believe? What do I think? As a matter of fact, who am I? It is a feeling I recognize, this renunciation of self in favor of another, my other.

When I tell Steve and Mady we are going to Europe, they seem surprised. After all, they know how much I make teaching: very little. And Taik is working as an elevator operator. We are hardly in a position to be traveling all over Europe as though we have money to burn. But we have always managed to travel, to drink the best wine, to meet the most interesting people. Our tastes are so simple. All we need is a bed, a little bread and cheese, a few changes of clothing. I don't need money in Gorica, where Taik was born, and Bruno, the near mute, who can only speak with difficulty, yet is the main spokesman for his nation. I will see the spot where Taik and his band of hajduci cooked stolen chickens, the čemer, and I will find the old tree trunk which contains his initials, carved when he was only eight years old. You have to look for two pieces of stone set about a foot apart, and around ten inches high, he tells me. We used them as a toilet when we had to shit. Each of us had his own pair of stones and we'd go out, position our butts on them, and sit around and talk while we did our business. I laugh as I imagine asking his family about these stones. What will they think of us, of Taik for telling me where and how he used to shit when he was small? They do not share such intimacies, even those couples who have been married for forty, fifty years. Married couples in the village still sleep in their clothes, Taik says. They've probably never seen each other naked! But I am certain that what they have shared, their history of suffering, the pain of barely existing in the rocky, sere mountains of Hercegovina, is a thousand times more intimate than bare skin, bodily functions.

I wonder, too, if I will have problems with the secret police. After all, I am a convicted political criminal, whose name is no doubt on all the computers, especially since I have married the evil manipulator who put me in prison in the first place. Taik tells me to check in at the American Consulate as soon as I reach Zagreb, to provide them with my itinerary. His brother, Ante, who lives with his family in Zagreb, will take me there. The thought of being thrown in prison again, this time for marrying Taik, which is probably a crime in Yugoslavia by now, makes us both laugh. I wonder how long they'd give me for that! I say, and we laugh until our faces turn red and our stomachs ache.

Because I have tried to banish all thoughts of a hijacking from my mind, it is only days later that something Taik said the night in the restaurant occurs to me. I replay his words, remember what he told me, about how sacrificing our freedom will illustrate to the public the desperation of the Croatian nation. Sacrificing our freedom…what exactly does that mean? I reach the horrible conclusion that it means prison, that we will be arrested, thrown in cells, apart, for a long time, a number of years. Certainly for such an offense as hijacking, the penalties would be severe. The idea of spending years in a cell is unfathomable to me. I feel I would rather die, that such an existence is not preferable to death, not at all.

I bring up the subject with Taik, I can't hold it inside any longer. Anyway, I am running out of room, so much do I keep to myself, keep back, deny. He seems to believe that we needn't worry about that prospect. If we are arrested in Europe, he says, we will only be in prison for a few years. The sentences there are much shorter than in America. Besides, you will only do a few months, because you are a woman and you're only showing loyalty towards me. But I haven't agreed to go! I tell him. I think it's a bad idea, it will hurt the Croatians and us! He doesn't tell me whether he wants me to go or not, he leaves that decision up to me, but I feel I have no choice, no options. I don't sit down and analyze the situation, determine what I want, what I need. What I do is what I have always done with him: allow my love for and trust in him to determine the course of my life.

In the back of my mind, though, I harbor a small hope that it is a passing notion, an idea born of fear and frustration with our life; it can't be true that we could become involved in such a thing, that we would ruin our lives and cause our families to suffer, that we would subject innocent people to terror. But what is the alternative? Will Taik be assassinated otherwise? These questions are too large for me. I feel as though I am choking on the air around me, that life is suffocating and incapacitating me. I have to act and cannot. How have I come to this?

In order to make the best possible impression on Taik's family, on Bruno and anyone else I may meet during our trip to Europe, I decide to go to a salon and have false fingernails applied to my ravaged stubs. When I arrive and have been seated, the woman who is assigned to me takes a look at my nails, shakes her head. I don't know if you have enough nail here to glue the false ones on, she says. But she decides it's worth a try, gets out her supplies, the cremes, the acetone, emery boards, cotton balls, pieces of gauze. What color polish did you want? she asks me. I hadn't even thought about it. How about white? I say. White? She is incredulous. Well, how about red, then, I tell her. That is more to her liking. We decide upon a bright red, but not too bright, the red of a ripening cherry tomato, say, or a drop of blood, just after it hits water. I watch her as she works, shapes the false nail, buffs it, trims it, glues it onto the tips of my fingers. And finally she is finished. I hold my hands in front of me, not recognizing them, marveling at their transformation. When I try to pick up the change I receive after paying the bill, I cannot, I must slide it with the palm of my hand to the edge of the counter, let it drop off.

Back in our apartment, I proudly show Taik what I have done. He doesn't laugh, though I can tell he wants to. What do you think? he asks me. I'm not falling for that, though, his trick of asking me first and fashioning his answer from mine. Never mind, I say. It doesn't matter. The main thing is that I won't be self-conscious in Gorica, I won't have to tuck my fingers under my knuckles or fold them together so that the nails are hidden. It doesn't occur to me at all that I could be self-conscious about other things I do or say, that my ways of behaving or speaking, moving or dressing, will set me apart, isolate me. My only concern is my fingernails and that they not be hidden away, covered over, as though they are a character flaw or a family scandal. And you can keep your opinions to yourself, I tell Taik. I jump up, hold my talons in the air in front of him, as though to scratch his eyes out. They give me the creeps, he says, and looks away. Me, too, I admit. And we are quiet.

When I play and wrestle with Taik, I sometimes notice that he refuses to let me touch his face or make wild and unpredictable movements with my hands. What's the matter? Don't you trust me? I ask him with some asperity. And then he becomes docile, allows me against his will to hold his face in my hands, to run my fingers over his eyes, one of which is smaller, darker than the other. Why are your eyes so different? I want to know. He tells me that when he was small, a cow kicked him. That is why one is set more deeply into his face, as though someone had taken the heel of a hand and shoved the eye into soft, yet-unformed baby skin. I won't hurt you, I tell him. Trust me. He tries, but is unable to believe that if he allows me full access to his face, his eyes, something horrible will not happen, that I will not lose control, scratch or poke him, perhaps even blind him. I trust you with my life, I say. You can do whatever you want to me! Though I have said this to make him feel guilty, I realize it is also true, that I do trust him without reservation and believe my life, my being, is safe in his hands.

But he resists the feeling of vulnerability, won't surrender more than he has to. I've never seen you fight with anybody, I say. Have you been in many fights? I used to fight with my sister, he tells me. But I never punched her or anything because it would've hurt her too much. Does he avoid physicality for fear of inflicting too much damage or because violence repels him? I find it difficult to imagine Taik hurting anybody physically, though he moves through the world with a purposefulness which can be intimidating to those who oppose his ideas and desires. It is nearly impossible to refuse him anything. Whatever he proposes he has thought through to the tiniest detail, he can provide one hundred arguments, one hundred intricate analyses for every action he undertakes, whether it be packing a piece of roast in a thick coat of flour and water paste and then cooking it for four hours in tinfoil over a small flame (wait until you taste it, he tells me, it is so juicy, so tender!), or throwing anti-government leaflets from a skyscraper, it is all the same. He seems to feel that the world was created for him and for the implementation of his ideas. And I find myself anxious to play a part, any part, in this magic world.

The time for our trip has finally arrived. A Croatian friend drives us to the airport, where we go into the bar for a drink while we wait for our flight to be called. The feeling of leaving is a comfortable and familiar one for me. I am well acquainted with what it requires from me emotionally: an utter lack of attachments, material or otherwise; a willingness to surrender myself to the strange and inexplicable forces of Fate, in the guise, I often believe, of Taik; and, last, a desire to escape. From what I am not sure. I only know that in most of the places we have lived, the moment of departure has been the moment in which I have felt most free. And so it is with New York. I harbor a secret hope that we will never return, that we will begin a new life in Bonn, or Liege, or perhaps a tiny town in Luxembourg. Everything else can be left behind.

Our flight is called, so we say our goodbyes and head for the plane. We are flying Loftleidir once again, and the plane is cramped and stuffy, as we knew it would be. Babies crying, their little fists balled, punching the air; entire families spread out over the plane, calling to one another up and down the aisles. It is truly like the hold of a refugee ship; so many languages, some unidentifiable, a word or phrase here and there rising above the general babble, like a tiny bird breaking from its formation, setting itself apart for the world to see or hear.

We try to make ourselves comfortable, take off our coats and fold them neatly above our seats, move the armrests up and down, do all the things one does to prepare for a long siege. Shortly after takeoff, we doze. It seems we doze most of the flight. It is not sleep, we are too aware that we are thousands of feet in the air, enclosed in a rickety piece of metal, and that there is nothing but miles and miles of treacherous ocean beneath us. When we finally land in Luxembourg, we feel disconnected from our bodies, as though we know the two people who are wearing our clothes and speaking in our voices, but can't bring ourselves to initiate conversation. Instead we drag ourselves to the train station, buy tickets for Cologne, and, to pass a few hours time until our train arrives, watch a gangster movie at nearby theater, featuring Shelley Winters as Ma Barker speaking French to her three moronic and sociopathic sons.

Why are we going to Cologne? I ask Taik. He tells me that we are to meet some Croatian friends there, people I don't know, some I have heard of, i.e. a well-known Croatian activist who has been the victim of numerous failed assassination attempts. The last time they shot through his window and missed him, wounded a German on the street below. The time before that they hit him, but they didn't kill him. We're going to his place? I ask. No, she will pick us up, he says. We have to wait near a kiosk for her. This apartment seems like a most unattractive destination to me, and I consider telling Taik I will meet him later, somewhere else, in some other city, another country. But I go, I am the consummate partner. The wife finally arrives at our kiosk and we learn that she had driven by earlier without stopping, in order to compare us with a photograph she had. We had matched; therefore, we were safe. When I see the apartment building, I am surprised at how bourgeois, how respectable it appears. It is a German building, full of proper,

law-abiding, hard-working, judgmental Germans. How they must hate
the scandal and the inconvenience his near death has caused them!
They are certainly scheming, trying to rid themselves somehow of his
and his family's presence in their otherwise irreproachable dwelling.

But he is not home, since we have arrived unexpectedly. I will try to
get in touch with my husband, the wife says. He is out of town at the
moment. We sit in the living room, which is well-furnished, spotless, like
the rest of the small apartment. There is a balcony overlooking a garden,
sliding glass doors. I wonder about the glass doors. It would be so simple
to break the glass, to come in at night with a gun... But anything is possible, I realize. It is possible to break through iron doors, through a
fortress, if only one has the requisite weapons. There is only so much one
can do to protect oneself. After that, one becomes a prisoner of one's
own creation. And his wife is not allowing such a situation. She is warm,
she is charming. Of course she has heard of Taik, perhaps even of me. I'll
call some other friends, she says. They will want to talk to you.
Meanwhile, we sit and wait. Perhaps an hour later, some men come and
take Taik with them. I am left behind to make hours of polite conversation. We are back in Europe.

If the husband ever shows up, I don't know about it. I go to bed late,
without having seen Taik, though I wake up at some point and hear
many men's voices in the living room, one I can identify as his. In the
morning, I turn over to find an empty space beside me. Moments later,
Taik comes through the door. Time to get up! he says. We have a train to
catch. I pull myself up to a sitting position, look around, not remembering where we are, not even the continent. Oh God! I say. Are we still
in Cologne?

After I have gotten dressed and we have had coffee in the kitchen, we
take a taxi to the train station. We are going to Saarbrucken to search for
Bruno, who is somewhere in Germany or France, traveling surreptitiously, trying to keep a low profile and evade Yugoslav agents. Franjo
Goreta is living in Saarbrucken, Taik tells me. You can meet him. I recall

the case of the Croatian, Goreta, who had killed a Yugoslav consul rather than assassinate Croatian dissidents, a task the consul had tried to blackmail him into performing. After Goreta had exposed the Yugoslavs, though he still had to serve eight years, they put out a contract on him. But they missed and shot his sister instead; he survived to testify in court about the methods of the Yugoslav UDBA, or secret police, and against his would-be assassin, who was given a long prison sentence in Germany. Franjo Mikulic would be there, too, Taik told me, a former Communist official and an old friend of Bruno's, who had spent many years in prison in Yugoslavia as a result of his anti-government activities. These stories are difficult for me to assimilate. I tend to compare them with experiences I have had in Gearhart, or at the university. But it doesn't work, I have had no such experiences. The only violence I have ever known is the fistfights I have had with my younger brother, Rick, or the slaps I received from time to time from my father, for my "tone of voice". I once saw a dead whale on the beach, and a wounded deer on the Sunset Highway, twitching, trying to drag itself off into the bushes. And when I was eight, a bicycle kickstand got stuck in my leg. There was so much blood that my friend, who had been riding next to me, burst into tears and rode away, leaving me by myself at the side of the road. But political violence is something altogether different, so premeditated; it cannot be explained away by fits of uncontrollable passion or an irresistible urge. It is so much more…

Saarbrucken is a lovely little city on a river, whose name I don't know. Taik calls a number from the train station, and moments later, an older, graying man with kind eyes, a sweet smile, picks us up and drives us to a Croatian restaurant. Outside, there is a terrace with ten tables, all shaded by green canvas Cinzano umbrellas, and inside, two levels, a bar, pinball machines, a jukebox. The place is packed, though it is only mid-afternoon, and many of the men I see are already drunk, eyes bleary. The only language I hear is Croatian, as though the place has been quarantined by xenophobics. Taik leads me to a table where three others are sitting. Julie, this is Franjo Goreta. He points to a block-headed man, who stands and extends his hand. His eyes are tiny and set wide on an expansive, pale face. There is about him a look of danger, of cunning. He doesn't strike me as the type to be threatened or intimidated into doing anything he doesn't want to do. His hair stands up in spikes, a strange cut for a Croatian. I think I see scars on his skull, but I can't be sure, I am not able to get close enough and don't want to stare or ask. And this is Franjo Mikulic, Taik says. Another man stands and offers a hand, whose first two fingers are badly stained with nicotine and tremble slightly as well. His face is jowly, the thin hair slicked back. He reminds me of my Uncle Rus, a rumpled, disheveled man who has more important things on his mind than washing and ironing. But his face is kind, he endears himself to me immediately. Madame, he says, in French, and tilts his head. The third man, whose name I don't catch, tells the others that I am the one who threw the leaflets. But they already know. It seems everybody knows. I wonder briefly whether, were it not for my notoriety, their behavior towards me would be different, less obsequious, more Croatian. But I don't care. I am notorious, I will never know the answer for sure. Meanwhile, I enjoy their attention and respect. It's not often I feel I have done something noble.

We sit and talk, drink and eat, until the early hours of the morning. Then I am taken to an apartment to sleep, alone. The next day, a door opens to my room. Time to get up, Taik says, shaking the bed. Where are we? I ask him woozily. We're going to Karlsruhe to meet my brother, my uncle and Bruno! he tells me. This is shocking news. I am awake immediately, tingling.

22

"I love him who maketh his virtue his inclination and destiny: thus, for the sake of his virtue, he is willing to live on, or live no more." Nietzsche

When we arrive in Karlsruhe, we go to a hotel to meet Stjepan, Taik's youngest brother, and his uncle, Bosko, who lives in Linz and is a Austrian citizen now. They greet me with hearty enthusiasm, laughing and hugging me, complimenting Taik on his choice of wife. The three men have not seen each other for many years, so I let them go ahead to a restaurant while I stay behind and clean up. But I am more exhausted than I realize, because I lie down for a few moments and, against my will, fall into a deep sleep. The insistent buzz of a telephone on the bedside table rouses me at some point. I reach for it, hold it to my ear. Hello? It is Taik. What are you doing? We're waiting for you! He gives me the address of the restaurant, tells me I can walk over; it is only a few blocks from the hotel. Is Bruno there? I ask. He is. Suddenly I am filled with anxiety. I go to the mirror, comb my hair. The false fingernails from New York City are holding up. Good. My sweater is nice, understated, in shades of pale blue, and the denim skirt I wear is American, as I am. After all, what can be expected of me? I can hardly be something more, something other than, myself.

The restaurant, Wacht am Rhein, is on a quiet corner. The proprietor's name, Gojko Bosnjak, is above the door. It is somehow familiar to me. Is this the same Bosnjak who survived a fire-bomb attack several years ago? And then an assassination attempt one year after that? The Yugoslav secret police had been found responsible and a certain Vlado Misic was sentenced to ten years in prison. But it is broad daylight. Certainly nothing can happen to me now. I open the door, go inside.

Heads turn at the bar. A woman hurries over to me. Are you Julie Busic? she asks in Croatian. Yes, I am. She takes my arm, pulls me along, past the tables, past the bar, to a room in the back, in which at least thirty men sit, around a long, rectangular table. The room is smoky, raucous. On the table are large platters of steaming meats, loaves of bread cut in brick-sized chunks, salads of green pepper, tomatoes, onion. I see Taik before he sees me. Next to him is a gray-haired man who sits quietly, listening, his legs crossed. I go over to Taik, tap him on the shoulder. Here I am, I tell him.

Taik turns around, pulls me to him. This is my wife, Julie, he says to the gray-haired man. And Julie, this is Bruno. The first thing I notice about him is that he has a tie-clasp with a little pistol on it, an intricately detailed miniature of the real thing. The second is his smile, which lights up not only his whole face but the room, the restaurant, the entire world. He stands and takes my hand, holds it firmly. I am smiling, too. We feel an instant bond with one another, as though we have been bosom friends since birth, have shared all our joys and sorrows. This is the famous and formidable Bruno Busic the writer, the statistician, journalist, politician, ex-political prisoner, exile, Croatian. At least he doesn't say "So you're the one who threw the leaflets." My act pales compared to what he has done, suffered, accomplished for his people and country. He doesn't say anything at all, as a matter of fact. He just looks me over in a loving way. When he does finally speak, he says one word, which, in spite of the strange speech defect, I am able to recognize as "nevista". "Nevista" means daughter or sister-in-law; in actual speech, however, it can be used to imply a close bond with another woman, who is often not related in any way except emotionally and spiritually. And Bruno has already called me "nevista", only moments after our introduction. I am suffused with warmth and happiness. I sit down, the men make me a spot at the table. It is not surprising that I am the only woman in the room, excepting the waitress, an exuberant and red-cheeked Croatian named Terezia, who seems capable of doing one hundred things at once and maintaining her good humor. A plate is put in front of me, piled high with cevapcici, raznjici, Croatian spiced meats. And Dzuvec rice, liberally dosed with paprika, as well as various stuffed vegetables, french fries. French fries? I ask Taik quizzically. They like french fries, he says. I assume "they" means everybody else besides the Americans. But I am really too excited to eat. If I chew or look away, I might miss something Bruno and Taik are saying. It is difficult enough to understand Bruno, but I am anxious to hear and comprehend every word. It is such a strain for him to speak, the sound he makes is that of a blocked pipe suddenly flushed by a burst of heavy pressure. When I can't understand something he says, he repeats himself patiently and slowly. If that fails, he writes to me on a piece of paper.

Stjepan and Bosko talk to us as well. Here we are, five Busics! Taik announces. Who knows when these five Busics will be together again? We are all delighted with his observation. Many more times! says Bosko, lifting a glass of wine to his mouth. It dawns on me that I, too, am one of these Busics, and, again, I feel special, set apart from the others at the table. It seems to be something extraordinary, this being a Busics. Everyone is eager to acknowledge it, to confirm the reality.

Julie's going to Gorica tomorrow, Taik tells Bruno. Stjepan is driving her there! I look at him. This is news to me. But I recover, smile in agreement. Tomorrow! I have hardly gotten over the shock and excitement of meeting Bruno and I'm already on my way to Taik's village and family, practically in the car. On my way to Croatia, for whom so much blood has been let, so much passion spent. Will I understand why, this time? Will I finally comprehend the reason for all the sacrifices? I hope so. I long to know these things, to feel them with my whole heart and being. It is different for me now, I am not the girl in the Zagreb cell, who cried soft tears under her pillow at night and trembled when an angry word was spoken to her, who had to be liked by one and all. There are seldom tears now; I am strong, invincible, inured to it all!

Later, Taik, Bruno and I go for a walk along a park near the restaurant. I am surprised that no precautions are taken, that they are oblivious to danger, to the possibility of our being followed. From time to time, I look behind us, for a dark or suspicious shape lurking in the bushes. We should be careful, I say to Taik. We are, he says. I certainly can't tell. They are discussing my trip to Gorica. I will go through Zagreb, spend some time with Taik's brother, Ante, and his wife and children. Taik will stay behind with Bruno. Will you do Bruno a favor in Zagreb? Taik asks. Will I do Bruno a favor? He might as well ask me if the Pope is Catholic. I will do anything for Bruno, I say. It seems he was forced to leave important papers behind in Zagreb when he fled the country. He needs them for work, for his political asylum status; he needs them because they are his, they constitute the identity from which he has been forcibly separated.

The papers are in one of two places. He writes down both addresses, with a note from him personally by way of introduction and explanation. Anything having to do with his credentials, his schooling, any identification documents—this is what he wants. I take the piece of paper, fold it carefully and put it in my wallet, aware that the people whose names and addresses Bruno has given me can easily land in prison for hiding his papers, any of his possessions. And perhaps I can be imprisoned for having the piece of paper upon which Bruno has written. But I suppress violently this thought. If I allow it free rein, I will not be able to help Bruno, who needs my help so badly.

We walk along companionably and, as we walk, I watch Bruno's face. I remember the stories I have heard about him, how he was published at a very young age in all the student magazines, and later prohibited from attending any high school in the country due to political activities. As a child, he was not ridiculed about his speech defect; he had a certain nobility about him even at that age which precluded the usual pre-adolescent cruelty. He was held in awe by the village children, for his humor, his spirit, his awesome ability to experience life and put this experience into his timeless writing. Bruno had been Taik's hero. He was, in fact, the hero of many of the villagers. And each time the government imprisoned him, he grew in stature, became a symbol. It is no wonder that, once he fled the country, he was looked to by the majority of the Croatian exile population as their savior and leader, the one who would deliver them from their agonies, restore their country, their identity to them.

There is nothing hard about his face; to the contrary, his eyes are soft and tender, his mouth mobile, full, given easily to smiles which expose a set of large, white teeth. There is a child-like quality about his smile, an innocence which belies the torture, the suffering he has endured. His hair turned white in prison, Taik had once told me. He's only in his mid-thirties! It is hard to imagine Bruno without the full head of wild, gray hair. It is one of many reminders he carries with him of his prison years, perhaps the most benign.

That night we sleep above the restaurant, where the Bosnjaks have their apartment. We sleep in the building that has been firebombed by the Yugoslavs, with the family whose head has been a victim of two assassination attempts. Taik and I are on the floor of the living room, blankets and pillows spread out on the rug. Down the hall is Bruno, who is presently the number one Croatian enemy of the Yugoslav government and is a prime assassination target himself. And what of Taik? And the threats made against him in the recent past, the messages friends have brought him from Croatia, from government people, that he should stop his political activities or lose his life? I am in a dangerous position. But somehow I am able to reconstruct this reality, to persuade myself that it has all been a mistake, that nobody could seriously consider Taik, Bruno, Gojko Bosnjak, a serious danger to an entire government, to that government's existence. They have done little, in my opinion, to merit such an exalted position in the Yugoslav gallery of political enemies. Every government has its critics. What I do not understand is that the Yugoslav government admits no criticism. The fabric of this government is so thin and ragged, so worn, that the tiniest tear will bring it down, leave it standing naked. I am unable to accept that decent and honorable people are summarily murdered for exercising their freedom of speech, that these murders are often unavenged and the murderers unpunished. Because I am unable, I have no difficulties in falling asleep, on the floor of Bosnjak's living room, Taik at my side, Bruno down the hall. Each day that we awaken, without being blown up or shot, affirms my belief that it is all just a misunderstanding, a game, a cruel exaggeration intended to intimidate but not destroy. I have forgotten the past, the shots fired at Taik and me in Berlin. It was all a mistake, a misunderstanding. After all, we are alive and healthy, we have done nothing for which we need be ashamed or frightened. We are decent, honest, generous people, especially Taik and Bruno, who want what everybody wants: freedom, happiness, a life free of torture and oppression. We want to be left alone.

We are up early in the morning. I have slept only sporadically, too excited about Bruno being just down the hall from us, in the same building; apprehensive, too, about the trip to Gorica, to Taik's village and parents. Downstairs, we have coffee and bread, fixed by Ana, the young daughter of the Bosnjaks. The restaurant is closed until early afternoon, so it is dark and peaceful, like the inside of a church. Stjepan, Bosko and I will drive first to Linz, Austria, where Bosko lives with his wife, Mara. From there we will continue on across the border.

I am concerned about the fact that I am permanently banned from entering Austrian territory. You have an American passport, Bosko tells me. They won't even check it on the computer. And I have an Austrian passport and car registration. Don't worry, there will be no problem! I have heard these words before, prior to my arrest in Zagreb, for example. But since I have been unfairly banned from Austria, simply for being in Taik's company, I have no ethical qualms about entering the country. After all, Vienna had been my second home for a number of years; I had worked there, in a candle shop, and as a nurse in the eye clinic, caring for Austrian citizens, emptying their bedpans, bathing their musky, bed-ridden bodies with a smile. I paid rent in Austria, bought clothes and food there, contributed to the economy. Rarely did I avail myself of their socialized medicine or take advantage of their system. I was a good citizen. The only complaint the Austrians could justifiably have about me is that I had a penchant for sitting on the grass, going barefoot, and drying my hair out the window. All right, let's go! I say. I am ready for whatever happens. We all march out to the car. Bruno comes, too, and hugs me for a long time. He says something which I do not understand. How I wish I were quicker, smarter, so that he does not have to repeat himself. He takes out a piece of paper, writes "Be careful, nevista" on it, holds it out to me. I nod seriously. And then Taik holds me, but not for too long, lest he become sentimental or emotional. He says "pazi mi zenu" to Stjepan, "take care of my wife". As we drive away, Stjepan turns to me, tells me how solemn and momentous a responsibility has been given him by Taik. It's not something one says lightly, he tells me. He'd kill me if something happened to you.

And then we are gone, heading towards Austria. It is hard for me to leave Taik and Bruno behind, knowing they cannot go to their own country and village, that I must go in their place, greet their families, take care of their personal affairs. A horrible injustice. What kind of person would accept this arbitrary disenfranchisement? Certainly not

Taik, not Bruno. None of the Croatian exiles has appeared satisfied with a permanent life in West Germany, Austria, France or the United States. They are forever talking about buying a piece of land in Ljubuski, Rijeka or Vukovar, or about building a house there once they have enough Deutsch Marks saved. On weekends they gather at train stations, watching trains from Croatia disgorging their passengers. They drink too much, cry a lot. All they want is to go home.

As we drive we talk and, from time to time, stop for a coffee or a beer. Just before the border, Bosko pulls over to the side of the road. He feels the necessity for a pep talk. You and Stjepan just sit quietly, don't say a word unless they ask something, he tells us. We nod our heads. I notice that the mountains around the border are green the and undulating, hardly an obstacle for those who might wish to cross illegally. You can always go over the mountains if they check the computers, Bosko adds. I relish the idea somehow. It doesn't strike me as being wrong, only exciting. We drive off once more, reaching the border crossing about five minutes later. An official strolls over to the car. Bosko rolls down the window, says Guten Tag, hands over his passport, along with both of ours. The official looks them over carelessly. He goes behind the car, checks the license plates. Here you go, he says, and hands the passports back to Bosko. We drive off, elated. I am bouncing up and down on the car seat, laughing, and and Stjepan are smoking cigarettes, feigning nonchalance. They knew we'd make it all along. I am traveling with professionals, after all. But they are unable to contain themselves, pull over once more a while beyond the border so that we can have another drink, celebrate. Now there's the Yugoslav border to worry about! I remind them.

Linz is a picture-perfect Austrian city. It lacks the fastidiousness of Germany, the enforced order and sterility, but it's still clean and wholesome in its own way. The Austrian accepts well-intentioned deviation; the Germans do not. So I feel freer here, as though I have unbuttoned pants which are too tight or taken off my shoes to wiggle my toes. There are few people on the streets. After all, it is just mid-afternoon. The shops are still closed, people still napping after the heavy noon meal. A plump woman wearing a dirndl and a green fringed scarf comes out of a Tabak Trafik, holding a string bag in one hand and a baby in the other. The sun is beating down on the pavement. My head begins to ache. We drive and drive. How much longer can it be? Linz is not so wide across, not so long. We must be in another city by now! And then we arrive, turn into a parking lot, stop the car. Mara has been watching for us. I see her face in a window, moving behind a lace curtain, dark and shapeless, like a raincloud.

But Mara in person is sweetness and light, with a smile so brilliant that it must be real. She has prepared a lovely table for us, probably the night before, with her best plates and glasses, her softest tablecloth, and has invited Croatian friends to meet me and stay for dinner. It is an orgy of food and drink, which continues until the early hours of the morning. We leave the table in ruins, it looks as though a violent battle has been fought and lost. There are bones, bits of flesh everywhere—red wine stains dot the cloth, some large, some small, like tracks of blood in the snow. I stagger to the bed Mara has made up for me in the next room, manage to take off my clothes before I fall asleep. When I am awakened only hours later, it seems that I have not slept at all, so exhausted am I, so difficult is it to open my eyes. It is an impossibility to face the question of the Yugoslav border today. Let me sleep! I beg Stjepan. But he persists. We have a long drive and many things to discuss. I can sleep on the train. I peel myself from the bed, dress, and march to the car. Mara and Bosko wave from the window. They, too, want nothing more than to go home. I want to sleep.

Stjepan and I decide that when we reach the border of Austria and Yugoslavia, I will take the train across into Maribor, the first town on the other side. There Stjepan will be waiting for me. This way, there will be no difficulties for him, traveling with an enemy of the state and former political prisoner. Stjepan has not been active politically, though he takes pride in the history of his family and their contributions to Croatia. He can still go home, on vacations from his job as a pipefitter in Hamburg, but anyone who has exiled dissidents in the family has to put up from time to time with interrogations, sometimes even beatings, by the UDBA about their relatives. Parents are often pushed around, punched and berated about their offspring, as though their influence extends into foreign countries, into the minds of their adult children. Why can't you force your son to stop his activities? the secret police asks. Don't you have any control over him? Don't you know he's going to get hurt? But the parents haven't seen their children for years. They know nothing of their activities, nothing of their lives in the West. All this is irrelevant to the UDBA officials, who thrive on creating an atmosphere of terror and persecution. Their machinations are not means to an end but simply an end, performed for their own sake, for the fun of it, the excitement, the sense of power they afford the cowardly bullies who have risen in the ranks of this execrable agency. What other reason for frightening and abusing the innocent, who want nothing more than to plant their tobacco, grind their corn and have enough to eat and drink when they finish their work?

It makes no sense to expose Stjepan to danger. I will buy a ticket for Maribor, ride across the border, disembark, and be picked up by him at the station. But as we are waiting for the train to leave, I notice a well-dressed man a few meters away, watching me, not bothering to hide his curiosity. Is he staring at me? I ask Stjepan. Or is it my imagination? It is not my imagination, Stjepan notices him as well. There is nothing to be done about it. I have no choice but to board the train, leave Stjepan on the pavement.

It is not surprising that the man follows me to my compartment and asks me in English if he may join me. I don't mind, I say, though I do, very much. When two young Slovenian kids come in a few minutes later, I relax a bit. They speak German, too, because they work in Austria, where it is possible to earn more money, so we chat with each other, about America, the clothes we wear, the movies, the music. I pointedly ignore the man who is following me, spying on me. Of this I am certain. But he refuses to be ignored. Where are you going, all by yourself? he asks. To Maribor, I say. I'm on vacation. Do you know somebody in Maribor? he wants to know. I tell him I don't. To change the subject, I ask him where he learned to speak English. My daughter goes to school in America, he says. This is hardly the answer to my question, but I am not surprised. It is the typical answer of an incompetent undercover agent, who underestimates his opponents. You don't speak Serbo-Croatian? he asks. No, I don't, I say with some impatience, and turn again to the kids, who have been listening politely, as they have been taught to do when their elders are speaking. And then the strangest thing happens. This spy, this agent provocateur, turns to the kids and says, in Croatian, that I do, in fact, speak the language, that I can understand every word he is saying, I'm just pretending that I don't. As he talks, I look at an American magazine I have brought along and attempt to block out his words, force myself not to react, to maintain a look of utter blandness on my face. It is horrifyingly difficult to pretend incomprehension. I long to shoot this revolting man a look of unmitigated contempt, to tell him what an ass he is and to mind his own business. My heart is racing and it is almost more than I can bear to remain silent, to allow this donkey to continue spewing forth. But I keep my mouth closed. It is a nightmare to do so when every instinct of my being is ordering me to burst out in a stream of Croatian profanity designed to shut him up, not just for the moment, but for all time. When it comes to ingenious and imaginative profanity, the Croatians have no equals. What other nation could come up with a phrase such as "fuck the soup made of Jesus' bones"?

The conductor comes, mercifully, and puts an end to the diatribe of Agent X by asking for all our passports. The noble agent smirks as he hands his over, so certain is he that complications are in the offing. I hand mine over as well and so do the young Slovenians. Though I have nothing to fear, at least according to the other four Bušićs, I am loath to part with my passport, symbol of the government which is duty-bound to stand behind me in times of trouble and even stupidity. After about a quarter of an hour, during which the four of us have sat in uneasy silence, looking out the window or at our knees, the conductor returns with three passports, one for the agent and two for the kids. The failure of the conductor, who is, after all, a representative of the regime, to return my passport has confirmed the vague suspicions Agent X has planted in the minds of the two Slovenians, who now regard me with a mixture of awe and stupefaction.

I wait and wait, without appearing to wait; that is, I open my magazine and read the same words a hundred times, not understanding any of them or what possible connection they might have to one another or to me. It is difficult to remain seated; my first instinct is to jump up and track down the conductor, to shout and scream, in a loud, indignant, and dictatorial English, that I refuse to be treated in such an offhand manner, I have my rights, my international rights, that the agreements which exist between states are being violated. Can I sue? I am uncertain about this. But it is not in my nature to cause scenes. I am the type who simply endures.

The train comes to a slow and grinding halt. Out the window, I see a sign, Maribor, and small groups of people waiting on the platform. We have arrived. Where is my passport? The worthy agent gathers his belongings together slowly, forcing me to disembark before him. But I see the conductor hurrying down the aisle. Where is my passport? I yell out. I'm getting off here! He tells me in German to report to the police office at the station. Everything will be explained to me there. Stjepan is milling around in a dark doorway near the platform, I spot him from the window.

I return to the compartment, grab my bag, and drag it down the aisle to the exit. Stjepan sees me step onto the platform and walks out into the light. But I am headed for the police station, so I ignore him and he gets the message, lights a cigarette and waits to see what I am doing.

Meanwhile, the honorable agent has sidled up to me. Are you lost? he asks. Can I be of any help? No, thank you, I tell him. I'm sure it's just a misunderstanding. Of course, he says, but remains standing, watching.

The police station is brightly lit and the big doors are open. It gives an impression of warmth and I feel myself drawn to it, against my will, like a small, cold animal creeping up to a bonfire. Inside there are three officers sitting at three desks. When I enter, all three heads look up at me. They seem to know who I am immediately, which I expect. Agent X has probably thrown bits of paper out the window along the way, coded strips that have been retrieved by his cohorts. Is this your passport? one of the beefy officers asks. He holds it up. I don't know, I say. You have to open it up so I can see if my picture is inside. He chuckles. Hahaha, aren't you the clever one? he seems to be thinking, and opens it. It's my picture, all right, so I tell him so. Where are you going? he asks. To Zagreb and then to Gorica, I answer. He makes notes in a small pad. When are you leaving the country? I am not sure, I say. Perhaps in a week or ten days. He writes this down as well. Report to the American Consulate in Zagreb, will you? It is not a question but an order. All right, I say, I will. He hands me my passport. Have a good trip! he tells me and seems to mean it. I put the passport in my purse and throw my bag over my shoulder.

Stjepan is waiting just outside the door, his back pressed against the wall in case he has to make a move on somebody. After all, he has been entrusted with my life and safety. Let's go, he says. The car is over here. He walks on ahead, leaving me to trot behind him. I look back one last time. The venerable agent is still standing on the platform, now joined by a small girl and a woman. It crosses my mind that he is a simple family man, curious but harmless.

When I am safely seated in the car, my passport in my purse, I can finally relax. It is already dark and people are hurrying down the streets to their apartments, heads down, as though afraid of being recognized, by anybody. Stjepan tells me we'll arrive in Zagreb in a few hours, by some back road that he feels is faster than the regular route. But before we have gone two blocks, a man dressed in farmer's clothing, an old hat and baggy pants, a torn sweater, jumps right in front of our car, flagging us down.

Stjepan steps on the brakes, puts his arm across my chest so that I don't crack my head on the windshield. The old man comes to my side of the car. Open the window, Stjepan tells me, but I refuse. Who is this man? What does he want with us? Open the window, Julie, come on! he repeats. And he is supposed to be taking care of me. Wait until Taik hears of this lunatic request. So I open the window, since he obviously does not plan on driving off. Give me a ride to the next village, brother! the old man says. He is a hitchhiker? I am indignant. We are not that stupid, we don't pick up strangers who flag our car down only blocks from the station. Stjepan tells the man to climb in the back seat. I am beside myself with indignation, can't even berate Stjepan because the old man will understand. If only he spoke German or English, what I would say to him! As we drive, the old man, who is perched on the edge of the seat, sticks his head between Stjepan and me, talking, pointing his index finger here and there. He smells of tobacco and hay, not an unpleasant smell, but the fact that he is so obviously working for the Yugoslav secret police prevents me from granting him any concessions. I try to unravel the details of his scheme, the purpose of his mission. What is to be gained by hitchhiking with us to the next village? It is baffling, perplexing to be so sure, yet so incapable of getting to the bottom of things. Perhaps a car is waiting in the village to follow us as soon as he gives them the signal. That must be it. How can Stjepan be so trusting and gullible, this is what flabbergasts me, Stjepan, who was born and raised in this country, whose family has such a history... Here, brother, this is the place! the old man says. I get out here! Thank you! Stjepan stops the car, he scrambles out, waving, and disappears into the night. Stjepan turns to me, sees my black look. What's wrong? I don't believe you did that, I say. It was just an old farmer, he tells me. Don't be so suspicious! Could it be that I have behaved like an idiot about an old and harmless farmer?

Though it is too dark to see details, I sense a certain exotic quality to the landscape we pass; things appear to be larger than they should be, a different shade of blue or black, a different texture. The sky, which, in other countries, stops abruptly at the horizon, has a strange depth here; it is as though I can see all the way around the earth. It accounts, perhaps, for the different vision of the world these people have, the conviction that they can accomplish the impossible on their own terms. A contagious notion. I feel it myself, feel I have been given a power, an insight into the mysterious workings of the universe.

We are quiet as we move through the blackness. I am recording impressions, conjuring up similes, metaphors, synecdoches, for the story I will someday write, or for the one I will tell. Time flows, smooth and sweet, and then we are in Zagreb, driving around and around, trying to find, among the cluster of gray stone monoliths, the apartment building in which Taik's brother lives. The complex is far from the inner city and is reminiscent, at least in the dark, of a concentration camp or an insane asylum: bleak, drab, purely utilitarian. No trees, no flowers... These are luxuries superfluous to those working for "brotherhood and unity". My parents hate visiting here, Stjepan tells me. They think it's unnatural living up in the air. And it is, I realize. How perceptive they are!

We park the car and get out, go door to door searching for the building numbers. Here it is! I say. Number 29. The elevator takes us to the fifth floor. Surprise! Stjepan says when his brother opens the door. The family is exuberant, grateful that we have broken the monotony of existence. We eat, drink, talk, play with the two little boys, Goran and Ante. There is hardly room for this small family to live. They waited years for the apartment, Stjepan had told me. They're lucky to have it! I am unable to imagine life in this tiny space, in a country which makes no room for its people. Stjepan and I, as guests, are given the only bedroom, so the entire family must sleep together in the living room, a curtain separating them from the rest of the apartment. I don't sleep well. Stjepan snores loudly above me and I feel shame that I, and not the family, am sleeping in the only bedroom.

23

"Nobody dies nowadays of fatal truths, there are too many antidotes to them." Nietzsche

Zorislav Dukat, my attorney during the leaflet trial, is still alive and well in Zagreb, and the next morning, I persuade Ante to take me to his apartment so that I can say hello. Afterwards, I will report to the American Consulate to present my travel itinerary, just in case I should suddenly disappear or be arrested. It is my luck that Dr. Dukat is home, is in fact just leaving for an appointment, or so he says when he realizes who I am. I sense his discomfort, but also his desire to hug me and practice his English, to find out what I have been doing since the day of my release when the two of us eluded reporters in his car and hid out in a tiny cafe, drinking tea with lemon. He is truly torn between his natural inclination to sit and talk and his fear that we are being surveilled, that he might be accused of some vague crime against Yugoslav brotherhood and unity simply by being polite to his guests, one of whom has obviously unmasked herself as at least a semi-impostor by marrying the agent of her near destruction, Zvonko Busic. After all, my defense was that I had succumbed to Croatian charm. What better proof than to marry the charming person after my imprisonment and trial? When we leave, we all shake hands firmly and exchange wishes of good luck and prosperity. Back in the car, Ante turns to me and asks if I noticed how frightened my Dr. Dukat seemed. Yes, I did, I tell him. Isn't it a shame?

Then we are off to the American Consulate, which is located across the street from a lovely park whose trees are heavily laden with pink blossoms. I present my itinerary to one of the consular officials, who yawns and looks away when I talk to him, not out of boredom, I feel, but because of a huge arrogance he has developed as a minor personage in the Department of State. I am a small fish, a guppy, in his heady world of espionage, international relations, geopolitics. Because I need his help and also want to shock him out of his languorous complacency, I call him over to a corner of the office where we cannot be overheard by the secretaries, locals who are doubtless in the employ of the UDBA. I have to get some important papers out of the country, identification papers of a Croatian dissident who was forced into exile, I say. Is there any way they could go in the diplomatic pouch? The official opens a file cabinet and begins to rummage through some papers. There is an aimless quality to his ruffling, as though it is an activity designed solely to fill blocks of time and enable him to continue ignoring me. After a lengthy hesitation, he stops, hands still on the files, resting there as though they are piano keys, and looks at me against his will. We can't become involved in something like that, he tells me. There is a finality to his statement which admits no arguments or entreaties. He is not a man to be reasoned with. I'd like to know what you do get involved with, I think to myself as we go down the stairs to the car. Covering up torture cases, assassinations, and illegal imprisonments to preserve U.S./Yugoslav relations? Pumping billions of U.S. dollars into a collapsing economy? I'll get the papers out somehow. I don't need a government to do it, not even my own.

On our way back to the apartment, Taik's brother suddenly makes a turn into a large wood, pulls over to the side of the road and stops. Let's take a walk, he suggests. I have to talk to you. So we get out and walk silently deep into the forest, along a wide, well-trodden footpath. There isn't a single soul around, not even a small animal or a bird, and the silence is somehow ominous. Ante gets right to the point. Taik is in danger because of his political activities, he tells me. He has to stop or he is going to get killed. I want to know where he heard this. Many of the villagers have relatives working in the UDBA, he says. Some of them are still Croatian patriots and try to protect their friends when they can. One of them had a talk with me the last time I was in Gorica. But I have no power to influence his activities! I tell him. I wish I did! Then at least try to make him see that he must be very, very careful, he says. I promise to do this, knowing that the presence of personal danger has had no effect on Taik whatsoever in the past. Why should it be any different this time?

As we walk back to the car, I reflect upon a society in which the exercise of basic freedoms is a danger, leading more often than not to a long term of imprisonment, preceded with torture, depending upon one's transgression. Taik had once told me that a friend of his was imprisoned for damaging Yugoslav brotherhood and unity. His offense: displaying the Croatian coat of arms in his house, an object he had bought freely in a local store. Singing old Croatian nationalist songs which have been passed down through the centuries is also a crime. One is not allowed to be oneself in this country. Everything is a sham, a facade incapable of hiding what lies behind it: a seething resentment against the Serb-controlled government that threatens at any moment to explode. Of what can simple conversation exist when anything critical of one's very existence must be articulated deep in some forest or on a deserted street, an empty beach? Of what does life consist when Taik must be killed simply for thinking and articulating his thoughts?

When we arrive back at the apartment, I stay in the car because Stjepan and I must go over to one of the addresses I have been given by

Bruno, collect his papers. We don't tell Taik's brother about this. There is no need to involve additional people in what could be an dangerous and incriminating assignment.

What is the first address? Stjepan asks as we drive off. I give it to him. It's near the center of town, he says. I know these students. Two of them are from Gorica. We pull up, some minutes later, in front of a low, red building, which resembles a deserted warehouse more than anything else. But the inside of the apartment is homey and cosy, and there is a pleasant atmosphere of productive activity within. Everyone is home, all five of the inhabitants, sitting around, drinking Turkish coffee. They are happy to see visitors, especially one from another continent, and bustle around making more coffee, producing liqueurs and small cookies, chitchatting. But the time for our real business must come sooner or later. Stjepan clears his throat, tilts his head in my direction. She needs to talk to you, he tells one of the girls, the one whose name Bruno has given me. She is confused, looks at me strangely. I don't understand! she says. The others shift in their chairs, unsure of the situation but not wishing to appear discomfited, as though this were not cool. She finally gets out of her chair, though, to break the uncomfortable silence that has descended upon us, and motions me into the other room. I pull out the note Bruno has written. She begins at first to read it hesitantly. When she realizes who has written these words, she breaks into a brilliant smile, murmurs something to herself. You have seen him? she asks anxiously. Yes, just a few days ago, I tell her. He's doing fine? She hopes for a positive response, which I am happy to give her. Thank God, she says. Thank God.

Well, we'd better go through his boxes, she tells me. They are in a closet, covered by some books and papers. We pull them out, open the flaps. Since I am unable to quickly scan the papers for the pertinent ones, I leave this task to her and to Stjepan. They pull out stacks and stacks of documents, go through them one by one, setting some aside, pushing the others under a chair. When they are finished, we have only a small pile consisting of perhaps ten or fifteen pieces of paper. I hope these are the ones he wants, the girl says. I'm sure they are, I tell her, and gather them up, fold them gently and put them into my purse, thankful that I will not have to go to the second address of Bruno's cousin, Ante Petric, and put him also in danger. She walks us to the car, shakes our hands somberly. Tell Bruno to be careful, she says. It seems everybody must be careful, one can't simply live one's life unmolested.

The next day we are finally on our way to Gorica. We'll take a back road, Stjepan tells me. It goes through Bosnia instead of Dalmatia. I think it will be quicker. As we drive, I take notes on a pad I have on my lap. What are you doing? he wants to know. I'm writing down things that I don't want to forget, I say. He gets a kick out of this. What could I possibly want to remember about a road, the fields on either side of it, the cows grazing peacefully, heads down, as though rooted to the earth? I don't have a clear answer, but I know somehow that what I am seeing can give me an answer to the questions I have often asked Taik. What is so special about a piece of land that can drive people to such sacrifices? Why can't people live on any piece of land? How is Croatian land any different? I had often asked why Croatians couldn't just buy a piece of land somewhere else and live there. And I had tried to conjure up the feelings I would have calling some piece of land in Nebraska or South Dakota by the name of Oregon. Would this be acceptable, could I make it home, make it be home? Home is where the heart is. Could my heart be in South Dakota?

As we drive, I find this country affects me as no other. Everything I see has an intimate connection to Taik—the cows grazing in the pasture (such a cow and such a pasture I had never seen before); the color of the grass, the color of the sky (these shades of green and blue were previously unknown to me)—everything has a certain unique feeling to it, from the banal to the very significant. I am aware that all I am seeing and experiencing Taik is not allowed to see and experience. It is forbidden him. This extreme injustice creates a violent bitterness within me, but, at the same time, intensifies my love and devotion to the landscape to which I am so symbolically linked. I feel that I belong to this country and that it belongs to me, in all its facets. I feel I have been born in this country and would die for it. Somehow the fact that it is denied to Taik and not to me intensifies my emotions, as though I have the responsibility to experience everything for the both of us. I understand as well that, had I not come, I would never have grasped to the core the essence of Taik's character.

As we drive, we pass low, stone houses along each side of the road. In front of one is standing an old woman in a kerchief, watching the cars whizz by, eyes inscrutable, and in an overwhelming moment of revelation, I am aware that everything has fallen together, I understand. And I will never be the same again. The woman, the land, they belong together, as long as both exist.

This is Bosnia now, Stjepan tells me, Hercegovina's neighboring republic. Here they do everything backwards! I wonder if they tell Bosnian jokes here, just as Polish jokes are told in America. To our left is a river, a stagnant ribbon of mercury, behind which stand black mountains under a full, pale moon. A giant shelf of rock overhangs the road, and as we drive under it, I experience a pleasant claustrophobia, the sensation of being trapped in a long, dark tunnel, but seeing a light at the end, being certain of imminent liberation.

The landscape evokes a feeling of majesty, a sense of omnipotence—as though we are in the kingdom of some great ruler, or are, in fact, ourselves the rulers. Because it is dark, I cannot make notes in my pad, I am forced to file away my impressions, metaphor upon metaphor, like stacks of tiny blocks which threaten at any moment to topple in my mind.

After a number of miles on the main highway, we turn off onto another, pock-marked road for the remainder of the trip, the back way into the village. My window is open, we are driving very slowly, in order to preserve the undercarriage of the car. I stick my neck out, breathe in the air, which is so crisp it makes my throat ache, my eyes water. We are surrounded by a blackness so total that is seems to exclude anything living. There are no sounds anywhere except the labored breathing of the engine and the pounding of my heart. All the night animals are silent. Perhaps there are no night animals in this soundless vacuum, and we are the only living beings, making our relentless way forward into the inky darkness. I can barely make out low, sparse bushes scattered over the dry, stony land like clumps of tumbleweed thrown around at random.

Suddenly, ahead of us, we see a car circling around as though the driver were lost or drunk. We stop. On the car is a sign: Driving School. I look at Stjepan in amazement. It is three in the morning, in the dead of night, and whatever small population is hidden away in this wasteland through which we are driving has rarely ever seen a car. Where has the car come from, where is the driving school? Who is learning to drive inside? Why here, why now? Stjepan explains this bizarre sight in one sentence. After all, he says, we're in Bosnia.

I recall the sign we had seen many miles back, as we had been speeding along the highway. Caution: Potholes Ahead. And immediately, not more than five feet beyond the sign, we were jolted into the first of a long series of huge craters in the road. Stjepan had cursed as we bounced up and down in our seats. Why don't they put the sign at least a few hundred feet in front of the first pothole, to give people a chance to prepare? I had asked reasonably. We're in Bosnia, remember? he had answered.

And now, a driving lesson at three in the morning. What a strange and wonderful land! But it is time for a drink, and it so happens we are approaching a small, lit stone house at the side of the road. Over the entrance door is a sign too dim to make out. We get out of the car, walk into a tiny room in which five men are gathered around a dank-smelling counter spotted with spilled beer and wine. Cigarette smoke curls upward in small snakes. The men have cracked and gnarled hands and their fingers are stained yellow. They remind me of plump frankfurters spread thinly with pale German mustard. Their teeth, I notice as they talk, are stained, at least the ones they still have. From their ears sprout small, curly hairs and their heads are covered with dirty, sweat-stained hats. These are Croatian farmers, up before the sun rises on their tobacco fields, their grapevines. Somehow they personify the nation and all its struggles and weaknesses. A symbol I can one day use to say something profound!

They smile at us only because I smile first. They seem to say to them-selves, Why not? What harm is there in it? They figure we must have more than a passing connection to this land, this nation. The barren strip of land upon which we all stand and drink wine does not attract tourists, travel writers, professional tour guides.

We drink our wine companionably and, when I have finished, I go to the bathroom to which Stjepan directs me. It is a small cubicle and the floor consists mainly of a huge hole with just enough space around it to stand without being swallowed. I place my feet on either side of the abyss and hope for the best. Toilet paper is not available to anyone but high Party members or government officials in Yugoslavia. What is offered in its place in this little stone bar in the dead of night is a big pile of neatly-folded comic strips from some local newspaper. Is it a joke, a philosophical statement, a political protest? I will never be certain. I take the top sheet, read it and then consign it to a graceless death. But where is the string to flush this hole? I look around. It is hanging behind me, a battered wooden bead attached to it. I give it a strong pull. Suddenly water floods out of the gaping hole in undulating waves. I squeal and jump up and down, trying to escape the torrent. Finally, it recedes, leaving my shoes spongy wet. When I open the door and go out, I find Stjepan alone except for the proprietor. The customers have faded into the black night to similar stone houses lit with one bulb to awaken their sons, daughters, wives, or to gather their shovels, their wheelbarrows, before heading into the cold fields.

I thought I was going to drown in there! I tell him. He smiles, pre-tending sympathy. He knows nothing else. And I, I know even less.

Back in the car, we continue to bump along, and I begin to feel that we will never, can never arrive, that it is a cruel scheme to raise my hopes or to teach me patience, perseverence. When I least expect it, when it seems as though we have, in fact, no destination, that there is no end to the road, Stjepan announces that we are almost there. He pulls over and stops. Look to your left, he tells me. I look out the window and see a small copse of trees, stumps really, surrounded by bare, rocky hills. This is the "gaj", he says. This is our land, and part of it belongs to you, as Taik's wife. I look at the scrawny patch of land which reaches beyond where I can see in the dark. My land. This then belongs to me? I am overcome completely. I have never owned a piece of land before. Suddenly I feel a fever of love and possessiveness, as though I would fight any number of armies to protect my small plot of land, I would sell all my valuables to preserve it, what would I not do for that piece of land! The feeling of longing deep in my stomach I cannot identify; it transcends the spoken word, it is beyond all forms of human communication. And if I truly belonged to this land, this entire land, and it to me, if I had been born and raised here, what would I be willing to do for it? If I were a Croatian, here or in exile? I understand, once and for all, the man I have married and his entire nation. I am transformed by a passion I have only heard about in the past; now I feel it in my own soul. I have been given access to a great and profound secret.

Our village is just down the hill, Stjepan tells me. We're almost there now. I stick my head out the window once more, it seems as though I am always peering out the window, as though I can somehow make sense of things without the glass barrier between me and the outside. There are no lights below to indicate that we are anywhere near civilization, no sounds of human activity, just dark shapes against a dark sky, different shades of black. The car bounces down the hill slowly, comes onto a stretch of flat road, and then begins to climb a gently sloping dirt path. This is our street, Stjepan says. Haha! I think to myself. This collection of loose stones and gravel thrown over a pitted, muddy piece of earth cannot, by any imaginative leap, be called a street. A street is what my family house is on, a wide, paved thoroughfare with sidewalks, curbs, flowering cherry blossom trees on either side, driveways, gutters... A street indeed! But it doesn't matter, I certainly don't care about the name of this patch of geography. All that is important here is that this is the place of Taik's birth, on this street, or road, or alley, or strip of mud and rock. On the right, now, is his house. Gorica 21. I know the number by heart, though it is too dark to see. We stop in front of the low stone house. Stjepan goes in to wake his parents, tells me to wait in the car. I hear a low growl in front of the car. A village dog. I recall stories Taik has told me about the dogs, how they are never completely tamed, how they would kill to protect their masters, their territory. I figure this is a true Croatian dog and that I should get to know it, so I get out, try to approach this growl. "It's all right, puppy", I say soothingly. The dog continues to growl, then breaks out into a series of loud yips. He is coming closer. I can't see him, can't tell how big, how dangerous he is. Just as I decide to make the acquaintance of this fierce beast in the daytime, when he will no doubt be transformed into a scrawny, unprepossessing beast who, like all disenfranchised beings, has to make up for a lack of real power by putting forth a brave and intimidating facade, I see blurred forms approaching me. Stjepan is carrying a lantern. Behind him follow his parents, hesitant. They look as though they are in shock, eyes wide and unblinking, and approach me as they would a strange animal they have never seen before, even a Negro! I know exactly what to call them: his mother is not Iva, but "Kendusha", after her native village. And his father is known by all as "Peija", an affectionate form of his name, Petar. Kendusha and I lock eyes, but only for a moment. Then we are in each other's arms, sobbing. Kendusha! I wail, between sobs. Peija stands stoically, but I can see that he is moved. We go into the house, arms entwined.

There are three rooms, two bedrooms and a combination living, kitchen and dining room. I am struck by the smell of hickory-smoked meats, yeast, and clean dirt, a healthy smell, unadulterated by smog, chemicals, or the fumes of factories, mills, Corvettes or Subarus. The floor is packed earth. There is a single naked light-bulb hanging from the ceiling, of very high wattage, because it throws a stark, bright light over the room. We all look at each other again, as if for the first time, and we are pleased. There are sparse furnishings; two chairs, a large wooden table, a few cupboards and, incongruously, a fancy radio perched on one of the shelves. The only window in the room looks out onto grapevines hanging down from the roof and onto the road as well.

Peija pours us a glass of wine. They all toast me. The wine goes down my throat like silken water. And then I remember the pictures. I brought pictures of our wedding! I tell Kendusha and Peija, and pull them out of my purse. These are for you! I tell her. This is in New York. And the priest is Father Romich! Taik and I had decided to have a religious ceremony before our trip, in the Catholic church. I had actually converted, for the sake of his family. It is difficult enough having a foreign daughter-in-law. A non-Catholic daughter-in-law would be anathema. Kendusha takes the photos, bursts into fresh tears at the sight of Taik. My son, my son!, she cries as she holds the pictures against her heart. I too begin to cry, softly but with determination. Why can't Kendusha see her son? Why is there so much evil and injustice in the world? I sit quietly, patting her on the leg. Stjepan continues to drink. He is used to this.

Finally we go to bed, emotionally exhausted. I am given Taik's old bed in which to sleep. As I lie awake, I hear the same sounds I am sure he must have heard as he lay there as a child; a dog barking in the distance, muted breathing from the next room, a rooster crowing inexplicably. A barrage of sharp and sweet sensations, all connected to Taik, all bringing me closer to him, allowing me to share his consciousness, his reality. Against my will, I doze off into a fitful sleep, only to be awakened a short time later by a rooster crowing, a donkey braying. For a moment, I am unable to fathom these sounds. Where can I possibly be? And then I remember, it all floods back to me, and I am out of the bed, afraid I have missed something profound, anxious to spread myself out in every direction. I look out the window. There is a stable right underneath me. I am living with animals in the same house! What a strange and attractive notion! And the dog from the night before, I am sure it is the same one, is sprawled across the road. From time to time it opens one eye and looks around. It spots me and wags its tail. Is this the beast that had approached me so menacingly the night before? I wonder. But, like everything else in the village, things are not what they appear to be.

I am alone in the house. There is an atmosphere of activity in the air which leads me to believe the entire village has been up and working for hours. Of course the American would have to sleep in, is not accustomed to working early, working hard, living hard. But I am different! I want to tell somebody. I want to be up, I want to suffer! Where is everybody? And then I see Kendusha, plodding slowly up the road, a bucket in her hand. She is heavy, dressed in layers. Her face is round and her eyes dark and piercing. Kendusha! I yell. Wait for me! I run out and up the road, catch her and take the bucket from her hand. Where are you going? I ask. She is going to milk the cows. I'll help you, I tell her. She smiles, humoring me. I'll show her. How hard can it be to milk a cow? All you need to do is grab the teats and pull up and down.

As we walk up the road, people come out of their houses and stare at me, an alien from the farthest galaxies. The news has spread throughout the village that a foreigner, an American, is here, and, what's more, she is the wife of the notorious Zvonko Busic. Old women in black come up to me, smile, pat my arm, tell me stories about Taik. He stole bread that was cooling on the window ledges, he took chickens and roasted them up in the woods with his band of Hajduci, he was always organizing the boys in the village, a leader, a charmer, an entertainer, but also a brooder. He would read until all hours, one of the crones tells me, I used to see his lantern still burning in his window when I got up at four in the morning. He swore he would never marry! she adds with a cackle. And I always wondered who could possibly handle him! I'm trying, I tell her, but it's difficult at times! Then Kendusha begins to cry and the others join in. Oh God, oh God, they wail, hands covering their eyes. Everybody in the village has at least one relative who cannot return, who lives in exile or is in disfavor with the government. When one cries, everybody has a reason to join in, to mourn the loss of love, companionship, familial joy.

I discover that cows are not so easy to milk. With my first pull, I manage to squirt everybody standing over me and myself, in the eye. The second pull is unsuccessful in that nothing whatsoever comes out. The cow, a mangy, manure-encrusted and matronly creature, turns her head and regards me woefully. Kendusha, you'd better do this, I say. I think she is going to bite or kick me if I don't stop. So she finishes and we take the milk back to the house. And then it's time to plant tobacco. I'll help, I offer. Peija is in disagreement with this plan, I can see it in his pinched expression. It isn't seemly for me. I am a guest, a foreigner, who is dressed inappropriately and will probably plant the seeds wrong, too deep or too shallow. But I persevere, imagining the stories I will tell Taik and Bruno when I return to Germany, how I planted tobacco, how I milked the cows…As we walk down to the tobacco fields, I notice that there are no garbage cans in the village. There is really no garbage. Everything is grown in the garden, slaughtered, made by hand. It all biodegrades. But strangely, there are old shoes everywhere, of every style, color, shape, crumpled along the side of the road, resting under bushes, lying in ditches and one even hanging from a tree branch.

After I take a long rake-like tool and create lines in the earth for the tobacco seeds, (I have decided this constitutes planting tobacco), I prepare to take a walk to the next village to deliver a letter to the parents of a Croatian friend living in New York. They have a horse, I have been told, and I mean to take a ride on it. The plan to go to the village, unfortunately, necessitates an escort. It would not look right for a guest and a foreigner to walk alone in the area. I might get lost. I might embarrass myself. So Stjepan goes with me, and, even though the village is a mere quarter of a mile down the road, we take the car, make a big entrance. Once again we are surrounded by villagers. The recipients of the letter burst into tears, both the father and the mother, and, when they have composed themselves, ask me one question after another about their son, greedy for details, impressions, hungry for descriptions, every little thing, the length of his hair, whether he is losing any of it, whether he has a girlfriend, whether she's Catholic....They offer us coffee, liqueurs, platefuls of pastries and trays of smoked meats. But all I want is to ride their horse. Ride the horse? they ask incredulously. Animals in the village serve a purpose, they are not to play with, to ride, to pet, to pamper. They have a role like every other member of the family, and the loss of or injury to one of them represents a great tragedy to the owners. Just for a few minutes! I tell them. I know how to ride! They reluctantly lead old Blaze, a raggedy yet robust chestnut, with long forelock and clotted tail, out of the barn. There is no saddle, of course, so they throw an old blanket over his broad back. When I am astride, I take the reins in my hands and give him a kick. He is baffled for a moment until his primordial memory kicks in. He is a horse and he is being ridden. Old Blaze takes off at a canter up the hill, leaving my entourage behind, slack-jawed and frozen with fear. The horse is running away with her, the American is going to fall off and die! Her death will bring dishonor upon her hosts, and, by extension, the entire village, all of Croatia! They begin to chase me up the hill, as though they mean to grab old Blaze's tail and pull him to a stop before I am catapulted into the air prior to breaking my back. But Blaze and I are one, I could no sooner fall off his back than a star could fall out of the sky. We come to a stop at the top of the hill, both breathless with excitement. Blaze has not had this much fun in years. Oh, we thought he had run away with you! the anxious parents say as they scurry up to us. You'd better walk back down the hill, they urge me. It's better. So I dismount, pat old Blaze on his soft muzzle and walk back down the hill. I am finding it very difficult to have what I consider fun in the village.

My nieces and nephews live down the road from Kendusha and Peija. They are the children of Taik's oldest brother, the one we had visited years ago in a worker's camp in Germany, and they want to play with me, listen to me speak Croatian so they can snicker behind their dirty fists. Let's go for a walk! they tell me. Since I am not alone, Kendusha and Peija approve. The two of them, Milena and Zdravko take my arm and pull me behind them as though I were a household pet, parade me in front of their friends, who laugh and turn red in the face when I look their way. We pass a pigsty, something I have never seen close up. Wait, I tell them, I want to look at the pig! It is a hilarious and filthy animal, obscenely grotesque, from its crusty snout to its strangely dainty hooves. The children are astounded that I have any interest whatsoever in a common pig; they stand behind me impatiently, shuffling their feet in the dirt and smirking. At the top of the road, we come to a small house on the left. A peasant woman emerges and walks right up to me. Who are you? she demands. I tell her. She gives me her name, which I recognize. Her son and Taik are old friends. We have visited him often in West Germany, where he now lives. I even know her son's childhood nickname. You're Kutlesha's mother! I exclaim. She screeches with pleasure, grabs me in her arms. I must tell her everything I know about her son, I embellish upon much of it, just to provide her more pleasure. Who knows when or if she will see him again before she dies?

By the time we return to the house, word about my encounter with Kutlesha's mother has spread throughout the village. Peija is filled with mirth, proud of me for knowing these little details of Gorica's history. Nevista knows everything! he says. I do, I tell him, I know all about the woman down the road who used to get thrown out of the window, I know about Ikina, Panjac, everybody… They are amazed and delighted. Now I am even more a part of the family and the village, the intimacy we share grows moment by moment.

Stjepan suggests that we pay one of his uncles, Panjac, a visit. I agree, so we set off down the road to his house, which is in the middle of a flat, dry field. He greets us effusively. Who has not greeted us so? This nation is a nation of hosts and hostesses, people who delight in the company of others, who delight in giving and sharing what they have with others. We are sat down by Panjac' wife while refreshments are prepared. Stjepan and Panjac reminisce about the past, including me from time to time, especially when Taik's name is mentioned. I daydream, though, as they speak, because I am not able to understand much, their speech has fallen into the local dialect. At one point, however, my attention becomes focused on their conversation. First, I hear Taik's name and, second, the word "eye". Am I mistaken or are they discussing Taik's eye? I listen closely, hoping for more details about the terrific kick in the eye Taik had received from the cow when he was a small boy. They are talking about a tree or a stick, though, and a big snow, which prevented Taik from being taken to a hospital. Or did he finally go? He could have lost them both! I think I understand Panjac to say. I am frustrated, unable to grasp the fine details of the narrative, too proud to ask questions. After all, as Taik's wife, I should be privy to this information, I should have no need for further clarification. If only we could leave and return to Peija and Kendusha! I am finding it impossible to accept the horrible reality of what I think I have heard: Taik, the man I have lived with for over five years only has one eye. This can't be true, though, because a wife would know such things, a husband would tell a wife if he were missing something, if he had some disease, some disability, just in case the wife lacked character and wished to exchange him for a more perfect specimen. A wife should know such things for a hundred different reasons! Finally Stjepan gets up, tells me it's time to go. We make our farewells, head up the path to Taik's house. Stjepan, I begin slowly, tell me all about when Taik lost his eye. Didn't he tell you all the details? he asks. Yes, he did, but I want to hear what you remember, I manage to say, your version. It is true, then. I have been at least half blind myself, did not know that my own husband has one eye, couldn't figure it out for myself. The shame of it, the thought that I, his own wife, did not know such an elementary fact about him! I feel faint and dizzy at the enormity of my ignorance. Do I know this man at all? If his physical reality escapes me, what of his inner life, his inner essence? It is as though I am suddenly confronted with the possibility that I know nothing whatsoever about the man I love, my husband, my confidant and best friend. What are the reasons for his secrecy, his silence? I am assailed by doubts. He doesn't trust me, he doesn't believe in my love, perhaps fears abandonment if his infirmities are known? An insulting proposition. I am forced to abandon it as being unworthy of him and of me. When we were in grade school, Stjepan begins, we were playing in the field near Panjac's house. We had branches in our hands, pulled from one of the small trees, and were fighting with them. Somehow, Taik fell on one of them or else got poked in the eye, nobody knows exactly. His eye got infected, but there was so much snow that the roads were impassable, my parents couldn't get him to a doctor. By the time the snows melted, the eye was too far gone. He almost lost the other eye as well. So he has a glass eye they put in when he was small? I ask. Yes, Stjepan says. I can see his two eyes in my mind, the larger one, which has a lot more white in it and moves around more quickly, and the other, the impostor, which has a charm, too, all its own. It is smaller, darker, but gives his face in profile a certain impish quality I had noticed when we had first met. I just didn't know why. He hasn't outgrown the eye he got as a child, though. It fits him somehow, it is part of his allure, his mystery. Against my will, I begin to cry quietly, at the injustice of Taik's silence, about his suffering, both as a one-eyed child and a one-eyed adult, at his suffering in general, and for myself, who suddenly feels she knows nobody, and nobody knows her. Stjepan walks ahead of me, singing softly, oblivious to my pain.

It is Tito`s birthday and in every village we pass in the car, long banners are stretched from building to building proclaiming "We are Tito's and Tito is ours!" I find this an obnoxious manifestation of the cult of personality and say so. Stjepan tells me the population is forced to do this; they have no choice. We are driving around the area, stopping here and there to deliver messages from exiled sons and daughters in America to their aging parents and disenfranchised siblings. There are so many tears, so many tortured faces begging me for information, for details about the loved ones who cannot return home. It is an exhausting task, but one which I do gladly. After all, Taik cannot come home, either. I am the link between the lost sons and daughters and the families they can neither see nor touch nor comfort.

When we are finished, we decide to have a glass of wine at a roadside bar up in the mountains. The family that owns this bar is a very well-known nationalist family, Stjepan tells me. It seems they are notorious in this part of Hercegovina. We go in and sit at the counter. There is a table of four men in the corner, playing cards quietly; otherwise, the place is empty. A man comes out from a back room and asks us what we want. We get into a conversation with him as we drink our wine. I'm from America, I tell him. He has relatives in Chicago and New York, asks me questions about people he knows there, as though America were a small village where everybody knows everybody else. The card players stop their game and come to the bar, sensing that something interesting might be about to happen. We buy them drinks, continue to talk, about America, Boston, Florida, about their relatives who cannot return. On the wall of the bar is the obligatory picture of President Tito. Emboldened by an excess of wine, I ask the men if they have to keep the picture up there. They seem stunned, as though they had just been confronted with the existence of the picture which had, no doubt, been hanging over that same rectangle of wall for many years. The man behind the bar suddenly says No! We don't have to keep the picture up there! and runs into the back room, coming out with two other dusty pictures, one of the former Croatian Peasant Party leader, Stjepan Radic, and one of the first Croatian King, Tomislav. He yanks Tito off the wall and throws him under the counter, replacing him with Radic and King Tomislav. By now, the men are talking loudly. Two of them are singing Croatian songs, heads together, a drink in one hand. The bar has been transformed. We finish our drinks and leave quietly. Nobody seems to notice.

Back in Gorica, I sit in front of the house, leafing through my nieces' and nephews' schoolbooks. They are divided into chapters, one of which is titled "The Return of the Communist Heroes". Curious to read this account, I turn to page 29. It is missing. So is page 30. On page 31 begins another unrelated chapter. What happened to the chapter on the Communist heroes? I ask one of my nephews. I don't know, he says innocently. Somebody must have ripped it out! His attitude is similar to that of one of the village women, who tells me she never listens to her fancy radio sent by her son from West Germany. Why not? I ask. After all, there are no televisions, no stereos, in the village. It seems to me that a radio would be a highly-coveted item, one which would enjoy extensive use. Who wants to listen to their lies all day long? she had answered. So the fancy radio gathers dust. After all, the government cannot force them to turn it on, just as they cannot be forced to read a book they are issued in school. It is a freedom they zealously protect and exercise, children and adults alike.

Stjepan tells me we will have one more night in Gorica. Then we must head back to Germany to meet up with Taik and Bruno. I regret having to leave the village, the new friends I have made, I don't want to be parted from Peija and Kendusha, who have taken me to their hearts as though I were their own daughter. Gorica is a magical spot, a bright patch of earth unlike any other; in spite of its barrenness, its rocky hills and dry fields, in spite of its poverty, the force of the collective personality of its inhabitants, the bony donkeys and the barnyard dogs, the gangs of dusty kids and the old women dressed like ferocious crows, draws one to it involuntarily. It attracts. One wants to stay there forever; at least I do.

We sit up and talk until very late in the morning, aware that our time together is slipping away. When I finally lie down in Taik's old bed, I cannot sleep. After lying awake for at least an hour, I need to urinate, so I head for the outhouse at the top of the hill above the house. It is raining and the stone steps are slick. There are no lights, it is a black and stormy night, and I am guided only by a narrow footpath extending beyond the top of the stairs. The door to the outhouse is open, so I enter and position myself in the air, hoping I will hit the hole and not spray myself instead. When I am finished, I head back down, but the steps are so slick that I slip on the top one and bounce down the entire flight on my rear end, landing at the bottom with a thud. I am grateful that there are no lights and that nobody can have been watching me from a window or a porch. My dignity, along with my rear end, has been damaged. But that isn't all, I realize when I wipe my gravelly hands on my legs. One of my long, red, false fingernails has been knocked off in the course of my downward journey. I feel around for it on the ground, moving my hands over the stones inch by inch, but it is pitch black and the rain is pouring down on my back. I am finally forced to give up the search; it is too dark, too unfamiliar. But I can't simply leave it there to be found later! What will Peija and Kendusha think? Will they even know what it is if they come upon it in the morning? I will have to put a bandaid on the nailless finger and hope for the best. And if the impostor nail is discovered, perhaps it too will play an integral role in one of the many mysteries of Gorica handed down from generation to generation.

In the morning, we are all glum, knowing we are soon to be separated. Nobody feels like speaking or making conversation, though we force ourselves to do it. Peija goes out to kill a chicken so that Kendusha can boil it for us to eat along the way. Meanwhile, she pulls some fresh onions and picks some tomatoes from the garden. A fresh loaf of bread is included as well, with a chunk of cheese to go along with it. There! she says when everything is packed in a big paper bag. We walk together to the car, avoiding each other's eyes. Peija trails behind us, a grim expression on his face, as though he is being asked to witness a gruesome crime or to kill the family dog. But there can be no storm without rain and no farewell without tears, as much as we wish to be brave and stoic.

I hold Kendusha tightly in my arms, my tears spilling out onto her ample shoulder upon which I rest my cheek. She, too, is weeping with full abandon, her chest heaving, her body shaking. We will come back soon, I tell her. And Taik will be with us, too, you'll see! She wants to believe me, but what she knows of life tells her otherwise, and she shakes her head violently back and forth. There, there, I say, and push her gently away. Peija steps up, holds me for a short moment in tense arms. Take care of yourself, Nevista, he says, and steps back. And then we are gone, bouncing down the dirt road, heading for Germany, away from Gorica, from Hercegovina, from Croatia, from Taik's home, to which he may never return. The desolation and despair I feel is almost intolerable. How can the Croatians, or any exiled nation, live day to day with such feelings, how can they survive this suffering? I feel I want to die if life is so unjust, so cruel. Who can love life, knowing what arbitrary pain it contains?

The journey back towards Austria goes quickly. I take no mental notes, refuse to notice the scenery we pass, the cows grazing, the old women selling cheese by the side of the road, as though, by refusing to acknowledge the reality of my departure, the feelings of loss and rage cannot exist.

We're coming to the border, Stjepan tells me. I suddenly realize that Bruno's papers are still in my purse. Perhaps that is the safest place for them. I decide to leave them there, come what may. But the Yugoslav guards are more concerned with those who are entering and not leaving the country and barely glance at the contents of our car or our passports. And the Austrians don't care, either. I am somehow disappointed that my secret mission has been completed so uneventfully. I almost wish to be thrown into prison once again, so that I will not have to leave the country. If Taik cannot return home, I can at least stay, keep the bond strong.

As soon as we reach the train station, we stop so that I can call Taik and tell him we are out of Croatia and on our way to Germany. He is happy to hear my voice, but wants to wait until we are together for a report on my visit. Did you get the papers? he asks. I think so, I tell him. Everything went smoothly. Good, good! he says. I'll see you soon!

At least I have accomplished something of value on my trip. Bruno will have his papers, his identification, so that he can verify his accomplishments, justify his need for political asylum. Will this be enough for him? He, too, wants more than all else to go home.

It is early in the evening when we arrive at Bosnjak's restaurant, where we are to meet Taik and Bruno. I feel as though I have been on a long odyssey, traveling not only through space and time but a different consciousness as well. I jump out of the car, go into the restaurant, anxious, searching the room for Taik's familiar form. I feel I will perish if I am not reunited with him without further delay, I need him, I want him, I have revelations to share with him, about our love, our life, our destiny. He is standing by the bar, his back to me. Taik, I call out, I'm back! He turns around, sees me running to him with open arms. I jump into them, kiss him full on the mouth, in spite of the customers and Croatians watching us. He maintains a cool facade, but I am not fooled, I can see the emotion in his eyes, and he is trembling slightly with anxiousness or perhaps joy. And then Bruno emerges from one of the back rooms. Nevista! he says, and gives me a tremendous hug. We missed you! But Bruno and Taik were with me the entire time, I saw through their eyes, felt with their hearts. Can they see that I am changed? I am a person transformed. Now I know their suffering, and it has become my own.

The three of us go for a walk. I begin to tell them of my journey, which, however, has only just begun. And I give Bruno the papers, proudly, confident that I have done him a great service. He shuffles through them, clearly disappointed. What's wrong? I ask nervously. Aren't they the right ones? He doesn't want to hurt me, but he is too honest to dissemble. These will help a little, but they aren't the ones I was hoping you would bring. It's OK, Nevista, you did your best! He touches my cheek with the back of one of his hands, so gently that I want to cry.

This man is such a tender and loving being! There were boxes and boxes of papers, I didn't know what to look for, so I left it up to the others! I tell him. It's not your fault. You did your best, he says. But I am not to be pacified. I can go back tomorrow, I want to, I don't mind at all! I can take the train and be back in a day or two! I say. They consider this idea and decide it is unwise. Why push my luck? This time I might be followed, the papers could get confiscated, I could be arrested.

Taik tells me the three of us are going to Paris tomorrow. But first I have to get a visa in Frankfurt, he says. There's no consulate here in Karlsruhe. Paris! I am thrilled. And Bruno can show us the city in which he lived and studied for three years. He speaks French fluently, at least with those who take the time to decipher his speech and don't automatically assume he is retarded or worse.

In Frankfurt, though, Taik is denied a visa. He has only his green card and the French, for some abstruse reason, refuse to grant him one without lengthy consultations with an official who is out of town for the next week. Now what can we do? I ask them. We can't go to Paris! We'll think of something, Taik says. Meanwhile, Taik and I go to a coffeehouse while Bruno makes some phone calls. I have not yet spoken to Taik about my discovery that he has lost an eye, have been waiting for the perfect moment. I feel both the anger and the tenderness welling up within me once again as I think about his deception and the possible reasons for it. We order two coffees and, when we are served, I begin to talk to him, tell him about Gorica, about the horse, the missing pages in the book, the bar high on the hill. And we visited your uncle Panjac, I add nonchalantly. He told me about how you lost your eye. I am stirring my coffee, trying to dissolve the sugar, but I can't help looking up at him for his reaction. Yeah? he says. And this is all. He has nothing more to say, seems to expect me to go on. But I am lost. What more is there to say? So he has only one eye. Has anything changed? It hasn't. Would anything have been different if he had told me? It would not. You should have told me! I blurt out. I have to do something with the anger I feel towards him for the humiliation I suffered in Gorica. I have to travel to another continent to only accidentally stumble over the truth! If it were left up to Taik, I would never know. You never wanted me to touch your eyes, I tell him sadly. He looks at me, as though trying to understand exactly what I am feeling. I didn't need to tell you, Julie. It wouldn't have made any difference, would it? He is right, after all. But if this is just one of many things I do not know, the man I love and have married will always be a mystery to me. The certainty of having finally understood the essence of Taik, the truth I discovered in Gorica and driving through Croatia has now become only a possibility, a possible truth. But Bruno returns before we can say anything more. I am relieved. What more is there to say? Let's go back to the hotel, Taik suggests.

The hotel we are staying in is next to the train station. We have taken just one room in which all three of us sleep. It is safer this way. We can keep an eye on Bruno. As we walk to the hotel entrance, a husky man in a gray, somewhat rumpled suit approaches Bruno. They seem to be acquainted, because Bruno stops and talks for a few moments. Who was that? I ask him when he rejoins us. It was an UDBA agent I know from home, he says. What did he want? I demand, immediately protective of Bruno, aghast that it is so simple for one of his enemies to approach him. He could have shot him, he could have had a gun! He just wanted to make his presence known, put a little pressure on me, Bruno answers with a slow smile. He and Taik are used to these psychological games; in fact, they welcome them as an opportunity to hone their skills and use their resources.

I am unnerved, though, that Bruno is so accessible. When we go into our hotel room, Taik automatically checks the little odds and ends he has positioned around the door to ascertain whether anybody has been in the room. It seems the room has not been disturbed, we can safely enter.

But before we leave, Taik decides to call his old friend from Gorica, Kutlesha, so that I can tell him about my encounter with his mother in Gorica, how I was the talk of the village for knowing his nickname. But when he calls, Kutlesha tells him it is better not to see each other. It seems the last time he was home, he was called to Mostar to be interrogated by the UDBA, who told him to invite Taik to dinner the next time they met. Other dissidents had been in prison, many several times. Some had been murdered. Taik had escaped their fate. They wanted to make sure it befell him as well, Kutlesha was told. We decide not to go to Kutlesha's. We are all in foul moods.

One of Bruno's Croatian friends solves Taik's visa problem, tells us that he and his family often drive over a little-used border crossing to dine at a restaurant which lies just on the other side of the border in France. The guards know him and he believes they will simply wave us across if he were to drive us. It sounds like a good idea, so we set off in that direction. It is as easy as he has described it. The guards wave us through, hardly giving us a glance, and we find ourselves in France! From here we will take a train to Paris.

Bruno knows a good, small hotel near the Luxembourg gardens, the Hotel des Mines, and it is here we will live for the next month or so. The proprietor knows him and is aware of his situation. He never gives out information about whether Bruno might be registered and does not allow strangers to loiter around; he also has some vague connection with the French police and is therefore able to pass on information to Bruno from time to time. I am a little curious about our reasons for being in Paris, but I know that sooner or later I will be enlightened. Perhaps it is to visit Dane, one of the more well-known victims of Yugoslav assassination squads, a friend of Bosnjak's. The Yugoslavs had tried twice to kill him, the first time in Karlsruhe, where they had shot at him and missed, and the second time in Paris, this time pumping him with bullets from head to toe. Yet he had refused to die. He had gone underground, though, and was rarely seen in public. Bruno and Taik surely know his whereabouts, though, and most likely want to see him. Perhaps Bruno simply wants to relax and enjoy Paris, his favorite city in Western Europe. He needs to be able to relax, to have some moments of happiness and solitude and forget about the reports he has received of his imminent death. I am often overwhelmed by the situation in which Taik and Bruno find themselves. And I, I am right in the middle of it.

Bruno insists that we have separate rooms in the hotel. After all, we will be living there for at least a month, and married people must have their privacy! He will be just down the hall, he can call out if he needs something or make a loud noise. Our rooms are on the fourth floor, overlooking the Boulevard Saint Michel. They are simple yet clean, containing beds, a small table with chairs and the ubiquitous bidet. The toilet is between our room and Bruno's, halfway down the hall, and there is a room with a bathtub on the ground floor.

The first day we walk all over town, led by Bruno, who remembers this and that spot from his student days, La Palette, for example, where he used to see Francoise Sagan drinking coffee in the morning; we go there and have a beer, but it is loud and smoky and we don't stay long. He takes us through little side streets to restaurants that are cheap but good, little holes in the wall that are frequented only by Parisians or those who have lived there. He points out an apartment above one of these restaurants, a corner room on the second floor. I used to live there, with a Basque woman, he tells us. He is lost in his memories, which I can tell, by the soft look around his eyes and mouth, are tender.

Bruno loves women, loves to look at them and flirt with them. He comments on their gestures, their physical condition, the clothes they have chosen on that particular day, the shoes, whether they match or not, whether the entire impression is aesthetically pleasing. I am envious of the attention he shows for other women. What's wrong, Nevista? he sometimes says. He is sensitive to every nuance of one's behavior. It is difficult to hide things from Bruno, who, after all, is an artist, a writer, whose life's passion depends upon knowing people and writing about them. Nothing, I say, but I am certain he can read my every thought. He must, for he immediately focuses his attention on me, talks to me about

Faulkner, Pablo Neruda, who are two of his favorites, asks me which writers I like, wants to know why...

Bruno has a friend in Paris, Vladimir, whose brother has been in prison in Yugoslavia for many years and is permanently crippled due to torture by the Yugoslav police. Vladimir's mother lives with him in Paris. Unable to visit her imprisoned son, she has sought comfort from the other son living in exile. We are going to pay them a visit, say hello. Bruno knows the son in prison as well, doesn't expect him, he tells us confidentially, to get out of prison alive. He's been damaged too badly, he says. One of the few times his mother was allowed to visit him, he didn't even recognize her.

Vladimir and his mother are delighted to see us. The mother disappears immediately into the kitchen, returning soon thereafter with large platters of smoked ham, cheeses, peppers, fresh scallions. Bottles of wine and beer are brought out as well, good French wines and German beer. The men talk with each other in low voices and I am able to understand very little. But I know what to do in such situations: drink wine and eat. Before too long, I am lost in daydreams and don't care whether anybody talks to me or not. This time, though, I am drawn to the conversation, especially when the little wrinkled raisin of a mother returns and sits down with us. She wants to be congenial, to laugh and talk and be carefree, here in Gay Paree, but the subject inevitably turns to the imprisoned son. Before too long, she is weeping uncontrollably. The men try to comfort her with quiet words, but she will not be comforted nor quieted. My son, my son! she wails. He doesn't even know his own mother when she goes to visit him! He can barely open his eyes! How many more years does the son have to serve? I ask Taik in German. Eight more, he says. He'll never make it.

Walking down to the Metro after our visit, I hold tightly to the arms of both Taik and Bruno, as though in this way we cannot ever be separated and no harm can come to either of them. After all, I am an American, with the weight of my entire government behind me. Yugoslav agents wouldn't dare lay a finger on us as long as I am with them!

It seems Bruno has many friends in Paris, and we visit most of them in their apartments or meet them in cafes. One of the men lives in Belleville, a section of Paris inhabited mostly by Arabs; a decidedly un-French atmosphere pervades the entire quarter. On every corner there is a table with a group of dark men standing around it, playing some obscure card game or watching the others. The smells are different, too; spicy and exotic ribbons of aroma drift out of tiny, cavernous cafes along the street. The Arabs smoke cigarettes that evoke cinnamon or cloves and wear hair oil that seems to have been squeezed from the bark of an olive tree. It is dark and noisy in Belleville, and one feels the proximity of danger; the danger of incomprehension, of intolerance, or perhaps it is the danger of being separate and different. We don't belong.

Bruno's friend, an older, kindly man by the name of Brnadich, appears, however, to feel at home in Belleville. There seems to be a sense of camaraderie among those who don't belong, even though they don't belong to each other, either. When we leave for our hotel, I am relieved. The visit has been exhausting somehow, and I have found it difficult to lose myself in daydreams, despite the many glasses of wine I have drunk.

The next morning, Taik and Bruno want to visit this man who survived by sheer will so many Yugoslav bullets. Though I would like to meet him, I feel I can't possibly endure another story of pain and suffering, injustice, oppression, assassination attempts, bullets, blood…. Instead I stay behind to walk the streets of Paris, to sit in cafes and write postcards, buy strange French foods, such as sandwiches dipped in egg batter and deep fried. (I eat one and take one back to the hotel with me.) There are street people everywhere, there are acrobats, mimes, musicians and artists drawing pictures with colored chalk on the sidewalk. I feel I could live the rest of my life in Paris. I feel I could live my life in Gorica as well. How is it that I can simply lay my heart down all over the world? Is it that I truly belong nowhere? But the bond I feel toward Gorica and, by extension, Croatia, is not imagined. And I somehow feel a part of Paris as well. This strange sense of belonging—its essence escapes me. I only know what I feel.

When Bruno and Taik return, they find me lying on our bed eating the second of the egg-dipped sandwiches and wiping my greasy fingers on a towel. They both want to take a nap, immediately, so I leave them to sleep. The visit with the man who refused to die has taken their strength from them, left them withered and pale.

The hotel includes breakfast in the price of the room. Every morning, the proprietor calls to our rooms to wake us, and we file downstairs to have golden, fresh croissants, sweet butter and strawberry preserves. The coffee is dark and strong, even though we have it made with milk and not water. One rainy morning, the proprietor pulls Bruno aside and speaks to him in a low voice. When Bruno returns to the table, he tells us that the French do not want him in the country, that they are afraid for his safety. They have gotten reports that the Yugoslavs have sent somebody to kill him. Well, as you know it's not the first time I've heard that, he says. They told me the same thing the last time I was here! But Bruno loves Paris and keeps coming back, even though they refuse to grant him political asylum in France.

The days pass with long walks around the city. When we are tired, we spend hours at one of the larger coffeehouses, such as the Deux Magots or the Select, watching people and drinking coffee. Sometimes we have our pictures taken, arms draped around each other, standing on one of the bridges or sitting on a stone wall near Notre Dame. We feel like a real family together, sharing everything, looking out for one another, but behind it all is a sense of transience which colors everything we do and say. This can't last forever! I tell myself, though I don't know why. It is simply something I feel deep in my soul.

We have finished whatever we had to do in Paris. I include myself, even though I have no idea what it was we did. As far as I can determine, we ate many meals in obscure but excellent restaurants, drank dozens of cups of coffee in cafes all over the city, visited Croatians who had been tortured, shot, threatened and lived to tell about it. We talked and talked, until late into the night at times, about our childhoods, about authors we like and why, bought French pastries, French wines, wrote lots of postcards (at least I did), and went to one museum, the Louvre. (I went alone.) Are we simply spending time with Bruno in case we never have the opportunity again? This is what I believe. We will return to New York and Bruno will stay behind, moving around from country to country, a step ahead of his pursuers....

He is sitting on our bed in the hotel, his hands in his lap. Bruno has beautiful hands, his fingers are long and slender, artist's hands, and his wrist bones delicate, like smooth shells covered with sand. He always knows what to do with his hands, they never look awkward or ill-placed, just as he always knows what to do with himself, where to be and when, what to say and exactly how to say it. But it comes naturally, it is all effortless for him, anybody can see that. And yet he provokes no envy; he is liked and respected by everyone we meet, worshipped even.

So we are leaving tomorrow? I ask. Are you sad, Nevista? Bruno wants to know. Yes, I tell him. I love Paris. He understands. He, too, loves Paris, but he can't stay any longer. He will always have to go. Taik tells me we are taking a train back to Cologne, and from there we'll go to a small town outside the city, to a hotel near a Croatian restaurant owned by friends of Bruno. We can eat all our meals without cost at the restaurant and the hotel bill is taken care of for a month, he says. I wonder who is paying for all this and why, but with Bruno along, I suspect we would never have to pay for anything.

When we have gathered all our belongings together and gone to the train station, we board the train and settle down into one of the compartments before anyone has a chance to take the window seats or to make themselves at home. Before I know it, we have arrived in Germany.

The name of the small town is Porz. I have never heard of it before, but it is strangely attractive, not unlike a resort or a place where one might come to cure an allergy or heal the lungs. There is a river running along one side of the town, and small, colorful pleasure boats sail up and down all day long. The center of Porz includes a post office, a theater and various small specialty shops. Like the rest of Germany, the streets are spotless, everything is sterile. I long for the disarray of Paris, for the absence of rules and expectations, it is soothing somehow, allows for the possibility of change and creation, perhaps even revolution. But we are in Porz now and must make the best of it. Our hotel is nothing more than a large, well-kept house with a bar on the ground floor. We have two rooms adjacent to one another and our room has a balcony overlooking a garden. Right away, we want to walk to the restaurant, so we take a path along the river. The restaurant is a fancy affair, with a half-moon terrace outside and a split level dining room on the inside. The food is a combination, both Croatian and German, but we, as usual, prefer the familiar Croatian dishes, the spicy goulash, the shish kebabs and the paprika rice. Word has spread that Bruno is here. The place suddenly fills up with Croatians, they have come from all over, out of curiosity, respect, a sense of duty and loyalty. I am introduced, too, as both Taik's wife and as the one who threw the leaflets from the skyscraper. A balding, congenial man dressed flamboyantly in a peach, three-piece suit hands Taik two hundred marks. Buy your wife some flowers! he tells him expansively.

We drink and eat and talk with one Croatian after another. Most of them must content themselves with sitting at adjoining tables, we have room for only four people. There are ex-Partisans, ex-Ustashi and Domobrans; names such as Crljen, Mikulic, Beban, Jelic are mentioned. Some are young, some are very old, so old that they must be helped up from their seats. Bruno seems to have brought them all together, eradicated their political and philosophical differences. Now they are willing and ready to work with one another toward their common goal: an independent Croatia. The atmosphere surrounding Bruno is one of respectful attention. Nobody dares to ask him to repeat himself, as though it is a secret that he has a speech defect. But I am proud that I understand most of what he says and also that I could ask him this without embarrassment. He has allowed himself to be vulnerable to me and I have reciprocated. Only with Taik have I known this type of intimacy. It comes as a revelation to me that it can happen twice in a lifetime.

After we eat, we return to the hotel. It is dark outside, and the path we walk along is deserted. Shouldn't we take the street back? I ask Taik. But he and Bruno seem to think we are safe, so I swallow my apprehension. After all, they are the ones in danger, Bruno even more than Taik. They must know how to take care of themselves. Bruno carries a gun, I have seen it, but it does not fit him, it looks funny in his hand, as though there should be a pen, a paintbrush there instead of the cold piece of metal. I am sure he can use it, though, or he wouldn't have it around. He may not look like a gunman, but if he has to learn something, he learns it well.

Sometimes he puts it in my purse, not as a joke, which is what I first think, but as a sign of complicity, a way of including me in everything that is happening in his life. When I hang the purse strap from my shoulder, I can feel the extra weight, which is like an friendly anchor, and when Bruno is not with me, this piece of metal serves as a bond between us.

The days at the hotel pass, punctuated with meals three times a day. Much of the time, Bruno is writing in his room. In the mornings, he and Taik go over some of what he has written, which, as far as I can tell, is a political document. Pages and pages of paper are scattered over his bed, some wadded into balls, some marked with red pencil, and on top of his small desk is a stack of books and more paper. One night when we are in bed, Taik tells me Bruno is writing a leaflet to be used in an eventual publicity event. Like the hijacking of an American plane? I think to myself. Perhaps Bruno, too, must feel that desperate action is necessary, and this thought depresses me. I would much prefer to believe that Taik has been suffering a sense of personal desperation which will wane in time. If Bruno were to share his view I would be stunned. Are there no other alternatives, in his experience, which could prevent future assassinations and focus the world's attention on the plight of the Croatians? I cannot think of any. The Croatians have a strange, unfounded faith in America. But I have been at Croatian demonstrations, consistently ignored by the American newspapers and television stations; I have seen the paid ads in major publications, forgotten by the readers the next day or even the same afternoon. Croatian political prisoners languish in prison, lose their sight, their minds, their sanity, often their lives, and nothing is heard about them anywhere. But one can always read about Scharansky or Mandela, whose imprisonments somehow suit the myriad political machinations of the American government. Taik and perhaps even Bruno believe a hijacking, begun on American soil, is the only hope, that the basic fairness and decency of the American public will prevail, leading to a complete investigation of all allegations and a total renunciation of all U.S. ties to the terrorist Yugoslav government and its paid assassins. After all, they reason, Croatians are essentially anti-Communist and have always identified with Western culture. They subscribe to all the highest ideals of American thought: self-determination, freedom of speech and religion, democracy... It all makes sense to me, everything they say makes sense, but they have forgotten one thing: Americans have not been the victims of recent imperialism. They find it difficult to identify with the passions underlying all liberation movements. Americans don't like hijackings, I say reasonably. For whatever the reason. But it has been decided. And others have probably agreed, perhaps the Paris Croatians or the Cologne Croatians. It is also possible that noone else has been consulted. After all, they can hardly take a vote among the exiled Croatian community!

One afternoon we take a trip by streetcar into Cologne, visit the huge cathedral in the center of town, buy a few books and some writing paper. After we finish, we have a cup of tea in one of the little cafes we pass during our walk. Bruno is quiet, stirs his tea slowly and thoughtfully. Then he looks up at me. What are you thinking about, Nevista? he asks. I am thinking, but don't tell him, about the hijacking, that I will get on the plane with Taik and suffer along with him any possible repercussions. Imprisonment, death, humiliation? Somehow the latter bothers me most, the loss of dignity one must invariably suffer when one thrusts oneself into the public eye in such a way. Meanwhile, it appears that I have committed myself to this act. It is done. I am reminded, to my displeasure, of the colonist in George Orwell's essay, "Shooting an Elephant", whose motives and intentions were noble, but thoroughly and completely misunderstood by all but himself.

Bruno and Taik have to meet somebody, so they leave me behind to take the streetcar back to the hotel. While I am standing on the platform, a familiar face from America suddenly appears in front of me. It is Ante from Chicago! What are you doing here? I ask. He is here to visit friends, he says. That can cover almost everything, and we both know it. Where's Zvonko? he wants to know. Gone to meet somebody, I say. Is Bruno with him? he asks. I hesitate. Is it safe? Yes, he is, I answer. After all, I have got to trust my intuition from time to time. Taik and Bruno cannot always be with me, monitoring my every response. Tell them I'll see them in a day or two, will you? he says. I agree to deliver the message and we part. Sitting securely in the streetcar, it occurs to me that I could simply disappear, apply for a work visa and find a job in some small town. Taik and Bruno would never find me and I would never again be confronted with such things as hijackings, murders and political intrigue, all of which are entirely outside my realm of comprehension. It is a tempting daydream. Instead, I get out at the hotel stop and return to our room. I am alone. At one in the morning, I climb into bed, but the strange consciousness which overcomes me whenever Taik is near awakens me from a deep sleep. I sit up and listen. Outside, there is dead silence. But I cannot be wrong, this strange telepathy has never failed me before. Sure enough, after about five minutes, I hear somebody climbing up the side of the hotel, I see a hand clamped over the railing on the balcony, Taik's hand. What are you doing? I demand, hands on hips. You locked us out! he says. Well, go back down to the door before you break your neck! I tell him. Bruno is below, a dark figure, but I hear him laughing. How did you know we were there, Nevista? he asks me when we are all inside. She always wakes up when I'm near, Taik says. Isn't it bizarre?

Bruno has finally finished the document he has been writing and it is time for us to return to America. Packing our things, I stop many times, unable to continue. It doesn't seem possible that we can simply leave Bruno behind, he has become such a part of our lives, my life. We are a family. We need each other. And Bruno is so vulnerable. Who will watch out for him? Who will make him laugh and talk about books with him, listen to his stories about this or that girlfriend? He plans to stay a few more days in Porz, so we say our goodbyes at the hotel door. He and Taik throw their arms around each other, pat each other on the shoulder. I can't look at Bruno or I will begin to cry, so I look at Taik, at the ground, at my suitcase, which I suddenly notice is not completely zipped. Nevista! he says softly. I must look up, just to see his face one more time. He cups the back of my head in his hand, pulls it to his shoulder. We hold each other for a long time and the words we say are lost to me, I only know intuitively that they are the words everybody says to assuage the pain of separation and loss. And then we are gone, and Bruno is gone, a memory now, not a physical presence. I lean on Taik, tearful, bereft. Oh, oh! I say. There are no other words which occur to me, which can possibly express the desolation I feel.

At the bus station, we buy some newspapers to read on the way to Luxembourg, where we will catch our plane to New York. I am shocked to see that on the front page of one of them is a long, sensationalist article about a wide police sweep in Cologne in the early hours of the morning of several activist Croatians' houses. A Croatian newspaper office has been closed down and it is rumored that a cache of weapons was found. Some individuals are under arrest, though no names have been released. What does this mean? I ask Taik. It's just another Yugoslav provocation, he tells me. They provide the Germans from time to time with alleged "documentation" about Croatian activities and the Germans roust the Croatians. Then when the Germans need something, the Yugoslavs return the favor.

I am quiet during our bus ride, trying to figure things out. It is still so confusing to me. I find it difficult to fathom all the intrigues, the political games and arbitrary disruption to people's lives, to their families and friends. While I am thinking, we pull up to the border and our passports are collected. What should be a quick procedure drags on and on. The other passengers begin to shift in their seats, complain first in muted and then strident tones. What's going on here? one beefy man asks. We're going to miss a flight! There's a slight delay, the driver says. It won't be much longer. But it is. After another half hour we are still sitting on the bus, which is now parked at the side of the road. Finally, one of the border guards climbs up into the bus. Will Mr. Zvonko Busic and Mrs. Busic come with me, please? All heads turn wrathfully to regard the individuals responsible for this outrage. We get up, go down the aisle. Taik is self-assured, as always, and I am contrite, as though the mere fact of my existence is enough to justify the actions of the border guards. Must I really be sorry for living? Our bags are removed from the hold of the bus and taken to an office in the border control building. Several officials paw over our belongings, removing each item individually and shaking it in the air with great fervor, as though they were dogs with a particularly juicy bone. Another hour and they are finished, obviously dissatisfied that they have been unable to uncover a devious plot, a message in code, a bloody dagger among my underwear. We climb back onto the bus and are greeted with hostile silence. Finally the same beefy man asks loudly, to noone in particular, if we could please get the goddamn bus on the road. And we are off again.

Part Three

24

"There is no pre-established harmony between the promotion of truth and the welfare of mankind." Nietzsche

The flight to New York is painlessly quick. It seems to have taken us longer to reach Luxembourg from Germany than it has to reach New York from Luxembourg. Being back in New York feels like being dropped from a great and glorious height and landing in a pile of garbage. My spirits sink, my eyes cloud over. How can I possibly survive? Sleepless nights loom once again on the horizon. There's nobody outside the door! I will have to tell Taik again. Go to sleep, go to sleep! At least we slept in Europe, we felt secure and safe, against all probabilities, since most of the political murders have, in fact, taken place on European soil. I feel I will do anything to get out of New York, where I don't belong, never have belonged...

And Bruno, what is he doing, what is he thinking, can the people around him understand what he is saying? Are they humoring him, pretending comprehension? Is he being careful, does he carry his gun with him as he should at all times?

It is summer in New York. I laugh cynically at the idea of summer as it applies to sweltering, foul-smelling New York. Summer is hot garbage, hot dog shit. At least it's frozen in the winter, doesn't emit noxious fumes into the air, befouling the atmosphere, making breathing nearly impossible. It has been decided that I must translate the document Bruno has written into English. It is a monumental task. Bruno's Croatian, while not convoluted or overly abstruse, has a special style of its own, hard to render into English, harder still for an American whose grasp of the language leaves much to be desired. But I will do it, no other will apparently do. Someone else will translate it into French, I am told, though I do not know who this person will be or whether he or she will know what use will be made of the document.

So I put on my bathing suit every day, gather together my tablet, a pen, a dictionary, a big towel and my sunscreen and go lie on the grass next to the Hudson River to work on the translation. If only the other sunbathers knew what I was doing, I often think as I lie there. And I wish I were a mere sunbather, with nothing more on my mind but a tan or a cold, refreshing drink. How easy such a life would be! But such a life is not for me. I know this, though I do not yet know why. I wonder how this knowledge can finally be imparted to me, I who have waited so long and so patiently.

The translating is tedious. Extracting meaning from the layers of text is like trying to free a coatsleeve from the teeth of a committed dog. The dog pulls. You pull harder. And then both of you pull, back and forth, until the sleeve comes free, suddenly, effortlessly, and each regains his sovereignty. What a light and airy feeling when I am able to make the words transcend cultures and continents. And I can feel Bruno in each sentence, as though he were dictating to me. Anyone who knows him knows he wrote this text.

Each day I go out in my bathing suit to work on the translation. It takes me about two weeks to finish and edit, and I am pleased with my effort. It sounds solemn yet lively. I have managed to retain Bruno's spirit and style in each sentence, a not inconsiderable feat, as his writing is like he, a combination, perfectly assembled, of disparate yet harmonious parts. Taik, too, is pleased, though his English isn't yet fluent enough to judge my effort. He trusts me to have done an excellent job. It is enough that I tell him so. And he has gotten back the French translation as well. I scan it, though my French is rusty. It looks impressive, but I wouldn't know if it were riddled with mistakes. The translation project has kept me too busy to contemplate the course our life is taking, to sit down and ask myself what I am doing and exactly why. There is still time for Taik to change his mind or for some cataclysmic event to take place which would render the hijacking plan unnecessary, such as a Russian march on Belgrade or an American decision to cut ties with Yugoslavia for human rights violations. Hahaha, what a joke, I know neither will happen in time to prevent what I have come to realize is looming in the near future. And I am powerless to assert myself. There are demons within me which prevent me from risking the possible loss of Taik's love and dedication. And the thought that Bruno might have concurred with Taik's idea makes my rebellion even more impossible. Who am I to set myself up against these two, whose knowledge and experience of the world, and especially the capabilities of the Yugoslav Secret Police, is so much greater than my own? I can only hope for the cataclysmic event, but I take little comfort in this eventuality. I may be possessed but I am still in touch, to some extent, with external reality.

Taik is in and out of the apartment constantly, sometimes gone for most of the night or even for days. The last thing in the world I want to know is where he is and what he is doing, and I am relieved that he offers me little information on the subject. He does mention, though, that he is deciding who else will be participating in the hijacking. It is an important decision, one which could mean success or tragedy, and he spends much time talking to Croatians who, unbeknownst to them, are being considered for inclusion in his plan. I don't care who they are, I tell him. I don't want to know. And then I attempt to carry on with a life which has become nothing more than a curtain pulled across a stage where the real action is taking place. Nothing I do has any meaning anymore, there is no continuity in the face of the upheaval our lives will soon undergo. The people I meet, with whom I talk and have things in common, have as little connection to me as the characters I see on television shows, the Gomer Pyles, the Ralph Kramdens, the Victoria Barkleys. Everybody in New York City, everybody in the state of New York, and most probably in the entire North American continent, will soon be excised from my life, probably forever. I can only look to myself, so I withdraw into a small room in my mind, a tidy, self-contained space in which nothing enters and nothing leaves.

And time is racing past, transforming itself into something other than the little divisions we have invented to organize our existences; it has become an amorphous mass, undistinguished by lines or sounds or angles, in which seconds, minutes, months and years are superfluous. All I know is that I am able to rise in the morning and fall into bed at night, and that the space in between the rising and the falling seems constantly to be shrinking. Soon it will be unnecessary to do anything but wait, prone, for the end of time.

It is agony to talk to my mom and dad. We take turns calling one another, I call one week, they call the next. Their voices are like blue, clear water in a dry and dying desert, echoing across the continent and coming to rest in the heart of their only, their lost daughter. There is little I can say, knowing the suffering I am soon to inflict upon them. If only they could sense my desperation and order me home, immediately, without further delay, to undergo intensive sessions of whatever magic treatment might render us safe and the action unnecessary. My mom would hold me, my dad would stand to the side frowning, a book in one hand, glasses resting on his nose. Why, that's ridiculous! they would say. You're going to do no such thing! Instead, I tell them I love and miss them very much! We hang up and I place the receiver gently into the cradle. All I can think of to do is sit, so I sit and sit, until the sun sets and the moon rises. I sense a vague connection between myself and the sun and moon, something to do with time, but it escapes me, time goes on without me.

Everything speeds up. Taik tells me the only demand he plans on submitting to the authorities is that the text be printed in major U.S. newspapers. The American public will ask why it is necessary, in a country with freedom of speech, to commit such a desperate action for publicity! he tells me. They will want to know the truth about the assassinations, the rights violations, the oppression of the Croatians, all of which are supported by American dollars, billions of American dollars! It's the only way to focus attention on these issues! He's also not just going to sit around waiting to be killed. The message I have brought him from his brother in Zagreb has strengthened his belief that his death is imminent, and has provided him with further justification for the action. There won't be weapons on the plane, nobody could possibly be hurt, he says. If I were a passenger on a plane and somebody hijacked it for the same reason, I would understand, I would support it. So would I, I tell him, but most people can't identify with your situation. It is beyond their comprehension. And what people don't understand, they fear or judge! I talk on and on, knowing nothing will change. The decision has been made. And I am unwilling to change the course our lives are taking, to take the responsibilty for what could happen otherwise.

Taik tells me to go out and buy a new dress. Is this for the hijacking? I ponder the type of dress that is appropriate for such an event. It is something I have never before contemplated. I go from store to store, trying on one after another, until I finally decide on a blue corduroy dress with a patterned insert and an empire waist. It is expensive, though, over fifty dollars. But what need do I have for money? It seems the only attachment I have is to Taik. The shopping distracts me from thinking about more germane issues, issues I cannot bear to consider. And what if I am pregnant? It is a possibility. At least we will all be together, wherever we end up. I have even heard that in some European

prisons, mothers are allowed to keep their babies with them for the first
year. And in Sweden, there are co-ed prisons, in which men and women
can live together in the same cell. I don't want to go to prison. It is
inconceivable that I could be imprisoned a second time. It occurs to me
that promises made to whatever deities in times of extreme and dire
need are quickly forgotten when the crisis subsides. So is it with me,
whose memory has faded over the years, who can't now remember the
fear and suffering of the Zagreb prison, the supplications tearfully made
to God to deliver me immediately from not only the prison, but the city,
the country, perhaps even the continent. In return, I had sworn to be
good, very good, for the rest of my life, to be kind and loving to family,
friends and even perfect strangers. I have been kind and loving. But I
have been loyal and faithful as well, to my husband, who needs me and
whose life, as well as the life of his nation, is in danger. Surely I will not
be punished too severely for this? The thought is disturbing, so I push it
all back into the darkest corners of my mind, cover it with layers and
layers of other memories, words from popular songs, faces of people I
knew long ago; the day I met Taik. Suddenly I think of my little red knit
hat, which had blown off my head as he had carried me across the street
the night of our first date. My cap, my cap! I had screamed. My mother
made it for me! But the cap was never found. I found Taik instead.

25

"There are no moral phenomena at all, but only a moral interpretation of phenomena." Nietzsche

It becomes increasingly easy to ignore what is happening around me, to deny it. It has nothing to do with me. I don't want to know anything. It is difficult enough knowing what I do and attempting to stuff it into my subconscious, or to justify it. There are so many arguments for and against, all of which are perfectly rational and valid, depending upon one's subjective viewpoint. I myself can fully sympathize with what Taik and perhaps even Bruno believe, as well as with the outrage innocent victims would surely experience. There are innocent victims on both sides, though; on one side a nation, symbolized by Taik, and on the other, hostages, who have no connection with the injustice being perpetrated on the Croatian people, at least on a personal level. It is difficult for me to decide how much responsibility, moral or practical, a citizen must assume for the unjust acts of his government. I would be proud to be a hostage for such a cause! Taik had told me. Any decent human being would. To help a suffering nation? To expose government murderers? He is sure of himself. Taik, the idealist, always ascribing the purest and noblest of motives to mankind, endowing them with superhuman compassion, understanding, the ability to transcend physical and transitory suffering in order to reach a higher, more spiritual plateau....I know better. There are few such people. On an airplane, perhaps three or four. The rest will excoriate Taik, all of us. We will be terrorists, they will demand revenge and compensation and say horrible things about each of us in the first public forum they can find.

The movies and television programs I have seen about hijackings reinforce my beliefs. The hijackers are invariably portrayed as foul-mouthed scum, they push the innocent people around, force them to wet their pants, to do cruel things to one another, and then they laugh about it, the animals, the bloodthirsty thugs. Their motivations are never given serious attention, the issues which lie behind their desperate action ignored, belittled. It is important to portray them as mindless sadists. The less the public identifies with them as human beings, the less sympathy can be garnered for them or their cause. It makes a certain amount of sense to me. But the more important issue is the lack of serious attention to matters such as genocide and murder, gross violations of human rights, which, when denied or rationalized, lead to greater tragedy than a single hijacking or the occupation of a consulate.

A great weariness has descended upon me, an exhaustion which cannot be eradicated by any means, except, perhaps, death. Sleeping, waking, eating, moving, standing, talking, everything is interchangeable, nothing stands out as being different than anything else. All I can do is wait and try to feel as little as possible. It is not difficult. I have already had years of practice.

The people have finally been chosen by Taik, though he doesn't give me their names. One of them I know, he says, the others I do not. It is amazing to me that three young men, with their lives arranged neatly, soccer on weekends, a steady job, perhaps a girlfriend from the old country, would simply give it all up, plunge themselves into uncertainty and perhaps danger, to become involved in a plan that could end in tragedy or even death. But I do not know what Taik has told them, though it is difficult to imagine him misrepresenting anything to them, it is not his nature. Besides, it is too serious a matter. That I am simply allowing myself to be carried along with the hijacking plan does not, however, amaze me. It seems inevitable, it seems as though everything that has come before in our relatively short time together has had to lead to something like this. It is true that I have tried to dissuade Taik from this undertaking, it is true that I am not in agreement with it. But it is also true that if Taik were to tell me to decide whether it should happen or not, I would be incapable of making that decision. I could not bear the probable repercussions of an incorrect decision. Either way I am in despair.

One night Taik comes home late, with a package in his hand. He gets one of our chairs, pulls it over so that it is right under a storage space we have above the bathroom, climbs up on it, opens the small door to the space, and shoves the package in. What's that? I ask him. Why? he says. So I forget it, I am used to this. I am the one, after all, who didn't know her husband had only one eye. And anyway, the less I know, the less I can be forced to tell, as Taik had told me years ago. I am a good student, I have learned my lesson well.

I quit my teaching job; my heart is not in it. How can I conduct lessons on the future tense when my own future is in question? When the chance exists that I will soon be deprived of one? My students are unhappy about it, we have become close and they have even managed to learn a little English! I tell Steve and Mady that we are moving back to Oregon. I harbor a small hope that this is, in fact, what might ultimately happen, that the cataclysmic event, the coup or the uprising, is on the horizon, heading our way like a benevolent storm cloud. And when it happens, we will be safe in Gearhart, reading about it in the papers or watching it on television, and not in some foreign prison, living amid filth and squalor and career criminals paid to attack the political people and make their lives even more miserable, if possible, than they already are.

Taik wants to move the package he has put in the storage space, so he climbs up once again on a chair and retrieves it. Let's go out for a walk, he says. But it's freezing outside, I tell him. It has rained most of the day, a cold, chilling rain which hits the skin like tiny slivers of ice. Put on your coat and gloves and get your muffler, he says. So I go ahead and do it, put on layer after layer of clothing, when all I had really wanted to do was go to bed, pull the covers up over my head, lose consciousness. He places the package in a canvas bag with a hand grip and we head outside, down the street to Riverside Drive, where we turn right. Where are we going? I ask him. I hope it's not far, because I'm freezing already. My hands are buried deep in my pockets and my chin is tucked tightly against my chest. Even so, all my extremities are beginning to go numb. Put your arm around me, Taik tells me. He does the same, drapes his arm across my shoulder, as though we are in our early courtship days, strolling along, in love with each other and the rest of the world as well. This way we won't look suspicious, he says. We didn't look suspicious before! I protest. Just keep walking, he answers curtly. We turn right about five blocks from our street, then right again to the landing of an apartment building, where Taik rings a buzzer. The outer door opens and we go up three flights of stairs, to another door, which opens slowly, revealing a face puffy with sleep. It is a face I have seen once or twice before, a Croatian, whose name I don't recall. I need to leave something here, Taik tells the man. Come on in, he says, closing the door behind us. He doesn't turn on the light, though, maybe because he is in his white jockey shorts. They look spooky; they are the only shape I can make out in the blackness, and they look as though they are walking around by themselves. He doesn't ask Taik what is in the bag, just tells him to put it under the bed, which Taik does, just shoves it under. Thanks, he says. No problem, the man answers. On our way home, Taik walks quickly, hands in pockets. Oh, you don't want to hold me now, huh? I say. He laughs, says, Of course I do, Punky! and pulls me to him. So we walk back home as though we are young lovers. But we are young lovers, after all. As I lie in bed later, it occurs to me that the man in the dark apartment did not ask Taik what was in the bag. And neither did I! If we don't know, we can't tell anyone else. He, too, has learned his lessons well.

There are a few other things Taik wants me to do. One is to type a list of demands. He wants it to be perfect. So I sit down at a typewriter we have borrowed from a friend and Taik dictates to me. He wants the document to be published in four major newspapers, the Los Angeles Times, the New York Times, the Chicago Tribune and the International Herald Tribune. There is also an additional leaflet, written by a friend of his, which is entitled "Appeal to the American People". He wants this published as well. If these two statements are not published, he dictates, many lives will hang in the balance. This part I do not like and tell him so. But it's only to force them to print these things. Nobody could possibly get hurt, he says. We won't have any weapons on the plane! I know that Taik would be incapable of harming innocent people. This I do know, it is as certain as the tides, the waxing and waning of the moon. So I continue to type the words he says to me, fixing them up as I go along so that they are grammatically, syntactically correct. Where are you going to put this list? I ask him. And the documents? He is going to put them in a locker, along with some explosives, just so the authorities will think there are more of the same on the plane. This information numbs me. What if something happens and they go off accidentally? Or if somebody breaks into the locker and pulls the contents out? Taik assures me that this will be impossible, he has taken extensive precautions, trust him. Don't I trust him? Of course I do, I tell him, that's not the point, that's not the point at all. I don't feel as omnipotent as he does, there is always an element of uncertainty and doubt to anything anybody plans, it is the nature of the universe that something can always go wrong, in spite of the best plans. Nothing can possibly happen, he repeats. And that's that. I finish the page and hand it to him. My head is pounding, pulsating, as though an exotic virus entrapped within is replicating wildly and has begun to penetrate the layer of skull which holds it hostage. I am close to collapse. But there is only one thing I can do if I want to put a stop to everything and that is to call the police. This thought enters and exits my consciousness faster than the speed of light. It will never happen. I have only two choices: stay behind in New York or go with Taik. The horror of staying behind, the shame, is intolerable to me. He may need me! I am his wife, his partner and best friend. And the passengers might need me, might feel more frightened of foreigners with strange accents than they would of me, an American, a former nurse, former teacher, one used to comforting people when they are suffering or struggling. I choose to go with him. That is where I feel I belong. It is the better of two impossible choices. The consequences do not occupy my mind at the moment. My only concern is that nobody get hurt, that everybody come out alive and healthy and, if at all possible, that the passengers understand and sympathize, at least a little, with the circumstances which led normally law-abiding, decent and humane people to become involved in such a desperate act. The thought of what might, what will come after, I banish from my mind. It is enough trying to cope with what I already know for sure.

After reviewing the pages I had copied months ago from the Jane's Aircraft book in the main library, Taik goes to the airport to buy tickets for the appropriate type of plane, one he figures can make a long flight without having to refuel. It is a New York to Arizona flight, with a stopover in Chicago. It should have plenty of fuel on board, enough to reach the European continent. Taik wants the leaflets he has had printed, thousands of copies in French, English and Croatian, to be dropped from the airplane over the major European cities we will fly above. There's a big religious celebration on a Croatian island at this time, Taik tells me. It would raise the morale of the Croatian nation to have these leaflets dropped over the island. So he plans to have the plane fly over Yugoslav air space? This is another thing I refuse to contemplate. Too many things could happen. The Yugoslav government is too paranoid and too fragile to allow such a event to take place. They wouldn't dare shoot down an American passenger plane, Taik assures me. He is talking about a government that shrinks from nothing, that would commit, and has committed, an endless list of atrocities upon its peoples, ostensibly in defense of Yugoslav "brotherhood and unity". When this alleged "unity" is in danger, I believe there is nothing the Yugoslavs would not do. Taik is strangely confident that they wouldn't dare go this far. I cannot agree. Too many of my illusions have been shattered.

It is a relief for me to talk about all the little details, it prevents me from contemplating the disaster that is soon to strike at the very essence of our shared life. The more I try to fit all the little pieces together, the more sense and logic I labor to imbue the plan with, the less time I have to acknowledge the feelings of fear and nausea that overwhelm me daily. For no matter how noble the underlying motive, no matter how desperate Taik's situation and the situation of the Croatian nation, my merciless conscience is finding it difficult to make peace with a hijacking, the two cannot be friends or even civil to one another.

It is time for the other men who will be going with us to see each other. Taik has invited them, there are three, to meet us for dinner at the top of the Gulf Western building on 59th and Broadway. I would prefer to stay home but Taik wants me to come; no matter what he might be doing, he has always taken comfort in my presence, would rather have me with him than someplace else. So we get dressed, take a taxi to the restaurant. When we arrive at the top floor, we go into the bar, where the others are already waiting, as arranged. We look each other over. Taik lights a cigarette, sits down. I sit, too, at a low table, so low that our knees are bent dangerously close to our chins, we look like grasshoppers which have folded their legs together. Such a stupid idea, I think to myself, making tables like this. But this is hardly a critical issue at the moment. More important are the three men sitting across from me. One I know, Slobodan, whose parents I had visited during my stay in Gorica. It was their horse I had ridden, galloped him up the hill despite their protestations, left them openmouthed on the road below us. The other two I don't recall ever having seen. Frane is small and dark, with deeply set black eyes which dart back and forth like those of a clever animal. The other, Petar, is tall, with big features, big hands, big jaw, the type one would pick out in a crowd, just because he is not innocuous like so many others. We have a drink, make small talk, and then go in to the dining room. The meal is delicious, the appetizers varied and imaginative, the service excellent. But throughout the meal, the subject of the hijacking is not mentioned. We talk about soccer, the political situation in Yugoslavia, the food, the view from our table. When we have finished, we all take the elevator down to the street. Taik tells me I can go home, he will be back soon. While I am waiting to flag down a taxi, he takes the men aside, one by one, talking to each quietly, handing them something. I am grateful that I am able to make my escape. The scene had been strained and unnatural. I had more than once wanted to ask why we had been called together. We surely could have eaten alone in our apartment, just Taik and I. Who knows how many more meals we will be able to share? I begrudge spending our time with anyone else, for any reason. We haven't had nearly enough together, and already it is in danger of ending.

I suppose I should pack our things in boxes, I say to Taik the next morning. He agrees, wants me to do it while he goes out to buy a few things. There is no organization to my packing, I just throw everything in the boxes indiscriminately, as though I know I will not be the one unpacking it. It is tempting to simply throw it all away. None of it can mean anything to me again, all associations I will make with objects or people, feelings, ideas, this color or that smell, will relate to life before or life after the hijacking. All I own and all I do or become will be classified as pre-or post-hijacking, like an age, the Stone Age, the Iron Age, placing me in a particular phase of my evolution from which I can never disassociate myself. Some human acts and endeavors can stand by themselves, for themselves. I can say that I finally understood the theory of dream interpretation last week or that I ran ten miles this morning, and neither defines who I was before or who I will become. But if I hijack a plane tomorrow, that moment, the moment the control of the plane is passed from the pilot to us, can never stand alone. All I did and was before, all I will do and be in the future, will be forever linked to the person I am at that fateful moment.

Taik comes back with some iron pots and tape, which he will use, he tells me, to simulate bombs on the airplane. The items look somehow malevolent, the type of things one would expect to find in a torture chamber or an S&M parlor. Black electrical tape, to tape a mouth shut while heinous acts are perpetrated, a big pan to hit somebody over the head with should he try to escape, or perhaps to boil water in the possibilities are endless. The tape and the pans do not inspire trust or confidence, do not engender tender feelings within my soul and heart. The packets of leaflets go into small hand suitcases which we will take with us on the plane. There is room for little else. What need will we have for clothes? I think to myself sadly. Our wardrobes will consist of black and white striped uniforms, just like in the movies. Strange how many things turn out to be just like the movies, contrary to one's expectations and hopes, which dictate that life does not, should not, imitate art.

Everything is packed, the leaflets, the pans, tape and even some clay which Taik will use to fashion phony sticks of explosives. He has already left the real explosives somewhere in a locker, along with the note he had dictated to me. The thought of Taik bouncing along in a taxi with a bag of explosives horrifies me, and I hasten to erase it from my mind, deny that such a thing could have happened in our world. But I have an unnatural trust and faith in Taik, I believe without question that he is capable of doing exactly what he plans, that he has attended assiduously to every detail, anticipated every possible obstacle and complication, thereby eliminating all twists of fate or quirks of nature which could otherwise interfere with his intentions. I have attended to the little voice within me which insists upon asking what if? what if? every few moments. I have told it that I have complete trust in Taik. He has taken care of everything. Hasn't he taken care of everything in the past? How many times have I surrendered myself to his judgements and evaluations, put my life in his hands? This is just another one of those times.

We are finally ready to go. I have put on my new blue corduroy dress and Taik is wearing a brown corduroy suit and sunglasses. We take the typewriter we have borrowed, too, which we will drop off on our way to the airport. How will you be sure that the leaflets have been printed in the newspapers? it occurs to me to ask Taik. They could trick you and say they had and you wouldn't know. I've arranged for someone to call in a code word, which can then be passed along to the plane, he tells me. He really has thought of everything. And my mind, in comparison, is as blank as I can make it as we drive off, leaving our small apartment behind, leaving New York behind, perhaps never to return. I take Taik's hand and hold it tightly. The thought of leaving him behind is ludicrous; how could it ever have crossed my mind?

We reach our friend's house, drop off the typewriter. Have a good trip, he tells us. I wonder what Taik has told him. Where are we going? Could it all be a joke or a test, to see how loyal I can be, to gauge the limits of my understanding, fidelity and love? It would be a cruel test, but an effective one. Perhaps to see if I can be trusted with something even more critical, more momentous to come in the future? My head is ready to explode, it is filling up rapidly and against my will with all types of unconnected, grotesque and horrific propositions which insinuate themselves steadily into my consciousness from moment to moment. I must close my eyes, try to get some sleep. But we are in a taxi, on our way to the airport! I lose track of where we are, who I am. If only I could sleep. It is not death, but it's close enough.

At the airport, we check in and then go sit in the waiting area. I see that the other three have already arrived and are all sitting separately, one reading a magazine, the other staring straight ahead, the third composed, hands folded in lap, eyes partially closed, as though he were daydreaming. I suddenly feel that I must throw up. I have to go to the bathroom, I tell Taik. I go into one of the stalls, sit down on a toilet seat, head between my knees. Everything is fuzzy before my eyes, even my hands, which are clasped in front of them. When I return, Taik is sitting already and has saved a seat for me. Are you all right, Punky? he asks. I'm ok now, I tell him with a faint smile. At my feet is my bag containing part of the leaflets and the molding clay. I lean my head against Taik's shoulder, imagining for just a moment that we are taking a trip, to Oregon, perhaps, to visit my family, to see the ocean….I search the faces of the passengers who are shortly to board the plane with us. There are many men, mostly men, business types, in suits and ties, looking as though they'd prefer to be anywhere but here, waiting for a plane to windy Chicago or the stultifying heat of Phoenix. If only they knew, I think to myself, if only they knew…. Taik is silent. I find it difficult to imagine what might be going on in his head, am afraid to ask, don't want to know that he, too, might be frightened or nauseous. I require total invincibility from him right now. It is the only way I can survive.

Our flight is called, so we get up and file into the plane. I am sitting in the aisle, Taik is in the center seat. Shortly after takeoff, he transfers the molding clay from my bag to his, gets up and goes, with his bag, to the restroom. I take the flight magazine from the pouch in front of my seat and pretend to read it. Is Taik coming back to the seat? Will he change his mind while he is in the bathroom, think of our walks along the river, our bike rides, remember the strange towns and countries we have discovered together, understand that it is in his power to restore or deny us those tender days? But he has chosen to sacrifice one thing so that another might exist, he has decided to make a trade. Without even looking in my direction, he suddenly passes by, heading towards the front of the plane. I get a glimpse of wires and black tape on his chest. I close my eyes. A moment later I hear a voice. Would you please come to the captain's cabin? A male steward is bending over me, talking. The captain's cabin? I ask. Yes, please, he says. He looks agitated but keeping it under control, believing his state of mind is still a secret, though it has already betrayed him. I follow him to the cabin. He knocks, and the door is opened. Taik is sitting directly behind the captain, wired up to give the illusion that explosives are hanging from his neck. You did it, I say inanely. There is a co-pilot to my right and a flight engineer at my side. At this point, they are shapes and sounds, they don't yet represent anything to me, the thought that they, too, are human beings is something I cannot consider at this point. But it bothers me to be rude and to ignore them and their feelings. It isn't the way I was brought up.

Go back and get Matanic, Taik says. Tell him to come up front. I obey woodenly, anything to occupy my mind and to create the impression that I know what I am doing and have not lost control. He is in the first class section. Well, that was a waste of money, I think irrelevantly. He comes with me, silently, calmly. He and Taik exchange some words while I wait outside. The passengers, I notice, have realized something is amiss. They will have to be told soon. It isn't fair to leave them in a state of ignorance. Nobody is talking to me, so I decide to sit back down. Perhaps I will simply be forgotten. I can pretend to be asleep or ill. As soon as I have taken my seat, though, the pilot comes on the loudspeaker. Well, folks, I have an announcement to make! The passengers sit up straighter, put down their magazines, as he continues. This plane has been hijacked. There are a few scattered gasps, but nothing extreme. Everyone appears more incredulous than frightened at this point. The hijackers have some demands and will be explaining to you what is happening, he says. Please try to remain calm so this thing can be concluded quickly and safely. Thank you! My seatmate looks at me suspiciously. Am I a part of this? Why did I go to the front of the plane? I am still hoping to be found superfluous, refuse to admit anything.

But I am involved and can't deny it to myself or to others any longer. Matanic comes to my seat and tells me Taik needs me up front. I get up and follow him, give a wan smile to my seatmate, who is clearly angry at being misled into thinking I was a nice and pleasant person. Go back and get Frane, Taik tells me when I reach the cabin. So I go down the aisle way to the back, where I find him and Slobodan sitting wired up with what appear to be explosives. The passengers around them are rigid, barely even turn their heads as I pass. Hostages have been shot for less on the TV movies they have seen. Taik wants you in the cabin, I tell Frane. He follows me silently. He, too, is rigid, and his knuckles are white. I myself feel as though I have no substance, as though a hole has been cut in my leg or arm and somebody has pulled all the bones from my body one by one, leaving me a mass of undirected, limp flesh. As I walk up the aisle, a cute girl with short hair and a bright smile stops me. Excuse me, she says, but I am a stewardess on this plane and I'm not sure what I'm supposed to be doing. Do you want me to sit down or take care of the passengers or what? She is asking me, as though I am the boss around here. I feel unhappy to be perceived as the orchestrator of the actions of strangers. She looks apologetic. It's just that this is a new situation for me, she explains. You know? I can't help but smile at her. a She's so sweet and natural and clearly would prefer to be up and about, doing her job, being of assistance. Because Taik is in the cabin and the others speak little English, I decide to tell her what I feel would be best. It's fine for you to do whatever you want for the passengers, I say. Oh, good! My name is Basia Reeves, she adds, as she heads down the aisle. I notice that the two other stewardesses are sitting together near the front of the plane. They have withdrawn, apparently feel no desire or responsibility to minister to the passengers. They are hostages like everybody else, they seem to have decided, and refuse to lift a finger. Another of the passengers raises a feeble hand as I walk by. Excuse me, he says. May I go to the bathroom? Hostages have been shot for going to the bathroom without permission on the TV movies, too. He is not taking the chance.

I am frustrated and embarrassed that anyone should ask my permission to relieve himself. Of course you can go to the bathroom! I tell him. Anybody who wants to can go to the bathroom whenever he wants! What do they think, that I am the kind of person who would make them wet their pants or wait for hours in agony to relieve themselves, enjoying that illusory and obscene power over my fellow human beings? The reasons behind this hijacking, the very understandable and valid reasons, Taik's fears of being assassinated, his concern about further murders of Croatian dissidents, the tortures, the suffering of his people. I can't think of them at this moment. All I see are the faces of the frightened passengers, all I can identify with is the suffering before me now, not the centuries of suffering Croatians have endured before I was even born.

Another of the passengers asks me who we are, what group we belong to, and it occurs to me that I should pass out the English leaflets to the passengers so that they will have an idea what lies behind the hijacking. I'm going to pass out some leaflets, I tell Taik. The passengers want to know who we are. He agrees that this is a good idea, so Petar and I pass them out, one by one. The passengers read them avidly, as though the words contain clues about when they will be released from this flying piece of metal and reunited with their families. You aren't Arabs? one man asks. No! I say. I'm American and the others are Croatian! Some of the passengers appear relieved to hear that we are not Arabs. They won't have to hide their identification after all! They won't be shot or tortured arbitrarily for being a Goldstein or a Friedman!

When the passengers have finished reading, I am barraged with questions. What are the demands? Who wrote the leaflet, which appears to be very well-reasoned and articulate? Why don't we ever read about the Croatian situation in the newspapers? Where is the plane headed? What can we do to help? The last question stuns me. How reasonable these passengers are, how compassionate! They understand, they want to help! I tell Taik that the passengers are on our side! My mood transforms itself from one of depression to one of jubilance. The passengers aren't angry at us! They sympathize, they too are indignant about the situation of the Croation nation. It is true what Taik had told me. Any humane and compassionate person will understand why this desperate action has been taken. What free person would not wish others to be free? I hadn't believed him, hadn't shared his faith in my own countrymen. But he is right after all, his understanding of the human heart is, as always, superior to mine.

I head back down the aisle, eager to answer more questions, to explain everything to these wonderful passengers. I notice a distinguished graying man on the right. He reminds me of Melody's father, who is now deceased. You look just like my good friend's father, I tell him. He has been writing something and hurriedly puts it into his pocket. I do? he says. What were you writing? I ask. I am simply curious, always like to know what people are writing, a poem, a short story, a journal? He is unnerved, though, he believes I am going to grab his pages, uncover something he has written, perhaps about us, something critical or derogatory. I'm only asking out of curiosity. I don't care what you're writing, really! I assure him. He looks me over for a moment, and then tells me he is writing some things to his family in case he never sees them again. Oh, don't even think that! I say in desperation. Nothing is going to happen to anybody! I give you my word! It is appalling to me that anyone might think we will harm them in any way. Can't they see what kind of people we are? I am not pretending to be nice and to care about them. I am nice, I do care! The man and I chat for awhile. I feel very secure with him, as though we have known each other for years. One of my daughters is about your age, he tells me. I can imagine her getting involved in something like this, too. It could happen to anyone's daughter.

Yes, I agree, it could! I'm no different than any other girl. It's just the circumstances. I felt I couldn't do anything else. He nods his head, seems to understand, as though he has lived through many such situations in his own life and is fully aware of the contradictions which confront mankind at every turn.

Basia Reeves hurries by, carrying drinks in one hand and a pillow in the other. The passengers are standing around talking, some are laughing, telling stories of trips they have taken or women they have known. A few are drinking whiskey. Basia is obviously bringing them whatever they want from the plane's kitchen. Anything to put them at their ease, to keep them calm and confident. Excuse me, I tell my new friend, whose name is Rudy Bretz. I have to go to the cabin for a minute. In the cabin, the atmosphere is tense. If only Taik could charm them as he is so capable of doing in any other situation! The captain, whose name tag reads Dick Carey, is gray-haired and soft-spoken. He asks Taik questions calmly and listens closely to his answers, as though they are partners collaborating in a business deal. The co-pilot, Lou Senatore, wants nothing to do with Taik. He looks out the window, ignoring what is going on around him, disapproval showing clearly on his face. The flight engineer, Tom Sheary, is friendly and smiles a lot, but it's not an obsequious smile. He's simply a good-natured guy, regardless of the mess he now finds himself in. Hi, I say to the three of them. They return my greeting in their three individual ways. Taik has given Dick Carey a piece of paper explaining where the explosives are located in New York City, how they are put together, how they can be rendered harmless. Dick Carey has relayed all the information to the authorities in New York City, so that they can verify what Taik has told them and also so that they will believe there are real explosives on the plane. This way, the demand that the leaflets be printed will be met more quickly.

Dick Carey explains to us that we will have to re-fuel somewhere in order to fly to Europe. The plane was scheduled for a re-fueling in Chicago, which will not now take place. So much for our assumption that the plane could fly directly to Europe. If we had been aware of this complication, the plane we are on would have been in Chicago by now and we would have been elsewhere. Where will we stop? I ask. He tells us it will have to be Montreal. What choice is there? Taik gives the approval for this change in his plan. Can leaflets be dropped from this plane? he asks Dick. It seems they can't be dropped from our plane. It would disrupt the air pressure in the plane and we could crash. But we can give the leaflets to another plane that is equipped for such a thing, Dick suggests. You just tell them where you want them dropped. This sounds like a good idea, so we get the packets of leaflets ready for when we arrive in Montreal, pile them just outside the door to the pilot's cabin.

Meanwhile, I prefer to talk to the passengers. They seem to be helping me more than I am helping them. But I notice a few of them are crying, something that had so far escaped my attention. There is a German couple with a small child. The mother, obviously terrified, is holding her child tightly against her breast, weeping. She speaks no English, so I try to comfort her in German. As much as she would like to be comforted, she finds it impossible to be reassured by a person who is obviously capable of all types of deviousness, dishonesty, and treachery. Why else would I be here? And strangely enough, there is another German national in the back of the plane, a small, plump, white-haired gentleman, who is sitting patiently, waiting to be told what is happening. One of the other passengers has determined that he speaks no English whatsoever and that I speak German. So far nobody has been able, or has had the heart, to explain the situation. Hello, I say. Hello, he answers with a delightful smile, are you the stewardess? Yes, I tell him. Why tell him the truth? It would only upset him. Do we have a mechanical problem? he asks. Yes, I say. It's not serious, but we'll have to re-route some of you. You'll be in Chicago soon, just a little later than you had expected. He rewards me with an exuberant pat on my arm and settles back in his seat, prepared for a great adventure. If only he can remain in total ignorance until he arrives in Chicago! At least one person will be spared the fear and anxiety.

Before I know it, we have arrived in Montreal, where we will refuel for the next leg of the trip. The authorities on the ground have asked

Dick Carey to try to persuade us to change to a plane that can fly further without refueling. It is dangerous to take this plane across the ocean, they say. But Taik is suspicious, can't take the chance that they won't simply shoot us as we walk across the landing area into another plane. There's no reason why this plane can't fly across the ocean, he tells Dick. We'll just have to stop again for more fuel. Dick doesn't press the point. In fact, he seems relieved that we don't have to make a big move from plane to plane, as though he is ethically incapable of perpetuating the charade he has been called upon by the authorities to act out. But this is just my impression. Perhaps the plane cannot, in fact, make it across the ocean. I don't think about it. I have to trust Taik, there is no other alternative.

On the ground in Montreal, the plane is quickly refueled and we are once again on our way. It has been decided to allow some of the passengers to disembark at our next stop, which Dick has told us will have to be in Gander, Newfoundland. As I walk up and down the aisles, I am approached by those who have emergency situations to attend to in the States, who are on their way to a son's wedding, a medical conference, a christening. Some are simply scared and say nothing, such as the German couple with the child. I relay each request to Taik, bring each individual case to his attention, though it is just a formality. I am confident that he will leave most of these decisions to me; after all, I am the one who has been talking to the passengers and who knows better the circumstances of each one… He has spent the majority of his time in the pilot's cabin, listening to the transmissions between the plane and the ground.

And then we are in Newfoundland. As food is brought aboard for those remaining, and the fuel tanks refilled, those who are leaving the plane get up and gather their things together, relieved to be escaping the plane and any possible tragedy and trauma which might loom in the future, but committed to seeing that our demand is met so that the others are released as soon as possible. A few of the passengers carry packets of leaflets, which will be transferred to their plane for later distribution over Chicago and Montreal. Don't worry, they tell us, we'll see that they all get dropped as soon as possible. We'll go right to the media if they refuse to do it! One Jewish couple tells me they had hid their passports in the beginning, thinking we were Arabs. Another says he was embarrassed to ask to get off the plane, though he felt his medical condition was serious enough to warrant it. I just feel that I should stay, he whispers to me quietly. I'm a man, after all. I feel like a coward somehow just getting off. This strange confession touches me deeply. It confirms that I can still be perceived as a human being and not a monster, that he feels comfortable exposing his vulnerabilities to me. I am not evil and vicious, I am none of the other things which will no doubt be written about us after this nightmare is over. Don't worry about that, I tell this suffering man. You have every reason to get off, more than most! All in all, about thirty five people disembark. As one of them, an attractive black woman, heads down the steps, I tell her I wish I were going with her. She smiles a sad and even sympathetic smile. The thought of being despised and disliked by the passengers and crew torments me, so I attempt to simply be myself with them, whatever that might cost me.

As soon as the passengers have disembarked, we take off again, heading east. I notice that Basia is carrying a lot of the little airport bottles of whiskey and wine down the aisles. We're going to be out of liquor in a few minutes, she tells me. Oh well, I say, as long as it helps them deal with this situation it's OK with me. And most of the passengers are dealing with it quite well. They are either standing around in small groups, drinking, talking, or reading a book or magazine. One young boy is even taking a nap, dead to the world, sprawled across three seats, his long, awkward legs hanging out into the aisle like the legs of a grasshopper, bent at the knee. One of his friends, a cute, blonde kid of about nineteen, approaches me with a serious expression on his face. My name is Steve, he tells me. I have a problem I wanted to ask you about. Sure, I say, what's the matter? (Other than the obvious, I think to myself, that you are on a hijacked plane and we could all be dead before morning). Well, me and my two friends, the one sleeping and the other guy down there—he points to a dark-haired boy who is sitting by the window, just staring out—were on our way to Chicago to report to duty in the Navy. Uh huh, I say, waiting for the rest. But there is no more. I wait and so does he. Finally he realizes he must not have explained his problem adequately. Well, he says, what I'm worried about is, will they consider us AWOL (away without leave)? I am tempted to laugh, but he is seriously worried that his military career will be over before it has started. I reassure him as best I can that there is no way in the world that the authorities will penalize him and his friends for something that is out of their control. He is relieved, gives me a broad smile. I feel a lot better now, he says. That's good, I tell him. I feel better, too. Can I ask you something else? he says. Sure, I tell him. Whatever you want. He hangs his head and even though he isn't shuffling his feet, he looks as though he would like to. Well, I was just wondering how you got mixed up in all this. I mean, you remind me of my sister. I feel real comfortable around you, like we've known each other for a long time. There is nothing I would like more than to explain everything to this young boy, so that he will understand how I came to my decision. But where could I begin? It is a story that needs time and patience to tell, more than I have at this moment. Someday I will tell you everything, I answer. Let's just say I felt I had no other choice under the circumstances. This seems to satisfy him. He nods his head in understanding, as though to say that this is exactly what he had thought all along.

I head up towards the cabin, to make sure Taik is all right. It seems weeks, months, since I have talked to him. On my way I am stopped by a short, blonde, baby-faced man who introduces himself as Ron, a talk-show host from Nevada. He is flying with a man who appears to be his boyfriend, and they would like to take some pictures of them with us, just "for souvenirs", they say. There is really nothing I would not do, short of betraying Taik in some way, for these passengers. Of course, I tell him. I don't mind. So I stand with my arm around Ron's boyfriend while he shoots several pictures of us. Then others get the same idea. It seems everyone who has a camera wants a picture as well. Let's get one of the other men, too, one of the passengers says. Frane and Slobodan are sitting together at the back of the plane, still wired up, looking wan and tired. I go behind their the seat and stand over them, elbows resting on the top of the seat. We are told to smile, so we do. I can imagine how ludicrous the three of us will look in some newspaper, perhaps the "Enquirer" or the "Star", the men with what appear to be explosives hanging from their necks, the bubbly blonde above them. "The Happy Hijackers", the caption will read, or "Bombs Can Be Fun!" I try to smile for the camera, it is the least I can do, but it's difficult when what I would really like is to wake up and find that it is all a hallucination, that everything is fine, that Taik will not be assassinated, that his friends will not be hunted down, tortured or killed, that he can go home to his village and family and be free, and that the passengers have not been hijacked, they are all in Chicago or Phoenix or St. Louis, at their weddings, operations, family reunions, conferences....

Back in the cabin, the situation is less than cordial. Dick is trying his best to be patient and calm, but Lou is not so disposed. He speaks only when spoken to and otherwise sits quietly, a grim look on his face. Tom is going in and out of the cabin, apparently uncomfortable being stuck in such an uncompanionable group. His is an exuberant Irish temperament which demands high spirits and lively conversation. Even Taik, who can generally charm anybody over to his way of thinking, is quiet, his features drawn and tense. The men tend to talk to me about the situation instead of to Taik. It is because I am a woman, an American and so obviously obsequious and apologetic. Besides, they sense that I have a certain amount of influence with Taik, which surprises me at first. I myself had never really believed that I exerted any appreciable influence, but these strangers had intuited otherwise. And they were right, I realize as Taik summons me more and more often to the cabin for consultations. He trusts my opinions, he values my suggestions and ideas more than those of the others, who, for the most part, remain in the back of the plane, sitting stiffly, fake bombs resting in their laps. Petar is the exception. He is the type who needs to talk with people, to comfort them and reassure them. Though he is big and cumbersome, he is not the least bit intimidating. He regales the passengers with stories about his soccer days, about his village in Croatia and the atrocities committed there against Croats during the last war. We have made the mistake of believing that because the passengers are not spitting on us or calling us names, they agree with what we are doing and are actually our compatriots. It is hard to believe otherwise, so congenial is the atmosphere, so understanding the passengers. How can I help? they ask me again and again. I know this congressman in my state. I could get in touch with him! Another is a friend of a Senator. They ask me how it could be that they have never heard of the Croatians before, how their situation could have been completely ignored by the press, the politicians, the government, for all these years. They find it hard to believe that someone would go to such lengths in order to get the manifestly reasonable demands for publicity met. Are you prepared to go to prison? they ask. I tell them I don't want to go, but I don't see how it can be avoided. Many shake their heads, as though completely perplexed by the abstruse motives which underlie human behavior, or perhaps they are simply sad. What a waste! one says. I am reluctant to ask for further clarification. Better to be left in ignorance about such things.

There is a Catholic priest on board, Father O'Rourke, who is ministering to the needs of the Catholic passengers. At one point, he waves me over to his seat. Sit down for a moment, would you, please? Of course, I say, and take a seat. You know, he begins, the people on the plane are innocent of crimes against the Croatian people. Can't you use your influence with your husband to allow them all to be released? I reply that I understand his concerns, but that it is too late for that. We are in the air and I don't even know exactly what is happening next, I tell him. He talks on and on, using every argument available to him, philosophical, ethical, moral and religious. I nod my head until it feels as though it is attached to my shoulders by a big spring and will never again come to rest. I agree with everything, Father, I tell him helplessly, but there's nothing more I can say or do.

Meanwhile, everybody is watching the escort plane which has been flying with us and will eventually drop the remaining leaflets over London and Paris and, if all goes according to Taik's plan, Croatia as well. But first we have to refuel again in Iceland. How many times do we have to refuel? I ask Dick fearfully, aware that every time the plane lands, troops could possibly swarm the plane, shoot people or prevent us from taking off again. We have no control over the decisions the authorities of each land take. That is the truly frightening part, that whatever might be undertaken will be without exact information or input from the flight crew, whose responsibility the plane and passengers are. But the Icelandic ground crew is more curious than anything else. They bring us box after box of food, thick sandwiches, cheeses, fruit, they refuel the plane in record time and even wave as we take off again for England.

All the liquor is gone from the plane's galley and many of the men are slurring their speech. A few are sleeping, heads hanging down like heavy fruits on a particularly fragile branch. Rudy Bretz, I notice, is sitting calmly and quietly, jotting down notes on a piece of paper on his lap. I don't approve of hijacking, regardless of the cause, he tells me quite openly, but that doesn't mean I can't sympathize with you or like you as a person. This seems a consummately reasonable conclusion for any decent human being to have reached under the circumstances. I wish everybody felt the same way, I say. Sitting next to Rudy, I feel secure and safe, feel that I can express my anxiety and doubts without fear of rejection. And in fact this is so. I tell him I am scared, that I don't want to go to prison, that all I would like to do is cry. And dear Rudy listens patiently, patting my arm and even hugging me tightly at one point. Did I tell you remind me of the father of one of my best friends? I ask him.

Yes, you did, he says. He was a wonderful man, I tell him. He played the classical guitar and he loved to be on the ocean with his boat. He killed himself, I add. Suddenly I am so exhausted that I can barely speak. It seems as though I have lived my entire life on the plane, that the only people I have ever known are the eighty or so passengers which surround me. This is my world, this will be my world until the end of time; I know nothing else. Is this what Hell is like? Is this Hell? The thought terrifies me. At this point, anything is possible.

Back in the cabin, transmissions are going back and forth between our plane and the escort plane, which will soon be dropping leaflets over London. Lou makes a terse comment from time to time, but otherwise remains silent. He isn't rude to me, he doesn't give me dirty looks or anything like that, but he is definitely resisting the impulse to become friendly with his captors. I understand how he feels, I can sympathize with his antagonism and don't hold it against him, not in the least, even though Dick, in contrast, is friendly and open and doesn't show any signs of hostility whatsoever. They are two different people, shaped from different experiences. Each has his own way of coping. As for Tom, he tells me that he is Irish, so of course he can identify somewhat with the aspirations of the Croatians. Not that he agrees with the action; he can identify, that's all. Have you heard anything from New York? I ask Taik. We relayed the instructions, but haven't gotten any news back yet, he tells me. Taik looks tired and tense, not enjoying sitting in the cabin and giving orders to innocents. He will do it, though. Otherwise, what has this all been for? I prefer to be the soft one, to be the gentle counterpart to these big and determined men whose accents, more than anything else, set them apart from the passengers, proclaim that they are not Americans, they think differently, they act differently, they are a world apart. Of course the passengers turn to me with their fears and anxieties, I, the obsequious one, the reasonable conduit. Have you ever been a stewardess? one of them asks me. I deny having been one, but am complimented nonetheless for having those qualities. Basia is the real stewardess. The two of us work together, consulting, taking turns doing things. She is indefatigable, unquenchable. Her energy is boundless. Not once do I see her sit down, sigh or allow the bright smile to fade from her face.

26

"When the house burns one forgets even lunch. Yes, but one eats it later in the ashes." Nietzsche

Slobodan and Frane have been invisible for most of the flight. They haven't spoken much to the passengers or to me and Petar, but have simply sat silently in their seats, cradling the heavy pots in their laps. We have been without sleep now for at least thirty hours and I haven't been able to eat anything at all. Food is an unnecessary luxury at the moment, and the act of fixing something, standing and eating it would be totally inconceivable to me under the circumstances. All the liquor is gone, has been gone for hours, and those who indulged most freely are still sleeping it off, perhaps entertaining the fond hope of awakening and finding themselves hung over in Chicago or Phoenix instead of on a hijacked plane, flying haphazardly from country to country and still ignorant of the final outcome.

I go back to the cabin, though I can expect little comfort from Taik, who is as tense as the others. Stay here, he tells me. I have to go to the bathroom. So I stay with the three men, who want to know what is still in store, where it will end, whether I can persuade Taik to surrender when we next land. I outline the plan to them, tell them about the religious gathering in Croatia, the importance of dropping the leaflets. Nobody will get hurt, I assure them. That will never happen. Lou points out that some things are out of our control, such as the foreign authorities attacking the plane without letting the flight crew know. This is something I do not want to contemplate. I'll do whatever I can to bring this to a quick conclusion, I tell them with as much sincerity and determination as I can muster. Dick is exhausted. He has been flying for at least twenty hours, hasn't let either of the others take his place for long, as though to say that he is the pilot and he will do the flying. I take the liberty of putting my arm over his shoulder and squeezing him. He seems so vulnerable and accessible, one can tell by the body language. I'm so sorry, Dick, I tell him. He folds his arms in front of him and rests them on the controls. Then he puts his forehead on his arms. Lou looks away discreetly, then gets up and leaves the cabin. I hug Dick again, whisper to him in his ear that everything will soon be over. I feel such affection and tenderness towards Dick, who is tired and spent and doesn't quite know what he is supposed to do, how he is supposed to feel. His is such a kind and gentle face that it tears my heart to look at it in such exhaustion. I would understand if he hated me or called me names. Lou could perhaps do this, but not Dick, it is simply not in his nature to act unkindly to somebody who is kind to him, even if that person happens to be the hijacker of his plane.

Lou returns, looks at the both of us, and decides it is safe to sit down again. He asks me more questions, which I answer gladly. As we talk, I realize that Lou, too, is unable to be mean to me. He is mad, indignant, has nothing good to say about this whole event, but still, I am a young girl and he is a man and this biological imperative takes over, this urge to protect what he considers the weaker species. He finds himself comforting me, calming me down. I would like nothing better at this point than to be held in their collective arms, to be told everything, everything is going to be fine, but the need to be strong is more compelling. The crying I do will have to be later or not at all or only in the dark secrecy of my heart.

There is a problem about landing in Paris, which is our next stop before Croatia. The French don't want to let us land. Finally they agree to accept us at an old military airport outside the city, which is not generally used for commercial traffic. As we approach France, the mood in the plane becomes charged with nervous exuberance. Is the end approaching? the passengers seem to be asking. Will we soon be on our way back home? Some of the passengers tell me they have never been to Europe and thank me for allowing them to come for free. I probably would never have gotten around to it otherwise, one man tells me. Those who have been sleeping are suddenly awake and bright-eyed, and even the sitting stewardesses have gotten out of their seats. Look out the window! Rudy tells me. Flying alongside our plane as escorts are the most delicate and beautiful planes I have ever seen. They look like fragile, silver insects gliding through the air, their noses refined, aristocratic, their bodies designed for speed and grace. It is a breathtaking sight and all the passengers watch, enthralled, from their windows. Our landing is smooth, but no sooner have we coasted to a stop than there appear around the plane what seems like hundreds of sharpshooters, guns held at an angle from their shoulders, faces dark. This sight disconcerts everybody. What do we need them for? someone says. Dick is on the radio, requesting food, fuel and emptying of the plane toilets. They did what? he yells into the phone. That's amazing, he says. I can't believe it. What's the matter? I ask him. Jesus Christ! They shot holes in the tires of the plane as we were landing! Dick is furious, can't comprehend that such an action should be taken without consultation with the flight crew, without a thought to the safety of the passengers. I didn't feel anything, I tell him. Maybe they're just saying that so that we'll forget the idea of flying on to Yugoslavia. I don't know, Dick says. I don't know. He rests his head on his folded arms once again, too overcome by what is happening around him, shocked at the loss of authority he has suffered at the hands of the French. I'm in charge of this plane, he yells into the radio. You don't do anything without clearing it with me! Are they at least bringing food and emptying the toilets? I ask. They say they are, but who knows at this point, he answers. Lou is sitting disgustedly next to Dick, silent, brooding. Tom is standing behind us, as though preparing in the immediate future to disembark and leave this nightmare behind. Taik carries on a steady stream of conversation with Dick, telling him what to say, asking questions. But whoever is in the control tower is not accommodating, refuses to do what is asked, refuses to give the information requested. They do tell us that there still has been no message communicated to the American authorities confirming that the leaflets have been printed according to the demands.

And the passengers are restless. What's happening? they ask me. Why aren't we getting food? I relate what I have learned, that the tires have been shot, that the French are refusing to comply with our requests for food and sanitation measures. The toilets are full, I am told by Rick, who suddenly isn't having as much fun as he was before, when he was cavorting up and down the aisle in his shorts and rugby shirt, shoeless, laughing, thinking about what a great talk show he was going to make out of his experiences on the plane. I'm sorry, I say, but we can't force them to come if they don't want to! There is a minor insurrection brewing among many of the passengers and the entire flight crew, and it is directed bizarrely against the French. What do they think they're doing? Dick says. Do they want us all to get blown up over some leaflets? Tempers are exploding all over the plane, and I hurry back and forth, trying to persuade everybody to be patient just a little longer. I am strangely gratified, though, that the antagonism and anger of the moment is directed not at us, but at the French, who have shamelessly usurped the power of the crew and are subjecting everybody to unnecessary suffering and discomfort.

The longer everybody sits, the darker the mood that suffuses the plane. It isn't fun anymore, it's not an exciting adventure. The fact is, they are hungry, exhausted, emotionally spent and, besides, they want to relieve themselves and can't even do that. Those damn French! The idiots! I hear over and over again as one passenger after another finds it necessary to focus his anger.

Steve wants to know if we're still going to try to fly over Croatia, as planned. I hope we don't, I tell him. But I don't say that I'm scared the Yugoslavs will shoot the plane down. They don't care if it's a passenger plane or not! And minutes later, I hear in the cabin that the Yugoslav government has, indeed, issued a threat to the French and the Americans that they will shoot the plane down the moment it enters Yugoslav air space, and they don't care how many passengers are on board. It is a relief to me to hear that; first, because it means a take-off is highly unlikely, but mainly, because it clearly illustrates the type of government that is in power in Yugoslavia. They'd just shoot down a whole planeload of innocent people? I am asked. Sure they would. They go around murdering them all the time on the ground, I say. Besides, the government is scared of the effect the leaflets could have on the population. They'd rather shoot down this plane than allow pieces of paper into the country. That's how fragile the government is, I tell them. Meanwhile, the sharpshooters still surround the plane, row upon row of green, bent figures hidden behind a rise in a hill, an old truck, whatever they can find to partially obscure our view of them.

There is still no word of a message from the control tower and no signs, either, that the French are planning to bring food or to empty the toilets. An aura of doom and despair permeates the plane, of hopelessness and anger and frustration. Suddenly, on the loudspeaker, I hear the voice of Father O'Rourke. Friends, those of you who are Catholic, it is time for us to prepare to meet our Maker! Thinking I have heard incorrectly, I ask one of the passengers what the priest said. He's giving us the last rites! he cries. I look around me, see that many of the passengers were now in a state of panic. Some look back at me hysterically, as though I had been deluding and tricking them all along, had been withholding vital information which was now, finally, being imparted to them by the good father. I jump up, furious at the father for taking it upon himself to inject this needless hysteria into the group. He's doing this on his own! I tell the passengers one by one. He has no reason to be saying those things, nothing has changed, nothing has happened! They want desperately to believe me, but find it difficult to imagine why the priest would arbitrarily visit such fear and suffering upon them. Priests are supposed to comfort, not terrify. He's just taken it upon himself! I tell those who are most visibly affected. They dry their eyes, still upset, but choosing to believe me instead of the prophet of doom. Why in the hell did he do that? I hear along the aisle. Dick is angry as well. He hadn't known what purpose the priest meant to make of the loudspeaker, he says. If he'd known, he wouldn't have allowed it.

The hours pass excruciatingly slowly. One would expect such a set of events to provide a constant input of stimuli, that the level of excitement would be almost intolerably elevated, but the fact is that we, who have been completely relieved of our power to make decisions, the hijackers as well as the passengers and flight crew, find ourselves not exhilarated by the tension or even energized, but simply bored by the tediousness and irrationality of it all. Why can't we have some measly sandwiches? Why can't they empty the toilets? This isn't of international importance, it's not something that has to be negotiated. So why make things worse than they have to be? And the general feeling is that the French are to blame. It seems everybody's Senator, everybody's congressman is going to hear about this.

Taik has called Slobodan to the cabin for a quiet discussion. The control tower won't cooperate, they won't do anything we ask, Taik tells him. He is really at his wit's end. We have to show them we're serious. They don't seem to believe that yet, he says. They talk a bit longer and then Slobodan leaves. Dick has, I am certain, never been so tired in his life. He is not a person anymore, but a nerve end, even in his exhaustion. Lou tells me something has to give, we can't go on like this forever. We need food, we need the toilets emptied. And what of the message telling us the leaflets have been printed? I don't know, I say. We should have heard something by now.

I hear a loud voice back in the plane, so I leave the cabin to see what's happening. I am shocked to see that the passengers have been grouped around Slobodan, who is sitting on top of one of the seats, the iron pot in his lap. What is going on here? I demand. I am appalled at this turn of events. I rush back to the cabin to find Dick yelling into the radio that we are all about to be blown up, that they don't understand the situation on the plane, it is volatile, it is dangerous, the demands have to be met, that's all there is! They won't listen, he tells Taik. They aren't going to involve anyone in their decisions. It's out of our hands, no matter what happens in the plane. Taik is white with anger. What is it we are asking for, anyway? Some food, some fuel, news from the States about the leaflets....He shakes his head, looks out the cabin door at Slobodan, who still has the passengers huddled around him. Dick's voice is cracking as he tries to reason with the people in the control tower. I am the pilot of this plane and you are completely cutting me out of everything! You aren't here on the plane, you don't have any idea what's going on here. We're all going to get blown up because you won't fulfill a few simple requests! Tears have come into Dick's eyes, tears of frustration and anger and exhaustion. Oh, Dick, I'm sorry, I tell him inadequately once again. They won't listen, he says, shaking his head. They won't listen to a thing I say.

Go back into the plane, Taik tells me tiredly. We have to keep talking to the people in the tower. So I leave him, return to the passengers. Don't worry, I tell them, nothing is going to happen! How sick I am of saying these words. How sick they must all be of hearing me say them, hour after hour. I go to Steve, who is looking at me beseechingly. Julie, I'm so scared. I hate to admit it, but I am. He is close to tears himself, but won't allow himself to cry. Steve, listen, do you trust me? I ask him. He nods his head, his eyes blinking rapidly. Then believe me when I say that nothing is going to happen, you are going to be on your way home soon, I give you my word, OK? He is silent. OK? I repeat, looking into his eyes. He gives me a wan smile. OK, he says. There is another man, whose name I don't know, he has been quietly reading and writing for most of the flight, and he is standing only a foot from the bomb in Slobodan's lap. He is obviously hyperventilating, breathing in short gasps, and his upper lip and forehead are spotted with heavy beads of sweat. His glasses, too, have clouded up, and there are dark patches of sweat under his arms. He is in very bad shape, so I go over to him as well, put my arm around his shoulder, tell him that this is just a show, so that the people in the tower will meet the demands. I swear to God nothing is going to happen to you. You'll be home with your family tomorrow, I tell him as strongly as I can. All right, he says, all right, and his breathing seems to slow a little, though it could just be my imagination, what I would like to believe. Rudy Bretz stands close to Slobodan, too, but he is predictably calm in the face of imminent death. He is the type of person who has long ago come to terms with his mortality and, if he were to die today, would have no regrets whatsoever about the way he has lived his life. I run from passenger to passenger, reassuring each one that nothing will happen, that it is just a show, that they will be home tomorrow. Who knows what these people believe at this point? But I must continue to repeat the same words, as though they alone have the power to prevent great tragedy and to control the actions of everyone else, the sharpshooters, the faceless, nameless tower people, the authorities in the States.

Finally the passengers are allowed to return to their seats. The show hasn't impressed the people in the tower, who have only witnessed it vicariously. Dick could have made the whole thing up for all they know, and perhaps they even believe that he has, just to force them to abandon their self-righteous and inflexible opposition to any kind of negotiations with "terrorists".

Almost without my knowledge, the sun seems to have set. It is dark outside, black, and for all I know, sharpshooters could be creeping up at this very moment, preparing to storm the plane and shoot all the hijackers. If they happen to hit a few of the passengers, this is the price that must be paid to combat terrorism, the lesser of two evils! I doubt the passengers would agree, but they are not being asked their opinions.

Petar comes over and tells me one of the men is very sick, he has severe abdominal pains and wants to be taken off the plane so that a doctor can examine him. After lengthy consultations with Taik, Dick, Lou, and the control tower, Petar escorts the man off the plane, practically carrying him under his arm, to an ambulance that has driven up alongside us. When Petar is back aboard, it occurs to me that he could easily have been shot dead by the soldiers outside. What was to prevent them? One less terrorist to deal with. A good terrorist is a dead terrorist. But I am certain their restraint has less to do with humanitarianism than with whatever opportunistic scheme they are presently concocting. Otherwise, Petar would be lying bloody on the tarmac, just to remind us of the eventual fate of all terrorist thugs!

And now the talk show host has developed pains as well. He is more petulant than anything else, as though he has suddenly decided that the cover charge for the entertainment he was promised was too high, he wants his money back, he is going to complain to the management. He has curled himself up into a fetal position on his seat, moaning and crying, but not convincingly. His boyfriend even seems to be disgusted at his display and, after murmuring a few desultory words of comfort in his ear, abandons him and walks to the back of the plane. Are you going to take him off the plane, too? one of the men asks me. I don't know, I answer truthfully. I had nothing to do with the decision to take the other one off. But somehow, the talk show host is forgotten. I have the feeling that he has often been forgotten in his life, that it is difficult in general to take this man seriously and also that we are not the first to question his authenticity. As if to acknowledge our suspicions, his symptoms subside almost as quickly as they have surfaced. If he can't leave the plane, he certainly doesn't plan on lying curled up uncomfortably while everyone else is roaming around and looking out the windows. Without warning, a sharp fist of guilt hits me in the stomach. He has every reason to want to leave the plane. After all, who wouldn't want to leave? I want to leave myself, and I'm one of the hijackers! The argument moves me intellectually, but when I go deep into myself, into my heart, I find nothing there for him but a black and noiseless void.

Everyone is ready to explode. They can't take much more. If I weren't one of the hijackers, I, too, like so many of the passengers, would be in the cabin offering suggestions as to how we can bring this to an end. But all I can do is go back and forth down the aisle and try to keep everybody calm. I am drawn again and again to the cabin, our only contact with the outside, the real world, though it is difficult to imagine anything more real and immediate than our existence on the plane, which seems already to have taken on a much greater significance than whatever lives we previously stumbled through. The French have given us an ultimatum, they have told us that we must surrender immediately or be sentenced to death by firing squad. I look at Dick incredulously as he relates this latest indignity. I'm just telling you what they said, he says with a weak smile. I know how ridiculous it sounds. But the bottom line is that they won't negotiate with you under any circumstances. We have to do something, I tell Taik. This just can't continue, we aren't getting anywhere. And the passengers have just about had it. Besides, I have a feeling the French are going to attack the plane if something doesn't happen soon.

Taik looks out the window, though it is impossible to see whether the sharpshooters have crawled closer or whether they are even still out there. I don't understand why we haven't gotten the code word from the States yet, I say. I don't understand, either, he answers. And then I have an idea, a way to bring the situation to an end. Why don't I leave the plane with Lou, or Knudsen, and call the States to verify that the leaflets have appeared in the newspaper? That would work, wouldn't it? Taik thinks it over for a minute or two and then, with a resigned expression on his face, as though he realizes finally that it is the only option left to us, gives his approval. Lou, you go with her and take Knudsen, too, because he says he is close friends with the Senator in his state and wants to get him involved. Dick, call the tower and let them know what's happening, he orders. After you make the calls, come back to the plane, he tells me. All right, I say. I'll be right back.

Lou and I leave the cabin with Knudsen, who is standing just outside the cabin talking with Tom Sheary, and head for the rear exit. When the passengers are told what is going on, most are visibly upset. They don't want me to leave, I am a calming influence, anything might happen without me to keep things under control! But that's not true, I reassure them. The men aren't going to do anything to harm you, all they want is to find out about the leaflets and then they'll surrender and you'll all be going home. We're just trying to bring it to an end as soon as possible! Most agree that it is a good idea; they just wish somebody else could execute it.

As we descend the exit steps, a van pulls up next to the plane. The officials are clearly unaware that I am one of the evil perpetrators, they assume I am a stewardess and that the other two are flight crew members as well. How many of them are there? they ask us. Well, actually, I'm one of them myself, I say. Their mouths fall open. They have the grace to shift nervously in their seats. And there are five altogether, I answer. After this, the officials fall uncomfortably silent. When we get out, we are escorted to a room where I am to make my calls to America. Taik has given me his small address book containing the names of two people to call, both of them in New York, whom he can trust to tell me the truth about the leaflets. One is Marijan, a married father of three who, along with his wife, Alojzija, is very active in Croatian politics, and the other is Father Mladen, a Catholic priest who is a friend of Taik's. The calls take what seems like forever to go through, but finally I am able to hear the thin voice of Marijan over the wires. He assures me that the leaflets have been printed and that the others have been dropped over Chicago, New York, London and Paris. Then I call the Croatian church and ask for Father Mladen. He tells me he isn't sure whether they have been printed or not, he hasn't seen the papers yet. I hang up, tell Lou that one person confirmed it and the other couldn't. Well, can't you just tell Taik that both people confirmed it? he asks me. I can't lie to him! I tell him apologetically. He trusts me! Lying to Taik is an idea as inconceivable to me as my not accompanying Taik on the plane. Lou is angry about my refusal but he can't bring himself to yell at me or tell me I'm stupid or unreasonable or irrational. He sits down heavily in a nearby chair and stares at the floor until we are escorted up to the control tower, where, we are informed, the American ambassador, a certain Mr. Kenneth Rush, is in attendance. When we arrive, Mr. Rush does not deign to look in our direction. He is too busy being officious and unapproachable, delivering ultimatums over the radio to the plane. When he realizes that he must give over the radio to me, the one who has the message the people in the plane actually want to hear, he takes it in ill humor, stands back and glares.

The connection is very bad between the tower and the plane, but I am finally able to recognize Taik's voice. I relay the information I have gotten from New York exactly as I have heard it, in spite of Lou's request that I ought to lie, that it is the right thing to do. If only it were so simple to determine right and wrong, if only there were one answer to every question! Will you surrender now? I ask Taik. I have to discuss the situation with the others. I'll call back in a half hour or so, he tells me. Lou and I go back downstairs, to a small room adjoining a larger one, in which at least eight or nine soldiers pore over papers spread out on a long wooden table. I know instinctively what they're doing. They're planning an attack on the plane. Don't attack the plane! I beseech them.

They're going to surrender soon! One of the soldiers speaks a little English, asks me how I know. I just know, I spoke to them a few minutes ago. They're getting ready to come out! I'm certain of it! He returns to the others and tells them what I have said, but they continue, in spite of my protestations, to examine the papers. After all, I am just a terrorist who can't be trusted, why should anybody believe what I say? A bitterness overcomes me at the injustice of this assumption, as though I have not had a life before these last thirty hours, and every good thing I have ever done has been ruthlessly invalidated.

Lou has gone somewhere, leaving me alone in the room with one of the French officials, who stares at me the way one would stare at a somewhat familiar and odious bug he cannot name. I stare back until he averts his eyes. Nobody, it seems, enjoys being stared at. A few minutes later, another official comes into the room with a New York Times in his hand, obviously flown over from the states, and hands it to me. I am relieved that I can now personally confirm that the leaflets were printed. I take the paper, scan the front page. On the far right, there is a column saying "Bomb Blast Kills One Policeman and Wounds Three". I almost ignore it. What does it have to do with us, anyway? But my eyes are drawn back to it, against my will; a chill of horror spreads throughout my body as I read that a bomb left in New York City, a bomb connected to the hijacking of a TWA plane by Croatian nationalists, has exploded at the detonation site, killing police officer Brian Murray and wounding three of his associates. A complete and unequivocal denial sets in immediately. There must be some mistake. Taik took every possible precaution and also had Dick transmit over the radio all the information the authorities needed for the safe detonation, I had even heard part of the transmission. It's obviously a trick, a not-so-clever trick concocted by the government to force the men still in the plane to surrender. I'm surprised to have been even momentarily taken in by such a transparent piece of treachery!

When Lou returns, I bring the article to his attention. As he has no reason for denying or questioning the truth of the information, he allows himself the luxury of grief and shock. My God! he says, and looks at me for my reaction. But it's not true, Lou! I protest. It can't possibly be true! He is again too kind to claim otherwise, to tell me what this means to the life I once had. Instead, seeing the desolation in my eyes, he allows me to drape myself in his arms and cry, while he pats my arm and makes small sounds of comfort. Well, I need to cry, I tell myself, if only to release the tension. It doesn't mean the article is true! The enormity of its possible truth is akin to believing in the superiority of the Devil over God, the Devil, an entity whose entire being is dedicated to needless destruction and misery. If I don't believe, that evil force doesn't exist, it's as simple as that. And I do not, with all the strength of my will, believe. Therefore, it didn't happen.

When I call Taik again on the radio, I mention the article in passing, as though it is of little importance except to demonstrate the cunning of our adversaries. It can't be true, I say. Taik is silent. Though I have not solicited an answer or reassurance from him, I crave one nonetheless. It can't be true, can it? He lets about ten interminable seconds pass before answering. No, he tells me, it's not. The leaflets were printed, though, I assure him, I saw the newspapers. That's good, he answers, though his voice, even over the radio, sounds the way an old rag that has dried in the sun might sound if one were to pick it up and squeeze it. Let me talk to the ambassador now. So I hand the radiophone to the ambassador and go back downstairs to wait for the surrender, which Taik has assured me will take place shortly.

I am outraged to see that the soldiers are still poring over large sheets of paper spread out on the table, as though nothing I had said, none of my assurances of an imminent surrender, had fazed them in any way. But there are too many other things on my mind to worry about an assault on the plane. The men will be surrendering before they can even fold up all the papers. I sit and wait, wait, under the watchful eye of a guard posted just outside the door, a kind-faced, weary-eyed man who very clearly wishes I had not gotten myself involved in such a mess;

from time to time, he shares a sad smile with me, murmurs quiet words of what I instinctively know as encouragement. Suddenly I hear noises in the hallway, loud voices, shoes or boots on the tiles, a squeak, a door slamming. Then I look up to see the male steward from the plane. The surrender must have taken place!

But now everything has changed, he doesn't have to talk to me or even to look in my direction. I don't immediately realize the delicate balance has been upset to my disadvantage, and ask him immediately if he would take Taik's address book and hide it from the authorities, as though he and I were co-conspirators. He looks at me as though I were completely out of touch with reality, he has the sense to know what I have not yet comprehended: We are not on the same side. The camaraderie that had existed on the plane was an illusion, born of necessity, out of fear and desperation. But what about Rudy, what about Steve and Dick? It can't be possible that they were pretending, that they felt hatred for me, I would have known, I could have seen it in their eyes!

The steward moves away from me, as though I were contagious, and the benevolence, the generosity of spirit I had felt towards him on the plane dissipate and are replaced with a hot and searing anger. It is a transformation that amazes me. How can I be capable of such a total reversal of attitude? I see myself from afar, from a point removed in time and space, and I recognize with finality that what I am capable of cannot be contained, ordered, listed or summarized. The steward's eyes, deep and critical, look into me, through me, turn me inside out. I have to look away, I can't bear the thought that my essence has totally escaped him. Then the sick man, the one who was taken by Petar from the plane, walks in the room, looking fit, flushed, and healthy. Knudsen follows behind him, tells me the guy was faking, he just wanted to get off the plane. The sick but healthy man won't look at anybody, not at me nor at the others, as though the reality of what he has done is beginning to dawn on him like a huge sun in the east. Was he a coward? He will have to work this out for himself.

The French don't want me together with the passengers, obviously, for I am removed to another room, where a snotty, sharp-nosed and pale man of about my age attempts to question me in a barely intelligible English. His attempts at sarcasm and contempt in a language he has not mastered anger but do not intimidate me. Soooo, he says, you kill policeman. You receive death sentence, good for you. I am astonished to the very core of my soul by his scorn, unconnected to even the most basic knowledge of my self, but I do not let him know this. What name you? he asks as he takes out a pen. I look up at him slowly. Don't talk to me, I tell him. I don't like you. Ha! he says loudly. Ha! And then launches into an emotional tirade, conducted entirely in French. I close my eyes, lay my head on the desk for what seems like hours. When I open my eyes once more, he is sitting silently, in a rage, smoking a cigarette as though it were a pin he were poking into and then extracting from his clenched lips. I need to stand up, so I do, get up slowly, just in time to see Dick walking by, taking long strides, a shoulder bag hanging from his arm. My reaction is immediate and uncontrollable.

Dick! I scream, and run out of the room into the hallway towards him, arms outstretched. He turns, sees me, and drops his bag, opens his arms to me. I am crying, loudly, breathlessly, as we hug each other. My antagonist watches this inconceivable event with his mouth open, hands limp at his side. I love you, Dick! I say, and feel that these are the truest words that have ever escaped from my mouth. I love you, too, he says, before he is hustled away by strange men in suits and ties.

Back and forth, back and forth they take me, from one room to another. This time I go to a room in which Taik, Frane, Petar and Slobodan stand, handcuffed together. I look at them, dumfounded, as though I don't quite recognize them. They look weird in the handcuffs, like lions on leashes, diminished somehow, disenfranchised. I think they're taking us to Yugoslavia, Taik tells me. It isn't possible! I say. They can't send us there, we'll be killed! He shakes his head. They can do whatever they want, he says. Without warning, I collapse to the floor and begin to scream, as loud as I can, a high, piercing scream, one which brings people running down the hallway, guns drawn. My screams shock me. I have never screamed before and now don't seem to be able to stop. They're taking us to Yugoslavia, they're taking us to Yugoslavia, help, help, help! I repeat over and over between screams. I scream for Dick, for Lou, for anybody who can hear me. My legs go out from under me, I am being carried bodily out of the room, one man for each leg, one for each arm. I scream and kick, call them names, call for Dick and Lou, for people I have never heard of. Who are these people? We go into a room, the door is closed, I am put down onto the floor. Faces bend over me, some concerned, others exasperated. You aren't going to Yugoslavia! one of them assures me. Oh sure! I say, beginning to wail again. I realize the ludicrous picture I present crumpled on the floor, face red and snotty, so I sit up, smooth my dress. What would my family and friends think if they could see and hear me now? I must pull myself together, get a grip. My agonized screams still ring in my ears. Did I really lose control so totally?

Again I sit and wait, perhaps an hour, perhaps two, time has no meaning for me now, until I am taken out again to rejoin the men. This time I am handcuffed together with them, except I am at one end and Taik is on the other. I would like to be cuffed next to Taik, but don't know how to go about making this request. Common decency requires that husbands be handcuffed next to wives, but what would these people know about such things, these same people who refused to empty the toilets or bring food for the passengers, as though the passengers were guilty of something? The five of us are led outside the terminal, where hordes of photographers have materialized, cameras slung around their necks. Flashbulbs begin to pop, questions are thrown at us in a variety of languages, none of which we answer. I hang my head, pretend it is a mistake, a case of mistaken identity which will be cleared up later. A dull green plane is waiting not far from the building, a military jet which will take us directly back to America, or, as Taik still maintains, to Yugoslavia.

After the pictures are taken, we are driven by van to the plane, uncuffed, then cuffed individually for the flight. Our escorts, military police, decide I must not wear leg-irons like the men, who are taking little baby steps down the aisle of the plane to their designated seats. We are separated from one another, each assigned to one official, but we can still yell down the aisle to each other. Taik tells me not to admit anything, to be quiet. When one of the officials comes down the aisle and, improbably, as though this were a regular commercial flight, proffers a plate of before-dinner mints, which I am inclined to take, Taik yells at me not to touch anything, it could be poisoned, it could be anything! No, thank you, I say apologetically. My escort smiles. He seems to understand that the mints are simply out of the question. I eye them sadly nonetheless.

The flight is long, interminable, especially since our escorts cannot speak English and my college French is decidedly rusty. Taik has finally decided, though, that we are not going to Yugoslavia, he can tell by the sun. I am too confused and exhausted to know anything, too frightened of the possible truth in the article I had read back in Paris. It's not true, Taik reassures me over and over again. It couldn't possibly be true, it's a trick! And I allow myself to be reassured. After all, what is the alternative?

27

"The thought of suicide is a powerful comfort: it helps one through many a dreadful night." Nietzsche

Finally we arrive in New York, whereupon the plane is boarded immediately by a large group of FBI agents. They are not interested at first in speaking with us, they go directly to the French military police. Unfortunately, though, none of them can speak French. A clear case of poor planning. And since the French officials don't speak English, we all stand around and look at each other. My French escort tells one of the agents, in French, that our bags are in the back of the plane. He says our bags are in the back of the plane, I volunteer to the FBI agents. They are not pleased with my assistance. It makes them look stupid. What can they do, though, except go in the back and retrieve our bags? After all, it's evidence and they can't afford to overlook anything. Afterwards, they read us our rights, exactly like one sees in the movies, and then we are taken off the plane.

A sizable crowd waits impatiently behind ropes strung across a small square of asphalt in front of the plane. When we emerge from the plane and make our way down the steps, a murmur rises from the midst of the group, but I can't make out individual words, or don't want to. There is no time to look at one person or another, to get in touch with what I am feeling, because we are whisked into separate cars and driven off rapidly as the crowd scrambles and scuffles to get into better viewing positions. I don't look back.

At the FBI building, the five of us are separated immediately. I am assigned to a female agent named Margo, who warns me before one of the New York City policemen comes in to ask me questions. He'll talk tough to you, so be prepared, she says. This is the classic bad cop/good cop routine. And he does, tells me that they're going to lock me away for the rest of my life in some dark dungeon; that is, if I don't get the death penalty first. The bad cop, Coffey, is clearly a bad human being in general; this is not merely a role. He exudes a nameless yet incontrovertible aura of decay. He is the type who beats up suspects and then charges them with resisting arrest. He is the type who lies on his reports to make himself look better or writes false and tawdry, second-rate books about his more notorious cases, with himself in a role to which he will forever aspire: that of a brave and principled protagonist. Margo gives me sympathetic looks. Trust me, she seems to be saying, I don't want to hurt you, I want to help. My heart immediately hardens against the hapless Margo.

Are there any more bombs anywhere in the city, the surly bad cop asks me. Not that I know of, I answer. I vaguely recall a mention in one of the demand notes of other bombs in other places. No, I tell him more emphatically, there aren't any more. He wants to ask me more questions but I am not a good corn-fed, TV-raised American girl for nothing. I don't have to talk to them. I have a right to an attorney! Besides, I feel as though my head is floating up into the air like a helium balloon. Nothing I say would make any kind of sense. I want an attorney. I'm too tired to talk, I tell them. If only Taik and the others will remember their television! I lay my head on a table and simply refuse to say another word.

After what seems like hours later, we are taken to a newly-built federal detention center in downtown Manhattan. It's not so bad, good cop Margo tells me. You'll see. As I am being processed, I catch sight of Taik coming out of a small room. He is whisked past me, but manages to tell me not to admit anything, not to talk to them. I watch as they push him onto an elevator, watch as the doors close. Where are they taking him? When will I be able to see him? My fingerprints are taken again. I just had them taken at the FBI building, I explain, but nobody is interested. I am searched, every nook and cranny of me, but am simply too exhausted to be indignant. Some of the officers give me harsh, condescending looks, and others are simply curious. I have finally realized that it is true. Someone was killed and others were wounded. Taik was not right this time, it wasn't a ploy or a cunning trick to force the surrender. But I can't think about it, it is too much for me to handle, to assimilate.

I end up locked in a hospital room in the basement of the building. There is a small black and white television set in the corner, which is already tuned into a news coverage of the hijacking. I watch myself being led off the plane. I watch the five of us entering the FBI building. Dick Carey is talking, the Police Commissioner is calling us some names, the plane is shown in Paris, the passengers are waving from a van after the surrender. A voice outside my door wants me to come and talk, but I refuse to answer. Here's today's paper, the voice says as it is slipped under the door. You're on the front page! I stare at the paper as though it were a poisonous snake which has slithered between the door frame and the floor, feel an urge to kick it back out, get it away from me. The door opens, a physician's assistant asks me if I need anything. I begin to cry, my head drops against his shoulder. He is surprised to discover himself holding me, patting my back, my head. No, no, no, he says, no, no, no, over and over again, until my sobs subside. I want to call my parents, I say. But I irrationally tell myself that they don't love me anymore. I will tell them to disown me, to deny they have a daughter, have ever had a daughter. I will begin my punishment now, before anybody else has a chance to punish me, I will begin now to atone. Wait, I have to get permission for you to call, the P.A. tells me. Meanwhile, I sit on the bed. My mind, my sense of self has shattered into small, sharp pieces. I am close to hysteria, have to do something, do something now, at this very moment, to atone for what has happened, I have to surrender my life and all possible future happiness, but how can this be accomplished, what would be enough, how much? A thought flashes suddenly into my consciousness like a shooting star, streaks across the blackness of my being. I will become a nun. The rest of my life will be spent in isolation and contemplation. The joy of my life will be taken from me, no Taik. There will be no more joy in my life. This will be my punishment. I have been involved in something which has taken away someone else's joy. Now I must lose mine. Death would spare me the suffering I have inflicted, albeit unintentionally, on another. I have to live, I have to be reminded of it every day, every waking moment.

Come on, let's go make your call, the P.A. says. So we go to a wall phone and I dial the number with a shaky finger. My knees are shaky, too, so I lean against the wall, like a cripple who can't stand on her own. My mother answers the phone on the first ring. Mom? I say. She begins to cry or perhaps she has already been crying. Perhaps she has been crying for days already. Oh, honey! she sobs. They're charging us with murder! I say. She can't talk, can't answer. But she is on the line, connected to me in spite of everything. I'm so sorry, I'm so sorry, I tell her again and again. Nothing is your fault, I say, don't let anybody tell you that! It is critical that she understand that nothing is her fault, that I am taking responsibility for everything. We love you, she tells me, you are our daughter and we love you and we'll do whatever we can for you, OK? I can't talk. OK, honey? she repeats. OK, mom, I finally say. I love you so much, I tell her. I have to hang up now, I say. Call us as much as you can, honey, OK? I hang up the phone and shuffle back to the room. Though the P.A. gives me a sleeping pill, I cannot sleep, my head is full of nightmares and nightmarish thoughts, of horrors so vivid and intricate that I am hardly able to hold myself together, to contain the screams that threaten to erupt from within me at any moment. A nun, I repeat to myself, a nun, a convent, a nun, a convent.

The next day we are arraigned, and a bail of one million dollars apiece is set. And then an attorney comes to see us, one which has been retained by the Croatian community on our behalf. He is Michael Tigar, from the Washington, D.C. firm of Edward Bennett Williams, and right away he wants to know what our politics are. Taik says if we have to define ourselves, it would be as Social Democrats, which seems to please him. He will take the case. Besides, we discover that his aunt has lived in Gearhart for many years, an incredible coincidence.

I am moved to the fifth floor, with thirty other women awaiting trial. But they lock me in one of the rooms by myself, only let me out to make a phone call or to take a shower. The women feel sorry for me, come to talk to me through the crack in the door, slip me newspapers and magazines whenever the guard isn't looking. Taik and the others are on the ninth floor, and they, too, are locked in their rooms. It's because of the high bail and the escape risk, one of the women whispers to me through the door.

Stories of the hijacking and its aftermath are all over the papers, as well as on TV and radio. I see for the first time a picture of the policeman's widow, Kathleen Murray, with her two small boys. They are all dressed in black. She is wearing a hat and her head is down. The boys stand close to her, against her leg; they are bewildered, bereft. She looks so vulnerable and fragile, Kathleen Murray, and the boys are like small, tender animals at her side, who cling to her for comfort in the face of this inexplicable event which will change them forever. I wonder how much she loved her husband, find myself, to my shame, half hoping she didn't love him and is relieved in a perverse way that he is gone, that she can begin another life with someone else, someone not on the New York City Bomb Squad. But she loved him, I know it in the deepest part of my soul, and now he is gone and the little dark-haired boys are left to wonder all their lives what has become of their father, what they might have done to hold him. I hang my head between my knees, but then sit up straight again. I don't want the officer to log my actions, their duration, in the little book he is required to keep on my every activity.

At mail call every day, a huge pile of letters is delivered to me in my room. Letters from Croatians all over the world, from Venezuela, France, Australia, Germany, Belgium and Canada, congratulating me on my sacrifice, praising me for my bravery and humanity, pour into the prison. Huge bouquets of flowers are delivered as well, which I am not allowed to have. I am told that I am a heroine, I am a saint and a symbol! Poems are written in my honor and songs are sung for me. Money is raised around the world for our defense. It is confusing. I am a saint to a thousand people and a terrorist to five hundred others. What am I? All I know is that the pale faces of Kathleen Murray and her two boys haunt me. But so, too, does Bruno's face, dear Bruno, alone, hunted, and in exile, so do the faces of all the imprisoned and murdered Croatians, who only wanted to live in peace in their own country, the faces of those who live there now.

After a month, I am finally let out of my room to mingle with the other prisoners. One of the lieutenants, Mr. Holley, has decided it is unnecessary to keep me locked up any longer. He is from the south, Kentucky, I think, and we talk about the pictures I have tacked up on my bulletin board, one of the ocean, a small town in Italy, a field of poppies… You aren't what I thought you'd be like, he tells me. He is big, but soft and gentle in his speech and gestures. His small kindness to me breaks my heart and causes a lump to rise in my throat, as it is the first one I have experienced at the hands of the prison officials.

Our attorneys come to visit us regularly to discuss the trial and our options, but I am more inclined to use these visits to hold Taik's arm, or to rest my head against his shoulder. The prosecutor wants to make a deal with me. He sees me as the weak link. A woman, an American among foreigners… He'll give me twenty five years if I don't go to trial.

If I testify against the others, he'll sweeten the deal up considerably. There are many loose ends, many suspected co-conspirators, for example, where did the explosives come from? Who was supposed to call in the code word? Who wrote the leaflets and who translated them into French? Our offense carries an automatic life sentence or the death penalty. I venture to suggest to Taik that we make a deal for twenty five years without, of course, testifying against anybody else. He flatly refuses. We have to go to trial, he says, and that's that. Besides, Tigar reminds me, they didn't offer Taik twenty five years, they only offered it to you!

The letters, poems, flowers, money, continue to pour in from all parts of the world. Bruno writes to raise my morale and to assure me that all Croatians support us and will help us financially, morally, politically. He sends me pictures and cryptic phrases in Croatian which I take as secret codes relating to our imminent release. He also sends poems he himself has written and poems by others, such as Simic and Dragojevic, most of which deal with separation, loss, love, imprisonment, the force of will. The New York papers call us terrorists and murderers and call for the harshest of punishments available under the law. Meanwhile, I have been given a conscientious and committed public defender, David Rudolf, whom I decide, finally, to keep for the trial. After all, it is not a tricky case. I can't claim mistaken identity and there is plenty of evidence. There's no need to spend more Croatian money than is absolutely necessary. Besides, Taik needs the best representation. He has taken all the responsibility and refuses to allow us to contradict any of his statements, most of which were made in the FBI building shortly after our arrest. He and the others had forgotten their American cop shows, and had reacted from the gut, as they would have in Croatia, to avoid beatings and torture at the hands of the police. To them, police are all the same. When they ask you questions, you give an answer. It doesn't have to be the correct one, but if you don't want all your bones broken or your teeth knocked out, you don't get smart and ask for an attorney, you say, yes, sir, no, sir and I'll try to remember, sir.

Almost every day, we meet with our attorneys, go over everything again and again. Tigar wants to use a defense of diminished capacity for Taik; that is, that he was, due to his social history and experiences, unable to formulate the criminal intent necessary to commit the crime. Dr. Bernard Diamond, the originator of this unusual theory, interviews Taik and me and declares Taik the epitome of such an individual. The judge, John Bartels, refuses to allow his testimony, however, which deprives Taik completely of a defense. We will be judged like common criminals, our motivations ignored, given no weight whatsoever. We might just as well have done it for money or out of sheer perversity.

When we are taken out to court, there are sharpshooters stationed on the roofs and escort cars with heavily armed guards behind and in front of us, just in case any of our supporters should try to deliver us from federal custody. They are not here to protect us but to protect society from us. The sirens blare as we speed across town to our destination. People stop along the street and stare, wondering which important dignitary or movie star is traveling behind the dark windows. I feel ridiculous being the object of such excessive security precautions, but then I know that I am not, could never be, dangerous or violent. For that matter, neither could the four others. We behave politely and cordially at all times towards our guards and try to explain our actions as fully as we can when asked for explanations. Some of the guards grow to like us and look forward to seeing us from day to day. A few others make vicious comments under their breath, tell us they "hope we fry". The malevolence and brutality of such an sentiment stuns me. It takes an inordinate amount of cruelty to tell a perfect stranger you hope he or she dies. But we deal with it all, in our individual ways. We have no other choice.

The jury is composed of eight women and four men. One of the men is replaced in the beginning. He has fallen asleep during the prosecutor's opening statement. I can't blame him. I find it hard myself to keep my eyes open during his histrionics, and it is our trial.

The courtroom is packed every day with Croatians who want to witness what they consider an important piece of Croatian history. Some friends of ours, who happen to be nuns, are banished from the front row because of the prosecutor's belief that they could tend to influence the jury, and others are cautioned to refrain from applauding whenever we enter the courtroom. The press is present in large numbers as well, and there is even a courtroom artist, whose renderings of the key trial figures appear each evening on the news.

My parents have flown to New York for the trial, leaving Todd behind with friends. My mother cries when she sees me for the first time in the visiting room, wearing a baggy neon orange jumpsuit and rubber thongs three sizes too large. I am pale and quiet and find it hard in the beginning to talk to my sad-faced parents who have suffered so much because of me, but before too long, we have found each other again and are laughing at my prison anecdotes or at a joke my father heard back home. Their love and dedication to not only me but to Taik as well infuses me with new strength and optimism, and my spirits lift appreciably as the days go on. I visit with Taik as well, three times a week, though it necessitates a major logistical assault on my part to ensure that he is brought down to my floor at the proper time and on the proper nights. I beg, I whine and wheedle, I practically sell my soul to get him to me on time so that not a single moment is lost in transit. Once I even call on the phone to his floor, represent myself as one of the Case Managers, and order the floor officer to send him down immediately. Until I see him step off the elevator, I am in a state of frenzy and utter chaos, I can't sit, I can't stand still, all I am able to do is will him to appear, with a single-minded and ferocious will which admits no obstacles.

We get strange news from all directions almost on a daily basis. Somebody calls up the state district attorney, Alan Broomer, threatening to kidnap him if he doesn't drop our case. He's bright enough to smell

Yugoslav provocation and lets the matter drop. And the Yugoslavs are accusing the "Jewish lobby, the FBI and the CIA" of organizing the hijacking. On the other hand, another anonymous source who has called the federal prosecutor claims that it was a Russian plan, and that the passengers were to have been held hostage in exchange for the extradition of a recent Russian defector pilot, Victor Belenko. Another "amazing coincidence", according to one of the newspapers, is the fact that the notorious international terrorist, "Carlos", was in Yugoslavia on the very day of the hijacking and that the Yugoslav authorities had released him. Bruno sends me clippings from Croatian newspapers, in which our case figures, and assures me that some of the most highly respected Croatian intellectuals and activists people are working undercover on our behalf and will continue to do so, even if something were to happen to him. One of these, he tells me, is a revered religious figure, the same priest who had confirmed me in Cleveland, Ohio. The mail continues to pour in, from all parts of the world. The other prisoners give me a hard time when the box of mail comes to our floor each afternooon. All the mail is for me. Give us a break, Julie", they say, mostly teasing but not entirely.

I agonize over the implications of going to trial. I am frightened, I don't want to go, but how much value does an idea have if it is not taken to the end? This is the question I am being forced to answer. I am being asked to risk my life for an idea. It is the ultimate act of sincerity.

Dick Carey is the main prosecution witness. We have provided them with so much evidence, it is difficult to understand why a prosecution is even necessary. But it is good to see Dick again, though the sight of his face brings instant tears to my eyes. The memories we share, the agony we endured, the anger, the fear and doubts—all of it floods back into my mind, as though a huge dam in my consciousness has suddenly been blown to bits. He smiles at me, but not too heartily. He is, after all, a witness for the prosecution. But his testimony is not damaging to us; rather, he states the facts which are known to everybody and refuses to embellish upon them, refuses to paint a picture of terrorists and thugs, or bloodthirsty jackals with no regard for human life. He is here to tell what happened. He allows no deviation from those bare facts.

Other witnesses are called, but I find myself disconnecting from the proceedings. There is an excess of external stimuli which tends to deaden instead of invigorate my physical and emotional being. My parents are in the front row, as they have been every day. The sight of them keeps me going. My mother blows me kisses whenever she can and my father gives me the victory sign, discreetly, so that the marshals cannot see. They are constantly trying to catch our supporters engaging in partisan behavior, the better to be able to eject them all from the courtroom. But they are sly, my mother and father. I intercept all the kisses, all the victory signs, I get the winks, the waves, the nods, and the silently clapping hands when a certain fact is brought out on the witness stand, or a particularly revealing observation.

We learn that the Croatian community has raised over five million dollars and many have signed over all their property and possessions in order for us to be released on bail during the remainder of the trial. They have also gathered tens of thousands of signatures of support throughout the world, which amazes Judge Bartels. He comments on this huge show of support in the courtroom, and also about the hundreds of people who have also volunteered to serve our prison sentences for us, in the event that we are convicted. But the bail is refused, as the prosecution has raised so many obstacles that the trial would be over before they can be resolved. And, as we knew, there is no provision in the law allowing others to serve our sentences. But the solidarity gives us strength and helps us to survive, to transcend.

During the lunch break, which we spend in dank and grim bullpens in the basement of the building, our friend Stipe, owner of a French restaurant, a la Chandelle, brings us delicacies: stuffed filet of sole, filet mignon, salads, breads, rich and heady desserts. Instead of salad dressing, he has substituted red wine. We drain the bowls and drink it down,

368 Lovers and Madmen

quickly, before his ruse is discovered. But it never is. We drain our bowls day after day, and return to the courtroom infinitely more relaxed than we had been in the morning.

The trial goes on and on. Expert witnesses are brought in, bomb specialists, all trying to solve the mystery surrounding the explosion. Officers testify as well, those who were there and those who were not. None seem to be able to agree with one another. I begin to wonder if there are, in fact, any absolutes in the universe or whether everything depends upon, is contingent on, is relative to.... And then the strangest looking man enters the courtroom. His face is a Dali or a Picasso face, off-center, the angles all wrong. Nothing matches up, one side sags, the other looks as though the skin has been stretched over a bumpy canvas. What's the matter with his face? I begin to ask my attorney. Suddenly I stop. A horrifying mystery of the universe is suddenly revealed to me. This is McTigue, the head of the bomb squad, the one whose responsibility it was to safely defuse the bomb. I had heard his name over and over again and now he sits on the witness stand, only feet away. He doesn't look in our direction, not once, but my eyes are drawn to him against my will, something deep within me is forcing the fact of his disfigurement into my consciousness.

The technical testimony baffles and bores almost everybody in the courtroom. McTigue's answers to our attorneys' questions are incomplete, evasive, and when he finally leaves the stand, the question still remains: What happened? Why did the bomb, which was not designed to explode, suddenly blow up in his face? Why had he ignored the detailed instructions Taik had given him from the plane? We'll never get the truth out of them, Tigar says. It's a cover-up.

Taik still believes the Yugoslavs are somehow responsible, that they had been informed about the bomb and had gone to the site in advance of the bomb squad, fashioned some remote-control device so that they could detonate the bomb just as the police officers were approaching it, thus branding most effectively all Croatians fighting for independence as terrorists, murderers, lunatics…. His explanation is every bit as plausible as McTigue's. Who could imagine a professional bomb disposal "expert" approaching what he believes could be a live bomb without any type of protective clothing, without gloves, without a vest, and proceed to poke around the bomb with his fingers. How could he allow his men to follow him into the disposal pit and to ignore basic safety procedures known to every rookie?

Various passengers from the plane are called, but their stories are basically the same. They have no need to embellish on an experience only the vividest imagination could conjure up. They are surprisingly free of bitterness or resentment, and when they speak of their fears and terror during the worst moments, it is in a calm and even voice, as though the fears and terror had belonged to someone else, someone close, related perhaps by blood, which accounts for their obvious empathy but precludes, naturally, any histrionics on their part.

We return exhausted after each court session to our cell blocks. There is always a pile of letters from Croatians awaiting me at the officer's station, letters from around the world, many of them saying I am a heroine, I am the Croatian Joan of Arc, a symbol of freedom and sacrifice for the entire Croatian nation! Bruno writes, telling us he will be behind us until the stars fall from the sky. The New York newspapers call us thugs, murderers, terrorists, madmen… My mother holds me in her arms in the visiting room, tells me I'll always be her sweet little girl, strokes my hair, my face. This is who I really am, my mother's sweet little girl.

"Perhaps nobody yet has been truthful enough about what truthfulness is." Nietzsche

Our attorneys do such a good job defending us, they believe in us, respect us, want to perform a miracle in spite of the overwhelming evidence against us. My attorney, Dave Rudolf, puts his entire heart and spirit into the case. I see it transforming him as the trial continues, shattering some of his illusions, some important ones, sapping him of his idealism. But he is so imbued with enthusiasm that I find myself entertaining the possibility of an acquittal, or at least a term of probation in lieu of imprisonment. Michael Tigar is dazzling in the courtroom, endearing in his cowboy boots. The jurors warm to him immediately. The other two, Rochman and Elefant, are conscientious and capable and fight indefatigably to "protect the record". We makes jokes about our attorneys, one a Tigar and one an Elefant. Because the case against Taik and me is a capital case, we have two attorneys each, we have added Michael Asen and Pierce O'Donnell, who is also from Bennett and Williams. What a merry bunch we are, carrying on in the face of the greatest adversity and tragedy. It

wouldn't do to present grim faces to the courtroom full of our families
and supporters. They want to see determination, confidence, self-assur-
ance, so that is what we give them. The necessity for this enforced piece of
theater oppresses me. Surely the Croatians, surely our families, must feel
our despair and sadness and wish to share it with us. It is hard to imagine
that we have succeeded in deceiving everybody!

All of us have decided to testify on our own behalf. We have a story
to tell and explanations to offer for our actions, reasons any thinking
and feeling person can comfortably accept. When the time comes for
our testimony, however, I am horrified to discover that our reasons
are disallowed. Did we do it or did we not, that is all that matters in
this courtroom. And if we did it, how? And when? Surely somebody is
interested in the whole story! I am unable to discover that person, all
I know is that whenever any of us attempts to explain how we became
involved in this desperate action, the prosecutor, Peter Schlamm,
whose last name in German translates, appropriately, as "muddy,
murky", jumps up in feigned indignation. Objection! he bawls,
rolling his eyes at our shameless attorneys, who dare to try to defend
us, who, for doing so, are automatically, in his opinion, no better than
we, the scum of the earth, the detritus of a decaying universe.
Sustained, sustained…Everything is sustained. We are unable to get
anything of substance before the jury. By the time I take the stand, I
have abandoned all hopes of communicating the despair of the
months before the hijacking. It isn't relevant. Immaterial, irrelevant.
Objection! Sustained.

Judge Bartels wants to be kind and understanding, but is prevented
by the prosecutors from doing so. They cite the law, endless case docket
numbers, appeal decisions, all of which preclude our deviating in any
way from established defenses, orthodox testimony. Our character witnesses are paraded through the courtroom. They all attest to our good
characters and integrity, our work records, standing in the community,
history of law-abiding behavior. Steve Sunshine looks abashed as he

takes the stand, tries to loosen up the jury with a gentle jibe, thinking, as I had in the beginning, that any normal, reasonable person would immediately know that we are not terrorists or criminals, that any kind of testimony disputing that fact would be somehow superfluous, even insulting. The jury, though, is uncomfortable with his manner and regards him sternly. This is not a joke. This is reality! I look down at the table as he speaks of my good qualities. I feel ashamed that I must ask friends to defend me in this way to strangers. After Steve, Esther Ewart and Maria Boyer, friends from Oregon, speak on my behalf. They are articulate, sincere, devoted to me and my welfare, but their testimony is not the stuff of which great trials consist. The last thing anybody wants to believe is that we are possibly good people involved in a bad situation. They want to hear and see evil, in its most unadulterated form.

It is difficult to remember specific days. The trial goes on and on, like a ball of string which is rolling downhill, becoming smaller and smaller, more and more insubstantial. And finally it is over, all the witnesses have lied or told the truth, all the evidence has been entered. We return to the prison to await a verdict. My parents are holding up well, though their faces are drawn, as is mine, from the constant tension and uncertainty we suffer from one day to the next. I find myself more concerned with the particular marshals who escort us to court than with the verdict. One, a young female marshal, is haughty and insufferable, one of those hopeless types who heap their hatreds on the first available victim, who blame everyone but themselves for their ineptitudes and insecurities. But there are others who are truly a joy to be around, both among the marshals and state detectives, who escort us from time to time. There is Mary, an effervescent, kindly, mothering soul, who makes each day a little more bearable. There are the state detectives, Kelly and McGinniss, who seem to know instinctively that we stumbled into this whole thing and try to be kind, or perhaps they don't even have to try. When I see them waiting to escort us, I feel as though I am being delivered into the hands of my family instead of to snarling and implacable beasts. I am concerned with details in the picture, at this point, and not the picture in its entirety.

The jury asks question after question about the instructions the judge has given, and we try to divine their thoughts from what they are asking, but it is all pure hypothesis, we have no clue as to what is going on in the jury room. Whenever a question is asked, we must be brought back into the courtroom. Meanwhile, we wait in the fetid holding pens adjacent to it, on hard and stained wooden benches upon which desperate messages, names, numbers, have been carved throughout the years. Do the time or the time will do you...; La Skippy, New York Rican; Justice Sucks; I wouldn't know what to write if I were to write on this bench. What could possibly be sufficient to express my state of mind, sitting, waiting for a probable mandatory life sentence in this decaying cement hole, where thousands of others have wept and made brave jokes and fought and shaken the bars vainly?

When they take me from my holding cell, I pass the one in which the men are held. Taik moves up to the bars, puts his lips between them so that I can give him a fleeting kiss. Sometimes he doesn't get up, he is talking to the others or not paying attention, and then I am angry for the rest of the day and too proud to tell him so.

After four days, the jury finally reaches a verdict, and we are taken from our cells over to the courthouse. It is eleven o'clock at night, and I am already in bed when they call me, tell me to get dressed. The men are waiting below by the time I come off the elevator, in a tight group, smoking cigarettes and laughing. Taik tells me not to worry, that whatever happens we will handle it and the worse it is, the sooner we will be out. The Croatians won't allow us to sit in jail for too long! he tells me. As always, his optimism and faith buoys me, and I feel prepared to accept the direst of verdicts.

When we are finally seated in the courtroom, the jury files in and sits down. They don't look at us, which is always a bad sign, I know this from Perry Mason. When the verdicts of guilty are read off for Taik and me, I sit stonily, unsurprised, and refuse to allow myself any overt emotion whatsoever. Taik does the same. Our anguish and despair will be acknowledged only in the darkness of our cells when everyone else is sleeping. Peter and Frane haven't been found guilty of the death, as we have, so they are jubilant and so are their attorneys. But we, we are guilty of everything. I feel that I must be guilty of whatever crimes remain unsolved in the entire history of the universe. How else could a life sentence be justified? The marshals take us out of the courtroom after the jurors are polled. My parents sit bravely in the front row, but I am unable to do more than give them a faint smile. I will see them later in the visiting room, in my pumpkin suit and floppy thongs. My mother will stroke my forehead and call me her little girl, and my father will entertain me with his cynical observations on Schlamm and anyone else who has incurred his wrath on this particular day.

Slobodan has been spared the agony of the trial and taken a plea beforehand. But he has shared the everyday events with us after each daily court session. He has accepted a thirty-year sentence and concurrent state time, so we all assume Petar and Frane will get at least that much on sentencing day. Taik and I know already what we are by law required to receive, but the idea of a life sentence seems so bizarre, so ludicrous, designed for mass murderers, for psychopaths and the criminally insane, people like Charlie Manson or the Boston Strangler, and not for us, never for us!

While we are waiting for sentencing day, which will be in approximately one month, we work on our sentencing statements. As I am sitting at my desk on a sunny and cold morning (I know this because the free people on the streets are bundled up and walking hunched over, heads down, like shells with legs, though the sun is shining and the sky is a mindless blue), I find myself suddenly being locked in my room. What's going on? I ask the officer. She says she doesn't know, she was simply told to lock me up. I go to my radio, turn it on. There must be something happening on the outside, it's the only explanation. And before too long, I hear a report that some Croatians have taken hostages in the Yugoslav consulate in Manhattan. My heart begins to race. I must know these people, we know all the Croatians in this area! I try to guess who these Croatians might be, what their demands are. The reports come fast and furious every few moments. The Yugoslavs refuse to let the American police officers into the building. The Yugoslavs have guns and are going to shoot the Croatians when they are finally forced to surrender. When the Croatians finally do surrender after what appears to be an attempt at gaining media attention for human rights violations against Croatians in Yugoslavia, there is a pitched struggle between the Yugoslavs, who want to shoot the Croatians, who have surrendered and are unarmed, and the Americans, who frown on the Yugoslav style of justice and insist on taking them into custody. The Americans ultimately prevail, probably because the entire event is being filmed by television crews for posterity, and the Croatians are whisked away. It turns out I do know at least one of them, Marijan, one of the men I had called from the Paris control tower to verify that the leaflets had appeared in the American newspapers.

Before too long, my door is unlocked at the orders of the kind Lieutenant Holley, whom I have come to regard as my protector. He even calls me on the telephone to tell me he let me out as soon as he was aware that I had been locked down. Now I am able to watch the circus on the television. It is chaotic, there are people running in all directions, in and out of the consulate building, people in dark coats, sunglasses, people wearing bulletproof vests. At one point, smoke issues forth from one of the upstairs windows. A women comes rushing out of the front entrance, a trench-coated blonde who has her head down, as if afraid of being recognized. But I do recognize her! It is Margo, the good FBI agent. What on earth is Margo doing in the Yugoslav consulate? Why is she afraid of showing her face to the cameras? It occurs to me that she is a double agent, a Yugoslav plant in the FBI, who has suddenly found herself in a building in which she has no business, all because some

Croatians decided at that very moment to take hostages. All sorts of sce-
narios occur to me. It is because intrigue has become so much a part of
my life.

Sentencing day has finally arrived, and Taik and I are prepared with
our lengthy sentencing statements. Petar and Frane have been
sentenced already, the day before, to thirty years apiece, so there is little
doubt in our minds that we are in for the worst. In fact, there is little if
nothing Judge Bartels can do. Our life sentence is mandatory. When we
are all finally seated in the courtroom, the judge begins his remarks.
Much to the chagrin of the prosecutor, he states clearly on the record
that, after having heard all the witnesses and viewed all the evidence, he
does not consider us terrorists or criminals, and sympathizes with the
Croatian desire for independence; in fact, he states that he considers our
cause a "noble cause". However, he says that he does not and cannot
condone illegal acts in furtherance of that goal. He tells us his decision
was an extremely difficult one, but that his options were few, in spite of
the strong support we have received from Croatians and Americans
who know us well. He then proceeds to sentence Taik to life
imprisonment, with a recommendation that he be considered for
parole after serving the minimum of ten years. In regard to me, he
mentions the over twenty five letters of support and pleas for leniency
he has received on my behalf from passengers on the plane, one of
whom has written that he would be "proud to have me as a daughter".
I am to have a somewhat different decision, a life sentence but with
parole eligibility after serving only eight years. Eight years! I want to feel
grateful for this concession, but the idea of eight years in prison is
inconceivable to me, and I must force myself to express my thanks to
the judge. A ludicrous notion that I will, that I must, spend eight years
of my life imprisoned! But I won't think about it now, I'll think about
it later, in the solitude of my room. And Taik, how does he feel about
this? He gives me a hug as we are taken from the courtroom. Don't
worry, sweetheart, he says, we'll be out sooner than they think. And, as

usual, his optimism is infectious and I find myself able again to suffer the gravest indignities, to survive the most unthinkable tragedies, if only we are not separated, if only we can comfort one another.

My parents and brother Todd finally return to Oregon. They have been brave and loving and have shown themselves to be the best human beings imaginable in the face of this abrupt upheaval in their, our, lives. The two older brothers, Stewart and Rick, have also given me their unstinting love and support, both in letters and on the telephone. And not only have they given it to me, but to Taik as well, which is an amazing show of understanding and compassion. My family, my family, only three syllables, perhaps four, but they are more than the sum of their parts, more than the sounds and the hieroglyphics; they exist, one by one, as a unit, and it seems to me now, in this very moment when my need is so great, that they exist solely to love and forgive me, that their strength and resources are focused on this goal alone: to help me survive. I will survive. I will do more than that.

29

"The holiest and the mightiest that the world has hitherto possessed have bled to death under our knife—who will wipe the blood from us?" Nietzsche

There are many ways of talking about time and how it is taken from us. Sometimes it is gently taken, it slips away like sand between one's fingers, each grain a minute, until the hand is empty, and then one discovers that it is not only an empty, but a foreign and unrecognizable hand. Sometimes time is taken with violence, as though a hole has been ripped in the cocoon of our universe and all the life is being sucked through it by some invisible and malevolent force, and we are left drawn and withered, wondering if we will survive, wondering if we want to survive.

Time passes, one way or another. I struggle merely to exist, believing I can do no more than that. But something new always comes up, always a letter arrives from Bruno, from Mikulic, telling me what is being done for us in Croatia, assuring me it won't be long now, we'll be free, we'll be living in independent Croatia! Bruno writes that most responsible people in Croatia are working for you and give you support, and that they have promised to take care of you and they will. When they are able to speak openly, they will. I am troubled but not surprised when he writes that "I don't know how much longer I will be alive, perhaps not long, but as long as you hear I am alive, don't be afraid, I won't forget you". He adds that he is going to Paris and that his friend Ivo had telephoned him, saying that three Yugoslav agents had been sent to assassinate him. "It would be strange if that were not true" he writes. It occurs to me that these reports are intended perhaps to damage Bruno only psychologically, to render him ineffective. Maybe they don't want to kill him, only incapacitate him mentally.

Bruno always manages to find a card for me with a blonde girl on it. She is riding a white horse, or sitting on a rock like the Lorelei, luring the sailors to their deaths or suspended in air, her long hair flowing beneath her. One time he sends me one of those newspaper headlines one can order for a price. It reads: Julie Busic Crowned Miss Universe! Bruno, who tells me that assassins have been sent to kill him, but nonetheless finds time for cards, poems, manufactured headlines to lift my spirits.

Sometimes I translate interviews to keep busy, interviews which have been done outside Croatia with renowned dissidents such as Franjo Tudjman, Drazen Budisa, Vlado Gotovac, Marko Veselica and so many, many others. Bruno writes that, for the first time, they are interviewing the most respected Croatians and that everybody had spoken under his real name and had come out in support of a Croatian state. Eventually, most of these dissidents are thrown into jail as a result of the interviews, are sitting in their cells as I sit in mine, translating their words of resistance, their calls to action. Because of a Swedish television program for which Bruno and others had given a lengthy interview, he hears that "there is a big uproar in Yugoslavia. They are threatening to take off my head. They're right to be angry. This program is the beginning of a new political resurrection in the homeland."

But meanwhile, the state terror against the dissidents still in Croatia continues. Against all those whose consciences ordered them to act. What good is an idea if not taken to the end?

I continue to have a steady stream of visitors, more than I can psychologically accommodate, with the exception of my family, which is a constant source of support and comfort. My middle brother Stewart visits regularly from Oregon, bringing along his sleeping bag and pitching it wherever he stops for the night before hitchhiking to the prison. Passengers from the plane come to see me as well, Alan and Rudy and Warren. We all feel awkward the first time we meet under these changed circumstances. I am now a prisoner, they are free to leave. The tables are turned. But they do not exact revenge, they were not just acting out of fear or psychologically need on the airplane. They are only interested in exchanging feelings about the hijacking, reactions of our families, the effect it had on our lives. It is like a high school reunion in some strange way. The guards are shocked, as are the other prisoners. Such a thing is unheard of—victims visiting the perpetrators—and, as a result, I am regarded differently by all from that moment on, as a sorceress, or a witch perhaps, manipulating the minds of my hapless victims in some inscrutable way. It is too difficult for them to imagine that these passengers might well understand what circumstances brought me to this drastic act, that they are aware that it could be they, their children, were the situation reversed. Croatians from all over the world show up at the prison as well, wanting to visit, and I let everybody come in. We take pictures together, arms draped around one another. I introduce them all to my convict friends, I practice my Croatian. A Croatian Jew named Mladen Schwartz arrives unexpectedly, saying he has formed a Croatian-Jewish Society, and is in America to try to forge improved relations between Jews and Croatians. I find this a good and constructive idea and let him in. He is strange, and somewhat suspicious, with a wild head of hair and a continual smirk on his pale face. I never see him again. He too asks to take a picture together and I agree, although Taik has counseled me against taking pictures with strangers. It could be used against you later, he had often said, but I find it rude somehow to say no. A Croatian boxer, Marko Ecimovic, comes to visit from Australia. His hands are huge, like ham hocks. Not only can he box, but he can bend spoons by concentrating and does it with a plastic spoon from the visiting room, right in front of my eyes. We take pictures as well, he making a huge fist and resting it against my cheek as though I am his next contender. People come and go, Hans Peter Rullman, the German journalist, shows up. So does Zeljko Urban, a kind and intelligent man from Monterey, whose wife, Zdenka, sends me lovely embroidered cloths. Croatians from around the country, even many from outside the United States, come to visit, as regularly as the tides, the waxing and waning of the moon. In one bizarre twist, an FBI agent, who is investigating Croatian political groups in the California area appears one day, but instead of asking to question me about Croatians, ends up baring his soul about his drinking problem, his conflicts with his Greek son in law, and the book he wrote about his first love and was never able to get published. If you want, I'll send it to you, he offers. I accept, and the book arrives days later, pages yellowed with age, spotted, perhaps with tears.

On October 16, 1978, my counselor calls me to his office. There has been a death, he tells me gently. You are supposed to call this number. It is the number of a Croatian friend living in California. I lift the receiver slowly, with great effort, dial the number. What's the matter? I ask my friend, Velimir. Bruno has been murdered! he says raggedly. They shot him in Paris! No! I scream, and throw the telephone against the wall. My counselor watches me with a concerned curiosity, not moving from his chair, not jumping up or pushing the alarm buttons on his radio, just sitting, watching. No, no, no, I repeat over and over again, crying, falling to the floor. The world has come to an end, and I too must die now, I think irrationally. Bruno has been murdered! Bruno has been shot! My face is against the rough nap of the office carpet, my hands spread out at my sides, as though I have fallen in the snow and am trying to make an angel. I stay there for a long time, the time it takes to run out of tears, and then I pull myself up, pull myself up the stairs, to my room, fall onto the bed, numbly, heavily. I have to go back and call Taik, I realize. And then voices outside my door, soft voices, harsh voices, unfamiliar voices. A key in the lock and the voices are nearer. Do you want some medication? I tell them no. Want them to go away and let me suffer for Bruno, cry for him. Perhaps it isn't true? The World Series is on television below in the lobby. Somebody has just hit a run and the women are screaming. They don't know, I realize, they don't know the tragedy that has happened today in Paris. My room is dark, my life is dark, all the light in the world has been extinguished.

And incredibly, I find myself once again full of tears to shed, as though the barren wasteland of my soul has suddenly been flooded with the reserves of a hundred oceans. And my room is all of a sudden too small to contain all the sadness and desolation, so I stagger to the hallway and down the stairs, out onto the compound, which is already dark. But I am confused and don't know what to do with all the suffering, I stand and look around me, for something or someone I recognize, if only vaguely. I recall the crazy girl on the New York street corner who seemed of another world, perhaps not a better one, just another one. I am that crazy girl now, I understand her and why she had to stand motionless all day long, why she refused to speak to anybody. She, too, must have been confronted with the undeniable and inescapable existence of evil and had chosen to withdraw from such a world into her own.

For two days and nights I do not sleep. My system fills with appalling regularity with the liquid necessary to supply my tears. Excruciating visions of Bruno's head, riddled with dark holes, skip through my mind, haunting me. Dear, kind, loving Bruno, with the soft brown eyes, like a doe, and the sweet way he had of laughing at himself.

There are small articles about Bruno's assassination in the American newspapers, but the English tabloids, because he had been living there and had asylum from England, ran the story on the front page. "Defector's Date With Death", they read, or "Who Killed Defector Bruno?" He had come from a date with a mysterious female, they claimed, who had set him up. The assassin had been waiting in the shadows of the building, under the stairs. Taik, Bruno and I had gone together to this very building just a few years ago, in Belleville, to visit this Croatian acquaintance of Bruno's, Petar Brnadic. He was staying with him when he got shot. Someone had been following Bruno and had learned his schedule. I'm not going to spend my life in hiding, he had told me many times. letters insert If they want to find me badly enough, they will! The police speculate, say the articles, that the Yugoslav secret police is responsible for the assassination. No arrests were made. No suspects were named.

Taik takes the news of Bruno's assassination with outward calm, but I learn later how the shock affected him, so much so that he was placed in an isolation unit on his floor for refusing to obey an arbitrary order one of the guards had given him. He simply hadn't the strength to react, wanted only to be left alone to mourn.

I get out all the letters Bruno had written me, all the pictures we had taken together in Europe, the poems he had copied and the ones he himself had written. I look at everything five, ten times, read every word he wrote and look for hidden meanings, something which might have escaped me until now, until his death, and which could possibly provide comfort. I hold out a vain hope that there are other letters on their way to me, written before his murder, and that I haven't yet heard the last from him, he is still alive somewhere over the ocean, on a sheet of thin paper tucked into an airmail envelope. I simply can't let him go.

Something unexpected happens one day, the courage of it thrilling. Kathleen Murray has filed a negligence suit gainst the New York City Police Department for its mishandling and detonation of the explosives.

She has based it upon statements made to her by bomb disposal experts and her husband's colleagues—that documents had been destroyed, potential witnesses threatened, cover-ups had taken place—as well as on conflicting testimony by the head of the bomb squad, Terence McTigue, who had, incredibly, refused to speak to Mrs. Murray after the death of her husband. The suit reads that the bomb was "designed not to explode and that, absent negligence, would never have exploded. The grossly negligent manner in which McTigue attempted to defuse the bomb thus caused the death of Officer Murray." It further states that "as McTigue became aware of his own potential liability, his story changed" and that his "eagerness to blame the Busics stems from his fear—realistically based—that he, McTigue, was negligent and that his negligence resulted in Brian Murray's death." It alleges in closing that "Given McTigue's supposed prominence in bomb demolition work, McTigue has a strong personal reason to avoid acknowledging his own role in Officer Murray's death. Instead, McTigue contrives, incorrectly, to place blame on the Busics." It is a great psychological help that Kathleen Murray knows there was no harm intended by us, that we are not those kind of people. If only I could convince everybody else of what I know to be an indisputable truth.

Because I expect to be transferred soon, I write a letter to the prison warden, Larry Taylor, who has been kind and accessible. I counsel him to treat the prisoners as human beings, I, in what I feel now is my infinite understanding of human nature and the workings of the human heart, tell him that we are not numbers, but people of flesh and blood, no different than he and all the others who guard us. I refuse to be discounted, even for a moment. I am either disliked or held in awe by everybody, there is no middle ground with me. But I am not, will not allow myself to be, discounted.

The transfer list is brought up to our floor and pinned on the bulletin board by one of the trustees, and every night the prisoners rush to the board to read their fates. This day, it is my fate which appears in black and white: Busic, Julienne, 4:30am, WAB. The dreaded WAB, With

All Belongings. I arrange hastily for a last visit with Taik, don't even know where I am being sent, so I can't give him an address. The reality of a separation is impossible to fathom, so invincible had I believed our bond to be, so impervious to external forces. It can't be true that we will be taken from one another!

We have our visit on the second floor, under the eyes of one of the guards. Taik is in a red jumpsuit and I am in a mustard yellow one. We sit intertwined, Taik is talking with a false enthusiasm about what the Croatians are going to do to get us out of prison, what we ourselves must do, that we have to be strong and use our time constructively. But I want only to talk of love, I want to remember how we met, how I lost my cap the first night and in what restaurant he first kissed me. It was the Esterhazy Cellar, I know this for certain; the music was playing and one of Taik's friends was dancing. Suddenly, when everyone seemed to be looking away from the two of us, Taik had taken my head, turned it gently towards him, and kissed my lips. Then we'd laughed, so pleased with ourselves but not exactly knowing why. We sit together, but apart, alone with our thoughts, and before we know it, the guard tells us it is time to go. In the elevator, we stand very close, arms around one another. I'll take him to his floor first, the guard tells me. That way you can have more time together! We will have an extra fifteen seconds together. We will simply die a slow instead of a quicker death. When we reach the ninth floor and Taik gets out, I begin to wail. I hold him in my arms, refuse to let him go, feel as though no force on earth can dislodge him from my grip. All shame has abandoned me, I cry loudly and wildly, and Taik, who would like nothing more than to do the same, makes quiet sounds to me, strokes my face. Something has happened, I don't know what, but I suddenly find myself back in the elevator, alone with the guard, and going down, down, away from Taik. Where is he? What have they done with him? Oh, let me die, I say, and press my wet face against the wall of the elevator. My arms hang limply at my side, my knees can barely hold me up. I feel my very essence already spiraling into a vague and black nothingness from which there is no escape. But we have been wrenched from each other. And I am bereft. It is August 23. It is the end of the world.

Epilogue

February 2000—From my table at the Mala Kavana on Ban Jelacic Square, I am facing the skyscraper, or Neboder, from whose heights I had, almost 30 years earlier, dropped the notorious "unfriendly" leaflets which had called for all the victims of Yugoslav/Greater Serbian oppression to "rise up and fight", to take a stand against state terror, political imprisonments, assassinations. The Neboder regards me accusingly, turning upon me a cold eye whose gaze has frozen in time and space, has frozen on me.

But I cannot be held any longer against my will, so I pick up my newspaper and scan the headlines. After the recent death of Franjo Tudjman, the first President of the now independent Republic of Croatia, new elections have taken place. Among the candidates to succeed Tudjman were former political prisoners and dissidents, including Drazen Budisa and Stipe Mesic. Stipe Mesic has won and the inauguration is to take place in two days, on the historic St. Mark's Square. Madeleine Albright will head the U.S. delegation, in a show of support for the new government.

I turn to Taik to speak to him of these mysteries and miracles, of what Nietzsche has called the eternally recurring, but he has disappeared or perhaps just dispersed. He has violated all architectural concepts of support and load, concentrated his power. Like you, like me, like Croatia, he is now rooted only to the universe.